Empirical Studies in Institutional Ch [...] [...]
cal studies by fourteen scholars. Dea [...] [...]
evolution of secure markets in seven[...] [...] [...] to the origins of property rights in airport slots in modern America, the contribu-
tors analyze institutions and institutional change in various parts of the
world at different periods of time. The volume is a contribution to the
new economics of institutions, which emphasizes the role of transaction
costs and property rights in shaping incentives and results in the economic arena.

To make the essays accessible to a wide audience, including students
of economics and other social sciences, the editors have written an
introduction to each study and added three theoretical essays, including
Douglass North's Nobel Prize address, which reflect their collective
views on the status of institutional analysis and where it is headed.

EMPIRICAL STUDIES IN INSTITUTIONAL CHANGE

POLITICAL ECONOMY OF INSTITUTIONS AND DECISIONS

Editors
James E. Alt, Harvard University
Douglass C. North, Washington University in St. Louis

Other books in the series

Alberto Alesina and Howard Rosenthal, *Partisan Politics, Divided Government and the Economy*
James E. Alt and Kenneth Shepsle, eds., *Perspectives on Positive Political Economy*
Jeffrey S. Banks and Eric A. Hanushek, *Modern Political Economy: Old Topics, New Directions*
Yoram Barzel, *Economic Analysis of Property Rights*
Robert Bates, *Beyond the Miracle of the Market: The Political Economy of Agrarian Development in Kenya*
Peter Cowhey and Mathew McCubbins, *Structure and Policy in Japan and the United States*
Gary W. Cox, *The Efficient Secret: The Cabinet and the Development of Political Parties in Victorian England*
Jean Ensminger, *Making a Market: The Institutional Transformation of an African Society*
Murray Horn, *The Political Economy of Public Administration: Institutional Choice in the Public Sector*
Jack Knight, *Institutions and Social Conflict*
Michael Laver and Kenneth Shepsle, *Cabinet Ministers and Parliamentary Government*
Michael Laver and Kenneth Shepsle, *Making and Breaking Governments*
Leif Lewin, *Ideology and Strategy: A Century of Swedish Politics* (English edition)
Gary Libecap, *Contracting for Property Rights*
Mathew D. McCubbins and Terry Sullivan, eds., *Congress: Structure and Policy*
Gary J. Miller, *Managerial Dilemmas: The Political Economy of Hierarchy*
Douglass C. North, *Institutions, Institutional Change, and Economic Performance*

Continued on page following the index.

EMPIRICAL STUDIES IN INSTITUTIONAL CHANGE

Edited by

LEE J. ALSTON
University of Illinois,
Urbana-Champaign

THRÁINN EGGERTSSON
University of Iceland

DOUGLASS C. NORTH
Washington University
in St. Louis

CAMBRIDGE
UNIVERSITY PRESS

Published by the Press Syndicate of the University of Cambridge
The Pitt Building, Trumpington Street, Cambridge CB2 1RP
40 West 20th Street, New York, NY 10011-4211, USA
10 Stamford Road, Oakleigh, Melbourne 3166, Australia

First published 1996

Printed in the United States of America

Library of Congress Cataloging-in-Publication Data
Empirical studies in institutional change / edited by Lee J. Alston,
Thráinn Eggertsson, Douglass C. North.
    p.   cm. – (Political economy of institutions and decisions)
Includes index.
ISBN 0-521-55313-X (hc). – ISBN 0-521-55743-7 (pb)
1. Institutional economics.   2. Organizational change.
I. Alston, Lee J., 1951– .   II. Thráinn Eggertsson, 1941– .
III. North, Douglass Cecil.   IV. Series.
HB99.5.E5   1996
330 – dc20   95-47278
                                                    CIP

A catalog record for this book is available from the British Library.

ISBN 0-521-55313-X Hardback
ISBN 0-521-55743-7 Paperback

Contents

Contents

Contributors

Lee J. Alston, Professor of Economics, University of Illinois, Urbana-Champaign

Steven N. S. Cheung, Professor of Economics and Head, School of Economics and Finance, University of Hong Kong

Thráinn Eggertsson, Professor of Economics, University of Iceland

Joseph P. Ferrie, Assistant Professor of Economics, Northwestern University

Robert Higgs, Research Director, Independent Institute, San Francisco

Anne O. Krueger, Professor of Economics, Stanford University

Brian Levy, Principal Economist, World Bank

Gary D. Libecap, Professor of Economics and Director, Karl Eller Center, University of Arizona, Tucson

Douglass C. North, Professor of Economics and History, Washington University in St. Louis

Ricardo Paredes, Professor of Economics, Universidad de Chile

William H. Riker, late Professor of Political Science, University of Rochester

Itai Sened, Assistant Professor of Political Science, Tel Aviv University

Andrew Stone, Private Sector Development Specialist, World Bank

Barry R. Weingast, Senior Fellow, Hoover Institution, and Professor of Political Science, Stanford University

Jan Winiecki, Professor of Economics, Europa University Viadrina, Frankfurt (Oder)

Series editors' preface

The Cambridge Political Economy of Institutions and Decisions series is built around attempts to answer two central questions: How do institutions evolve in response to individual incentives, strategies, and choices, and how do institutions affect the performance of political and economic systems? The scope of the series is comparative and historical rather than international or specifically American, and the focus is positive rather than normative.

The nine path-breaking empirical studies in this volume capture the state of an important field, institutional analysis, in rapid transition. Institutional analysis focuses directly on the connection between institutions and economic performance. It emphasizes incomplete information and the costs of measuring performance and enforcing property rights. Unlike other books on property rights that deal specifically with particular political problems (e.g., the commons), regions (e.g., the developing world), or types of property (e.g., intellectual), this volume is concerned with property rights in general. It stresses the importance of history and the significance of adjustments on unanticipated margins. Several chapters document the creation of new political institutions, public policies, and forms of contract, all important kinds of institutional change, while the remainder explain the costs of extant regulations. The result is an impressive array of studies showing what we know about the origins and effects of institutions, which create the incentive structures in societies.

Like the earlier collections in this series, *Perspectives on Positive Political Economy* and *Modern Political Economy,* this one addresses both organizational development and the interaction between existing institutions and outcomes. All the chapters in this volume share the underlying purpose of integrating the concerns of economics and political science in areas where the interdependence of the two is evident.

Acknowledgments

This book has had a long gestation. We conceived the project as we hiked in the mountains outside of Boulder, Colorado, in the fall of 1992 while attending the Economic History Association annual meeting. We thank the Association for providing such an inspiring locale.

Naturally, we owe debts to many people. In particular, our students gave us invaluable feedback on the material in this book. We only hope they learned as much from us as we did from them. For their comments in our courses: Alston thanks graduate students at the University of Illinois and M.B.A. students at the U.S. Business School in Prague; Eggertsson thanks graduate students at the University of Hong Kong and undergraduate students at Indiana University in Bloomington; North thanks graduate and undergraduate students at Washington University. Alston is also grateful for feedback he received during an economic history workshop at the University of Illinois. Our colleagues at our respective institutions also gave us helpful comments; without meaning to slight anyone, we single out Ann Carlos, John Drobak, Larry Neal, and Elinor and Vincent Ostrom. Jim Alt, the series editor at Cambridge University Press, not only gave us insightful comments but was responsible for the selection of an anonymous referee from whom we received useful criticism.

For general research assistance and comments, we thank Bernardo Mueller and Tomas Nonnenmacher. For improving our prose, we thank Elisabeth Case. For final copy editing of the new material, we applaud the work of Mary Racine of Cambridge University Press. For preparing the index, we thank Randy Nielsen. Our editor at Cambridge, Alex Holzman, gave us valuable help. Finally, Alston expresses his appreciation for his supportive family, Mary, Greg, and Eric; and North thanks Elisabeth for all her encouragement.

xi

Introduction

LEE J. ALSTON, THRÁINN EGGERTSSON, AND
DOUGLASS C. NORTH

In recent years scholars and policy makers alike have paid increasing attention to the complex relationship between social institutions and economic performance. There are various reasons why it is important to understand the role of institutions: economic stagnation in many developing countries; structural problems in the old industrial economies; and the collapse of the soviet economies of the former Soviet Union, Central Asia, and Eastern and Central Europe. Institutional analysis is of paramount importance for guiding the transition to markets in formerly centrally managed economies. Many scholars now recognize that mainstream economic analysis, neoclassical economics, is of little help in restructuring economies that lack secure markets; the same criticism holds for other disciplines in the social sciences.

An interdisciplinary research program that deals explicitly with the link between institutions, institutional change, and economic performance is now emerging. The new institutional analysis is a line of investigation that departs from but does not abandon neoclassical economics. Central to the research agenda is an emphasis on property rights, the transaction costs of measurement and enforcement, and incomplete information. The research program has been further enriched through cross-fertilization with law, political science, sociology, anthropology, and history.

Although both theoretical and empirical contributions to this field are accumulating at an increasing rate and two pioneers of the approach recently received the Nobel Prize in Economics (R. H. Coase in 1991; D. C. North in 1993), the impression persists that the field is long on theoretical analysis but short on empirical work. It is probably true that the stock of knowledge would grow faster if the new institutionalists put more emphasis on empirical work, but excellent empirical studies are more abundant than many critics realize. The empirical studies are not

I

highly visible, because they are scattered through the journals of several disciplines. In contrast, major theoretical contributions are frequently published as books or reprinted in books that have a relatively wide circulation across fields and disciplines.

In this volume we bring together nine empirical studies by fourteen scholars. These scholars analyze institutions and institutional change in various parts of the world at different periods of time, and deal with issues ranging from the evolution of secure markets in seventeenth-century England to the origins of property rights in airport slots in modern America.

To make the empirical essays accessible to a wide audience, including students of economics and other social sciences, we have written an introduction to each study and added three theoretical essays that reflect our collective views on the present status of institutional analysis and where it is headed. The views expounded in our essays provide a re-search methodology for addressing the issues associated with the causes and consequences of institutions and institutional change. In the first essay, Thráinn Eggertsson outlines a general framework for the study of institutions and economic performance. Eggertsson makes clear that both formal and informal institutions affect decision making. He pays particular attention to two issues in the literature that have attracted criticism of the new institutional analysis: the role of power and the role of rational choice.

In the second essay, Lee Alston presents a guide to structuring and testing issues in institutional analysis. He argues that incomplete knowl-edge and unintended consequences warrant abandoning the functionalist approach to institutional change: explaining the causes of institutional change by their consequences. Alston advocates a research agenda that examines the independent causes of the birth, life, and death of institu-tions. The essays by both Alston and Eggertsson emphasize that the study of institutions involves layers of analysis, and different layers often require different theoretical and empirical tools.

Because the new institutional analysis is a rapidly evolving field, basic theoretical tools are still being shaped and important issues concerning institutional change, such as the evolution of informal institutions, are poorly understood. The third essay, the Epilogue by Douglass North – his 1993 Nobel lecture – summarizes past achievements and discusses the frontier of research in the theory of institutions.

In writing the introductions to the empirical essays we had several goals in mind: to place the studies in a broader perspective, to highlight relevant theoretical concepts, and to suggest questions for reflection by the reader.

Introduction

Institutional change is a multidimensional, multilevel phenomenon that empirical studies cannot capture in all its complexity. Therefore, empirical studies simplify in various ways. First, the *scope* of the analysis is selective. A study may focus only on economic processes and ignore the political domain or, alternatively, attempt to capture the interaction between economic and political processes but only consider the economic consequences for a single industry. Second, empirical studies in institutional change are usually framed in terms of one or a few *central theoretical concepts,* such as agency, collective action, or credible commitment. Third, the *treatment of time* varies. Sometimes institutional change is analyzed with the help of cross-sectional data, comparing institutional arrangements across space but at the same time. In other instances, the scholar uses longitudinal data for comparative statics or in an attempt to analyze a dynamic process. Fourth, the character of empirical studies in institutional change varies with the *nature of the political and social systems* that are investigated, which may range from a traditional authoritarian agricultural community with little specialization and exchange to an advanced, mature industrial democracy. The empirical studies in the present volume sample this variety.

The first study, by Gary Libecap, is a pioneering quantitative test of the naive theory of property rights, named so[1] because it assumes that potential opportunities to increase wealth induce the required institutional change. The study tests the thesis that, up to a point, property rights become more precisely defined as the value of a resource increases. The scope is sectorial, meaning that micro and political processes are not explicitly considered.

The second study, by Jan Winiecki, uses a simple model of an authoritarian state (based on the new theory of the firm) to explain the inability of rulers in the former Soviet states to radically reform their economies. The theory of agency is used to analyze the relative autonomy of mid-level agents who were responsible for implementing the reforms.

The third study, by Andrew Stone, Brian Levy, and Ricardo Paredes, is an example of a cross-sectional analysis. Again, the role of transaction costs in providing relative autonomy to local actors is emphasized. The authors ask whether local actors who are faced with a formal institutional framework, imposed by central political authorities, that generates high transaction costs are able to lower these costs by creating informal property rights. The essay attempts a limited empirical test by comparing various economic results and processes in a country with

[1]T. Eggertsson, *Economic Behavior and Institutions* (Cambridge University Press, 1990).

3

relatively efficient formal property rights (Chile) with outcomes in a country that relies more on informal arrangements (Brazil).

The fourth study, by Douglass North and Barry Weingast, is concerned with the political foundations of secure markets. In an economy where entrepreneurship is decentralized, economic actors will hold back on long-term investments unless the state makes credible commitments to honor its contracts and respect individual ownership rights. Because the state is usually the most powerful agency in a community, and because circumstances often tempt rulers to take the short view and expropriate private wealth, institutional arrangements for controlling opportunistic behavior by the state have profound implications for economic growth.

The fifth study, by Anne Krueger, is restricted to one economic sector and provides a longitudinal dynamic analysis of the process of regulation, explicitly considering the interaction between economic and political organizations over time. The study brings out the complexity and changing nature of the process, making clear that none of several competing economic theories of regulation applies all the time.

The sixth study, by Steven Cheung, also looks at the process of regulation in a single market – here, the rental housing market in Hong Kong. The study concentrates on unintended side effects of regulation and explores how, in a complex world, actors may respond to regulations with adjustments at various unexpected margins and create outcomes that generate further institutional change.

The dynamic process initiated by government intervention in a market or in some economic activity may converge on a tolerably low-cost solution and avoid extensive dissipation of resources. In the Hong Kong housing market new regulations eventually managed to limit dissipating behavior at the various margins. However, regulations can also create a dynamic process that converges on high-cost outcomes, involving the dissipation of the regulated resources and/or increasingly inefficient production methods and technologies. The seventh study, by Robert Higgs, analyzes a perverse regulatory path.

In order to exploit the wealth-enhancing potential of technological change, new types of institutional arrangements are often needed. The aviation industry provides good examples of technologically induced institutional change. The eighth study, by William Riker and Itai Sened, studies the emergence of brand-new property rights and stresses the relative role of political organizations in their creation.

The final study, by Lee Alston and Joseph Ferrie, takes a macro, or general equilibrium, view of institutional change in a democratic society and explains institutional change in terms of complex relationships between diverse economic and political organizations and sectors. Alston and Ferrie link production methods and technological change in agriculture in the U.S. South, the structure of Southern labor contracts, and the organization of the political system – particularly the U.S. Congress – to the growth of the welfare state.

A *note on the economics of institutions*

THRÁINN EGGERTSSON

1. INTRODUCTION

In this essay I argue for a research program in the economics of institutions that combines the best of all worlds. I argue for parsimony in structuring theories and a standardization of theoretical terms, but I also argue for the economic principle of judicious substitution at the margin when research methods are selected. As I see it, the maximization of net output in research requires a flexible use of the inputs, the matching of tools to the tasks at hand, while recognizing at the same time that eclecticism is not a free good. The optimal strategy involves a delicate balance that I outline in general terms.

The research program summarized and discussed here concerns the economics of institutions, particularly the relationship between institutions and wealth, the classic theme of Adam Smith. The following section contains a brief summary of a theoretical framework for the economics of institutions.[1] The core of the framework is a modified version of the neoclassical model in economics. However, I suggest that the optimal deviation from the basic model varies with the level of analysis and the type of variables to be endogenized. It is recognized that some lines of research will require extensive adjustments in the neoclassical model, perhaps to a point where the model becomes barely, if at all, recognizable.

In many instances, the basic neoclassical model, extended to include the concepts of transaction costs and property rights, is an effective tool

---

This is a shortened, revised, and edited version of an article published in *Acta Sociologica* 36 (1993), pp. 223–37, entitled "The Economics of Institutions: Avoiding the Open-Field Syndrome and the Perils of Path Dependence."

[1]The research program is discussed extensively in Eggertsson (1990), except that various ideas are elaborated here. We label the program alternatively *neoinstitutional economics* or the *economics of institutions*.

for studying the link between institutions and wealth. For other cases, especially for the study of changes in informal institutions, such as norms and customs, probably an alternative or a complement to the neoclassical model of choice is required. Furthermore, the appropriate mix of research methods obviously depends on the state of the arts in scholarship. A clear-cut breakthrough in modeling human decisions could justify a wholesale rejection of the rational choice perspective, but I am not aware of any such development. The third section of the essay considers criticism of the economics of institutions, paying special attention to the concept of power and the model of choice.

2. THE LINK BETWEEN INSTITUTIONS AND WEALTH

An analysis of the link between institutions and wealth can proceed at several levels, depending on which categories of variables are treated as endogenous. A research program for the economics of institutions that is based on an extended version of neoclassical economics capitalizes on the strengths of the neoclassical approach, maintains the continuity in economic analysis, and lowers the cost of transacting in scholarship. However, at the frontier of research there is also a need and scope for experimental work with an alternative paradigm.

To provide a role for institutions and organizations in neoclassical theory, the concepts of transaction costs and property rights are central, following the approach of Ronald Coase (1937, 1960); property rights economists of the Los Angeles–Seattle school, especially Alchian (1977), North (1981, 1990), Cheung (1969, 1970), Barzel (1989), and Demsetz (1988); a number of scholars working in economic history (Libecap 1989), law, and economics (Goldberg 1976a,b; Posner 1986); and students of the economics of organization (Williamson 1985).[2] Figure 1 presents a stylized schema of the main theoretical concepts that form the link between institutions and wealth, as seen from the short-term viewpoint of an individual. *Institutions* are defined as formal and informal rules that constrain individual behavior and shape human interaction; the *institutional environment* varies with a person's position in society (North 1990).

The economics of institutions employs the term *property rights* in a general sense (which does not correspond to its role in legal theory) to define the rights of an actor to use valuable assets (Alchian 1965). The property rights of an actor are embodied both in formal rules and in social norms and customs, and their economic relevance depends on how

---

[2]For a survey of the state of the art by several key scholars in the field, see Furubotn and Richter (1991, 1993).

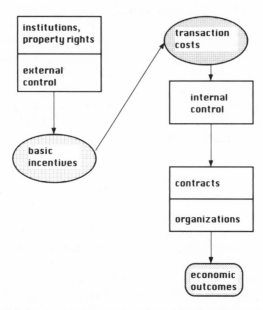

Figure 1. The link between institutions and wealth: the short-term viewpoint of the individual.

well the rights are recognized and enforced by other members of society. It is important to note that the ability (power) of an actor to use valuable resources derives both from external/exogenous control and from internal/endogenous control. *External control* depends on the property rights of an actor or, in other words, on how his or her institutional environment – constitutions, statutes, regulations, norms, enforcement, and sanctions – constrains and directs both the actor in question and outsiders. *Internal control* is established by the actors themselves through various investments aimed at gaining control over scarce resources, involving monitoring, fencing, hiring private guards, checking reputations, and other measures.

The term *transaction costs* refers to an actor's opportunity cost of establishing and maintaining internal control of resources. Transaction costs, the costs of measurement and enforcement, are incurred to protect values both in voluntary exchange and against involuntary exchange, such as theft. The transaction costs of several individuals can be aggregated, and theoretically one can contemplate the transaction costs of a whole economic system. At that level of aggregation, the distinction between internal and external control disappears (assuming an isolated economic system).

From the individual viewpoint, institutions and their manifestation, property rights, define the opportunity set, the basic system of incentives, and the transaction costs associated with various investments. As economic theory has elaborated for more than two hundred years, the creation of wealth is enhanced in various ways by cooperation, specialization, and exchange. These activities take place against the institutional framework and are constrained by transaction costs, as property rights never provide the actors with full protection and full certainty. Voluntary exchange involves the transaction costs of contracting. In order to lower their transaction costs in exchange, individuals resort to various measures that are embodied in *contracts*.[3] The structure of contracts reflects both the traders' institutional environment and various internal rules, which they set themselves. The state can play a very large role in lowering the cost of contracting of individual actors by providing clear and stable property rights, including a consistent system of enforcement, and also by supplying standards, such as weights and measures, which lower measurement costs. Economies of scale make the state relatively efficient both in lowering the cost of contracting and in disrupting contracting.

Finally, the term *organization* refers to a set of actors who cooperate or act jointly in production (North 1990). The output of organizations ranges from commodities (firms) and statutes (legislatures) to religious services (churches), and our approach makes an important distinction between the players and the rules (institutions) by which they play.

The behavioral link between institutions and wealth involves complex and only partly settled theoretical issues, but, at the risk of oversimplification, we make the following generalizations. The creation of value is curtailed:

1. when property rights to valuable assets are undefined or unclear because vague property rights tend to give rise to wasteful behavior;
2. when property rights to valuable assets belong to and stay with individuals who do not put the assets to their most valuable uses.[4]

For instance, the failure of the Soviet system can be characterized in terms of our framework as being caused by institutions that created vague property rights with high measurement and enforcement costs,

---

[3] As used in the economics of institutions, contracts are essentially a theoretical fiction. The view of exchange relationships as being embodied in a network of contracts, including ethnic trading networks, and the recognition that the structure of contracts involves informal rules, such as norms and even religious beliefs, suggest a need to study the role of social structures in facilitating exchange. Landa (1994) has studied how culture and ethnicity influence commercial morality.

[4] Barzel (1989) provides an excellent discussion of theory, explaining the link between property rights, incentives, and economic outcomes.

which increased over time. In the Soviet system, effective property rights were held by individuals who did not put assets to their most valued use, and the arrangement created an acute conflict between individual and group rationality (Eggertsson 1994).

Figure 1 illustrates how research in the economics of institutions can be segmented into analytical levels depending on which variables are endogenous. Various constellations are possible, but we consider the following three possibilities.

The first level of analysis attempts to explain how variations in institutional arrangements affect economic outcomes or wealth; and for this purpose institutions, organizations, and contractual arrangements are treated as exogenous variables. Traditional neoclassical economics, which assumes the existence of mature market organizations, is a special case belonging to this category.[5] However, in order to explore a variety of institutional arrangements (even variation within the category of mature market institutions) and to understand the consequences of institutional change (for instance, the transition to markets by former Soviet-type economies), the neoclassical model must be augmented by the concepts of transaction costs and property rights. Also belonging to this category is a substantial part of the work in law and economics that explores the economic consequences of various legal arrangements (Posner 1986; Cooter & Ulen 1988).

The second analytical level attempts to explain how the institutional framework affects the structure of economic organizations and contractual arrangements. The basic notion here, as illustrated in Figure 2, is that in each case the institutional framework defines and limits the set of practicable forms of economic organization available to economic actors. Pioneering work in this area was undertaken by Coase (1937) and Cheung (1968). Belonging here are contract economics (Werin & Wijkander 1992), the work of Williamson (1985, 1993) on the economic institutions of capitalism, and various contributions in industrial organization (Milgrom & Roberts 1992). These studies, although somewhat heterogeneous, are of the neoclassical tradition (albeit marginally in the case of Williamson), and all emphasize transaction costs. Relatively few studies have explored the adjustment of organizations to institutional arrangements other than the market institutions of capitalism, and the analysis typically focuses primarily on measurement and enforcement costs implied by the types of commodities exchanged and by the nature of the exchange. However, there are several noteworthy exceptions, studies that analyze the structure of organization in environ-

---

[5] Neoclassical economics also assumes that there are no transaction costs involved in using the price system or the firm.

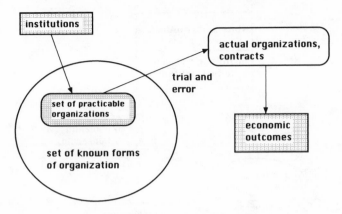

Figure 2. Institutions and organizations.

ments other than advanced industrialism, for instance applications to economic history by North (1981, 1990), Greif (1989), and Greif, Milgrom, and Weingast (1994), and work by Ostrom (1990) on common pool resources, by Bates (1989) and Ensminger (1992) on economic development in Africa, and by Landa (1994) on ethnicity, trading networks, and gift exchange.[6]

The third level of analysis, which opens a vast panorama of miscellaneous research, attempts to explain various elements of the institutional framework and the structure of property rights.[7] As the institutional framework consists of formal and informal rules and their enforcement, research at this level intrudes into the domain of political science, sociology, and anthropology, along with law and history. Consequently, the usefulness of the amended neoclassical model is more in question at this level than at the other two, at least for certain research topics.

To explain changes in formal rules it is necessary to understand the decision processes and structures of political organizations that produce formal rules. In this area a judicious application of the extended rational choice model with information and transaction costs has been rather successful, as witnessed by positive political theory (Shepsle & Weingast 1981; McCubbins & Sullivan 1987; Alt & Shepsle 1990). Also, the public choice literature and the economics of regulation have made valuable contributions (Mueller 1989).

For the analysis of institutional change, the short-run framework of Figure 1 no longer applies. Figure 3 illustrates a possible circular process

---

[6] Also see Eggertsson (1990).
[7] These issues are surveyed in chapters 8 to 10 of Eggertsson (1990).

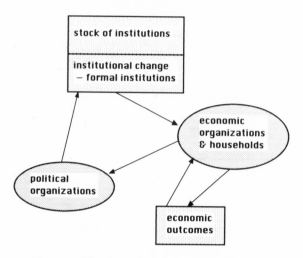

Figure 3. The dynamics of institutional change.

involving changes in formal institutions. Consider an exogenous change, such as technological change or changes in world markets, which upsets the political equilibrium in a community, causing changes in economic policy (institutional change). A change in economic policy usually creates both winners and losers. The effects of the change create a new economic equilibrium that feeds back to the political system, as winners and losers lobby political organizations, possibly giving rise to new economic policy measures that create a new economic equilibrium, and so on. The sequence of institutional change may move the economy either away from an efficient (wealth-enhancing) institutional structure or in the direction of such a structure (Krueger 1993). In a similar vein, recent formal analysis has shown that theories using commonplace assumptions about rational ignorance among voters, or about an uncertain distribution of costs and benefits of economic policy among groups of voters, can explain various apparently irrational cycles in economic policy and erratic shifts between the opposite ends of the policy spectrum – such irregularity as has been observed in various countries, such as in Latin America (Rodrik 1993).

Changes in formal institutional arrangements reflect the power (and the constraints) of the rule makers, who are frequently compelled by transaction costs to select institutions that do not maximize the size of the national pie and forgo arrangements that theoretically could make everyone better off (North 1981). The frequent inability of human groups to agree on institutional arrangements that could make everyone better off in material terms deserves more attention than it has been given in social science.

Formal rules are only a part of the story. We are concerned with both institutions and their enforcement characteristics, and enforcement depends heavily on informal rules, such as norms, customs, and conventions (North 1990). Arrow (1990: 139) has made the sensible observation that an economic system based on specialization and extensive contracting will not function properly unless the trading parties are imbued with commercial morality. Individuals who cheat whenever they expect to receive net material gains will always find circumstances where it pays to cheat: the presence of formal processes of enforcement (the police and the courts) and informal strategic considerations (such as reputation in repeated dealings) cannot by themselves account for order.

It is commonly believed that informal institutions, such as norms and customs, change relatively slowly, and therefore, in studies involving marginal changes in formal rules, informal institutions can often be taken for granted. Yet changes in informal institutions must be considered in studies with a long time horizon or studies of large-scale changes in economic systems, such as the evolution of efficient market economies in Northwestern Europe or the transition to markets of the former Soviet-type economies. A reasonable degree of Arrow's commercial morality and related norms (including informal institutions that restrain predatory behavior by the state) appear to be a necessary condition for the successful development of a decentralized economy based on private investment in specific capital and far-flung networks of exchange among unrelated individuals. However, the study of informal institutions puts a formidable stress on the neoclassical paradigm and the rational choice model, as discussed in the following section.

Finally, we must recognize the limits of our approach. Although various regularities and patterns have been and will be uncovered, we should not expect to discover a deterministic law of economic systems and economic history. Although the growth rate of an economy depends on various stocks, such as the stocks of institutions and knowledge, physical and human capital, and natural resources, economic prosperity also depends on external events, accidental circumstances, and apparently unpredictable political events and policies.

3. TWO CRITICAL ISSUES: POWER AND THE RATIONAL CHOICE MODEL

The approach just outlined has many critics, among both economists and other social scientists, who find it either too far removed from the neoclassical model or slavishly tied to it. Extensive discussion has centered on two issues: the neglect of power relationships in the economics of institutions and the relevance of the rational choice model.

Power

The central role of voluntary exchange and contracting in the economics of institutions has led critics to argue that the approach envisages a society where conflict and exploitation are absent and economic relationships are limited to mutually beneficial exchanges among equal and independent agents (Knight 1992). Critics have noted that some theorists have gone so far as to use contracts to characterize certain relations between slaves and their masters, which to these critics appears to be an outrageous attempt to cover up inequality and exploitation. However, this view is based on a misunderstanding, probably caused by a failure to appreciate the definition of property rights and the distinctions among the research program's several levels of analysis.

The economic implications of the institutional structure of society are manifested in the system of property rights, a term that refers to the distribution of effective control, by individuals and groups, of valuable assets, including human capital. In other words, the system of property rights describes the distribution of power in society. Consider stage 2 of our framework, where the researcher holds constant the institutional structure of society and studies how individuals use contracting to organize economic life, lower the cost of transacting, and increase their wealth. Slavery is an extreme example of asymmetric power relations. If there were no transaction costs of measurement and enforcement, the property rights of a slave master would be complete, and any form of contracting between masters and slaves would be irrational. However, in a world of positive measurement and enforcement costs, slaves sometimes acquire, because of the high cost of monitoring their activities, some limited control of the quality of their labor, minuscule property rights that they can trade.[8] It is conceivable that masters would offer slaves some improvement in their working conditions in return for their greater care and quality of work in activities where care is valuable (Fenoaltea 1984). Note the limited purpose of the theory in this instance, namely to explain the difference in the conditions of slavery in skilled

---

[8] In the economics of institutions, trade is defined as the exchange of property rights to various attributes of valuable assets – rather than as an exchange of the assets themselves. The value of an asset to an actor varies with the number of attributes he or she controls. A formal ownership but without the control of any valuable attribute has no value. Consider, as an example, the formal ownership of a residential building in a war zone.

and unskilled occupations. Also note in this context that contracting is essentially a theoretical fiction. As for the historical evidence, it indicates that slaves assigned to semiskilled or skilled work were frequently granted better living conditions than slaves engaged in unskilled physical labor, such as mining, stonecutting, and agricultural work with low care intensity (Solzhenitsyn 1968; Fenoaltea 1984).

Although high transaction costs may give slaves control over a few margins of their human capital that are valuable to their masters, it is obvious that the power relationship between the two sides is still extremely unequal. In other cases, the asymmetry of power is not as great, although the parties to the exchange may not have equal power. Laborers typically have less power than their employers, although free workers can rely on various property rights that increase their power of bargaining; for instance, the modern state usually protects workers from being outright enslaved by their employers. Scholars may disagree on the relative power of the two sides. Some may argue that usually labor markets tend to be competitive and confer considerable power on workers, as their cost of quitting and finding alternative employment is low, while other scholars argue that workers have very limited property rights because their human capital is firm-specific and prevalent unemployment further raises the cost of leaving a job. However, these are theoretical and, ultimately, empirical questions that can be settled within the framework.

Williamson (1985, 1993) and others have emphasized how highly specialized capital assets can create power asymmetries, as the suppliers of specific assets have no alternative valuable use for their assets and become dependent on the buyers of their services who have the power to hold up the suppliers or, in the jargon of economics, confiscate their quasi-rents. When credible commitments are lacking, such power asymmetries can discourage potentially profitable investments and retard economic growth. However, the dilemma is often solved through the merger of buyers and sellers into one firm or by government support of the enforcement of private contracts and regulations that strengthen the property rights of the weak party (Goldberg, 1976a,b). North (1990, 1993), North and Weingast (1989), Weingast (1993), and others have argued emphatically that unrestrained, undisciplined state power creates a strong disincentive for decentralized investors and maintain that the evolution of modern industrial economies in Northwestern Europe is closely related to success in introducing the rule of law and constraining the state from randomly overriding individual property rights.

Still, critics may argue that, by holding power relationships constant, the economics of institutions radiates an inherent bias, a secret (or perhaps not so secret) desire to preserve existing power relationships.

Consider for the moment the assertion that the structure of the capitalistic firm is designed not to minimize costs but to exploit workers, whom the capitalists have weakened and deprived of property rights by manipulating the institutional structure of society (Bowles & Gintis 1993). By focusing on exchange between the two sides and how they structure their relationships, the framework encourages scholars to turn a blind eye on what matters most for understanding the nature of the firm – the workers' limited property rights.

However, this view reflects the common phenomenon of confusing the values and conclusions of particular scholars with the nature of the tools they use.[9] First, an appropriate specification of the structure of property rights of workers and employers would bring out their relative power, even when the analysis focuses only on contracting within a given institutional framework. Second, the economics of institutions also provides an opportunity for explaining the institutional arrangements that affect the relative power of workers and employers and exploring how these power relationships emerged and how they are maintained.

To avoid the grave charge of economism, we hasten to add that the theoretical framework does not assume that all institutions are designed for economic purposes, although noneconomic institutions frequently have economic consequences, as suggested by Weber (1958 [1904]) in his controversial study of the Protestant ethic and capitalism (Coleman 1990: 6–10). Furthermore, informal institutions usually are not purposely designed but evolve through spontaneous interaction (North 1990). In the case of institutions that are explicitly designed to alter economic outcomes, the framework does not suggest that all institutional change is explicitly designed to increase aggregate wealth, as many critics seem to believe. Purposive institutional change reflects both the power and interests of those who control institutional change and the processes for making decisions in the political sphere. Only rarely do these forces combine to generate an institutional structure that supports rapid economic growth.

The modern theory of positive political economy, public choice theory, and the theory of regulation provide well-known explanations of

---

[9] If an economist is allowed to use the language of social psychology, it might be argued that criticizing the values and conclusions of frequent users of particular theoretical tools, while favoring the tools themselves, is liable to create unacceptable cognitive dissonance in the critics. In referring to the political discussion in France in the 1960s and 1970s, Elster (1990: 235–36) mentions that many intellectuals lumped together and rejected three concepts: methodological individualism, rational choice theory, and political liberalism. Elster (1990: 236) argues that these three concepts should be decoupled and refers to the propensity of people to "lump things together conceptually that have been empirically associated with each other."

the conflict between the individual rationality of those who control institutional change and collective rationality. All these explanations are related to information and transaction costs, which, for instance, are the source of the rational ignorance of voters in democratic societies and the impracticality of extensive contracting over the distribution of future gains from institutional change.

To conclude, the economics of institutions recognizes that individuals seek to better their position not only by investing in economic activity within a given framework of institutions, but also, in the long run, by investing in strengthening their property rights through altering the institutional framework. Far from failing to recognize the importance of self-interest and power, many economists studying institutional change may have gone too far by modeling the behavior of the actors solely in terms of unadulterated self-interest. Not all behavior in the political sphere can be explained satisfactorily in terms of pure self-interest. Obviously, humans are also motivated by considerations such as altruism and ideologies that stress values other than narrow self-interest, which brings us to the topic of rational choice.

Rational choice

In Figure 1, outcomes ranging from increases (or decreases) in wealth and the establishment of structured contracts, to the creation and enforcement of rules are the combined result of actions by numerous independent actors operating within an institutional framework.[10] The schema is clearly in the realm of methodological individualism, which requires that theories explaining aspects of the economic or social system be grounded in individual behavior. However, methodological individualism is interpreted loosely. Individuals do not act in isolation but are constrained by institutions, and the definition of individual actors includes decision units, such as firms, households, or even governments, although theories grounded in natural individuals are preferred. The behavior of decision units is modeled in terms of the rational choice model. As rational choice analysis has come under renewed attack for providing an impoverished psychological profile of humanity and failing empirical tests (Bell, Raiffa, & Tversky 1988; Cook & Levi 1990), a few words of explanation are in order.

We make four points about the use of rational choice analysis in the economics of institutions. The first point is the simple assertion that

[10] In his important study of the foundations of social theory, Coleman (1990: 1–23) argues that a theory of social systems should have a macro-to-micro component, an individual-action component, and a micro-to-macro component.

rational choice analysis is the best general method we know for modeling behavior at various analytical levels in the economics of institutions. A unifying theme of current research in this area is the ever-present conflict between individual and group rationality, the potential role of institutions in easing the conflict, and the pervasiveness of institutional failure. The rational choice perspective is a relatively effective way to analyze these issues.

The second point is that the economics of institutions has widened the narrow rational choice model of neoclassical economics by adjusting for transaction costs, which can be done by modifying either the constraints of individual actors or the choice process itself. We are inclined toward modifying the constraints rather than the choice process of the actors, a practice in economics that goes back to Alchian's (1965) work on property rights and information problems, and to Stigler's (1961) work on information and the so-called search models. The Simon–Williamson approach of bounded rationality is an alternative approach that focuses on the decision process but retains the assumptions of purposive action and (limited) rationality (Simon 1957; Williamson 1985). We contend that the two approaches are in the same category, and the choice between them a practical matter of convenience and usefulness.

The third point is that the rational choice model is more general than is often recognized. The rational choice approach only involves the assumption that individuals act consistently with their preferences when faced with alternative opportunity sets. The argument that the rational choice perspective is invalid in social studies because rationality is culturally defined is based on a misunderstanding, perhaps due to a mistaken association of rational choice with the economic man of neoclassical fame. Preferences and institutional arrangement may differ among cultures, but it is not helpful, as far as we can see, to visualize choice as being a different phenomenon from one culture to another.

Formally, there is no reason why we cannot make the rational choice model richer psychologically by introducing various norms, including altruism, except that giving each of two or more norms an infinite value severely limits the analysis of choice.[11] However, there is an opportunity cost of complicating the psychological profile of the decision maker. Although Hirschman (1984) has convincingly made the case that parsimony in theorizing is not a free good, neither is liberal complication of the structure. Complex theories are hard to maneuver, and as Coleman (1990:19) has argued, a scholar who studies social systems often must choose between a rich picture of social structures and a complex psycho-

---

[11] Consider a situation where any action or inaction involves ignoring a norm of infinite value.

logical profile of the decision maker. Also, the inclusion of particular values, such as altruism or the norm of vengeance, in individual preference functions to explain particular behavior invites the danger of trivializing the theory. However, competent scholars know both how to avoid tautologies and design theories that can be refuted, and how to weigh the benefits of complexity versus clarity and maneuverability.

The fourth and final point is that we recognize the inadequacy of the rational choice model, with its traditional assumption of stable preferences, in exploring certain important aspects of the economics of institutions, particularly the emergence, maintenance, and decay of social norms and other informal institutions (North 1990, 1993). The topic is not trivial, as informal institutions are a crucial component of the structure of property rights. Consider, for instance, the transition to markets of the former Soviet-type economies. After an initial period of optimism, many scholars feel that the transition process in many of these countries will take a longer time than originally expected, as institutional change involves more than the introduction of a set of formal rules imitating those in the West and the establishment of formal enforcement procedures (Eggertsson, 1994). A successful transition to markets may require the evolution of commercial morality and other norms, but little is known about how these traits appear. Various attempts to use game theory to explain how cooperation emerges through the interaction of selfish actors tend to rely on specific assumptions that deprive the explanations of general applicability – assumptions such as repeated play, a dual personality with one part selfish and the other nonopportunistic, or special circumstances that make monitoring behavior easy (Hechter, Opp, & Wippler 1990; Eggertsson 1992).

Informal institutions appear to be closely related to people's views of the world, both their moral views and their views of causal relationships. Changes in informal institutions are presumably related to learning, although people seem to draw different conclusions from the same experience, since they are subject to path dependence, just as social scientists hold divergent views of the same observable phenomena (Eggertsson 1993; North 1993). Furthermore, in many instances, people's experience provides inclusive evidence for rejecting their theories.

In a sense, the information revolution in economics and the other social sciences has yet to be taken to its logical conclusion. Until recently we have been concerned mostly with the transaction costs of collecting data and, in the language of computers, with the hardware problem caused by the brain's limited capacity to process large batches of data. However, costly information also implies that people may use different models of reality to process the data they receive, and, again using an analogy from computers, the mental models approach can be characterized as an attempt to reconstruct the software that people use for processing information. However, in order to understand learning and the paths of the human mind, we must shift to a new level of scholarship and study the individual (rather than society) as a system, which introduces lessons from the cognitive sciences. North's (1993) recent research has been concerned with mental models, their formation and change, and Schelling (1990:196) states, "If I were to start all over again, I think I would ask for several years to study recent developments in the brain sciences."[12]

The issue of mental models opens up a range of fascinating issues. It is clear that investigators in this field have asked the right question, but so far the "right" answer or operational models of general use have eluded investigators. The area is an important frontier of research and of great interest to all social scientists. It is conceivable that future scholars studying the economics of institutions will use models of the individual of various degrees of sophistication, depending on the nature of their work. For some purposes the narrow neoclassical rational choice model might be appropriate, for other uses the bounded rationality/transaction costs models, and in yet other situations models involving learning. It is interesting to contemplate whether future theories of the origins and evolution of mental models will be formulated in terms of purposive behavior and rational choice. One solution might involve two levels, an exotic theory explaining the emergence of mental models and another theory of the more conventional rational choice variety explaining actions in terms of given mental models.

4. CONCLUSIONS

We have been concerned with a research program for the economics of institutions – that is, exploring the relationship between institutions and wealth. Essentially the research program involves an effort to develop a general theory of economic systems, both a static and a dynamic theory. The word *theory* is used not in the sense of a grand theory of social systems but rather as representing a set of theoretical tools suitable for analyzing a whole range of questions at various analytical levels. The program attempts to integrate various theoretical contributions found in diverse marginal fields in economics, such as law and economics, eco-

---

[12] Schelling (1990: 196) adds: "Most of the work that attracts attention now in the cognitive sciences is pretty much in the rational choice tradition, but I don't think it has to stay that way." Schelling (1990: 197) also states: "I wouldn't abandon the rationality approach at all. I would instead like to enlarge it or enrich it by systematically relaxing certain assumptions of rationality. Because if I abandon the concept of rationality, then I have almost nothing left over."

nomic history, property rights economics, economics of information, and the economics of organization. Some of these contributions have already influenced mainstream economics. All of these theoretical developments share one feature: they reflect an attempt to reintroduce and work out the implications of information problems for economic activity. Information problems give rise to transaction costs and create a central role for property rights in economic analysis. As property rights derive from formal and informal institutions and their enforcement, the approach has obvious links not only to economic analysis but also to the other social sciences, such as sociology, political science, and anthropology, along with law and history.

In drawing on other social sciences, the economics of institutions has the limited purpose of explaining economic phenomena. Therefore, the approach displays some parsimony in portraying social phenomena and in modeling decision makers, which might be unsuited for other scholarly endeavors in other fields of social science. The narrow neoclassical model of rational choice, modified to allow for the cost of transacting (by either adjusting the constraints or assuming bounded rationality), is the main behavioral model of the economics of institutions. Although an obvious simplification of human behavior, the expanded rational choice model has proved a powerful tool for handling various aspects of economic systems. Its weakness is felt, however, when attempts are made to explain the evolution, maintenance, and decay of informal organizations that seem to be of critical importance for fundamental changes in economic systems. A substantial effort is under way to explain informal institutions, such as norms, in terms of the rational behavior of selfish individuals, usually in a game-theoretic context. The full evidence is not in, but many scholars doubt that phenomena, such as commercial morality, can be explained in these terms. These studies set up situations (games) where it is literally in the self-interest of opportunistic individuals to cooperate (for instance, because the gain from cheating is smaller than the cost of lost reputation). However, we need a theory to explain restraint also in situations where defecting has no such direct opportunity cost. The topic, which, for instance, is of vital importance for understanding the transition to markets of the former Soviet-type economies, is at the frontier of research in the economics of institutions. Some scholars have begun to explore these issues from a new analytical level, the individual level, drawing on recent work in the cognitive sciences in an attempt to study mental models, but so far this work has not given rise to new operational theories for the study of institutions.

I conclude with a few words on policy. Usually, economic policy involves modifying formal institutions, since it is not obvious that informal institutions are available policy instruments.[13] However, a better understanding of informal institutions as an exogenous phenomenon is of vital importance for policy. Formal and informal institutions are complementary in creating specific economic outcomes, and the design of efficient formal rules must take into consideration the interaction between new formal rules and existing informal ones. The game-theoretic framework can obviously be of considerable use here. A better understanding of informal rules could help us understand when the introduction of particular formal rules is futile – when they do not match the system of informal rules and therefore will not be enforced. Some of the serious mistakes made by the industrial countries in their programs of aid for developing countries may be due to a limited understanding of the relation between formal and informal institutions. Conversely, a better understanding of the role of informal institutions could be of help in designing formal rules that take advantage of existing informal rules to rely extensively on self-enforcement, leaving only pathological cases for the formal enforcement mechanism, the police and the courts.

REFERENCES

Alchian, A. A. 1965. Some economics of property rights. *Il Politico* 30, 816–29 (originally published in 1961 by the Rand Corporation); reprinted in Alchian (1977).

1977. *Economic Forces at Work*. Indianapolis: Liberty Press.

Alt, J. E., & Shepsle, K. A. (eds.). 1990. *Perspectives on Positive Political Theory*. Cambridge University Press.

Arrow, K. J. 1990. Kenneth J. Arrow. In Swedberg (1990), 133–51.

Barzel, Y. 1989. *Economic Analysis of Property Rights*. Cambridge University Press.

Bates, R. H. 1989. *Beyond the Miracle of the Market: The Political Economy of Agrarian Development in Kenya*. Cambridge University Press.

Bell, D. E., Raiffa, H., & Tversky, A. 1988. *Decision Making: Descriptive, Normative, and Prescriptive Interactions*. Cambridge University Press.

Bowles, S., & Gintis, S. 1993. The revenge of homo economicus: Contested exchange and the revival of political economy. *Journal of Economic Perspectives* 7, 83–102.

Cheung, S. N. S. 1968. Private property rights and sharecropping. *Journal of Political Economy* 76, 1107–22.

1969. Transaction costs, risk aversion, and the choice of contractual arrangements. *Journal of Law and Economics* 12, 23–42.

1970. The structure of a contract and the theory of non-exclusive resource. *Journal of Law and Economics* 13, 49–70.

---

[13] The desirability of governments adding the power to control norms and other informal institutions to their arsenal of policy instruments is a question left with the reader.

A note on the economics of institutions

Coase, R. H. 1937. The nature of the firm. *Economica* 4, 386–405.

1960. The problem of social cost. *Journal of Law and Economics* 3, 1–44.

Coleman, J. S. 1990. *Foundations of Social Theory*. Cambridge, Mass.: Harvard University Press.

Cook, K. S., & Levi, M. 1990. *The Limits of Rationality*. Chicago University Press.

Cooter, R. D., & Ulen, T. 1988. *Law and Economics*. New York: Harper Collins.

Demsetz, Harold. 1988. *The Organization of Economic Activity* (2 vols.). Oxford: Basil Blackwell.

Eggertsson, T. 1990. *Economic Behavior and Institutions*. Cambridge University Press.

1992. Review of Hechter, Opp, & Wippler (1990). *Journal of Institutional and Theoretical Economics* 148, 505–8.

1993. Mental models and social values: North's institutions and credible commitment. *Journal of Institutional and Theoretical Economics* 149, 24–28.

1994. The economics of institutions in transition economies. In S. Schiavo-Campo (ed.), *Institutional Change and the Public Sector in Transitional Economies*, 19–50. Washington D.C.: World Bank.

Elster, J. 1990. Jon Elster. In Swedberg (1990), 233–48.

Ensminger, J. 1992. *Making a Market: The Institutional Transformation of an African Society*. Cambridge University Press.

Fenoaltea, S. 1984. Slavery and supervision in comparative perspective: a model. *Journal of Economic History* 44, 635–68.

Furubotn, E. G., & Richter, R. (eds.). 1991. *The New Institutional Economics*. Tübingen: J. C. Mohr.

1993. *The New Institutional Economics – Recent Progress: Expanding Frontiers*. Special Issue, *Journal of Institutional and Theoretical Economics* 149.

Goldberg, V. P. 1976a. Toward an expanded economic theory of contract. *Journal of Economic Issues* 10, 45–61.

1976b. Regulation and administered contracts. *Bell Journal of Economics* 7, 426–41.

Granovetter, M. 1992. Economic institutions as social constructions: a framework for analysis. *Acta Sociologica* 35, 3–12.

Greif, A. 1989. Reputations and coalitions in medieval trade: evidence on the Maghribi traders. *Journal of Economic History* 49, 857–82.

Greif, A., Milgrom, P., & Weingast, B. R. 1994. Coordination, commitment, and enforcement: The case of the Merchant Guild. *Journal of Political Economy* 102, 745–77.

Hechter, M., Opp, K.-D., & Wippler, R. 1990. *Social Institutions: Their Emergence, Maintenance and Effects*. Berlin: de Gruyter.

Hirschman, A. O. 1984. Against parsimony: Three easy ways of complicating some categories of economic discourse. *American Economic Review* 74, 89–96.

Knight, J. 1992. *Institutions and Social Conflict*. Cambridge University Press.

Krueger, A. O. 1993. Virtuous and vicious circles in economic development. *American Economic Review* 83, 351–55.

Landa, J. T. 1994. *Trust, Ethnicity, and Identity: Beyond the New Institutional Economics of Ethnic Trading Networks, Contract Law, and Gift Exchange*. Ann Arbor: University of Michigan Press.

Libecap, G. D. 1989. *Contracting for Property Rights.* Cambridge University Press.

McCubbins, M. D., & Sullivan T. (eds.). 1987. *Congress: Structure and Policy.* Cambridge University Press.

Milgrom, P., & Roberts J. 1992. *Economics, Organization and Management.* Englewood Cliffs, N.J.: Prentice Hall.

Mueller, D. C. 1989. *Public Choice II.* Cambridge University Press.

North, D. C. 1981. *Structure and Change in Economic History.* New York: Norton.

    1990. *Institutions, Institutional Change and Economic Performance.* Cambridge University Press.

    1993. Institutions and credible commitment. In Furubotn & Richter (1993), 11–23.

North, D. C., & Weingast, B. R. 1989. Constitutions and credible commitments: The evolution of the institutions of public choice in 17th century England. *Journal of Economic History* 49, 803–32.

Ostrom, E. 1990. *Governing the Commons.* Cambridge University Press.

Posner, R. A. 1986. *Economic Analysis of Law.* Boston: Little, Brown.

Rodrik, D. 1993. The positive economics of policy reform. *American Economic Review* 83, 356–61.

Schelling, T. C. 1990. Thomas C. Schelling. In Swedberg (1990), 186–99.

Shepsle, K. A., & Weingast, B. R. 1981. Structure induced equilibrium and legislative choice. *Public Choice* 37, 503–20.

Simon, H. 1957. *Models of Man.* New York: Wiley.

Solzhenitsyn, A. I. 1968. *The First Circle* (transl. from the Russian by T. P. Whitney). New York: Harper & Row.

Stigler, G. J. 1961. The economics of information. *Journal of Political Economy* 69, 213–25.

Swedberg, R. (ed.). 1990. *Economics and Sociology. Redefining Their Boundaries: Conversations with Economists and Sociologists.* Princeton, N.J.: Princeton University Press.

Weber, M. 1958 (1904). *The Protestant Ethic and the Spirit of Capitalism.* New York: Scribner's.

Weingast, B. R. 1993. Constitutions as governance structures: The political foundations of secure markets. *Journal of Institutional and Theoretical Economics* 149, 286–311.

Werin, L., & Wijkander, H. (eds.). 1992. *Contract Economics.* Oxford: Basil Blackwell.

Williamson, O. E. 1985. *The Economic Institutions of Capitalism.* New York: Free Press.

    1993. The evolving science of organization. In Furubotn & Richter (1993), 36–63.

Empirical work in institutional economics: an overview

LEE J. ALSTON

1. INTRODUCTION

Most social scientists agree that an understanding of institutions is critical for understanding economic development and the economic performance of economies. Yet, despite this recognition, the research on institutions by many social scientists is either highly descriptive or so abstract as to render it useless for policy. The reason for the absence of the "happy medium" is that few scholars know how to do empirical work in institutional economics. It is seldom taught in graduate school and the practitioners have learned by doing. It is our goal in collecting the essays in this volume to further the development of work in institutional analysis by drawing out some lessons on how to perform research.

2. HISTORY MATTERS

Institutions are historically specific, and for this reason it is necessary to be sensitive to historical context.[1] This is particularly true for the dynamics of institutional change. Much of the developmental path of societies is conditioned by their past. Even after revolutions, institution builders do not start off in a historical vacuum. At any moment in time, actions are constrained by customs, norms, religious beliefs, and many other inherited institutions. This is as true for the leaders in Eastern Europe today as it was for Augustus Caesar.

An understanding of history is also important because the dynamics of institutional change frequently include unintended consequences that take on a life of their own. For this reason I warn against a functional-

---

[1] Stephen Jay Gould has advanced an argument similar to ours for the importance of historical circumstances in explaining the evolution of species. See, e.g., his "George Canning's Left Buttock and the Origin of the Species," in *Bully for Brontosaurus* (New York: Norton, 1992).

ist approach to institutional analysis whereby the motivations for particular institutions are judged from the consequences of the institutional change. For example, some scholars have argued that because the railroads captured the Interstate Commerce Commission by the early twentieth century, the railroads must have lobbied for the passage of the Interstate Commerce Act in the nineteenth century. Yet I believe the capture of the ICC by the railroads was an unintended consequence of the legislation.

3. INSTITUTIONAL ANALYSIS: AT WHAT LEVEL?

The analysis of institutions can take place at different levels, and much confusion in the literature can be eliminated if scholars are explicit about the analytical plane on which they are operating. The simplest delineation is between causes and effects of institutional change. Within the causes of institutional change further delineation can be made. Being careful about specifying the level of institutional analysis does not mean that scholars cannot address an issue at different levels. Indeed, most of the essays in this volume contain elements of both causes and consequences of institutional change.

The effects of institutional change

At this level the analyst is performing a comparative statics exercise. That is, the analyst moves from a situation where one institution is in place to a situation where another set of rules is in force and then compares the results. This is an important component of policy analysis. Institutional change is taken as exogenous. For example, in his essay in this volume (Chapter 6), Cheung is interested in the effects of rent control: Does rent control lead to deteriorating quality? Does it reduce the amount of building? What are the many ingenious ways of evading rent control? What are the intended consequences? What factors can lead to unintended consequences? The essay by Stone, Levy, and Paredes (Chapter 3) is another example of empirical work that analyzes the effects of institutional change. The authors take as given the formal laws and regulations affecting the textile industry in Brazil and Chile and analyze the perceived costs of the laws and the ways in which business persons transact to minimize the costs of burdensome regulations.

The causes of institutional change

At this level the analyst is trying to uncover the dynamics of a system that led to change. Institutional change can be thought of as the result of supply and demand forces in a society. We can think of demanders as constituents and suppliers as the government. This does not mean that there is a unique outcome. In some ways bargaining is a more apt description. The rationale for using the terms *demand* and *supply* is that formal institutions emerge through a political process. That is, laws are legislated, enacted, or decreed through government entities. In this way governments "supply" institutions. In analyzing institutions, one has to specify the political power of the demanders and suppliers. In some instances demanders have disproportionate power and can influence institutional change. For these demanders, institutions are a choice variable. Frequently, individuals on the supply side of institutional change – that is, government actors – have some power to change rules independently of their constituents. In both of these situations the political power of either certain demanders or certain suppliers will lead to outcomes that differ from those that occur when political power by any individual or group of individuals is negligible. Institutional change results from the bargaining actions of demanders and suppliers. We can describe three pure cases. In reality most instances are a combination of all three, but the analysis is clearer when one is explicit about the relative weights of each of the following cases.

Institutional change as endogenous to the system but exogenous to individual demanders and suppliers. Institutional change is not seen as a choice variable for any individual but is the result of the aggregation of the preferences of individuals for change. Put another way, there is little scope for individual discretion. This situation is analogous to that of the individual consumer in competitive markets. Some laws or rules are the result of a general consensus that the new law is the right thing. For example, most U.S. citizens approve of flood relief legislation. Legislators who pass such laws are simply responding to the demands of constituents to do something. They can be thought of as having little scope for individual action. So too on the demand side: no one citizen has much political power to determine the level of assistance. Demand is the result of the aggregated preferences of citizens. Several essays in this volume take as given the premise that individual actors or special interest groups have little discretion in changing rules.

In Chapter 1 Libecap examines the impact on mineral law legislation of increases in the value of mineral discoveries. Libecap argues that, as the value of minerals increases, claim holders will "demand" more precision in property rights. In his model individual claim holders are not politically powerful and the suppliers of legislation simply respond to the demands of constituents on the basis of the aggregate wealth-enhancing impact of more precise property rights. In a similar way, North and

Weingast in Chapter 4 analyze the aggregate forces, in addition to the individual actions of the Crown, that led to the emergence of a more secure set of property rights in seventeenth-century England. In the North and Weingast model even the Crown had little power to act unilaterally but instead was responding to aggregate forces, generally the threat of war.

Institutional change as endogenous to the certain demanders. The analyst must specify who in society are the demanders for the status quo or institutional change. In specifying the demanders it is important to determine their relative political power, including that of citizens at large. The analyst needs to know who has the political power to "demand" change or maintain the status quo and what are the incentives to lobby for change. For example, in several Western countries and Japan, the auto industry is an important demander of trade policy. As such, if the institutional change considered is trade policy, the analyst must specify the incentives and constraints faced by the auto industry and other demanders of policy.

The authors of several essays in this volume carefully specify the degree to which certain actors are able either individually or collectively to change laws and regulations to their benefit. For example, in Chapter 9 Alston and Ferrie argue that for nearly a century Southern agricultural interests were able to control their congressmen so as to prevent the federal government from interfering in agricultural labor relations. In Chapter 7, Higgs argues that salmon fishermen with less efficient fishing gear were successful in securing the passage of laws that excluded from the industry those with the most efficient fishing gear.

Institutional change as endogenous to the suppliers. The analyst must specify the scope for discretion faced by the suppliers of institutional change, usually government actors. Where a dictator has a firm command over her constituents, the scope may be nearly absolute. On the other hand, constituents may have many ready substitutes for a ruler, and monitoring the behavior of a ruler is easy, resulting in little independent discretion for the supplier of change. The essay in this volume that best typifies the "supply side" of institutional change is that by Riker and Sened in Chapter 8. In examining the decision to allow property rights in airline slots, Riker and Sened specify the roles played by the Civil Aeronautics Board, the Federal Aviation Authority, the Department of Transportation, and the Office of Management and Budget.

4. TESTING

Once one has specified either the expected results of institutional change or the expected causes of institutional change, how does one test the "model"? Unfortunately, there is no easy answer. Institutional changes usually have some unique features limiting the data points and thus generally preventing conventional statistical analysis. But all is not lost.

Comparisons across countries

One approach to testing is to compare the effects of different institutions across countries. In Chapter 3 Stone, Levy, and Paredes "test" for the effects of different regulations (institutions) on the garment industry in Chile and Brazil. The authors started with the premise that regulation was more burdensome in Brazil than in Chile. They did not attempt to measure directly how much more burdensome. This is important, because sometimes measures of more or less will suffice. To test whether the regulations caused differences in behavior, the authors interviewed managers of firms in the garment industry. To define the historical context, the authors also interviewed lawyers, bankers, and some public officials.

Quantitative measures

In testing for the dynamics of change, it is sometimes possible to use quantitative proxies for the political power of the demanders or suppliers of legislation. For example, in Chapter 9 Alston and Ferrie measure the political power across time of Southern congressmen by measuring the number of committees chaired by these legislators in different time periods. In Chapter 7 Higgs lists the number of fishermen using various types of gear for catching salmon as evidence of their power in the political arena.

At times it may be possible to run statistical tests for the causes of institutional change. This is usually the case when institutional change is continuous rather than discrete. For example, Libecap (Chapter 1) formally tested the hypothesis that as the value of gold and silver increased in the Nevada Territory so too did the demand for more precise property rights to minerals. Libecap constructed indices of legal change over time – a proxy for the precision of property rights – and used this as the dependent variable in a regression with the quantity of output as an independent variable along with a control variable for complete precision of property rights.

Lee J. Alston

Case studies

Frequently, quantitative measures of the causes or consequences of institutional change are simply not available; even when they are available, better evidence may come from the qualitative historical record. Using the details of historical facts as evidence, we essentially are applying the case study approach. All of the essays in this volume rely to a greater or lesser degree on the historical record to provide evidence consistent with their hypotheses. For example, in Chapter 4 North and Weingast maintain that the Glorious Revolution led to a diminution in the rights of the Crown. This proposition seems to be generally accepted. In Chapter 5 Krueger maintains that the regulations affecting the sugar industry in the United States became more complex over time, which in turn raised the barriers to participating in future changes. The proposition seems to be reasonable. Indeed, one way to assess much evidence is to stop and ask, Is the argument logically consistent and does the evidence seem reasonable?

In arguing for the case study approach we are not abandoning science. We still maintain that the use of theory in developing hypotheses is important. Indeed, the intuitiveness of a hypothesis influences the standards of evidence that we must have before we "accept" the hypothesis.[2] The more compelling is the hypothesis, the lower are our standards of evidence before we become convinced.

Furthermore, the case study approach to institutions is attractive because it may yield the building blocks for more general theories of institutional change. With the present state of theoretical knowledge about institutions, the case study approach is often the only way to further our knowledge about institutional change. Given that an understanding of institutions and institutional change is central to understanding economic performance, the issues at stake are too important not to use whatever analytical tools provide insights into the complex relationships among institutions, institutional change, and economic performance.

---

[2] One reason for the success of economics in explaining much behavior in the world is the intuitive appeal of the theory of demand: as prices increase, individuals desire less of the item in question. Whether we are talking about bordeaux wine or going to war, the hypothesis about demand seems reasonable.

I

Toward an understanding of property rights

The structure of property rights critically affects economic outcomes by influencing the incentives of actors to create new wealth or to dissipate resources. In the economics of institutions, the term *property rights* refers to an actor's rights, which are recognized and enforced by other members of society, to use and control valuable resources. The control over resources also has an internal component. Various rules, and their enforcement by political organizations and by custom and social norms, provide external control, but usually actors also invest privately in control, depending on how much external enforcement the community provides. Although governments, for instance, outlaw breaking and entering and provide enforcement through the police and the courts, the level of external protection varies across polities, as does the level of trespassing. Owners respond by investing in various amounts of internal enforcement – with locks on doors, burglar alarms, guard dogs, and other measures. However, economies of scale make well-functioning social control, with formal and informal rules, a much more effective arrangement than heavy reliance on private (internal) control, and the economics of institutions pays much attention to the origins and nature of property rights because of their potential significance for economic prosperity and the creation of wealth.

The following essay by Gary Libecap is a case study of the determinants of mineral law in the western United States in the nineteenth century – a study of the evolution of property rights to mineral deposits. Libecap postulates that the law changed in response to changes in economic value: as the value of a resource increased, claimants of the resource had an incentive to "demand" more precision in the definition of property rights in order to capture more fully the potential rental stream from the resource.[1] Libecap tests his model by developing indices of the precision of property rights. His essay made a pioneering contribution to the use of statistical analysis to test the determinants of institutional change.

Individuals demand or value property rights because they allow them to capture potential rent. Actual rent is a function of the property rights that one possesses; the more property rights one possesses over a resource, the greater is the value of a resource. For example, with respect to land, the more secure one's property rights: (1) the more secure is the future rental stream that the land produces, (2) the better one is able to use land as collateral, and (3) the larger is the market for sale.

There seems to be some confusion in the literature over which way causation runs between property rights and value. The confusion is cleared up if we remember the following. It is true that a resource becomes more valuable the greater the rights one has over the resource, and in this sense value (or actual rent) is a function of property rights. But it is not actual rent, but rather potential rent, that drives the *demand* for property rights. Potential rent is a function of the inherent rental stream (e.g., world price of the resource) and some benchmark set of possible property rights that are culturally and institutionally specific to a time and place. For example, today it would be silly to think of the potential stream from labor services to include slavery, but it is reasonable to think of other issues in labor law – for instance, legal sanctions against the employment of illegal aliens – as being in the realm of possibility.

The model of property rights in which potential rent determines property rights is naive in part because it ignores the difference between potential aggregate gain and the distribution of the gains and losses from changes in property rights. It is important to recognize that changes in property rights generally involve winners and losers. In some cases the transaction costs of making the side-payments necessary to get growth-enhancing property rights are prohibitive. In these cases the status quo set of property rights remains in effect because the heterogeneity of the parties affected gives rise to transaction costs that prevent movement to a set of property rights in which the aggregate gains outweigh the aggregate losses.

In other instances the creation of or change in property rights is not very sensitive to potential rent because of factors on the supply side of property rights. By suppliers of property rights, we typically mean governments, because it is governments that generally specify and en-

---

[1] This demand-induced view of institutional change is what Eggertsson refers to as the naive model of property rights. See his *Economic Behavior and Institutions* (Cambridge University Press, 1990).

force property rights. If potential rent in the aggregate alone drove property rights, the whole world would be developed and continually developing. Surely this is not the case, even in the long run in many parts of the world.

In both representative and nonrepresentative governments, property rights may respond sluggishly to potential rent. In nonrepresentative governments, the rulers may lose from changes in property rights that increase the national wealth but primarily benefit the citizens. Again, it is an issue of not being able to make the side payments necessary to bring about change because either the transaction costs of collecting from gainers are prohibitive or the beliefs of the citizens would not allow the transfer even though they are materially worse off in the status quo.

In representative governments, there are a variety of principal–agent problems that prevent potential aggregate rent from causing changes in property rights. For example, voters at large are rationally ignorant about many potential changes in property rights that would improve their welfare at the expense of special interests. Furthermore, there are institutional features of representative governments that allow government agents to act in their self-interest rather than in the interests of their constituents. For example, in the United States the ways in which committees shape legislation give advantages to seniority, which in turn allows more senior members some scope to act in their narrow self-interest: for voters it is too costly to "vote the rascal out."

WHAT TO LOOK FOR IN THE ESSAY

These supply- and demand-side issues do not imply that potential rent is an unimportant determinant of property rights. Libecap's study illustrates that in the case of mineral rights potential rent may be a sufficient explanation for change. We encourage the reader to consider the following questions while reading the essay:

1. Why did mineral laws change in ways that encc•.raged economic growth, while other laws are often not so responsive?
2. Were the demanders of mineral rights homogeneous?
3. Were there any losers from change, and if so were they simply politically impotent?
4. What benefits did the lawmakers derive from change?
5. Was this simply a case where the change in potential wealth as a result of the richness of the Comstock Lode swamped the transaction costs of change?

Economic variables and the development of the law: the case of western mineral rights

GARY D. LIBECAP

Much of American legal activity during the eighteenth and nineteenth centuries centered on the transfer of a continent of natural resources – agricultural land, water, timber, mineral deposits – from public to private control. That transfer was crucial for the development of an economic system based largely on private incentives and market transactions. Legal policy at both the state and federal level regarding natural resource ownership and use has been the focus of work by Paul W. Gates, Willard Hurst, Harry Scheiber, and others.[1] Those studies have generally been aimed at describing the nature and impact of governmental support for private economic activities.[2] This paper is concerned with a somewhat different question – the timing and emergence of particular legal institutions (laws and governments). The framework for the study is that offered by Lance Davis and Douglass North in *Institutional*

This essay first appeared in *Journal of Economic History*, Vol. 38, No. 2 (June 1978). Copyright © The Economic History Association. All rights reserved. Reprinted by the permission of Cambridge University Press.

I would like to thank Joseph D. Reid, Jr., Richard Easterlin, William Whitney, Oliver Williamson, and the members of the 1977 Cliometrics Conference for their helpful comments.

[1] Paul W. Gates, *History of Public Land Law Development* (Washington D.C., 1968); J. Willard Hurst, *Law and the Conditions of Freedom in the Nineteenth-Century United States* (Evanston, 1956); J. Willard Hurst, *Law and Economic Growth: The Legal History of the Lumber Industry in Wisconsin, 1836–1915* (Cambridge: Harvard University Press, 1964); Harry N. Scheiber, *Ohio Canal Era: A Case Study of Government and the Economy, 1820–1861* (Athens, Ohio, 1969); Harry N. Scheiber, "Property Law, Expropriation, and Resource Allocation by Government: The United States, 1789–1910," *Journal of Economic History*, 33 (March 1973), 232–51; Gerald D. Nash, *State Government and Economic Development, A History of Administrative Policies in California, 1849–1933* (Berkeley, 1964); Gary D. Libecap, *The Evolution of Private Mineral Rights: Nevada's Comstock Lode* (New York: Arno Press, 1978).

[2] A general conclusion from those studies has been that governments were active supporters of economic growth in the nineteenth century in the United States.

Economic variables and the development of law

Change and American Economic Growth.[3] There they hypothesize that institutions develop in response to changing private needs or profit potentials: "It is the possibility of profits that cannot be captured within the existing arrangemental structure that leads to the formation of new (or the mutation of old) institutional arrangements."[4] Essentially the same model of institutional change is used by some American legal historians, notably Lawrence Friedman and Willard Hurst.[5] They argue that the law can only be understood by examining the surrounding economic, political, and social conditions. Those conditions mold the law, and as they change, they force legal institutions to change. Friedman ties this view closely to the Davis–North model in *A History of American Law,* where he argues that competing interest groups are the primary determinants of the nature of the law at any one time.[6] This view of legal institutional change is in sharp contrast to the common law tradition of legal history which sees the law as an *autonomous* institution passed on from generation to generation – an institution that molds the economic, political, and social inputs from society.[7]

The empirical evidence reported in this paper strongly suggests that the private mineral rights law in the American West did not evolve autonomously, but rather was continually shaped by external economic forces. Focus is on a leading mining state, Nevada, during the period of the Comstock Lode (1858–1895), which was its richest mining region. Nevada is important because portions of its mining law were incorporated into subsequent federal legislation which is still in effect. In addition, the Comstock Lode was one of the West's premiere mining regions, producing nearly $400,000,000 in gold and silver bullion.[8] By 1889 the Comstock Lode alone had produced over 12 percent of all the gold and silver ever mined in the United States. During its peak years in the mid-1870s the Comstock yielded nearly 50 percent of the total United States output of bullion and more than double the output of the entire state of

---

[3] Lance E. Davis and Douglass C. North, *Institutional Change and American Economic Growth* (Cambridge: Cambridge University Press, 1971), particularly chs. 1–4.

[4] Davis and North, *Institutional Change,* p. 59.

[5] For example, see Hurst, *Law and Economic Growth,* and *Law and Social Process in United States History* (Ann Arbor, 1960); and Lawrence M. Friedman, *History of American Law* (New York, 1973).

[6] See Friedman, *History,* pp. 10–14, for an outline of the model.

[7] The question of whether to view the law as largely evolving autonomously or as molded by external events is discussed by Robert W. Gordon, "Introduction: J. Willard Hurst and the Common Law Tradition in American Legal Historiography," *Law and Society Review,* vol. 10, no. 1, pp. 10–11.

[8] Bertrand Couch and Jay Carpenter, "Nevada's Metal and Mineral Production," *University of Nevada Bulletin,* vol. 37, no. 4, Geology and Mining Series (1943), p. 133.

California, the next most productive region.[9] In contrast to California the Comstock was primarily a deep vein mining operation and was responsible for much of the technology (such as square-set timbering) which later spread throughout the West. As in California and Colorado in 1859, the Comstock mines were on public land, and until 1866 there were no federal procedures for granting private ownership. Yet, since Congress did not evict the prospectors, *local* ownership rules developed, and the mines were operated for private gain.[10] This local property law, however, was not static. Indeed, as the record shows, the thirty-nine-year period from 1858–1895 was one of rapid legal change regarding mineral rights. The aim of this paper is to describe and quantify the progression of property law from general rules to highly specified statutes and court verdicts and to relate causally that progression to economic conditions in the mining camps. Research shows that the Nevada mine owners were advocates of this progression to highly specified mineral rights, and that in most cases they were supported by the general population.

1. THE MODEL

To determine the incentives mine owners would have for changing the legal rights structure, I focus on the *net gains* received by them from laws of varying specificity and enforcement.[11] On the benefit side greater

[9] Calculated from statistics in Richard P. Rothwell, "Gold and Silver," in David T. Day, ed., *Report on Mineral Industries in the United States at the Eleventh Census* (Washington D.C., 1890), pp. 33–42.

[10] The development of mining law in Nevada and Colorado, both leading mining states, is discussed by Gary Libecap in *The Evolution*. For a discussion of American land law see Paul Gates, *History of Land Law*; for mining see Gregory Yale, *Legal Title to Mining Claims and Water Rights* (San Francisco, 1867), Charles Shinn, *Mining Camps: A Study in American Frontier Government* (New York, 1948) and the Rocky Mountain Law Foundation, ed., *The American Law of Mining* (New York: Mathew Bender, 1974). Rodman Paul, *Mining Frontiers of the Far West, 1848–1880* (New York, 1963) is a general study of western mining. Finally, John Umbeck has studied the rise of mining camps in the California gold rush: John Umbeck, "A Theoretical and Empirical Investigation into the Formation of Property Rights: The California Gold Rush," (Ph.D. dissertation, University of Washington, Seattle, 1975).

[11] This view of the development of property rights law benefits from the following studies: James Buchanan, *The Bases for Collective Action* (Morristown, N.J., 1972) and *The Limits of Liberty* (Chicago, 1975); Harold Demsetz, "Toward a Theory of Property Rights," *American Economic Review* 57 (May 1967), p. 350; Armen Alchian and Harold Demsetz, "Property Rights Paradigm," *Journal of Economic History*, 33 (March 1973), p. 24; William Craig Stubblebine, "On Property Rights and Institutions," in Gordon Tullock, ed., *Explorations in the Theory of Anarchy* (Blacksburg, Va.: Center for the Study of Public Choice, 1972), p. 11. Focusing on the net gain calculations of mine owners is the most direct way of understanding the

precision in the law increases the probability a mine owner will maintain control of his claim. That is, greater definition and enforcement of his private rights reduces ownership uncertainty. First, as individual rights and property boundaries are more clearly defined, trespass and theft can be more readily detected and proven; second, state protection of private rights can be more easily obtained as the procedure for doing so is made clear; and third, violators of private claims are more apt to be found guilty when the obligations of enforcing officials are exactly described.[12] Increased precision in the law, however, involves private costs. Due to a lack of state or federal mining law to borrow from, there are learning costs in determining the appropriate statutory response to new conditions. In addition there are lobby expenditures for influencing legislators, judges, and other enforcing officials; and taxes from government operations. Private costs are likely to be affected by a number of factors such as the physical nature of ore deposits, existing institutional arrangements, and the number of claimants involved. With these private costs and benefits in mind, I argue that mine owners will push for greater

motivation for the observed legal change in Nevada. The historical record shows that the mine owners were the major proponents of greater mineral rights guarantees. This is not surprising given the high expected returns from exclusive control. The record also shows that in most cases there was support by the general population for the legislation. Economic growth and increases in mine output were highly regarded by Nevada citizens, and there is little evidence of efforts at income redistribution. Similar findings regarding the general support of the population for private property rights and economic growth in other frontier areas have been reported by Hurst and Nash. Willard Hurst, for example, argued that Wisconsin timber law emerged in response to local needs; that the lumber industry was influential in its development; and that the community supported the desires of timber owners in exploiting the forest. See Willard Hurst, *Law and Economic Growth*, pp. x–xiii, 42, 159, 240, 264. Gerald Nash stressed the power of the California mine owners in the legislature in obtaining favorable statutes. He concluded that "promotion of private enterprise has been the most common characteristic in the relation of government to the economy . . . creation of the legal framework, to allow for incorporation, for agreements on contracts and trading procedures, and for establishment of a money system have been important." Gerald Nash, *State Government and Economic Growth*, pp. 36–40, 350. In cases of conflict with other individuals Comstock mine owners had an advantage in the political process since, compared with the rest of the population, they were a relatively small and organized group whose interests often coincided. For a discussion of the effectiveness of small, organized groups see Mancur Olson, *The Logic of Collective Action* (Cambridge: Harvard University Press, 1965), pp. 53–65.

[12] Richard Posner and Isaac Ehrlich argue that rules will be made more precise the higher the level of economic activity. "An Economic Analysis of Legal Rulemaking," *Journal of Legal Studies* 3 (January 1974), pp. 257–86. Individual rights must be clearly defined for an owner to enlist state support against violation of those rights since he must convince officials that a crime has been committed. See Richard A. Posner, "An Economic Approach to Legal Procedure and Judicial Administration," *Journal of Legal Studies* 2 (June 1973), p. 408. See also, Gordon Tullock, *The Logic of the Law* (New York, 1971), pp. 47–50.

precision in the legal rights structure as long as there are private net gains from doing so.[13]

In applying this model it is not necessary to measure directly the private net gains in order to understand the incentive for legal change. Instead, one can follow economic events which would alter private costs and benefits and then determine if the predicted changes in the law occur. In particular, new ore discoveries within a mine would increase the expected present value of exclusive control. Because of the fluid, short-term nature of most mining camps, current ore production was likely the most important determinant of the expected present value of ownership. Ore strikes, however, would encourage competition for the land, leading to greater uncertainty. Accordingly, as ore strikes occur, increasing mine output, one would expect lobby activity by owners to make mineral rights law more specific and enforcement more elaborate as long as uncertainty exists. This expectation leads to two testable hypotheses. First, mineral rights law will be made more specific and enforcement more elaborate as the value of mine output increases due to ore discoveries. (The value of mine output is used as a proxy for the expected present value of mine ownership.) Second, when the legal rights structure is highly defined and enforced, further increases in the precision of the law will occur at a slower rate. As uncertainty is reduced, the private benefits from additional legal change decline.[14]

2. THE EMPIRICAL EVIDENCE

The development of mineral rights law – a historical summary

This summary is designed to illustrate the dynamics of legal change in Nevada, and preliminary evidence indicates that similar patterns existed elsewhere in the mining West.[15] Mining operations took place in western Nevada (just east of Lake Tahoe) through most of the 1850s, though the

---

[13] The model places most emphasis on economic factors in the .development of mineral rights law. Given the high expected returns from exclusive control and the lack of an existing ownership structure when ore was discovered, one would expect economic events to outweigh other social and political factors in the formation of the legal structure.

[14] Warren Samuels discusses the interaction of legal and economic systems around the case of *Miller et al. v. Schoene,* in "Interrelations between Legal and Economic Processes," *Journal of Legal Studies* (October 1971), pp. 435–50. A more general outline of legal-economic interactions in American economic development is given by Harry Scheiber, "Federalism and the American Economic Order, 1789–1910," *Law and Society Review,* vol. 10, no. 2, pp. 57–117.

[15] See also Gary D. Libecap, "Government Support of Private Claims to Public Minerals: Western Mineral Rights," *Business History Review,* forthcoming. That

region was marginal with total annual production less than $67,000.[16] About 100 miners worked in an area of approximately 40 square miles under *unwritten* and informal ownership agreements. Eliot Lord, who studied the Comstock for the U.S. Geological Survey, reported that the prospectors were "easy humored" and that conflicts over allotments were rare.[17] The land was not valuable enough for a more formal (and costly) property rights structure. This changed abruptly, however, after the Comstock Lode was discovered in January 1859, increasing the present value of land ownership. The Comstock Lode was a rich vein of ore-bearing quartz that ran with other parallel veins in a mineralized zone about five miles long and a mile wide.[18] Once mining in the zone began, output for the region jumped to nearly $260,000 by the end of the year and to $2,500,000 annually by 1861; the population rose from 100 to 20,000 during the same period.[19] Most of the 3,149 new claims made between 1859 and 1861 were to portions of the Comstock Lode or adjacent veins, and competition for the land was intense. This pressure led to a predictable change in property rights institutions to achieve ownership security and to avoid the potential losses of anarchy. Within five months of the Comstock ore strike, a formal mining camp government, Gold Hill, was established by prospectors at the site of the earliest discoveries. The Gold Hill District had written rules regarding the establishment and maintenance of private holdings, and the rules were enforced by a permanent claim recorder and an ad hoc miners' court.[20] Three months later a similar government was organized at Virginia City, and the Devil's Gate District followed in early 1860. Ore discoveries in the latter areas were made after those in Gold Hill, suggesting that more formal property rights arrangements were not developed until competition for the land forced the miners to do so – a finding which is consistent with the model. In general the mining camp regulations described the recording requirements for locating a claim, the size of

article describes specific miners' rules, statutes, and court rulings and their impact on private mineral rights within the context of general government support for private economic activities in the nineteenth century.

[16] Calculated from data in Grant Smith, "The History of the Comstock Lode," *University of Nevada Bulletin*, vol. 37, no. 3, Geology and Mining Series (1943), p. 2.

[17] Eliot Lord, *Comstock Mining and Miners*, U.S. Geological Survey Monographs (Washington D.C.: Government Printing Office, 1883), p. 35.

[18] See J. Ross Browne, *Reports on the Mineral Resources of the United States, 1868* (Washington, D.C.: Government Printing Office, 1868), pp. 341–42.

[19] Bertrand Couch and Jay Carpenter, "Nevada's Metal and Mineral Production," *University of Nevada Bulletin*, vol. 37, no. 4, Geology and Mining Series (1943), p. 133. 1859 population from Grant Smith, "The History," p. 2; 1860 population from the San Francisco *Alta California*, 14 November 1860.

[20] Claim numbers from Grant Smith papers, Bancroft Library, University of California, Berkeley. Mining camp rules are found in Eliot Lord, *Comstock Mining*, p. 40.

individual allotments, the procedures for marking claim boundaries, and the work requirements necessary for maintaining ownership.[21] By following the rules of the mining district, claimants were granted locally recognized possessory rights to mineral ground.

While the mining camps seem to have been established to provide more precise and secure property rights arrangements, continued ore strikes within mines made them only a short-run solution. The rise in output, increasing the present value of mine ownership, was accompanied by continued competition for control of the best claims, and the miners' courts were quickly swamped by the case load. Most of the conflict centered on the mines directly on the Comstock Lode, rather than on the mines located on parallel veins. The former were already the region's leading producers, a situation which never changed. The 7 March 1860 San Francisco *Alta California* (one of the early West's leading papers) reported:

There are very few claims of any value not in the utmost confusion of title and mystery of description. If there shall ever be established here a judicial system, there is a beautiful prospect of litigation; if there be no courts, then there is too much reason to fear force and violence.

The problems with the mining camp governments were accentuated by changes in both the nature and ownership of mining on the Comstock. While the early operations had been small-scale, placer mines (similar to California), by 1861 the surface ore was exhausted, forcing the Nevada mines to access the ore deep beneath the ground. To do so the mines became capital intensive since underground tunneling and elaborate milling processes were necessary to extract and separate the bullion from captive elements. Between 1860 and 1865 over 57 miles of tunnels were dug and over 90 custom mills were built to process Comstock ore.[22] The original claimants who lacked both training and capital sold out quickly, and the Lode's leading mines were transferred to San Francisco owners. By the end of 1861, 86 mining corporations had been formed in that city with an aggregate capital stock of $61,500,000.[23]

It is likely that both the lack of a permanent judicial system and the emergence of large-scale, absentee-ownership mining on the Comstock led to pressure for the establishment of a territorial government.[24] While the miners' courts might have been expanded as an alternative, judicial

[21] For a more detailed discussion of mining camp rules see Gary D. Libecap, "Government Suport."

[22] San Francisco *Mining and Scientific Press,* 29 September 1866.

[23] Ibid.

[24] There was also hostility toward the Mormon government in Utah which had official jurisdiction over the Comstock.

authority could have been a problem since it is doubtful the jurisdiction of such courts would have been recognized in other states – particularly California – where most of the owners lived. On the other hand, the territorial process provided a known and accepted procedure for creating a government with a more extensive judiciary, and that process allowed for part of the costs to be subsidized by Congress.

In March 1861 the Nevada Territorial Government was created, supplementing the mining camp as the major source of mineral rights law. The opening address of the president of the legislature's upper house captures the intent of that body regarding mineral rights:

We are called upon to make laws of a peculiar character, to protect and perpetuate interests that differ essentially from those of most of the other territories . . . the principal resources of this territory exist in its marvelously rich mines, which for their proper development and advancement require judicious thought and enactments by which titles to them can be secured and permanency given to that class of property.[25]

As the theory predicts, most of the mining laws passed during the territorial period focused on existing sources of uncertainty.[26] For instance, one of the first actions of the legislature was to set up the judicial system and to outline how the courts might be used to protect private holdings. That system quickly became the arena for contention over the most valuable ground. The record shows that through 1866, except for one case, disputes were always between mines on the Comstock and those off it and not between adjacent mines on the Lode. This was due to differences in production and in the way mining camp rules defined claim boundaries. By 1861 only those mines directly on the Comstock Lode were producing (though not all were), and they were surrounded by parallel and competing claims. Those Comstock mines most often in dispute were also the most productive: the Ophir; the Savage; the Gould and Curry; and the Yellow Jacket. The total production of these mines between 1859 and 1865 was $25,131,564, compared with $23,718,000 for the 36 other mines on the Lode.[27] Mining camp rules clearly defined subsurface claim boundaries between mines along the same vein, and they were not subject to much dispute.[28] Those rules, however, were less definite regarding boundaries between mines on *different* veins. This lack of precision for side boundaries was due to the

[25] *Journal of the Council of the First Legislative Assembly of the Territory of Nevada* (San Francisco, 1862), p. 8.

[26] For analysis of specific legislation, see Gary D. Libecap, "Government Support."

[27] Computed from data in the Grant Smith papers, Bancroft Library.

[28] For example the Comstock Lode was divided into successive segments or claims, ranging from 10 to 2,000 feet in length along the vein. The underground boundaries between those claims were the vertical extensions of the surface end lines.

practice of granting extralateral rights which allowed miners to follow their section of a vein wherever it traveled beneath the earth. Those rights, which became a central tenet of American mining law, made it possible for a mine to run under a claim of another as long as the two mines were accessing separate veins.[29] Because of their indefinite side boundaries, rich Comstock mines were open to competition from "vampire" claims which tapped the same ore deposit while asserting that it was in a separate vein. The difficult question facing the territorial courts was whether or not the veins were truly distinct. The Comstock mines were aggressive in using the judicial system to define their rights and protect their claims. They were the plaintiffs in 70 percent of all District Court cases through 1866, and most suits were actions of ejectment. By that year the leading mines had spent over $4,500,000 in litigation expenses or 11 percent of total production costs.[30]

While the debate over underground boundaries was occurring, new pressures were developing for further institutional change – the formation of a state government. By 1864 the small territorial judicial system of three judges was overwhelmed by the massive case load, sparked by competition for Comstock mines which were now producing $16,000,000 annually. The Virginia City *Daily Union* reported on 6 March 1864 that 304 cases – three-fourths of which involved mining – were on the docket of the District Court. The backlog prevented the rapid adjudication of disputes which would clear titles. The issue was put succinctly by a member of the state constitutional convention in 1864:

[The mining interests are] very anxious for a State organization, and why? The reason is very apparent; they want a judicial head. They want more courts, or more judges, in order to clear off that calendar which now contains six or seven hundred cases. As things now are, they expect to have to wait 3 or 4 years before the present litigation in respect to mining claims can be brought to a close.[31]

Another important source of uncertainty for Nevada mining rights was the federal government. By late 1863 both the executive office (departments of the Treasury and Interior) and Congress were considering taxing and selling the rich western mineral lands as a means of paying the Civil War debt. These proposed policies were observed nervously in the West because of their potential impact on a local rights structure that was not recognized formally by Congress. On 29 Decem-

---

[29] See Gary D. Libecap, "Government Support," for a discussion of extralateral rights.

[30] See Gary D. Libecap, "Government Support," for the calculation of litigation expenses.

[31] Andrew J. Marsh, *Official Report of the Debates and Proceedings in the Constitutional Convention of the State of Nevada* (San Francisco, 1866), p. 412.

ber 1863 the Virginia City *Territorial Enterprise* reported: "It is necessary that Congress be informed, that justice may be done, and a state organization with an honest and faithful representative in Congress is the surest safeguard against taxation, sale or the disposition of the mines by the Federal Government." The efforts to obtain statehood for Nevada were successful. The new state was admitted in October of 1864.

The state legislature continued to provide support for the mining industry by refining territorial legislation regarding mineral rights, by lobbying against feared federal attenuation of local possessory rights, and by expanding the judicial system. While territorial courts had been preoccupied with the question of underground boundaries, the state courts were not. By 1865 the question of subsurface boundaries between parallel claims was largely resolved through judicial rulings. With the issue settled, litigation dropped off rapidly; the remaining issues centered on claim abandonment and state mine tax policies. Accounts of conflict between mines in the Virginia City *Territorial Enterprise,* San Francisco *Alta California,* and Sacramento *Union* declined. The *Territorial Enterprise* of 29 November 1866 reported that court action was down and that the Ophir title was secure. By 1868 Comstock mining rights were well established. The record indicates that they stayed that way, with no evidence of major conflict, even though output, and the value of the mines, continued to rise through 1876. The model argues that such security should reduce pressure for further legal change. That seems to have happened. After 1866 the Nevada Legislature stopped meeting annually and began to meet every other year; a likely reason is that yearly legislative actions were simply no longer necessary. There was a similar decline in activity in the Nevada Supreme Court. While during the six-year period 1863–1868, the court had thirty-two mineral rights cases (60 percent of the total considered through 1895), there were only seven cases in the following six years; after 1880 Supreme Court rulings on Comstock mining rights almost ceased.

The historical progression of laws and governments in Nevada seems to fit closely the pattern predicted by the model, which indicated that mine owners would lobby for changes in legal institutions as a means of reducing ownership uncertainty. The fluid nature of the mining camp, with repeated ore strikes within mines, which increased the expected value of claim ownership, stimulated new rounds of competition and uncertainty, and forced successive revisions of mining law. This process continued until the late 1860s, by which time rights were relatively secure. Mineral rights law became highly defined through the enactment of 178 statutes and Supreme Court verdicts by 1895 – the situation stood in sharp contrast to the general, unwritten rules that had existed in 1858.

Gary D. Libecap

Indices of legal change

Activity in Nevada regarding mineral rights over the period 1859–1895 is condensed into the indices of legal change presented in Table 1. Columns 1 and 2 list indices of the annual-increase-in-precision of mining law due to statutes and court verdicts respectively. The indices were constructed as follows. To quantify the specificity with which private property rights were defined by the law it was necessary to isolate the central elements involved. After examining empirical accounts and legal studies of mining law, fifteen categories were selected as important in describing mineral rights.[32] The first seven related to the rights of individuals in staking, working, and selling mine claims, and the remaining eight dealt with the enforcement structure needed to protect those rights:

1. Physical claim boundaries;
2. Actions which the claimant can take to protect his holdings from trespassers or other competitors;
3. Procedures for establishing a claim;
4. Provisions for the transfer of ownership;
5. Actions which must be taken to maintain ownership of a claim (includes work requirements and the issue of abandonment);
6. Requirements for the formation of mining corporations and the power of such corporations over their members;
7. Requirements for the formation of mining partnerships;
8. Taxes – sharing mine revenue with the state;
9. Duties of judges in the enforcement of mineral rights;
10. Duties of sheriffs;
11. Duties of juries;
12. Duties of surveyors;
13. Duties of recorders of claims and mine records;
14. Duties of notaries and commissioners of deeds;
15. Provisions for jails for punishing law violators.

Using these fifteen elements or characteristics of mining law, the indices in Table 1 were computed in the following way. First, each statute and verdict was scanned to see which of the fifteen categories were covered. Then *within each* category the provisions of the statute or verdict were compared to previous laws. If those provisions were more detailed and precise in their definition of rights, a point was assigned for each category included. If the provisions essentially repeated earlier legislation

[32] Sources reviewed included: Rocky Mountain Law Foundation, *The American Law*; Gregory Yale, *Legal Title*; George Blanchard and Edward P. Weeks, *The Law of Mines, Minerals and Mining Water Rights* (San Francisco, 1877); Charles Shinn, *Mining Camps*; and Rodman Paul, *Mining Frontiers*.

44

or rulings without changes in specificity, no points were assigned. The total points assigned to each statute or verdict depended on the number of categories covered and refined. The sum of points for *all* statutes passed in a year formed the index of the annual-increase-in-specificity of mineral rights legislation shown in column 1; the sum of points for court rulings given each year formed the index of increased precision of judicial opinions shown in column 2.[33] The cumulative specificities of mineral rights due to the actions of the Nevada Legislature and Supreme Court listed in columns 3 and 4 are running totals of the corresponding annual changes from the preceding two columns. In the analysis, verdicts were compared with verdicts, and statutes with statutes. In deciding whether a law refined one of the fifteen categories, no general scale was used; instead, an ordinal comparison was made within the context of existing laws. This ordinal ranking procedure can be illustrated with changes in the Nevada law regarding the duties of claim recorders from 1859–1878. The first written statute concerning this important enforcement official was passed in June 1859 at the Gold Hill miners' meeting. Article 4 of the *Gold Hill Rules* required that the recorder list the names of all parties staking or purchasing claims, together with the size of their claim and date of location. This rule was given a value of 1 under the category of "Duties of Recorders" since it was the first written outline of duties. The first session of the Nevada State Legislature, meeting in 1864, passed a statute which listed in more detail the duties of recorders and was therefore assigned a point for that category as a refinement; similar laws followed in 1869 and 1871 and were also assigned points. Yet in 1877 a bill was passed which seemed merely to repeat an earlier requirement that out-of-state corporations register with the recorder. Accordingly, the bill was given a 0 for that category.[34]

The cumulative indices from columns 3 and 4 are plotted in Figure 1 and they provide a clear picture of the pace of legal change regarding mineral rights in Nevada in the last half of the nineteenth century. The

[33] There is a certain amount of subjectiveness in the construction of indices such as these. The selection of pertinent statutes and verdicts and the ordinal comparisons between laws involve personal judgments. There may, accordingly, be minor differences in index values computed by different people, but the general pattern of legal change reported in the paper should not vary. In addition, weighting schemes could be used in constructing the index to reflect different magnitudes of refinement. One statute might refine existing legislation more dramatically than a subsequent law, yet under the procedure used in the paper both would receive 1 point for each category affected. Such a weighting scheme would reinforce the conclusions reported in the paper regarding the fall-off in legal activity after uncertainty was reduced since the major refinements occurred prior to 1868.

[34] Eliot Lord, *Comstock Mining*, p. 42 for Gold Hill Rules. *Statutes of the State of Nevada*, sessions 1–8.

Table 1. *Quantitative measures of changes in Nevada property law*

Year	Annual increase in precision of mineral rights law due to statutes	Annual increase in precision of mineral rights law due to judicial opinions	Total precision of mineral rights law – legislative[a]	Total precision of mineral rights law – judicial[b]	Number of mineral rights laws passed	Number of Supreme Court rulings
1858	0	*	0	*	0	*
1859	6	*	6	*	6	*
1860	0	*	6	*	0	*
1861	7	*	13	*	11	*
1862	8	*	21	*	5	*
1863	4	2	25	2	6	2
1864	4	7	29	9	13	8
1865	8	5	37	21	6	5
1866	4	7	41	21	6	6
1867	0	6	41	27	0	6
1868	0	5	41	32	4	5
1869	0	2	41	34	0	2
1870	0	1	41	35	3	1
1871	0	0	41	35	0	1
1872	0	3	41	38	3	2
1873	0	0	41	38	0	0
1874	4	1	45	39	8	1
1875	0	1	45	40	0	1
1876	1	4	46	44	5	2
1877	0	0	46	44	0	0
1878	3	2	49	46	7	2
1879	0	1	49	47	0	1

Year						
1880	1	4	50	51	5	3
1881	0	1	50	52	0	2
1882	4	0	54	52	8	0
1883	0	2	54	54	0	1
1884	1	0	55	54	6	0
1885	0	2	55	56	0	1
1886	4	0	59	56	4	0
1887	0	0	59	56	0	0
1888	0	0	59	56	5	0
1889	0	0	59	56	0	0
1890	2	0	61	56	4	0
1891	0	0	61	56	0	0
1892	0	0	61	56	3	0
1893	0	0	61	56	0	0
1894	0	1	61	57	5	1
1895	0	0	61	57	0	0

[a] Computed as a running total of column 1.
[b] Computed as a running total of column 2.

Sources: Statutes from "Gold Hill Rules" in Eliot Lord, Comstock Mining and Miners, pp. 42–43; Laws of the Territory of Nevada (1861–1864); Statutes of the State of Nevada (1864–1895). Supreme Court Verdicts from the Record and Judgements of the Supreme Court of the Territory of Nevada and Reports of the Supreme Court of the State of Nevada (1865–1895). For a detailed discussion of the construction of the indices, see Gary D. Libecap, The Evolution of Private Mineral Rights: Nevada's Comstock Lode, Appendices A and B.

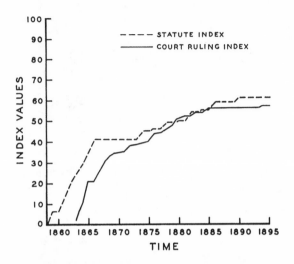

Figure 1. Legal change in Nevada, 1860–1895.

slopes of the curves illustrate the earlier finding that the most rapid increase in the specificity of mining law occurred in the early years, 1859–1868. This was also a time of both major increases in mine output (presumably raising the present value of mine ownership) and great uncertainty regarding control of the mineral ground. In response to this insecurity there was intense legal activity in the courts and the legislature. Figure 1 also shows that refinement in property law occurred more slowly after 1868, even though production did not peak until nearly ten years later in 1876. After the early 1880s there was almost no change in the precision with which private rights were defined and enforced – again supporting the conclusion that rights were secure after 1868 and that fewer legal guarantees were needed.

Statistical tests

These tentative conclusions regarding the pace and causes of legal change are supported by statistical analysis, using the data in Table 1. The theoretical model underlying those tests argues that increases in the expected present value of mine ownership will lead to refinements in mineral rights law as a means of reducing ownership uncertainty. Once that uncertainty is minimized, however, the pace of legal change will decline even if present values continue to rise. Accordingly, in the analysis the annual-increase-in-the-specificity of mining law (the sum of the yearly entries in columns 1 and 2) was regressed against the average value of mine output, $(Q_t + Q_{t-1})/2$, as a proxy for the expected present value of mine ownership, the cumulative level of legal precision (the sum of yearly entries in columns 3 and 4), and a constant.[35] The cumulative level of legal precision was lagged by one year to see if, as predicted, past refinements in the law would reduce uncertainty and lessen the need for further revisions. The use of the average value of mine output for the current and preceding year as a proxy for the expected present value of mine ownership seemed reasonable, given the fluid, short-run nature of western mining camps. Stock prices would, perhaps, measure more directly the expected present value, but they were not available for the entire test period. Correlations between the average value of output and stock prices for selected mines, however, showed the two moved closely together, indicating that using average output to represent the present value did not result in serious error.[36]

Regressions were run for three periods which corresponded to different phases in mining activity on the Comstock: 1858–1868, the time of the initial ore strikes and allocation of rights; 1869–1878, the period of greatest output; and 1879–1895, the region's terminal phase. In addition, two regressions were run for the entire period 1858–1895. The last

---

[35] Regression analysis was used because both the historical record and the theory suggest a dependence relation between legal change and the independent variables mine output and the cumulative precision of the law. The equation estimated was $Y = a + b_1 X_1 - b_2 X_2 + U$ where Y was the annual change in the precision of the law; X_1 was the average value of mine output; and X_2 the cumulative precision of the law. The coefficient b_1 showed the impact of mine output on annual legal change when the cumulative precision of the law was held constant, and b_2 showed the effect of the cumulative precision of the law when output was constant. The equation assumed a linear relationship between the variables, and there was no reason to believe that was not the case. Other forms of the equation, however, were tried with little effect on the results. For a discussion of the basic linear regression model see David S. Huang, *Regression and Econometric Methods* (New York, 1970).

[36] To see how closely stock prices and average output were related, output figures and share prices were assembled for two leading mines, the Ophir and the Gould and Curry, between 1859 and 1868, and correlations were run. For the Ophir the correlation between prices and output was .74 and for the Gould and Curry .69. Stock price data were assembled for 1859 and 1869 from the following: Grant Smith papers, Bancroft Library; Jones Collection, Huntington Library, San Marino, California; J. Ross Browne, *U.S. Mineral Resources*, p. 111; San Francisco *Bulletin*, 21 April 1860, 21 July 1860; San Francisco *Mining and Scientific Press*, 30 November 1860; San Francisco *Weekly Stock Circular*, 27 December 1862. Stock prices for 1861 through 1866 from the San Francisco *Alta California*; 1867 prices from the Virginia City *Territorial Enterprise*; 1868 prices from J. Ross Browne, *U.S. Mineral Resources*. An average stock price for each year was computed for the correlation. Similarly, output data were collected for the two mines as follows: Ophir, 1859–1868, Grant Smith papers as adjusted in Gary D. Libecap, *The Evolution*; Gould and Curry, 1860–1867, calculated from figures in the San Francisco *Mining and Scientific Press*, 12 January 1867; 1868 value from Rossiter W. Raymond, *Statistics of Mines and Mining in the States and Territories West of the Rocky Mountains* (Washington, D.C., 1870), p. 64.

Table 2. *Annual value of Comstock output*

Year	Output ($)
1858	67,000
1859	257,000
1860	1,000,000
1861	2,500,000
1862	6,000,000
1863	12,500,000
1864	16,000,000
1865	16,000,000
1866	11,739,000
1867	13,737,000
1868	9,442,000
1869	6,684,000
1870	11,382,000
1871	10,645,000
1872	12,631,000
1873	22,390,000
1874	22,525,000
1875	26,023,000
1876	38,048,000
1877	37,062,000
1878	20,437,000
1879	7,560,000
1880	4,332,000
1881	1,414,000
1882	1,675,000
1883	1,995,000
1884	2,621,000
1885	2,952,000
1886	3,430,000
1887	3,820,000
1888	5,665,000
1889	5,526,000
1890	4,062,000
1891	2,733,000
1892	1,963,000
1893	1,872,000
1894	1,281,000
1895	915,000

Sources: 1858 output estimated from Grant Smith, "The History of the Comstock Lode," p. 2; 1859–1895 production from Bertrand Couch and Jay Carpenter, "Nevada's Mineral and Metal Production, 1859–1940."

of those is a fit of the combined curves in Figure 1 to a Gompertz function, an adjustment function which assumes annual changes in the precision of the law are determined by the current precision of the law and the gap between the long-run equilibrium precision and the current level.[37] The estimated coefficients, the corresponding t-statistics, in parentheses, and the R^2s are given in Table 3.

[37] Trend functions such as the Gompertz, lognormal, and logistic can be used to describe economic activities which seem to be an adjustment to a long-run equilibrium. For example, Griliches and Mansfield use trend functions in the study of the adoption of technological change: Zvi Griliches, "Hybrid Corn: An Exploration in the Economics of Technological Change," *Econometrica* 25 (October 1957), p. 501; Edwin Mansfield, *Industrial Research and Technological Innovation* (New York, 1968). A similar study by A. D. Bain focuses on the purchase of consumer durables; see A. D. Bain, *The Growth of Television Ownership in the United Kingdom Since the War* (Cambridge: Cambridge University Press, 1964). See also Alfred Lotka, *Elements of Physical Biology* (Baltimore, 1925); and J. Aitchison and J. A. C. Brown, *The Lognormal Distribution* (Cambridge: Cambridge University Press, 1957). The curves in Figure 1 were fitted to a Gompertz function. That function assumes that annual changes in the precision of the law are determined by the current precision of the law and the gap between the long-run equilibrium and the current level or $dS/dt = AS_t(\ln S^* - \ln S_t)$ where S_t is the cumulative level of precision for any year and S^* is the long-run equilibrium. Regressions were also run separately for judge-made law and legislative enactments. For instance in the first case court verdicts, the dependent variable, was the difference of the natural logs of the current cumulative precision index for each year and the previous year's index (from column 4 of Table 1). The independent variables were a constant and the difference of the natural logs of the long-run equilibrium value and the current year's index. The results of the two regressions are shown below. In those regressions the long-run equilibrium values were the cumulative index figures when annual changes in the law dropped to and remained at zero (the horizontal portions of the curves in Figure 1). For the courts that was 56 (1885) and for the Legislature it was 61 (1890).

Dependent variable	Independent variable	Estimated coefficient	t-Statistic
Annual change in legislative law	Gap between current precision and the long-run equilibrium	.27	9.6
			d.f. 33
	Constant	−.02	−1.7
$R^2 = .70$			
D.W. = 1.269			
Annual change in judge-made law	Gap between current precision and the long-run equilibrium	.41	14.9
			d.f. 30
	Constant	−.04	−2.2
$R^2 = .88$			
D.W. = 1.190			

Table 3. *Statistical tests of the model of institutional change using data from Table 1*

Dependent variable: annual change in the precision of the law	Independent variables			Constant	R^2, D.W., d.f.
	Average output $(Q_t + Q_{t-1})/2$	Total precision of the law	Gap between equilibrium and current precision		
1. 1858–1868	6.1×10^{-7} (3.92)	-4.3×10^{-2} (−1.11)		3.18 (3.25)	.73, 1.92, 7
2. 1869–1878	8.0×10^{-8} (1.46)	-2.0×10^{-2} (−.22)		1.95 (.30)	.54, 2.22, 6
3. 1879–1895	-1.3×10^{-7} (−.96)	-1.4×10^{-1} (4.65)		17.76 (5.11)	.64, 1.83, 13
4. 1858–1895	2.0×10^{-8} (.29)	-8.9×10^{-2} (−3.20)		11.16 (3.95)	.80, 1.39, 34
5. 1860–1895			2.5×10^{-1} (15.2)	-1.0×10^{-2} (−.97)	.82, 0.97, 33

Though the index is a rough measure of legal change, and average output is an imperfect proxy for the present value of mine ownership, the results generally support the hypotheses. For the years 1858–1868 the test shows that the value of output was a significant determinant of annual adjustments in the precision of property rights law. The coefficient measuring the impact of output is statistically significant, and the sign is positive as hypothesized.[38] During those years the land was rich and becoming richer; competition was intense; and owners pushed for greater specificity in the definition of their rights to guarantee their holdings. For the later periods the tests show that output had less effect, with its coefficient positive as predicted, but not statistically significant through 1878, and negative and not significant after that year. These results are likely, due to the fact that after 1868 private mineral rights were relatively secure, reducing the need for further legal adjustments, even though deeper shafts led to new bonanzas with output peaking in 1876.

The total precision variable also behaves as predicted. It was hypothesized that the accumulated body of law would make rights more secure and dissipate pressure for further legal change. The results in Table 3 show that the sign of its coefficient is always negative, and the variable is significant after 1878.[39]

Regression 4 tests the impact of the variables over the whole period 1858–1895, and the results are mixed: The cumulation precision of the law has a significant and negative effect on annual legal change, as hypothesized; but while the value of output has the predicted positive sign, it is not statistically significant. The lack of significance for the output variable can be explained, at least in part, by the asymmetry of the process of institutional change. Figure 1 reveals that the legal rights system was largely built up before 1878, a time when output was rising. After that year output plummeted, and the Comstock (and Nevada) faded as an important producer; yet, there was no corresponding dismantling of the rights system as measured by the index. Laws and court verdicts were not repealed as the mines closed, and this strongly influences the showing of the output variable.

Finally, regression 5 shows that the pattern of legal change closely fits the Gompertz function. Though there are some autocorrelation problems, the gap between long-run equilibrium and current precision variable is highly significant, positive, and the R^2 is high. This finding supports the contention that Nevada mining law evolved as a result of an adjustment process to reduce ownership uncertainty. Viewed in that

[38] Significant at the .01 level.
[39] Significant at the .01 level.

Gary D. Libecap

way the Nevada experience can be summarized as follows: Until 1868 successive ore strikes stimulated both competition for the land and pressure for additional guarantees of private mineral rights. The lobby activity that followed continued until ownership security was obtained. These, however, were only short-run equilibria, since each was upset by additional ore discoveries which led to renewed legislative and judicial actions regarding mining rights. This reactive process of legal change continued until after 1868, when a long-run equilibrium level of legal refinement was reached. At that point rights were so well defined and protected that further ore strikes did not result in adjustments of the law.

Efficiency and equity effects of Nevada mining law

As we have seen, the support of private mineral rights allowed for the maintenance of large-scale mining activity on the Comstock. Besides this efficiency gain, the record suggests that there were also equity effects from the law. While it is not possible at this point to measure directly all of those effects, one can isolate the major sources of income transfer to better understand the equity impact of the legal structure.

Because federal policy allowed prospectors to appropriate public land in 1859 without payment, there is the possibility of a transfer in their favor from taxpayers. Yet the amount of income transferred was small due to low land values when privatization occurred. Because there was a general lack of knowledge about the location and extent of ore in early 1859, even the Lode's top claim, the Ophir, sold for only $50, and the 600 other speculative claims made at that time must have sold for less.[40] This means that the government could have raised no more than $30,000 from the sale of Comstock land. Comstock mine owners did receive more significant transfers from Nevada taxpayers. While the record indicates that both the territorial and state governments were set up at the insistence of the mining interests, these interests failed to pay their share of the general tax burden. The first legislature exempted mining from taxation, and subsequent legislatures through 1867 gave mine owners preferential tax rates. The owners lobbied hard to maintain that policy. Data for 1862 illustrate the nature of the subsidy received by the Ophir Company. During that year nonmine property was assessed at $1.30 per $100, while mine gross income was assessed at 30¢ per $100 or $5,040 out of a gross income for the Ophir of $1,680,000.[41] Had the mine been taxed at the former rate, the levy would have been higher. If

---

[40] Ophir price, Grant Smith, "The History," p. 7; number of claims, Grant Smith papers, Bancroft Library.
[41] *Laws of the Territory of Nevada* (1862), pp. 131–66.

one assumes that the value of mine property was roughly equal to the market value of the company on the San Francisco Exchange, or an average of $3,067,350 in 1862, then the tax would have been $39,874 – a difference of nearly $35,000.[42] Clearly mine owners were benefiting from the policy of the legislature. Nevertheless they resisted any payment, charging that the mines were on federal lands and therefore exempt from state taxes. In 1863 the Territorial Auditor reported that the Ophir and the Gould and Curry had gross proceeds of $8,600,000 but had paid no tax.[43] This resistance was generally upheld by the District Court, but never the Supreme Court. The anomaly may be explained by the fact that district judges were elected in Storey County (site of the Comstock Lode) and were therefore more sensitive to pressure from local interests than were supreme court judges who were elected state wide. Efforts to change the law were defeated. The 1863 Constitution, which required equal tax rates for all property, was soundly rejected 2,157 to 8,851. Nearly half of the negative votes came from Storey County. A revised document without the tax provision was accepted 5,448 to 142 in Storey County and 10,375 to 1,284 state wide.[44]

In spite of this successful lobby record the mine owners did not use the legal system to obtain monopoly control of the Comstock. After 1859 there was consolidation of mines from perhaps several hundred to 40–50 due to economies of scale, and the legislature aided that process by passing laws to facilitate title transfer, to recognize corporations, and to allow corporations to sue recalcitrant stock owners. Yet the number of mines remained roughly constant until the ore was exhausted in the 1880s, and while ownership became concentrated from time to time through stock purchases, that control was temporary. Competition among investors and variations in mine output prevented stable coalitions from forming. In addition, laws which would have blatantly and severely restricted access to a few were likely to have been vigorously resisted. Western miners had a tradition of requiring public land to be held open for the staking of claims by private citizens. Throughout the Pacific Slope they consistently established rules through the legal system to prevent monopoly control. On the other hand, competition for control in the stock market did not have similar opposition. Stock speculation was widespread and was apparently held to be a legitimate means

---

[42] Market value of the Ophir company calculated from stock prices listed in the 1862 San Francisco *Mining and Scientific Press*.

[43] *Report of the Auditor of the Territory of Nevada* (Virginia City, Nevada, 1864).

[44] Returns from Eleanore Bushnell, *The Nevada Constitution* (Reno, 1968), pp. 29–31, Myron Angel, *History of Nevada* (1881; rpt., New York: Arno Press, 1973), p. 85, and Andrew Marsh, *Reports of the Constitutional Convention*, p. xiv.

of obtaining ownership.[45] There is other supporting evidence that the legal system was not merely a tool that the leading mine owners could use to obtain control of the Comstock. Until 1865 the most significant issue facing the courts was that of determining underground boundaries between parallel claims. Despite pressure from the Comstock Lode mines, the courts refused in important cases to rule against the competing parallel mines until the evidence was clear regarding the location of ore deposits. After lingering for four years the controversy was settled only after excavations revealed that the so-called parallel and separate veins were in fact branches of the Comstock Lode and therefore, under mining camp regulations, within the original Comstock claims.

The record also shows that the legal system was used for attempted transfers away from holders of rich Comstock land. In every case, however, those attempts were successfully defeated. In 1862 resentment against the absentee ownership of the Lode led to a statute restricting out-of-state corporations. The mine owners responded by appealing to Congress to nullify the law: "Having invited and encouraged the citizens of California to undertake development of the mines in their Territory, they have waited until the moment of fruition to attempt to seize the prize which we have rendered valuable."[46] The statute was disapproved by Congress in February 1863. Later that year Congress, faced with a $1,000,000,000 debt from the Civil War, saw the Comstock (which was by then producing $16,000,000 annually) and other western mines as a potential revenue source. A 5 percent gross proceeds tax was considered, but it was eventually reduced to 0.5 percent after intense lobbying from the mining interests. Mass rallies of miners had been held in Virginia City, and the San Francisco Chamber of Commerce had sent memorials in opposition to the tax. The reduction lowered the 1865 Comstock tax bill by $720,000.[47] Congress, however, continued to consider raising income from the mines, leading owners to press for Nevada statehood. In 1866 a bill was introduced in Congress to sell the western mineral lands to raise an estimated $500,000,000. Opposition from the Comstock was sharp, and through the efforts of California and Nevada representatives, chiefly Nevada Senator Stewart, the measure was defeated and replaced in July 1866 by a law which recognized the possessory rights structure in existence in the West. While the law allowed individuals to obtain formal title from the federal government, few if any on the Comstock did so. The law removed the federal threat, making

[45] See Gary D. Libecap, *The Evolution*, ch. 5.

[46] U.S., Congress, Senate, *Miscellaneous Documents*, no. 21, 37th Cong., 3d sess., 1862–1863.

[47] See Gary D. Libecap, *The Evolution*, ch. 7.

such titles unnecessary, since Nevada already recognized the local rights structure.[48]

In summary, the equity effects from Nevada mining law seem to have been more limited than one might have expected given the economic and political power of the mine owners. That power was successfully used throughout the period to protect mine property. The major effect appears to have been a transfer from taxpayers to mine owners through Nevada tax law, with no observed use of the legal structure to obtain monopoly control of the Comstock. This leads to the conclusion that the pattern of legal change in Nevada from the mining camp through the state government was largely determined by efficiency needs – the need to reduce ownership uncertainty as competition for mine income grew.

3. CONCLUSION

The last half of the nineteenth century in the American West was a time of intense economic and legal change, as the mining industry boomed, spurred by huge ore discoveries. What had once been nearly uninhabited territory became the focus of a hurried migration of individuals attracted by dreams of mineral wealth. Soon population centers such as Butte, Leadville, Boise, and Virginia City dotted the region west of the Mississippi. The rapid rise in population and resource values placed pressure on existing legal institutions, particularly property rights, and forced new ownership structures to emerge. This resulted in the observed progression in mineral rights law from general, unwritten rules in the 1850s to highly specified statutes and court verdicts by the end of the century. This paper has examined one of the leading mining areas, the Comstock Lode, and has attempted to explain the nature and pace of that legal progression by applying the theory of institutional change outlined by Lance Davis and Douglass North. Both the historical record and the statistical tests suggest that the evolution of mineral rights law in Nevada can be understood as an adjustment process to reduce ownership uncertainty. While legislators, judges, sheriffs, and claim recorders were directly responsible for writing, interpreting, and enforcing the law, the major proponents of legal change were mine owners. Since there was little existing mineral law to borrow from (either state or federal), most of the Nevada statutes and court verdicts were written in response to local conditions. For any given amount of mine output there appear to have been short run equilibrium levels of legal support – levels at which

---

[48] U.S., Congress, Senate, *Congressional Globe*, 39th Cong., 1st sess., 1865–1866, pp. 3916, 3952, 4016, 4054.

there were no private net gains from further change. Additional ore strikes upset each equilibrium by raising both the benefits of exclusive control and ownership uncertainty. The latter was due to increased competition for the more valuable land. This led to lobby activity by owners who sought further legislative and judicial guarantees until a new short-run equilibrium was reached. This progression occurred until a stable long-run equilibrium of support was obtained where uncertainty was minimal, regardless of the amount of mine production. These efficiency gains seem to explain most of the observed legal change in Nevada. There were equity effects from the law as well, but preliminary investigation indicates that those effects were probably small, with the major transfer due to state tax policy.

The Nevada experience, then, offers empirical verification of a model of institutional change which emphasizes the net gain considerations of the proponents of change. The model promises to be a valuable tool for studying the development of the legal structure and the important interaction between legal and economic activities in the process of American economic growth. Finally, this study indicates that we can quantify qualitative changes in the legal structure, allowing us to examine the process with greater precision and to use techniques of statistical analysis and hypothesis testing.

2

Impediments to institutional change in the former Soviet system

REFORMING THEORIES OF REFORM

According to the modern theory of institutions, two factors are critical to the performance of an economic system: the information held by the various actors and their incentives. Yet in the past and even in our times, scholars have frequently ignored these factors in their proposals for reform.

In 1908 the Italian scholar Enrico Barone published an article entitled (in translation) "The Ministry of Production in the Collectivist State."[1] Barone's article encouraged economists and other social scientists to follow a path that took them away from the central issues of information and incentives. Barone, a pioneer in mathematical modeling, used his tools to establish a formal equivalence between the basic categories in a market economy based on private ownership and those in a socialist economy managed by a central authority. In the two instances, optimization involved solving a comparable set of equations.

Barone's vision of the fundamental issues of an economic system has been shared by many scholars in the twentieth century. In the 1930s the famous Lange–Lerner blueprint of a managed economy envisioned a system of "market socialism" where a central planning bureau (CPB) balanced supply and demand by using a trial-and-error method to set prices.[2] The managers of the state-owned enterprises were to be given instructions hailing from Econ 101: (a) pick a combination of productive factors that minimize average costs and (b) set marginal costs equal to the prices determined by the CPB. Similarly, many economists in the

---

[1] English translation in F. A. Hayek, ed., *Collectivist Economic Planning* (London: Routledge, 1935).

[2] Oskar R. Lange with Fred M. Taylor, *On the Economic Theory of Socialism*, edited with and introduction by Benjamin Lippincott (Minneapolis: University of Minnesota Press, 1938).

former Soviet Union and Eastern Europe, as well as in the West, believed that the advent of powerful computers would enable central planners and programmers to solve Barone's equations and provide a scientific solution to the economic problem.

Many of these proposed reforms were based on a notion of the optimal allocation of resources, which was seen as existing independently of economic systems. The scholars then proposed new institutional arrangements intended to align society with their models and bring economic systems closer to the theoretical optimum. Generally, the proposed reforms emphasized static rather than dynamic efficiency and ignored technological change, as might be expected of theories that deemphasized knowledge and information.

Not all economists agreed with this worldview. Probably the best known of the early critics were the Austrian economists. In 1920, Ludwig von Mises denied the possibility of rational economic calculations under socialism because important information required to make such calculations would be lacking.[3] According to von Mises, a market based on private ownership of the means of production provides at low cost vital information that would be unavailable in a system where the means of production are not individually owned and traded. Another Austrian scholar, Friedrich Hayek, wrote extensively on the role of information in economic systems and made a pioneering contribution to the economics of institutions and the information revolution in economics.[4]

AGENCY PROBLEMS IN THE SOVIET SYSTEM

Although many academic reformers were often not overly concerned with problems of measurement and enforcement and believed that national planning would be *simple and transparent,* the leadership of the Soviet Union learned from experience that incentives and the effective transfer of information were the toughest problems associated with central planning. The monitoring system invented by the Soviet leaders, which Jan Winiecki describes in the following essay, is perhaps one of the two most consequential innovations in organization in modern times – the other being the more durable and successful large-scale corporation.

The institutional structures for transferring information and monitor-

---

[3] Ludwig von Mises, "Economic Calculation in the Socialist Commonwealth." English translation in Hayek, *Collectivist Economic Planning.*
[4] One of his best-known contributions to the economics of information is F. A. Hayek, "The Use of Knowledge in Society," *American Economic Review* (September 1944): 519–30.

ing and coordinating behavior, which the Soviet leadership invented in the 1920s for rapidly building a centrally controlled industrial economy, were later introduced in other countries and became a leading alternative to the market system. Although the center never directly controlled the millions of identifiable products made by the Soviet economy, there were output plans for tens of thousands of products, which required a massive administrative system. In the new system, economic and political managers were merged into one gigantic agency of the state, which set the stage for agency problems of an unrivaled magnitude.

A NOTE ON THE THEORY OF AGENCY

In a world of costly information, contracts between principals and agents are necessarily incomplete and the problems of *adverse selection* and *moral hazard* are likely to emerge. For the actors involved, the extent of these problems depends on the institutional arrangements and various other aspects of their environment. Adverse selection occurs when contractual relations are established and is caused by the high cost to a contracting party of measuring accurately what the other side has to offer, with measurement being necessarily incomplete and, as a consequence, being frequently by proxy. When managers were hired in the Soviet system, much weight was given (for good reason) to outward signs of loyalty to the regime. However, the evidence suggests that unscrupulous, opportunistic, and incompetent persons paraded signs of loyalty in the hope of obtaining good positions. Moral hazard arises during contractual relations because it is too costly for one side to a contract to accurately measure the performance of the other side, which creates opportunities for cheating. The central managers of the Soviet system were not able to specify, monitor, or enforce quality at all valuable margins of each planned commodity. Instead, they issued a general description of the planned products and watched select margins such as quantity or weight, creating an opportunity for producers to ignore unmeasured qualitative margins. As would be expected, the resulting goods and services were usually of low quality.

WHAT TO LOOK FOR IN THE ESSAY

Although the early performance of the system of central management in the Soviet Union is often overrated, the system appears to have been relatively successful during the early years, with performance deteriorating over time. The deterioration was due to three general factors. First, the introduction of new products, new methods of production, and new industrial structures sharply increased the costs of monitoring, enforcement, and coordination. Second, the Soviet system had little capacity to innovate, and this became an increasing problem after the Soviet economies had gone through the early stage of catching up with the West and started accelerating their attempts to employ sophisticated technology. Third, over time the consequences of adverse selection and moral hazard accumulated: incompetent agents rose to the top of their hierarchies and a capital stock of inferior quality expanded.

Early in the postwar period the Soviet leadership realized that extensive reforms were required to preserve the regime and the relative position of its system in the world economy. The essay that follows explains in terms of the theory of agency why a series of reforms attempted in the Soviet Union and Eastern Europe failed. Winiecki's thesis is that the reforms were sabotaged by midlevel agents of the state.

Some people believe that many serious economic problems could be solved if only the national economy were run like one big firm. The Soviet economies tried central management, but perhaps they did not use the appropriate institutional structure. As an exercise in armchair economics, we challenge the reader to think of a workable way of managing a large (or small) industrial economy from the center.

Central to Winiecki's reasoning is the notion that the midlevel managers of the Soviet system embodied human capital that was *system-specific*, implying that these actors would be worse off under alternative institutional arrangements. Unfortunately for the rulers, the execution of their reforms was in the hands of these same midlevel managers. We ask the reader to consider the following questions: Is there any solution to the rulers' dilemma? For instance, could the Soviet leadership realistically have offered to compensate the managers (buy them out) if they agreed to give up their opposition to the reforms? The issue is relevant to representative democracies where powerful minority interests (such as French farmers) are often able to block changes that would be costly to these special interests but would increase aggregate wealth and even benefit the global economy.

Why economic reforms fail in the Soviet system: a property rights–based approach

JAN WINIECKI

1. INTRODUCTION

In analyzing the disequilibrium characteristics of contemporary Western economies, Mancur Olson (1982; 1984a; 1984b) agrees with the neo-classical macroeconomists in finding that, given the tendencies of markets to clear and given the rational expectations of economic agents, any disequilibrium indicates that all mutually advantageous transactions have not been consummated. Having made this point, however, he asks what can make agents ignore the potential gains from unconsummated transactions and turns his attention toward the structure of incentives, and thus of institutions and policies. Olson insists, and rightly so, that a satisfactory static and dynamic macroeconomic theory has to explain who, among key actors, has the incentive to generate economic growth and equilibrate the economy and who does not. Furthermore, no government, even an authoritarian one, has an incentive to generate serious recessions or disequilibria. Olson (1984a, 637) writes that "even in dictatorial systems, the dictator has an incentive to make the economy of the country he controls work better, since this will generate more tax receipts he can use as he pleases and usually also reduce dissent."

Olson's arguments about incentives, institutions, and disequilibria offer an ideal basis for an inquiry into why reforms fail in Soviet-type economies (STEs).[1] In Olson's theories of incentives, the old Roman

This essay first appeared in *Economic Inquiry*, Vol. 28 (April 1990). The author and the editor wish to thank Professor Hans C. Palmer of Pomona College for extensive editorial assistance. An earlier English version of this article appeared as a Seminar Paper No. 374, Institute for International Economic Studies, University of Stockholm, January 1987. The author gratefully acknowledges the use of excellent research facilities during his stay in IIES.

[1] The terms STE and Soviet-type state will be used interchangeably except when it is necessary to distinguish between specifically economic and political considerations.

principle of criminal law *cui prodest* (who gained) is applied to modern economies, and the results suggest that, contrary to widespread opinion, it is not necessarily the "small but powerful group of high and highest leaders" that stands to gain most in terms of power and privilege from "the preservation of the existing order."[2] A powerful political elite could satisfy its desires for both power and privilege through an alternative undemocratic system, one which involves authoritarian "don'ts" rather than totalitarian "dos." In that perspective, the inefficient system of economic control typical in STEs, involving centrally planned production goals and input rationing, would not be a *conditio sine qua non* of an authoritarian solution. Since totalitarian command and control systems persist, however, one must seek groups other than the powerful and privileged few which have incentives to resist reforms and keep the economy inefficient.

The following sections identify the membership and motives of groups having strong incentives to keep the STEs inefficient and prevent successful (i.e., market-oriented) reforms. We show how those groups operate, and analyze their effects on the economic performance of their countries. First the incentives for these groups to prevent decentralized management in the state sector are spelled out.[3] Then, their incentives to prevent the expansion of the more efficient private sector are outlined. Third, having identified who benefits from the status quo and why, the paper discusses when and how market-oriented reforms are aborted, limited or reversed by those who stand to gain from the reforms' failure. The last two sections consider the prospects of current attempts at economic reform in three specific countries: Poland, the USSR, and China and the prospects for economic reform in STEs more generally.

2. WHO GAINS FROM THE STATUS QUO AND WHY

Disincentives to decentralized management in the state sector

Most analyses of Soviet-style systems focus excessively upon the distribution of power and neglect the distribution of wealth across the ruling stratum. By contrast, in an incentives-oriented analysis the distribution of wealth becomes the focus of attention. Power and privilege are viewed as means to acquiring wealth, and the desire to acquire wealth motivates the actions of the ruling stratum.

This shift of analytical emphasis does not mean that power and its

---

[2]Thalheim (1986, 40). However, Bauer (1984) stresses the existence of a whole social stratum interested in maintaining the institutional status quo.

[3]"State sector" is intended to mean both the state and cooperative sector, i.e. the "socialized" sector in Soviet parlance.

distribution do not matter. On the contrary, the rulers of an STE may regard control over the working population as satisfying their need for power, either as an end in itself or as a means to attaining some long-run goal, such as the creation of "true communism." It is important, however, to realize that the means by which wealth is distributed is crucially important in determining the attitudes of elements in the ruling stratum toward decentralizing, market-oriented reforms. Without considering this issue, it is difficult to explain why economic reforms – badly needed by the rulers themselves to correct flagging economic performance – did not materialize or, if they did, why they failed or at best brought about very little improvement in economic circumstances.

At this point, Douglass North's explanatory framework for the structure and enforcement of property rights, as well as their changes over time, should be brought into the picture. Applying what North (1979) calls a predatory theory of the state to the Soviet-type state, two, sometimes conflicting, objectives of such a state are identified:

1. To provide a set of public goods and services designed to lower transaction costs and increase the efficiency upon which the growth of wealth is predicated. (In non-STEs economic growth is synonymous with the growth of wealth, but in the STEs the two are distinct. For this argument see Winiecki [1986a].)

2. To specify the fundamental rules of the property rights structure, i.e., the ownership structure in factor and product markets, in a way that maximizes the rent flowing to the ruler and the ruling stratum. The fact that this structure is extremely muddled in STEs is irrelevant, since such muddle, i.e., the dominance of non-exclusively owned resources in the state sector, actually facilitates the expropriation of rent.

At this stage, two of North's (1979) reservations about predatory states must be addressed. First, he saw complications arising for such states from the advent of representative government. Soviet-type states, however, despite their coexistence with states having representative government, clearly have pre-representative governments and, accordingly, can be easily analyzed within the basic predatory state framework. Second, North (1971) also pointed out that his model, predicated upon profit-maximization, does not hold if social reformers change institutions so as to benefit groups other than the rulers and profit-makers. However, contemporary Soviet-type states lack profit-maximizing institutions, and the existence or non-existence of social reformers at the beginning of such states is irrelevant. Indeed, any impulse for social reform in the founders of the Soviet-type states quickly degenerated, and the ruling stratum established property rights that maximized their rent.

The process has been criticized by insiders such as Trotsky (1937) and Djilas (1956).

The following hypotheses now arise from these considerations:

1. In STEs the fundamental conflict described by North (1979), i.e., the conflict between efficient property rights designed to lower transaction costs and increase wealth and inefficient property rights designed to maximize rent to the ruling stratum, is strongly in evidence; and
2. in such states the nominal ruler will avoid offending powerful groups in the ruling stratum, i.e., the *apparatchiks* and economic bureaucrats, who benefit most from the institutional and economic status quo.

In STEs the rulers agree to maintain a property rights structure favorable to those groups, regardless of the effect upon efficiency. In fact, modes of wealth distribution resulting from the STE structure of property rights differ so much from those in other pre-representative government states (i.e., traditional and "modern" autocracies), that institutional change leading to lower transaction costs and increased wealth is much more difficult to achieve. No STE, for example, has replicated the successful, efficiency-enhancing institutional changes of "authoritarian" South Korea or Taiwan.

In "old" autocracies the ruling stratum consists of either the traditional hierarchies or elites based on the military and the police. These appropriate to themselves a larger share of created wealth than they would obtain under a representative government. They get higher salaries and more "perks," while their status symbols (articles of conspicuous consumption or modern professional equipment) have a priority claim upon the state budget. According to Winiecki (1986), however, the rulers of an STE preside over a ruling stratum consisting of these four pillars of the system: communist party *apparatchiks,* economic bureaucrats, the police, and the military. All may (and do) receive a larger share of the created wealth than is true in representative states. Their salaries may be relatively higher and their "perks" relatively more important in the STE shortage economy.[4] So far, the mode of wealth distribution appears to be the same as in "ordinary" autocracies.[5]

In the STE, however, another mode of wealth distribution exists that maximizes the rent of two particular segments of the ruling stratum: party *apparatchiks* and members of the economic bureaucracy. This mode, unknown in other systems, enables these groups to benefit from

---

[4] Salaries and costs of various subsidized services for the ruling strata are usually kept secret in communist regimes.

[5] It may be added that status symbols in the Soviet-type systems are often grandiose, and include the white elephants of forced industrialization having little, if any, productive efficiency.

their protracted interference in the process of wealth creation itself. There are two interconnected ways in which this is done.

The first is through the principle of *nomenklatura*, i.e., the right of the communist party apparatus, from the central party committee down to the enterprise committee, to "recommend" and "approve" appointments for all managerial positions in the economic (and public) administration and all managerial positions in enterprises. These appointments are made primarily on the basis of loyalty rather than managerial competence, and *apparatchiks* usually appoint themselves and their friends in the party to those well-paid jobs. *Nomenklatura* has adverse effects for at least two reasons:

1. It signifies a severe limitation on the pool of talent from which managers are drawn; and
2. given the well-known negative selection process under totalitarianism, the pool of *nomenklatura*-included talents is not only smaller but also of lower competence relative to any other pool in the society with similar occupational, age, sex, and other characteristics.[6]

Since loyalty is the foremost concern, managers, once appointed, are evaluated on the basis of their loyalty as measured by their compliance with commands (e.g., achieving planned targets or meeting ad hoc commands) rather than their efficiency (e.g., producing desired outputs at least cost). Of course, loyalty to one's own superiors is not necessarily perceived by subordinates as involving an obligation to fulfill commands to the letter. Winiecki (1988a) reports that falsified reports on economic performance are the rule rather than the exception in STEs. Falsification continues, *perestroika* or no *perestroika*.[7]

Does the preference for loyalty to one's superiors over real performance signify the dominance of power or ideology over wealth considerations? Since the power of the party and the ruling stratum has rarely been threatened, while a relative neglect of real performance vis-à-vis loyalty has been a constant in STEs, the answer appears to be in the

---

[6] In analyzing aspects of negative selection involving character traits, a Polish organizational psychologist – without pointing his finger in the too obvious direction – offers the following version of what may be called the *Copernicus–Gresham Law:* "In bureaucratized, technocratic, punitive and pathological organizations, where fundamental laws of human behavior and human development are ignored, egoists, conformists, cowards and people without moral scruples begin to play more important roles than individuals concerned with everybody's welfare, people who are brave, honest and responsible. Under such conditions – in plain words – bad character drives out good character" (Jozef Kozielecki in *Zycie Gospondarcze* Nos. 51/52, 1986).

[7] Various Soviet sources questioning official plan implementation figures in 1987, as quoted by Marie-Agnes Crosnier (1987).

negative. Bureaucrats and *apparatchiks* learned long ago that their wealth does not depend primarily upon ideology or upon creating social wealth but upon the rents they extract through their control of the wealth creation process. Thus, loyalty to superiors is important in struggles between various coteries within the ruling stratum who position themselves to extract more benefits from the inefficient economic system (Hillman and Schnytzer [1986]). Power or ideology considerations alone, i.e., the attempts of any one group to set an ideologically different course for the party, rarely dominate.

A major mode of rent extraction involves the system of side payments or kickbacks from managers of (primarily industrial) enterprises. In a shortage economy these kickbacks are mostly of a non-pecuniary nature. Enterprise managers offer to those who appointed them, and to other superiors and colleagues who may advance their careers a variety of goods and services, and have the opportunity to benefit in the same way. More often than not these side payments involve goods in short supply which have a high black market price. These goods are, however, sold to favored people at list prices or even at reduced prices because of allegedly "lower" quality. (Actual lower quality goods do, indeed, reach the market en masse, but kickback-related goods are carefully selected for high quality!) These offers may include delegating workers from auxiliary factory divisions to build country houses at sharply reduced prices, to build one-of-a-kind furniture for the apartment of a superior on the same basis, etc. The relative unimportance of efficiency allows managers to absorb, without being held accountable, the costs of these kickback activities. Leakage of wealth thus takes place not only through the losses incurred and gains foregone by incompetent managers but also because of the time and effort spent on rent seeking activities.

Both types of rent extraction exist because of the muddled structure of STE property rights. Since the means of production are in theory, but not in fact, socialized, since workers are "the hegemonic class" in a socialist society and the communist party is "the leading force of the working class," any appointment through the *nomenklatura,* or any other decision process for that matter, can be justified. It does not matter whether or not STE property rights were originally devised to achieve a socialist purpose or to maximize rents for the ruling stratum. What matters is that muddled property rights allowing protracted interference in wealth creation serve the latter purpose very well.

Under the *nomenklatura* system personnel shifts from the ranks of *apparatchiks* to those of the economic bureaucracy are by far the most frequent. The reverse flow also occurs, however, since young economic bureaucrats perceive that their professional career is advanced by a spell in the party apparatus. On the other hand, such interaction with the

Why economic reforms fail in the Soviet system

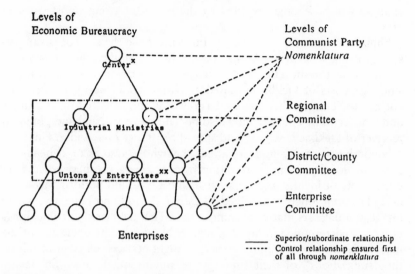

Levels of Economic Bureaucracy

Center[x]

Industrial Ministries

Unions of Enterprises[xx]

Enterprises

Levels of Communist Party Nomenklatura

Regional Committee

District/County Committee

Enterprise Committee

———— Superior/subordinate relationship
------ Control relationship ensured first of all through *nomenklatura*

Figure 1. The rectangle displays the levels of economic bureaucracy rendered superfluous by real decentralizing, market-type economic reforms. Dashed lines show also which levels of party apparatus lose the chance to get themselves appointed to the well-paid jobs covered by the *nomenklatura* in industrial ministries and unions of enterprises. *Center also includes certain functional ministries (finance, labor, technology and others). **Also called central boards or associations. Trusts and combines belong to the Union level as well.

party and the *nomenklatura* is much less common for the police and the military.

The different methods of rent maximization used by groups in the ruling stratum are of primary importance for the prospects of reform in the Soviet system. All segments of the ruling stratum prefer the status quo to the alternative of representative government. But two segments only – party *apparatchiks* and economic bureaucrats – have, in addition, a strong incentive to maintain the undemocratic, centralized institutional status quo in the economic sphere. To see why this is so, consider that decentralization assumes, as a first step, the substitution of parameters for commands. Since parameters (in contrast to plan targets), such as the interest rate, need not be input- or output-specific, intermediate levels of economic bureaucracy become superfluous. A look at Figure 1 shows clearly that the liquidation of the intermediate levels of economic bureaucracy (the dashed-line rectangular area) not only makes redundant the bureaucrats employed in industrial ministries and unions, but also reduces the pool of well-paid jobs to which *apparatchiks* may be appointed through the *nomenklatura*. It is only to be expected that such changes will be strongly resisted by the powerful groups most strongly affected.

Similar resistance appears at the enterprise level. For example, strengthening enterprises' budget constraints by holding them financially accountable for the effects of management decisions will be resisted, since the costs of kickback-related activities would begin to affect the enterprises' balance sheets as well as rewards and penalties for managers and workers. The effects would also be felt by every actual and potential receiver of kickbacks who would spread resistance even wider. Financial accountability could, in fact, affect the whole system of dependence based on loyalty. Conflict resulting from a divergence between the requirements of loyalty and those of financially sound performance is an everyday occurrence in modified STEs like Poland and Hungary, where financial indicators matter to some extent. That conflict's outcome, however, is predetermined in favor of loyalty because of the operation of the *nomenklatura*.[8] Simply put, managers caught between whether to follow the "suggestions" of their superiors or pursue other, more financially appropriate goals for their firm choose the former and ask for subsidies afterwards. Otherwise they might lose their jobs. That is why even in Hungary, the most reformed STE, the budget constraint continues to be "soft," to use Janos Kornai's (1979; 1980) well-known phrase.

Predictably, *apparatchiks* and economic bureaucrats would most strongly resist attempts to replace *nomenklatura* by selections based on merit. As a result, *nomenklatura* has never been abolished for managerial posts in the economic sphere, the sphere where efficiency gains are most important for the rulers.[9] While it is true that *apparatchik* and bureaucratic resistance is found throughout the STE, its intensity differs among sectors of the economy. Since the best paying managerial jobs under the *nomenklatura* (i.e., those enjoying best opportunities for kickbacks) are in industry, it is in industry that reform faces the strongest

---

[8] Therez Laky (1980) points out two most important sources of dependence in a modified, or reformed, STE such as Hungary: the multilevel institutional structure left intact in the 1968 reform and the rights of appointment and dismissal of enterprise managers retained by the superior levels of economic bureaucracy.

[9] The breaking down of large monopolistic enterprises would liquidate some well-paid posts, since pay scales are dependent on size. Not only these measures but also certain market-type measures resulting in equilibrium prices would be resisted because they could result in increased costs or reduced benefits for the privileged stratum. For example, a car that an *apparatchik* or any other member of the privileged stratum gets on the basis of an allocation coupon (*asygnata*) costs 110–130 percent more on the free market in Poland. Larger or smaller differentials between list prices and free or black market prices exist throughout Eastern Europe. Eliminating the coupons would automatically reduce either the wealth or the income of *asygnata* receivers.

resistance and, correspondingly, the highest probability of failure. The economic history of STEs shows some partly successful reforms of state agriculture, a sector in which opportunities for rent extraction are less frequent and the benefits smaller. To date, no reforms of state industry, based on general parameters, accountability, or merit, have been successful.

The wealth-maximizing interests of *apparatchiks* and bureaucrats in maintaining the inefficient economic status quo is in sharp contrast with that of the current ruling groups in the Soviet-type states. On the other hand, while a "small but powerful group at the top," to employ Thalheim's phrase, does not necessarily need central planning in its system of rule and wealth-maximization, those upon whom it depends for maintaining that rule – those who control the STE – draw considerable benefits from the existing economic arrangements.

Before proceeding with the argument, the term "control of economic activity" by the economic bureaucracy and party apparatus requires some further definition. In an STE, this function has little in common with guidance toward efficient achievement of desired economic outcomes, at least those desired by the public or even by the ruler. Rather, the goal most often is to maximize rent for the ruling stratum. Control is process-oriented, rather than outcome-oriented, and is based on detailed prescriptions of how, when, and with what means to produce what outputs. The obedience of subordinates is all-important, since this gives superiors a sense of control and of an ability to protect their rents. Ironically, control of the process does not confer control of the outcome because the consequences of following such detailed prescriptions are far from the expected ones: part of output exists only on paper; products are shoddy and obsolescent; deliveries are late; efficiency indicators miss plan targets and the managers are obviously unable to do anything to correct the situation (see Winiecki [1986a]). Another irony is that this style of control may impede realization of the ruler's own objectives, yet the ruler is also powerless because the *apparatchiks* and economic bureaucrats are essential for *his* (their) political control of the whole system. Controlling economic activity means simply that the *apparatchiks* and economic bureaucrats are able to issue commands ("suggestions" at the very least) affecting process or product. These commands are superficially in form, but not in substance, obeyed by enterprises.

The amount of effort expended on control by the economic bureaucracy and party *apparatchiks* will be lower with a simpler control procedure. For example, commands are preferred to suggestions, since the latter require bargaining. Commands may be, and are, often changed, but changes later need less arguing, since the disparity between targets and reality becomes more visible over time. The fact that making changes later is also more costly does not bother bureaucrats and *appar-atchiks* in the least. Thus, even if systemic modifications or reforms do not actually threaten maximum rent extraction, such changes may increase the effort needed to maintain (superficial) control of economic activity. Therefore, the *apparatchiks* and bureaucrats have incentives to resist change, however modest it may be.

The ruler-ruling stratum relationship clearly is crucial to understanding reform failure in the Soviet system. The juxtaposition of these two groups in this article should not be confused, however, with the oft-encountered "good czar, bad officials" approach to Russian politics. The rulers (or "ruling group") is actually representative of all the ruling stratum and reflects all the moral, intellectual and professional consequences of decades of system-specific negative selection. Thus, the czar is not any better than his officials. Nonetheless a great difference exists between the rulers and other groups in the ruling stratum. The ruler, alone within the ruling stratum, is interested not only in seeing reports that commands are fulfilled, but also, and more importantly, in seeing that the commands were actually fulfilled! No other group bears that ultimate responsibility. He will be blamed for any failure of the system by competing groups within the ruling stratum, and his interest in real performance makes the ruler more sensitive to falling efficiency and consequently more ready to reform the economy than is the average representative of the ruling stratum.

As a result, if rulers try to change the economic system significantly, they may face a revolt by functionaries who have the strongest incentives to maintain the status quo, placing their political dominance in jeopardy. Thus, rulers face both the rent-maximizing and the transaction cost constraints stressed by North (1979). In periods of declining performance, the ruler feels the transaction cost constraint. Inefficient property rights do not generate the increased wealth needed, for example, to sustain the superpower status of the Soviet Union, or to avert consumer dissatisfaction in all Soviet-type states. On the other hand, if the ruler attempts a significant revision of the existing property rights structure, he risks loss of support from important members of the ruling stratum who will turn to competitors for political power. It is, moreover, a special feature of STEs that even if competitive constraints on the ruler diminish and reforms begin, their implementation is in the hands of party *apparatchiks* and economic bureaucrats. Reforms, if not aborted or weakened from the start, may then be sabotaged, distorted or finally reversed.

Clearly and unequivocally it is the *apparatchiks* and bureaucrats of STEs who gain most from maintaining the institutional status quo, and they are the groups which resist change most strongly. Given the key positions of these groups in the STE system, we may predict a very high probability of failure of decentralizing, market-oriented, efficiency-increasing reforms.

Disincentives to expanding the private sector

Expanding the role of the private sector in an STE usually has the same objectives as decentralizing, market-oriented, efficiency-enhancing reforms in the state sector. Theoretically, private sector expansion could serve as a substitute for state sector reforms, and could provide the means to circumvent strong resistance to market-oriented change in the state sector. In actuality, attempts to reform the state sector have complemented simultaneous private sector expansion. Changes in policy toward the private sector have been numerous, however, since often the private sector has had to contend with various forced concentration drives in the state sector. In the course of these drives, large state enterprises often gobbled up small state and private enterprises alike.[10]

Analysts invariably cite ideology as the cause for the limited role of the private sector (except in agriculture) in Soviet type economies. The same ideological argument comes to the fore in two other circumstances: (1) when Western experts and journalists seek the sources of vilification campaigns and other obstacles to change that follow each official policy shift favoring the private sector, and (2) when rulers must explain the unsatisfactory results of pro–private sector policy changes. In the latter case, the rulers usually produce some type of circular memorandum aimed at the economic bureaucracy or party committees and lecturing them on the need to overcome the "old style," "dogmatic" approach with respect to the role of the private sector under socialism. These memoranda are usually ineffectual.

An ideological explanation for the failure to harness private enterprise to improve performance in a persistently disequilibrated and structurally distorted STE fails for two reasons. First, ideological fervor has generally subsided, although admittedly to differing degrees, since the imposition of the STE system. This subsidence has occurred in all spheres of the society and suggests that ideology is not a good explanation for un-abated hostility towards the private sector. Second, and more important, any ideological reservations have had to be overcome first and foremost at the top. When a policy to promote the private sector is announced, it is actually the ruler who has to "eat the toad," i.e., to confess directly or indirectly, that the state sector cannot do what the private sector is

---

[10] The concentration drive in East Germany (GDR) in the mid-1970s is relevant here.

expected to do.[11] Even policy changes announcing the most limited expansion of the private sector amounts to precisely such a confession. It would seem, then, that few lower level bureaucrats or party *apparatchiks,* whose position depends not on performance but on loyalty, will dare to sabotage the latest twist of the party line and remain ideologically hostile to privatization.

On the other hand, the ancient principle of *cui prodest* suggests that there must be strong disincentives for certain groups to follow the rulers' privatization lines. The two avenues of rent distribution, i.e., *nomenklatura* and kickbacks, operate simultaneously in a STE. However, in interactions between segments of the ruling stratum and the private sector, both are conspicuously absent, or extremely rare. There are no well-paid posts to be filled by *nomenklatura* appointment in small private enterprises, nor is there a "soft" budget constraint, so permissive to a variety of rent-maximizing kickbacks even under reform. A shift of activity from the state to the private sector reduces, therefore, the possibilities for party *apparatchiks* and economic bureaucrats to extract rent. Hostility towards the private sector is, therefore, based not on ideology or even actual rent losses, but on gains forgone when expansion of the state sector is curbed in favor of the private sector.

The story does not end here. A bureaucrat, or even an *apparatchik* who can indirectly influence each decision, *may* extract rent by taking a bribe for a concession to set up a private industrial firm, or to open a restaurant or a repair shop. But this way of extracting benefits violates private sector property rights, where resources are clearly exclusive, and is consequently much more dangerous. In plain words, taking bribes is a criminal act. By contrast, in an STE rent extraction from the state sector is either fully legitimized, i.e., through the *nomenklatura* and the rationing of goods at the center's order, or, as with system-specific kickbacks, belongs to the "gray area" between the improper and the criminal. Therefore, since negative selection assures that moral scruples are rare among ruling stratum rent-takers in an STE, something akin to a political earthquake, like the "Solidarity" period in Poland, is needed to threaten all who predatorially extract rent from an STE system. Otherwise, only a few luckless individuals whose punishment was decided upon by higher-ups will be the show pieces in trumpeted, but deceptive, anti-corruption campaigns.

It should be stressed that only so-called "secondary" corruption – that

---

[11] It is immaterial whether the state sector is completely unable to perform satisfactorily or unable to do so at the expected cost or in the expected time or at the expected place. It is just as immaterial whether the state sector is unable or unwilling to perform because this means that there are no incentives that would induce that sector to change its attitude and behavior.

not legitimized within the ruling stratum – is the type usually punished in an unreformed STE. Such secondary corruption arises from conflicts between the utility function of the ruler and that of his agents. This is readily understandable in light of North's (1979) property rights approach. The inability of the ruler to constrain his agents perfectly would result in the diffusion of some of the ruler's monopoly rent and would, therefore, call down sanctions on the head of the offenders. Barzel (1974) and Cheung (1974) note the ruler's problem is rendered more difficult, and the rent diffusion is greater, when the measurement of output is more difficult and more costly. Since in STEs this measurement is most difficult in industry, one would expect diffusion is greatest precisely in that sector; Winiecki (1982; 1986a) has confirmed this. Diffusion is so great in fact that it trickles down to some of the ruled as well, through widespread falsification of performance reports by enterprises. *Nomenklatura*-covered managers and, to a smaller extent, but in larger numbers, all employees of affected enterprises may all benefit from these falsifications.[12]

3. WHEN AND HOW REFORMS FAIL: THE STRATEGIES AND TACTICS OF "COUNTERREFORMATION"

Because decentralizing market-type reforms of the state sector and expansions of the private sector adversely affect rent extraction possibilities, the *apparatchiks* and bureaucrats who benefit from the existing STE arrangements embrace what may be termed a multifaceted "counterreformation" course. To understand how reforms may thus be reversed or aborted one must consider again the relations between the rulers (or ruling group) and key elements in the ruling stratum, especially the *apparatchiks* and economic bureaucrats.

In analyzing those relationships and the "counterreformation," however, it is necessary to consider the ability of the members of large groups to act in concert. Olson (1965; 1982) stresses that large groups are not always able to act as if guided by their collective interest, yet for STEs this generally valid point does not apply so fully to actions by the *apparatchiks* and economic bureaucrats. A large difference exists between, on the one hand, a large, perhaps opposition, group struggling to bring organized pressure on a government or a ruling party to effect certain outcomes and, on the other hand, a large group that consists for

[12] According to A. Shitov, the vice-chairman of the People's Control Commission of the USSR, every third enterprise out of those checked was found guilty of such irregularities (*Planovoye Khozyaistvo*, No. 11, 1981). It is assumed by the author that those caught doctoring their reports make up only part of those who paint a rosy (or only rosier) picture to obtain plan fulfillment-related rewards.

all practical purposes of the government and/or its ruling political party. "Counterreformers" in STEs, indeed, usually are in the party and often coalesce around members of the ruling group itself. There are always one or few top party figures who think that cracking the whip, tightening discipline and increasing control are enough to solve the problem of falling efficiency. The hostile group's capability to act collectively is much greater in such situations for the simple reason that theirs is a very unusual, often majority, interest faction with access to mechanisms of political and economic control. If such a group sets itself to thwarting reforms outlined by the rulers and their advisers, the organizational and descriptive capacity of the "counterreformers" may turn out to be markedly greater than that of politically powerful elements who are outside the mainstream of economic control.

Even if they do not act collectively but only individually, the "counterreformers'" unusual position in the party and the bureaucracy will help them throw sand into the machinery of reforms. Although they may not be members of a strong trade union or an influential professional association, they effectively govern and control the STE. Individual decisions of a minister, a regional party secretary, or a city administrator, all *nomenklatura*-linked functionaries, have serious consequences. For example, they can twist and distort decentralizing reforms pertaining to all state enterprises in a given industry or region, or they may forbid establishment of private enterprises in a given industry or region. These actions symbolize an Olsonian "free rider" situation in reverse: everyone outside the informally organized group of "counterreformers" brings his valuable individual contribution to the common cause of resisting reform.

The preceding considerations suggest that (1) aborting reforms costs less effort by the interested parties than reversing reforms later, and (2) reversing less consistent reforms (with inconsistency deliberately built into the systemic modifications) costs less effort than reversing more consistent reforms.

Although the counterreformers are very effective in adjusting their obstructive actions to different circumstances, they probably cannot always implement their first-best (i.e., completely reform-suppressing) solutions and may try to abort reforms, at least in part.

Aborting reforms means neither that no changes whatsoever are introduced nor that all changes are repudiated. It means, rather, that the reforms actually introduced do not threaten the property rights structure in the state sector through which *apparatchiks* and economic bureaucrats maximize their rent. Abortive reforms also do not alter either the institutions or the procedures of central planning. Examples of such abortive or sham reforms abounded in the 1980s in such STEs as Bulgaria, Czechoslovakia, and the German Democratic Republic. The 1980s Soviet reforms likewise belong to the category of abortive reforms.[13]

The second-best solution for the *apparatchiks*/bureaucrats is to introduce internally inconsistent quasi-reforms, which modify the system so inconsistently that they are doomed to fail. To the category of quasi-reforms belong the Polish reforms of 1956–1958 and 1973, and most of the East European reforms of the 1960s (excluding the Hungarian reforms to be discussed later). Quasi-reforms may increase the effort *apparatchiks* and economic bureaucrats must expend in controlling economic activity, but that increase is only temporary, since reversal of the quasi-reforms is assured because of problems created by the inevitable reform and system contradictions. In any case, the structure of property rights remains intact.

With inconsistencies often obvious from the start, beneficiaries of the traditional STE model need only wait until the first problems appear to begin their campaign for reform reversal. Usually they do not need to wait for long, since STEs always enter reform periods in a state of larger or smaller disequilibrium, and reforms can thus be blamed for the persistence of disequilibrium even if no other reform-related adverse consequences have appeared. Actually, major adverse consequences will, in any event, likely arise because of quasi-reform and system inconsistencies. To be sure, small efficiency gains may be registered, but they are temporary and disappear over time under the impact of the process of reform reversals.

To the dismay of the ruling stratum, some crises are so severe, however, that neither no reform nor abortive or quasi-reforms are possible. For example, in Poland in 1981–1982 popular pressure combined with economic disaster prevented the abortion of reforms and forced the ruling group to appear to permit fundamental economic reforms, largely in order to deflect pressure for political reforms. A genuine attempt to improve Polish economic conditions was needed, since the rulers realized that the people understood that not all of the problems were the outcome of Gierek's mistakes or of Solidarity-organized strikes (despite attempts to convince the general public otherwise). The pressure for political reform did not abate, however, and martial law was introduced to stave off fundamental political system changes. Ironically, as Winiecki (1986c) has explained real economic reforms are impossible in the Soviet-type systems without political reforms, at the very least without the shift from totalitarian to "ordinary" dictatorship. Real economic

---

[13] There are, even in the West, those who believe the official East German figures; but the author is not among them. See Winiecki (1986b).

reforms radically alter the structure of property rights and eliminate the role of the *nomenklatura,* thus sharply reducing the possibilities for maximizing rent. Combined economic and political reforms also reduce the value of many privileges. For example, the rent to be extracted from access to rationed, underpriced consumer goods would fall to near zero if the national economy operated at equilibrium prices and more of those goods were produced.

The Polish economic "reforms" of 1982 under martial law provide a classic example of how a ruling stratum can turn back even strongly-grounded reforms. The 1982 programs yielded an emasculated version of the measures envisaged in 1981, and threats to the *apparatchiks'* ability to extract rent were either eliminated or reduced. Even so, the remaining reforms demanded increased efforts to control economic activity, and the functionaries soon regarded them as unbearable. Taking advantage of the various built-in inconsistencies of the 1982 reforms, the *apparatchiks*/bureaucrats busily rolled back the remnants of the reform under the guise of "further perfectioning."

The Hungarian reforms of 1968, as well as their later modifications, belong to a special category, not because they attempted more far reaching reforms than did other STEs but again for basic political reasons. In fact, the economic reforms were not very great, nor were the adverse consequences of inconsistent reforms significantly smaller than in other STEs.[14] Also, the degree of control over economic activity by party *apparatchiks* and the economic bureaucracy did not change, even if their control efforts had to expand substantially. Rather, in Hungary it was the presence of certain visible concessions to the population that were a hallmark of what became known in the West as "goulash communism." These concessions extended beyond the economic sphere to include a certain depoliticization of everyday life and less obnoxious propaganda. Economic concessions included, among other things, the inclusion of non-party members in the pool of candidates for managerial positions.[15] Additionally, the more sensitive attitudes of the ruling stratum made them more receptive to other reform measures disadvantageous to themselves. For example, despite the *nomenklatura's* survival intact, certain well-paid jobs disappeared during the reforms' second phase in 1980, when the industrial ministries were amalgamated into one and certain large enterprises were broken up into smaller units. Moreover, with

---

[14] Cf. Bauer (1984) and Beksiak (1982), who describe the post-1968 and post-1980 Hungarian economy and the post-1972 Polish economy, respectively, in almost identical terms as "neither command nor market-regulated economy." Laky (1980), Antal (1978; 1982) and Soos (1985) describe Hungarian systemic modifications as belonging neither to the centrally planned nor really to the market economy.

[15] In the 1970s, the share was barely 10 percent.

Hungarian prices being much nearer to equilibrium levels than elsewhere in East European STEs, the value of perks such as rationed cars decreased.

The explanation for these outcomes is as follows. The Hungarian communists were the only ones in Eastern Europe who, after having taken power, found themselves, albeit briefly, in 1956, at the receiving end of repression. Consequently they learned one thing, namely, that in case of another popular uprising the Soviets might come quickly enough to save the system but not necessarily quickly enough to save each of them personally. It is this collective memory of the ruling stratum that results in Hungarian policies that often moderate, rather than aggravate, the adverse characteristics of the system. In substance the system itself has, however, changed surprisingly little.

The examples of Poland and Hungary suggest that economic reforms in the STEs, even those with strong popular backing, do not bring about systemic modifications seriously limiting the ability of the party *apparatchiks* and economic bureaucrats to extract rent. Reforms at most reduce the number of well-paid jobs in intermediate levels of the bureaucratic hierarchy and increase the effort required to control economic activity. Both "defects," however, largely disappear in the inevitable process of reform reversal.

As shown above, the timing of the "counterreformation" depends on circumstances such as the degree of deterioration of economic performance, the existence of popular pressure for reforms, and the strength of that pressure. Consequently, the most effective time to act cannot be selected a priori by the interested parties, since the timing depends on the dynamics of a given reform process. "Counterreformers" enjoy greater latitude, however, in the choice of measures that will allow them to retain control over economic activity and to ensure that reforms will not succeed. With each failed attempt at economic reform, the *apparatchiks* and bureaucrats become more effective in applying their reactive measures, largely because of learning curve effects. Some of the most successful strategies to thwart reform are analyzed below.

Pseudo-reorganization. This classically Parkinsonian measure makes it possible to maintain the institutional structure basically intact by shedding a few middle levels of the multilevel hierarchy. At the same time, it is preferable to add some functional institutions in order to keep the pool of well-paid *nomenklatura*-covered jobs as large as possible. Pseudo-reorganization was a typical maneuver of "counterreformers" in the Czechoslovak reforms of 1967, the Hungarian reforms of 1968, all Polish reforms of 1956–1958, 1973 and 1982, and the Soviet reforms of the 1980s.

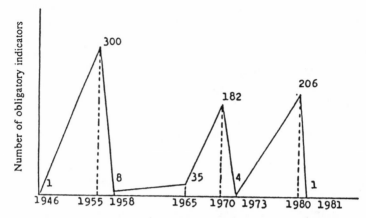

Figure 2. Changes in a number of obligatory indicators in engineering industries in Poland in the 1946–1981 period associated with the imposition of central planning and subsequent attempt at economic reforms and reform reversals. Source: Jermakowicz (1983).

Limiting the number of obligatory plan indicators for enterprises. This typical substitute for the abolition of commands has been widely used in most economic reforms under the rubric of simplifying enterprise management. However, with the STE's institutional structure intact and with government campaigns aimed at assuring the implementation of successive partial targets, many obligatory plan indicators are sooner or later reestablished while new ones were added in the process. An example of this in the Polish engineering industries from 1946–1981 is shown in Figure 2. The number of obligatory indicators has risen, fallen, and then risen again in a recurrent pattern.

An additional "counterreformer" device is to shift obligatory plan indicators to other categories instead of simply reducing their numbers. For example, in Czechoslovakia the number of obligatory plan indicators in industry was reduced from 1120 in 1965, to 66 in 1966, but at the same time 510 other items were added in two new classes of "orientating" and "auxiliary" indicators. The same happened in the Soviet reforms of the 1980s. A large number of indicators were shifted to a new category of "controlling figures," broken down to the enterprise level and then passed on the enterprises to "guide" them in their activities.[16]

Abolishing commands but retaining the rationing of inputs. Even if most production targets are formally abolished (which rarely occurs),

[16] *Czerwony Sztandar*, 31 December 1987.

allocation of scarce inputs by superiors in the multilevel economic bureaucracy constrains the pursuit of more profitable output mixes by
enterprise managers.[17] Managers understand that any output mix other
than that "suggested" by their superiors will reduce their prospects for
obtaining scarce materials, since those materials will be shifted to other
enterprises producing "priority" outputs, i.e., those desired by the economic bureaucracy or party *apparatchiks*. This pattern was typical of
the Polish reforms of 1982, where the share of rationed material inputs
increased to 90 percent.[18] The same was also true in the Soviet Union,
even with the USSR's smaller, less ambitious program of command
abolition. The modest room for maneuver secured by Soviet industrial
enterprises has in the 1980s been reduced to virtually zero due to continuing rationing of almost all inputs.

*Abolishing commands and rationing but retaining the right to appoint
and dismiss enterprise managers.* This "revolutionary" change – one at
least hailed as such – has happened to date only in Hungary. However,
as was pointed out above, the Hungarian command/rationing system of
central planning was not transformed into a decentralized, market-type
economy, since the property rights structure in the state sector did not
change. Even without production targets and input rationing, enterprise
managers continued to be dependent on their superiors for periodic
evaluations based on loyalty first and foremost. In such an environment
the strength of their superiors' "suggestions" was not much weaker than
that of commands.[19] With their position, salary, and bonuses dependent
upon the economic bureaucracy above them, managers in STE enterprises analyze performance in terms of efficiency and in terms of the
specific suggestions of their superiors. When these conflict, suggestions
prevail.

Furthermore, in Hungary the market did not really substitute for
central planning; therefore, the control void was filled by "suggested"
auxiliary or orientating indicators covering the whole range of enterprise
activities and by bargaining between managers and the economic bureaucracy for changes in the value of these indicators. These were accompanied by informal rationing and bargaining for inputs, by the

---

[17] Even with the formal abolition of commands in the Polish 1982 reforms, many
were retained in one form or another for military output and for a large part of
planned deliveries to other STEs. The situation is not much different with respect to
the more thorough Hungarian reforms of 1968 which – in theory – abolished not
only commands but also rationing.

[18] *Zycie Warszawa*, 16, June 1986.

[19] As Laszlo Antal (1982) remarked, suggestions (he used the term "expectations")
are less than commands but more than preferences.

participation of the economic bureaucracy and party *apparatchiks* in the preparation of enterprises' "autonomous" output plans, and by an amalgam of disguised or undisguised, formal or informal, persistent or ad hoc, interferences in enterprise activities.[20] Enterprises, although formally unconstrained in the pursuit of better performance, were, in fact, bound in a maze of mutually inconsistent constraints on their actions, which severely limited gains in efficiency. Consequently, according to Bauer (1984), patterns of economic development and foreign trade did not significantly differ from those in STEs not formally following the Hungarian reform model.[21]

Counterreform measures designed to maintain an unchanged degree of control over economic activities can be supplemented or reinforced by other measures. These may include expressions of various policy preferences or ad hoc regulations that contravene the thrust of reforms and, if implemented, reduce the ability of enterprises to react to profitable opportunities. These measures also raise costs, reduce quality, increase obsolescence of outputs, and otherwise make firms less efficient. Ironically, counterreformers use the adverse results arising from their interference as evidence of the failure of the reforms themselves during the next campaign for reversal.

Propaganda against reforms supplements these other measures. It often includes two types of arguments: "reforms increase inflation," although reforms usually only bring hidden inflation into the open; and "reforms increase inequality," although reforms usually, at least at the beginning, reward more efficient smaller enterprises and reduce existing, unjustified wage and salary differentials favoring employees of large enterprises. Also, isolated critical anecdotes by individuals or by employees in large enterprises are often overblown in the press and mass media, strengthening the campaign against reforms by conferring upon it a quasi-legitimacy.[22]

[20] Under traditional central planning, bargaining was usually more frequent during periods of plan implementation, whereas since 1968, it has become more frequent *exante* which is somewhat more efficient.

[21] This author has elsewhere shown (Winiecki 1986d; 1987) that the structural characteristics of the Hungarian economy are not different from those of other STEs.

[22] The author heard about a particularly humorous attempt at generating employee support. During the breakup of some large enterprises in Hungary (which threatened the jobs of those paid on the basis of the size of an enterprise), communist party *apparatchiks* in the Csepel Works in Budapest tried to sabotage the reform by organizing a protest strike. However, the time when communists could organize successful strikes in communist-ruled countries had passed, and they were not able to find more than a handful of followers. The attempt collapsed as a result. (Incidentally, in 1956 the unit from Csepel Works was one of those that fought the longest against Soviet troops.)

4. PROSPECTIVE FAILURES – IMAGINABLE SOLUTIONS

This analysis based on property rights, with special emphasis on the structure of incentives facing the ruling stratum in the Soviet system, not only explains the repeated failures of economic reforms in the STEs but also, given the argument's theoretical underpinnings, enables analysts to predict outcomes of ongoing reforms. This analysis has been applied to three industrial reform programs: the Soviet, Polish, and Chinese.

The Soviet Union

In the Soviet case the structure of STE property rights remains intact, retaining both modes of wealth distribution among the ruling stratum – the *nomenklatura* and kickbacks – despite exemplary punishments for "secondary corruption" handed out to a few improperly constrained agents of the ruler. As to the reforms themselves, Soviet responses display almost all the devices to ensure that reforms fail right from the start.

In the USSR, pseudo-reorganization and illusory limitations on obligatory plan indicators are the most common "counterreforms" in the measures promulgated so far. Changes at the top, ranging from traditional industrial ministries to committees playing the role of superministries, belong to the category of pseudo-reorganization, aimed nominally at decreasing uncertainty and shortages by integrating certain suppliers and purchasers under the same bureaucratic umbrella. However, this type of reform has never worked anywhere; the only thing it can do is *redistribute* shortages across enterprises. A given committee's "own" purchasers are relatively better supplied, while the plight of those under the aegis of another committee is ignored or worsened.

A shift of emphasis within the multilevel hierarchy from ministries to unions of enterprises (a measure that has failed many times elsewhere in STEs) is a similar non-performer. Ministries and unions are not interested in increasing efficiency but in showing improved *average* results from one year to another. Many analysts have shown that these bodies redistribute scarce resources for both current production and capacity expansion with the main intention of improving these average results. Therefore they shift resources from relatively more efficient to relatively less efficient enterprises. Soviet architects of reform in the 1970s and 80s showed an understanding of this point by early 1988.[23]

In the case of exports, emphasis has shifted from the Soviet Foreign Trade Ministry to industrial ministries, associations, and, in a very

[23] See an article by Gavril Popov, one of the close advisers to the present ruling group in the Soviet Union (*Sovietskaya Kultura*, 5, January 1988).

limited number of cases, to enterprises. Again, this measure has not succeeded because it is mainly redistributive, not corrective, and it cannot succeed in the future in an unchanged economic environment. Overall, in an STE shortage economy having strong disincentives to innovate and operating with low quality requirements, the costs incurred to turn out manufactures saleable on the world market far outweigh any possible trade benefits accruing to manufacturers.[24]

The STE experiment with limiting obligatory plan targets also has a long history of failure. The Polish reforms of 1956–1973, the Czech reform of 1967, and pseudo-reforms in other Soviet-type economies support this proposition. The much touted Soviet brigade system, which seeks to reduce inefficiencies by making contracts with small teams ready to implement specific tasks for specified remuneration, may improve the performance of some Soviet enterprises but only to a limited extent and not for long. The extent of improvement cannot be large because enterprises in the STEs are constrained, first of all, by system-specific excess demand, shortages and uncertainty, i.e., by the external environment of the enterprise; worker negligence and inefficiency are only a secondary source of enterprise inefficiency. Therefore, even if brigade workers were to exert themselves somewhat more, their efforts at the team level may not translate into effects at the enterprise level. This failure will raise costs without generating any compensating benefits and will bring conflict with higher levels of the economic bureaucracy. Workers will also have to be paid for their readiness to fulfill the contract even when, as frequently occurs, inputs fail to arrive, which again will increase costs. These problems lead to reservations being written into contracts or ad hoc interventions to reduce specified remuneration, actions which subvert incentives for workers to exert themselves.[25] The whole brigade approach then becomes another useless institutional fixture under which gains will first decrease and later disappear altogether. Ultimately, even cracking the whip over brigades through tightening labor discipline and more thoroughly checking plan implementation reports will cease to yield even paper gains.[26]

---

[24] Assuming that they try nevertheless to improve out of the penchant for change, they would fail anyway due to the low quality of domestic inputs for their (hypothetically) saleable products.

[25] The whole brigade system may even become a non-starter if – due to the reigning gigantomania – teams have too many members. In this case the classical "free rider" problem arises as happened in Bulgaria, for example.

[26] It is interesting to note that there is a strong correlation between reports of improved aggregate growth indicators and intensified campaigns against falsified reports on plan fulfillment. Incidentally, Winiecki (1986b) hypothesized that the 1980s, a period of decline, would become another period of greater overstatements of economic performance.

Finally, otherwise laudable Soviet attempts to reestablish *some* incentives for non-manual workers as means of eliminating plan targets will have as little, or less, effect on the enterprises' performance as will the brigade system. Both implemented and planned increases in wage differentials between white and blue collar workers in favor of the former are going to disappear rather fast. Winiecki (1988b) shows that STEs tend not only to generate excess demand for labor but also much stronger excess demand for manual labor. Such excess demand combines with a common industrial economy pattern of relatively reduced manual labor supply to *decrease* wage differentials between non-manual and manual workers. Actually, in some countries these differentials were already reversed in favor of the latter. Even ad hoc Polish and Czech interventions similar to those in the Soviet Union did not reverse wage convergence; they only delayed further narrowing of differentials by some two to three years.

Poland

The Polish reforms of 1982, despite attempts at counterreform under martial law, cannot be dismissed as completely sham. Although the structure of STE property rights did not change, the abolition of most commands, some limitation of rationing, and some reduction of price controls did occur. Even if the subsequent reform reversal process deprived enterprises of large parts of their freedom of action existing in 1982, the extent of decentralization was higher in the 1980s than it was in the 1970s. Also, the elected self-management bodies in enterprises still retained certain rights although those rights were strongly circumscribed from the start of the 1982 reforms. However, even with these positive aspects, the 1982 reforms *in toto,* to say nothing of their remnants, could not ensure efficient enterprise performance. Consequently, the failure of the reforms was assured. Nonetheless, the reforms increased considerably the effort expended by party *apparatchiks* and the economic bureaucracy in controlling economic activity.[27]

[27] An excellent illustration of this fact comes from instructions published by the personnel section of the communist party's Central Committee on the "consultative" procedure with respect to competition for managerial positions in those enterprises where the self-managing body has the right to select the candidate (who nonetheless has to be appointed later by the respective ministry). Although the interested party can always prevent "undesirable," incompetent (and critical) candidates from being appointed, and in most cases even from being selected, as well as force their own *nomenklatura*-selected alternatives on the (often unwilling) self-management body – the number of "consultations" among the selecting commission, the enterprise, the district and regional party committees, and a ministry superior to a given enterprise is much higher than under traditional *nomenklatura* procedure.

By 1987 the failure of the latest round of Polish reforms was glaringly visible even to the rulers. The propaganda apparatus, therefore, started a campaign for the "second stage" of the economic reforms; and the bureaucracy prepared a blueprint of expected changes. However, the blueprint had all the marks of a "counterreformation" move. It was quite radical in its verbal encouragement to entrepreneurship, innovation, autonomy in enterprise activities, and the role of prices in the economy, but fundamentally unchanged institutional structures and proposed interventionist policy instruments kept the "second stage" much like the first, having a similar probability of failure.

Because of the distinctive political situation surrounding the introduction of economic reforms in 1982, the Polish case is even more instructive about the probability of successful reform in an STE. The rulers apparently tried to "buy" the acquiescence of the ruling stratum (especially the most affected segments, the *apparatchiks* and economic bureaucrats) to the economic reforms it regarded as necessary to relieve the economic crisis. Therefore, the share of consumer goods diverted outside the regular trade channels increased sharply. The proportion of cars, the most coveted durable good, rationed through the system of centrally allocated coupons is said to have doubled from 20 percent in the late 1970s to 40 percent in the early 1980s.[28] Regional data for household consumer durables likewise showed a 45 percent share going to privileged access sales.[29] (The official figure for 1983 was 38 percent of all nonfood manufactured goods, including cars.)[30] Even if one considers that the rulers were also trying to "buy" members for the new government-sponsored trade unions by distributing various goods through trade union organizations during this period, these shares for the ruling stratum are shockingly high.[31] (It is noteworthy that cars were not among the goods distributed by union organizations.)

So far, only part of the Polish story has been told. During these years the number of posts covered by *nomenklatura* rose from about 100,000 in the 1970s to 250,000 in the 1980s.[32] Thus, the ruling stratum's access to well-paid positions improved considerably. In fact, in comparison with Voslenski's 1984 estimates for the Soviet Union (750,000 posts), the relative extent of formal control by the communist party over mana-

---

[28] Although in absolute terms it was less than before, given the fall in output and larger exports.

[29] *Zycie Gospodarcze*, No. 40, 1984.

[30] *Ibid.*, No. 10, 1986, quoted in the report of the Consultative Economic Council.

[31] This has been referred to in various research reports; see *Polityka Spoleczna*, No. 4, 1985.

[32] The numbers for the 1970s are from Smolar (1983) and these for the 1980s from *Polityka*, No. 24, 1986.

gerial posts seemed in the 1980s to be distinctly higher in Poland than in the USSR.

If the Polish and Soviet ruling strata behaviors analyzed above are the norm in acute crises, STEs could not often extricate themselves from dire economic troubles. In the first place, the ruling stratum aggravates the crisis when it compensates itself for an absolute fall in the nation's wealth by appropriating to itself a much larger share of the remainder. This action reduces the wealth that can be distributed according to merit, thus reducing incentives for good performance (even assuming that possible reforms could restore performance incentives). Second, the extension of the *nomenklatura* over the national economy reduces ex ante the capacity of enterprises to perform, especially given the effect of negative selection to managerial posts on enterprise performance (assuming that managers could choose among various production options).[33] Consequently, even in the case of true decentralizing market-type reforms – which the Polish reforms of 1982 definitely were not – parasitic *nomenklatura* behavior would preclude a positive outcome.

In comparative terms, acute economic crises can be handled more easily in market economies with a representative government than in Soviet-type economies with pre-representative governments. If one uses Schumpeter's term, "creative destruction," to characterize positive innovative behavior stimulated by crisis in representative market economies, one should, in parallel, use the term "destructive destruction" to identify crisis-induced behavior in STEs.

China

Ongoing reforms in China sparked the most excitement in the West until the beginning of similar Soviet developments. It appears, however, that the optimism of both Western observers and Chinese reformers reflects wishful thinking more than anything else. Deng Xiaoping, the prime mover of Chinese reforms, may have hoped that "if the reforms in the countryside worked out very well in three years . . . it will take five years for the reforms in the city," but as shown above, the assumption of a causal relation between rural–agricultural and urban–industrial reforms has no foundations whatever.[34] The amount and variety of benefits extractable by the ruling stratum through protracted interference in

---

[33] Interestingly enough, even the official control organ in Poland (the Supreme Chamber of Control) concluded that the same party-loyal mediocrities are being selected as managers as before the reforms. See the interview with a regional director from Wroclaw, *Rzeczpospolita*, 3, April 1986.

[34] In an interview with *Time*, 4 November 1985.

production are infinitely greater in industry than in agriculture; hence the prospects for successful reform in industry are much dimmer.

The partial success of agricultural reforms in China hence has no bearing on the possibilities for the success of industrial reforms. Hungary is a case in point. The success of Hungarian agriculture (relative to that in other STEs) was not followed by successful reforms in industry. Over two decades have passed since 1968, and Hungarian industry remains by and large unreformed. Whatever marginally greater efficiency it has enjoyed resulted not from a shift to a decentralized market-type economy but from a more cautious policy that alleviates some of the worst effects of the traditional Soviet system.

Reasons why the Hungarian ruling stratum has behaved as it has are clear. By contrast, there was no popular revolution and Soviet intervention in communist China and hence no ruling stratum victims to exert a moderating influence on the conflict between reforms and reactions. On the other hand, the domestic Maoist convulsions may have had a similar effect on party *apparatchiks* and the economic bureaucracy. Mao Zedong was a social reformer who, in his quest for a coercive utopia, also subjected many *apparatchiks* and economic bureaucrats (but not the military or the police) to often cruel and humiliating persecutions. Consequently, these functionaries, mindful of the not too distant past of the "Cultural Revolution," may have preferred a period of stability. They may have settled for gains in their own wealth proportional to those in the country as a whole, even if they experience a fall in relative position compared to, say, the new entrepreneurs.

Attitudes may change, however, as memories of the "Cultural Revolution" fade. The maintenance of reforms requires further limitations on ruling stratum benefits, including ultimately the abolition of *nomenklatura* in industry. In any case, the situation in a predatory STE state such as China, in which important segments of the ruling stratum are deprived of the power to extract rent through the structure of existing property rights, is inherently unstable. The transformation or liquidation of the totalitarian political party and of the Soviet-type economic bureaucracy is one possible outcome of such instability. Reform reversal is another one. Unfortunately the former is less likely than the latter.

In a previous paper, Winiecki (1987) predicted marked political changes resulting from China's instability in the early 1980s. That assertion proved prophetic in that the general secretary of the Chinese communist party was soon thereafter removed. Although his removal was associated with his support for greater political freedom rather than for economic liberalization, the counterattack of dissatisfied *apparatchiks* and bureaucrats reflected, and affected, economic reforms as well. Certain crucial pieces of legislation were withdrawn from parliamentary consideration (e.g., the law on enterprise activities and the bankruptcy law), and economic policy decisions supported old-style solutions to problems of disequilibrium and inflation. In spite of a measured critique of the "faulty views" of the antagonists of economic reforms by the general secretary, Zhao Ziyang, in the late 1980s, there was little forward movement. Reforms appear stalled for the foreseeable future.

5. CONCLUSIONS

Despite the pessimistic analyses offered in this article, one should not conclude that economic reforms in STEs will inevitably fail. Reforms, it is true, are much more difficult to achieve there than in other predatory states, largely because of the unique interface between the political and economic spheres in STEs. However, under certain conditions of long-term economic decline, such as apparently affected all East European STEs in the 1980s, political changes may positively affect the chances for the success of economic changes (see Bauer [1984] and Winiecki [1984a; 1986b]).

Winiecki (1986c) suggests two scenarios which could lead to real economic reform. The first involves the breakdown of consensus within the ruling stratum and the defeat of those interested not only in maintaining political power but also in maintaining the existing structure of property rights in the economic sphere, i.e., the party *apparatchiks* and economic bureaucracy. The other scenario assumes a gradual self-limitation by the communist party as the economic decline drags on and as the costs of maintaining the existing system increase as a result of falling absolute wealth and the augmented efforts needed to control economic and non-economic activities. Since the decline of STEs is multifaceted, combining falling living standards, rapidly increasing pollution, and increasing mortality, many hard questions will be asked within the ruling groups and the ruling strata. Accordingly, the probability of the occurrence of one of these scenarios may increase. Either scenario would enhance the prospects of successful economic and political reform in STEs as they approach the last decade of the 20th century.

REFERENCES

Antal, L. "Development with Some Digression." *Acta Oeconomica*, 23, 1976.
"Thoughts on the Further Development of the Hungarian Economic," *Acta Oeconomica* 29 (3–4), 1982.
Barzel, Y. "A Theory of Rationing by Waiting." *Journal of Law and Economics*, 1974.
Bauer, T. "The Second Economic Reform and Ownership Relations." *East European Economics*, Spring–Summer 1984, 33–87.

Jan Winiecki

Beksiak, J. *Change in the Economy*. Warsaw: PWN Publishers, 1984 (in Polish).

Cheung, S. N. S. "A Theory of Price Control." *Journal of Law and Economics*, April 1974, 53–71.

Crosnier, M. A. "L'économie soviétique en 1986: une image brouillée." *Le Courrier des pays de l'Est*, 318, 1987.

Djilas, M. *The New Class*. New York: Praeger, 1956.

Hillman, A. L. and A. Schnytzer. "Illegal Economic Activities and Purges in a Soviet-Type Economy: A Rent-Seeking Perspective." *International Review of Law and Economics*, 1986.

Jermakowicz, W. "Systemic Determinants of Organizational Structures," Parts I–II. Polish Economic Association, Warsaw, 1983, mimeographed in Polish.

Kornai, J. "Resource-Constrained Versus Demand-Constrained System." *Econometrica* 47 (4), 1979.

Economics of Shortage. Amsterdam: North-Holland, 1980.

Laky, T. "The Hidden Mechanisms of Recentralization in Hungary." *Acta Oeconomica* 24 (1–2), 1980.

North, D. C. "Institutional Change and Economic Growth." *Journal of Economic History*, March 1971, 118–25.

"A Framework for Analyzing the State in Economic History," in *Explorations in Economic History*, New York: Academic Press Inc., July 1979, 249–59.

Olson, M. *The Logic of Collective Action*. Cambridge, Mass.: Harvard University Press, 1965.

The Rise and Decline of Nations. New Haven: Yale University Press, 1982.

"Microeconomic Incentives and Macroeconomic Decline." *Weltwirtschaftlicher Archiv* 120 (4), 1984.

"Beyond Keynesianism and Monetarism." *Economic Inquiry*, July 1984b, 297–322.

Smolar, A. "The Rich and the Powerful," in *Poland: Genesis of a Revolution*, edited by A. Brumberg. New York: Random House, 1983.

Soos, K. A. "Planification imperative, regulation financière, 'grandes orientations' et campagnes." *Revue d'etudes comparatives Est–Ouest*, 2, 1985.

Thalheim, K. C. *Stagnation or Change in Communist Economies*. London: Center for Research into Communist Economies, 1986.

Trotsky, L. *The Revolution Betrayed*. New York: Pathfinder, 1937 (1972 edition).

Winiecki, J. "Investment Cycles and an Excess-Demand Inflation in Planned Economies: Sources and Processes." *Acta Oeconomica* 28 (1–2), 1982.

"Distorted Macroeconomics of Central Planning." *Banca Nazionale del Lavoro Quarterly Review* 157, 1986a.

"Are Soviet-Type Economies Entering an Era of Long-Term Decline?" *Soviet Studies*, 1986b.

"Soviet-Type Economies: Considerations for the Future. *Soviet Studies*, October 1986c, 543–61.

Institute for International Economic Studies Seminar Paper No. 374, University of Stockholm, January 1987.

"The Overgrown Industrial Sector in the STEs Evidence, Explanations, Consequences." *Comparative Economic Studies*, 28 (4), 1987.

The Distorted World of Soviet-Type Economies. London–Pittsburgh: Routledge–Pittsburgh University Press, 1988a.

"Narrow Non-Manual/Manual Wage Differentials and Excess Demand for Manual Labor in the CPEs: Causally Linked System-Specific Phenomena." *Osteuropa Wirtschaft,* 1988b.

Winiecki, E. D. and J. Winiecki. "Manufacturing Structures in Centrally-Planned Economics." *Jahrbuch der Wirtschaft Osteuropas* 12 (I).

3

Transaction costs and economic development

Institutions in society provide the rules of the game that determine the incentives for individuals to engage in growth-enhancing or redistributive activities. Institutions are both formal and informal. Formal institutions consist of the laws and regulations of a society. Informal institutions are the norms and customs of a society. Both impose constraints on behavior. The question addressed by Andrew Stone, Brian Levy, and Ricardo Paredes in the following essay is: To what extent do laws and regulations that ostensibly increase transaction costs in fact affect the costs of doing business? Or, put another way, in the presence of high formal transaction costs do businesses adopt informal institutions to lessen the burden of regulations? The work is innovative both theoretically and empirically. Theoretically, the authors recognize the interconnection and potential substitutability between formal and informal institutions. Empirically, they measure the effect of formal regulations by conducting field surveys in the garment industry in Brazil, a country noted for its regulations, and Chile, a country that has recently deregulated to a large extent.[1]

The degree to which formal rules constrain behavior depends on enforcement. Enforcement is effected by the coercive power of the state or by the norms of society. Coercion and norms are substitutes. If the members of a society generally agree that something is not appropriate behavior – for example, littering – society must expend fewer resources in enforcing laws against littering. Alternatively, if the members of a

---

[1] The empirical work follows in the footsteps of Hernando de Soto, who measured the costs of starting a business by the formal process in Lima, Peru. De Soto concludes that the high costs of doing business by the books accounts for the large informal sector in Peru. See Hernando de Soto, *The Other Path: The Invisible Revolution in the Third World* (New York: Harper & Row, 1989). Stone, Levy, and Paredes depart from de Soto not by measuring how firms could do business by the formal rules but by measuring how firms actually conduct business in the presence of the transaction costs imposed by formal regulations.

society generally believe that certain activities are not harmful – for example, within limits, gambling – enforcement of a law against those activities becomes prohibitively expensive. The costs of enforcement are higher if the illegal activity involves a transaction between two parties who stand to gain from the activity as compared with an activity between an individual and a government agent. But even when the activity is between government agents and individuals, bribery may be so acceptable that enforcement is impossible.

Governments seem to recognize the importance of informal norms or beliefs in enforcing laws and regulations. For this reason they frequently engage in campaigns to sway public opinion. For example, with respect to littering, we are told to "do the right thing" and, with regard to seatbelts, to "buckle up and live." No doubt governmental attempts to sway public opinion and affect norms have some impact; the question is, how much? The more government can influence norms, the greater is its power. Conversely, the more norms are independently formed, the more limited is government.

Because norms act as a constraint on government activity, do laws matter or are they simply a reflection of the beliefs of members of society? Although laws frequently mirror the beliefs of a society, they most likely have an independent effect, for several reasons:

1. As this essay will make clear, there are some costs to evading the law.
2. As long as the government has some legitimacy – for example, its officials are elected – the enactment of a law influences the beliefs of some citizens because politicians are, almost by definition, leaders.
3. Particularly during times of crisis, existing laws may act synergistically with norms to constrain behavior in a way that norms alone may not.
4. Crises may also enable laws to have a greater impact on behavior because during crises beliefs become uncertain and during periods of uncertainty some people may turn to the existing government for security.[2]

---

[2] Weingast argues that governments can credibly commit to secure property rights only if supported by the norms of society, yet this begs the question as to why laws matter. His answer is similar to ours: "The reason concerns unanticipated contingencies in which there are multiple interpretations of how to expand the current set of norms to the new situation. Such problems create a lack of equilibrium, and hence the strong potential for failure due to the resulting heterogeneity of attitudes. Hence explicit institutions are needed" (Barry Weingast, "Constitutions as Governance Structures: The Political Foundations of Secure Markets," paper presented at the 10th International Seminar on the New Institutional Economics, June 24–26, 1992, Wallerfangen/Saar, Germany, p. 38, footnote 37). Robert Higgs elaborates on the theme that crisis allows greater scope for government activity in *Crisis and Leviathan* (New York: Oxford University Press, 1987). Also see Chapter 7 by Higgs in the present volume.

WHAT TO LOOK FOR IN THE ESSAY

We encourage the reader to reflect on the following while reading this essay:

1. Do informal institutions allow businesses to operate outside the legal environment, within the legal environment, or both?
2. What types of transactions are better supported by informal norms and what types by formal regulations?
3. If bribery signals that citizens do not believe in certain laws, what maintains laws that citizens do not believe in?

Public institutions and private transactions: a comparative analysis of the legal and regulatory environment for business transactions in Brazil and Chile

ANDREW STONE, BRIAN LEVY,
AND RICARDO PAREDES

1. INTRODUCTION

How do complex, nontransparent laws and regulations and a somewhat inaccessible, expensive, and slow set of formal legal conflict resolution mechanisms affect business transactions? This study uses the approach of the new institutional economics (NIE) to contrast the impact of the complex legal and regulatory environment in Brazil with that in Chile, where regulatory and legal reforms have sought to facilitate market efficiency. In addition, the study examines the importance of legal and regulatory obstacles to the growth and operation of Brazilian businesses relative to other constraints. The results illustrate a central point: institutions matter economically in the actual costs (and benefits) they create for businesses, not in their compliance with ideal forms.

The study examines four basic areas where legal and regulatory institutions could create critical obstacles to efficiency:

- the start-up of a new business (entry);
- the regulation of business;
- orders by customers; and
- sales with credit.

The first two areas involve transactions between a business and the government, while the second two involve transactions between businesses. Interviews with garment firms were used to ascertain in as quan-

The views expressed in this essay are those of the authors and do not necessarily represent those of the World Bank, its Board of Executive Directors or the countries they represent. The work was carried out with the support and interest of Geoffrey Shepherd and Mary Shirley and benefited from the assistance of Roy Gilbert, Alberto Abu-Mohr, Karin Dhadamus, Thomas Magyar, and Fausto Lerner. Lisette Price provided useful comments on an earlier draft.

We gratefully acknowledge Polly Means, who created the graphics for this chapter.

titative a way as possible the costs and problems associated with particular transactions.

The results show that Chilean business transactions indeed benefit from legal simplicity and consistency of enforcement relative to their Brazilian counterparts, but these benefits are mitigated by the differences between formal law and the law in practice in Brazil. In two of the four areas examined, Brazil has evolved some effective institutional substitutes to reduce the costs that would otherwise have been imposed by inefficient formal institutions. In the entry of new businesses, professions have evolved to transform the process of registering a business from a potentially tortuous obstacle trail into a fairly affordable one-stop process. In debt collection, information systems obviate the need for the formal legal system in a vast majority of cases. In the remaining two areas, the existence of substitutes does not bring transaction costs down to the level of Chile. Brazilian businesses confront high transaction costs in regulation through more complex and resource-intensive regulatory processes and conflict resolution; and in orders, through greater uncertainty and frequent renegotiation. The net combination of these effects implies a somewhat inferior environment for business in Brazil.

Yet, even with these costs, our findings warn against a preoccupation with formal legal and regulatory reform as an immediate means to promote economic development. The relative ranking of obstacles to growth perceived by Brazilian entrepreneurs makes clear that problems relating to legal and regulatory institutions take a distinct backseat to macroeconomic instability, and that federal government economic policy imposes greater insecurity on property rights than does any regulatory or judicial institutional weakness. Once uncertainty of policy and prices has been addressed, an agenda of labor and tax regulatory simplification predominates. Only then do the obstacles imposed by defects directly tied to the formal legal system emerge as binding constraints on businesses.

2. SOME METHODOLOGICAL ISSUES

This section summarizes some of the theoretical controversies that motivated the research, clarifies the reasons for selecting Brazil and Chile as targets of study, and outlines how the field surveys were organized.

Formalistic versus new institutional approaches

Ideally, a market economy develops institutions (including markets, contracts, firms of various characteristics, and systems of regulation) that allow the highest value to be attained from its resources.[1] Traditionally, neoclassical economics has assumed that such institutions are in place, and consequently that transactions between buyers and sellers are cost-less, instantaneous, and based on perfect information.[2] Two distinct, but related literatures have increasingly begun to explore deviations from this ideal.

The field of Law and Development holds that rapid market-based economic growth depends on: a system of simple, transparent laws and regulations; consistent interpretation and enforcement (like cases are treated alike); just and rapid resolution of conflicts (justice deferred is justice denied); and a social attitude of respect for legal and regulatory institutions.[3] The common law systems of England and the United States, as well as the civil legal systems of Western European countries, are taken as ideals.[4] Deviations from the ideal obstruct development. The best-known recent example is the discussion in Hernando de Soto's *The Other Path* of the costs of starting a business in Lima, Peru. De Soto finds complex, strangling Peruvian law and regulation to be a powerful disincentive to formality, and hence a stimulus for the rise of a large

---

[1] This "ideal" would clearly depend on social goals for income distribution and other merit goods.

[2] "The former postulate [of neoclassical theory] evolved in the context of the highly developed, efficient markets of the Western world and has served as a useful tool of analysis in such a context. But those markets are characterized by the exceptional condition of low or negligible transaction costs. I know of no way to analyze most markets in the contemporary world and through history with such a behavioral postulate." Douglass C. North, *Institutions, Institutional Change and Economic Performance* (Cambridge University Press, 1990), p. 108.

[3] A World Bank official recently espoused this view as follows: "If the law is to be an effective vehicle for implementing policies and promoting orderly developmental changes in a society, the overall legal and institutional framework must be sound. That framework is of vital importance to all economic agents in the development process – from the large industrial conglomerates to the small entrepreneur and farmer." Ibrahim Shihata, "Law and the Development Process," *Bank's World*, March 1990, p. 12.

[4] In fact, it was Max Weber who first connected rational European-style legal systems to capitalist industrial development: "The rationalization and systematiza-tion of the law in general and . . . the increasing calculability of the functioning of the legal process in particular, constituted one of the most important conditions for the existence of . . . capitalistic enterprise, which cannot do without legal security." Cited in Kenneth L. Karst and Keith S. Rosenn, *Law and Development in Latin America* (Berkeley: University of California Press, 1975). In a recent literature survey, Imani Ellis-Cheek identifies a traditional qualitative literature, wedded to Western legal norms, and a critical literature of recent years demanding quantitative, empirical documentation of the merits of legal systems, foreshadowing the approach of NIE. *The Contribution of Law to Economic Development: A Literature Survey*, World Bank, Private Sector Development Advisory Group, Legal Department, September 1991.

informal sector unprotected by formal law.[5] De Soto's work stands out in its careful observation of the many effects of the legal and regulatory system on the poor and its attempt to document the costs of doing things "by the book."[6] The Law and Development literature is prescriptive in its conclusions: societies that are not ruled by transparent laws and consistent enforcement should be.

NIE has also observed the divergence of law and regulation from an ideal: that of the neoclassical economic model. NIE began with an emphasis on the proper definition and enforcement of property rights,[7] but has evolved to examine the impact of institutions on the cost of transactions. According to Williamson, transaction cost economics recognizes that the definition, comprehension, and enforcement by courts of property rights are all problematic. Therefore, nonmarket social institutions arise to provide "contractual integrity for transactions." Transaction cost economics, unlike the Law and Development literature, rec-

[5] De Soto observes the failure of Peru's Byzantine formal legal and regulatory institutions: "Taken together, all these setbacks show that legal institutions have ceased to provide the means to govern society and to live in it. . . . Moreover, lack of access to the protection and opportunities which legal institutions ought to provide seems to give most Peruvians the feeling that the system is unfair and that institutions discriminate among the population rather than unite it." *The Other Path: The Invisible Revolution in the Third World* (New York: Harper & Row, 1989), p. 232. Although chronicling the rise of informal institutions that have substituted for formal ones, de Soto and his organization, the Institute for Liberty and Democracy (ILD) prescribe a standard, formal Law and Development solution: "The ILD's paradigm for economic growth in the Third World stresses the need for democratic institutions to achieve market-oriented development. The ILD believes that accessible institutions which adequately protect property rights, facilitate public participation in the decision-making process and set forth facilitative law to promote private enterprise, are the only way to open up economies and political systems to all citizens. This is the foundation for sustainable growth." *ILD Newsletter* 1, No. 2 (October 1990), p. 1.

[6] De Soto's book briefly describes a study of 50 small industries in Lima and the regulatory costs they actually face. This study attempts to determine what different regulations cost businesses, finding that actual taxes paid form the minority of expenses imposed by government. Instead, labor is unduly burdened by regulation, biasing businesses toward capital-intensive production modes. However, it is his more formalistic study of the steps required to open businesses that has captured the greatest attention and publicity.

[7] Ronald Coase is commonly credited with fathering this school of thought: "One of the purposes of the legal system is to establish the clear delimitation of rights on the basis of which the transfer and recombination of rights can take place through the market." "The Federal Communication Commission," *Journal of Law and Economics* 2 (1959), pp. 1–40, cited in Oliver Williamson, "A Comparison of Alternative Approaches to Economic Organization," *Journal of Institutional and Theoretical Economics* 146 (1990), pp. 61–71. However, one could also attribute the attention to the legal definition of property rights to Jeremy Bentham: "Property and law are born together, and die together. Before laws were made, there was no property; take away laws, and property ceases." Bentham cited in Karst and Rosenn, *Law and Development in Latin America*, p. 695.

ognizes that formal law and courts do not and cannot, alone, resolve contractual problems relating to transactions:

> Transaction cost economics is specifically concerned with the governance of contractual relations (by markets, hierarchies, and by hybrid modes) and rejects the proposition that the courts can administer justice in an informed, low cost, and efficacious way. Rather than place the principal burden of contract enforcement on the courts, it argues instead that court ordering operates in the background role and that private ordering by the parties is the principal contractual arena. Thus . . . transaction cost economics focuses expressly on the comparative efficacy with which alternative governance structures manage transactions during contract execution.[8]

Transaction cost economics enriches the view of institutions by weighing the costs and benefits of alternative corporate governance structures and other institutions.[9] Thus, while NIE and Law and Development bear some family resemblance, NIE judges institutional arrangements on the basis of their empirical impact on the efficiency of economic transactions, not on the basis of their resemblance to rational Western norms of law and jurisprudence. Efficiency is achieved not only through low-cost exchanges, but also through the ability of businesses to commit assets to a series of transactions with another business – a dimension known as asset specificity. Central to efficiency is the low-cost availability of information needed to evaluate products being exchanged and to police and enforce agreements.[10] A central strength of the work of writers such as Douglass North is the recognition that informal institutions (besides laws and formal organizations) may play as important a role in determining the costs of doing business as formal ones.

---

[8] Williamson, "A Comparison of Alternative Approaches," p. 67.

[9] See, e.g., Oliver Williamson, *Economic Organization: Firms, Markets and Policy Control* (Sussex: Wheatsheaf Books, 1986).

[10] Describing the sale of a piece of real estate, North writes: "Institutions determine how costly it is to make the exchange. The costs consist of the resources necessary to measure both the legal and physical attributes being exchanged, the costs of policing and enforcing the agreement, and an uncertainty discount reflecting the degree of imperfection in the measurement and enforcement of the terms of the exchange. . . . Institutions in the aggregate define and determine the size of the discount, and the transaction costs that the buyer and seller incur reflect the institutional framework. . . . It is worth emphasizing that the uncertainties . . . with regard to the security of rights are a critical distinction between the relatively efficient markets of high income countries today and economies in the past as well as those in the Third World." North, *Institutions, Institutional Change and Economic Performance*, pp. 62–3. In an applied context, Cheryl Gray looks at the mixture of formal and informal legal processes in Indonesia in *Legal Process and Economic Development: A Case Study of Indonesia*, Policy, Research and External Affairs Working Paper No. 350 (Washington, D.C.: World Bank, 1990).

A. Stone, B. Levy, and R. Paredes

The field of NIE is relatively new and has only recently begun grappling with the difficult task of measuring transaction costs.[11] This study contributes to the growing literature devoted to the measurement of these costs by presenting several indicators of the costs involved in our four transaction areas. These indicators allow both comparisons among countries and among firms of different sizes. The information is used to evaluate the relative strengths of Law and Development and NIE. If bad practice (hence costly transactions) always accompanies bad law, the formalism of the Law and Development approach will prove sufficient. If, however, there are efficient transactions in the absence of good law, then an empirical approach of measuring the benefits and costs of institutional arrangements would seem justified.

The legal and regulatory environments of Brazil and Chile

Our study was set in two countries of fundamentally different policy and institutional environments: one that is highly interventionist in an exceptionally detailed way, and another that has engaged in systematic reform to reduce the size and role of government in markets and to impersonalize the rules of economic competition. Brazil's government has traditionally been heavily involved in the economy, both through direct ownership of public enterprise and through exquisitely detailed regulation, subsidy, and taxation of the private sector.[12] Rosenn describes a system in which laws are so complex and court procedures so expensive that formal institutions could not be relied on for dealing with day-to-day problems in regulation and business transactions.[13] He describes Brazil as a dualistic system, having simultaneously a rigid

[11] "The Department of Agriculture gathers data on the cost of growing peanuts, but we do not yet have a Department of Transactions to give us the crucial variables we need to operationalize the new institutional economics." James D. Hess, "A Comparison of Alternative Approaches to Economic Organization – Comment," *Journal of Institutional and Theoretical Economics* 146 (1990), p. 74.

[12] Claudio Frischtak observes that Brazilian industrial policy often ignored cost, saddling industry with "many internationally uncompetitive areas" and introducing rigidities into the economy in the form of barriers to entry and exit, "overdiversified production structures, and high mandated domestic content levels." See *Industrial Regulatory Policy and Investment Incentives in Brazil* (Washington, D.C.: World Bank, IENIN, 1990). For an analysis of the political economy of these interventions, see Michael Barzelay, *The Politicized Market Economy: Alcohol in Brazil's Energy Strategy* (Berkeley: University of California Press, 1986).

[13] Rosenn describes Brazil as a country "where laws and regulations are enacted upon the assumption that a substantial percentage will be disobeyed, and where 'civil servants, be they small or powerful, create their own law.' " Keith S. Rosenn, "Brazil's Legal Culture: The Jeito Revisited," *Florida International Law Journal* 1 (Fall 1984), pp. 2–42, at 2.

formal law and, quite separately, a "practical system for ordering affairs." Formal law is extraordinarily specific and is approved without reference to its consistency with existing law. Thus, a number of inconsistent laws may apply to an otherwise simple business transaction, such as the "1,470 separate legal actions with thirteen government ministries and fifty agencies" required for an export license in 1981.[14] He describes the use of the *jeito* (the fix) as a means of achieving a degree of simplicity, common sense, and speed (for both licit and illicit purposes) in a system that is tangled, illogical, and slow. The jeito is a way around the formal law, in the form of either an evasion by a private citizen or a sensible accommodation achieved with the help of a properly motivated government official. The *despachante*,[15] a professional go-between, facilitates the latter form of jeito, enabling business to proceed somewhat logically in a formal environment hostile to efficiency.[16] While Rosenn decries the erosion of the power and efficiency of law, he ultimately sees advantages to the informal institutions that have evolved. He suggests that these institutions, while more costly than a more rational formal legal system, allow business to process with "stability and predictability."[17] Yet, true to the Law and Development approach, he ultimately insists that the developmental benefits of legal reform toward a system with efficient laws, "a high degree of obedience to the rule of law, and impersonal, efficient administration of the laws" justify dramatic change.[18] While we fully sympathized with Rosenn's call for reform, we felt his claims about the relative costs and benefits of Brazil's system merited empirical scrutiny.

Given the complexity of Brazil's formal law and legal and regulatory

[14] This was *after* the process was "streamlined" in an "energetic campaign to stimulate exports." Ibid., p. 21.

[15] The word "despachante" means dispatcher, but refers to individuals whose job is to obtain government permits and authorizations on behalf of clients. Formally, their expertise derives from their knowledge of the legal requirements and administrative procedures for obtaining permits. Informally, their expertise also includes knowing which government officials can be persuaded to sidestep the rules in exchange for a gratuity. Despachantes are used not only by individuals and businesses, but also by lawyers and accountants, who regard them as distasteful but necessary agents for doing their dirty work while keeping their own hands clean.

[16] "In practice, the net effect of the jeito is frequently to push the government into assuming a more laissez-faire position than it is ideologically disposed to assume. . . . Permitting circumvention, as the Brazilians have done, enables the government to cater to popular pressures for restraining certain kinds of useful economic activities without actually preventing such activities." Ibid.

[17] "Industry and commercial activity is [sic] much less precarious when businessmen and industrialists have a sense that no matter what changes tomorrow may bring in the law, the jeito, be it corrupt or public serving, will insure business as usual." Ibid.

[18] Ibid., p. 43.

processes, we envisioned several possible states of Brazilian society. The first possibility, raised by a literature discussing elite power and oligopoly in Brazil, is that institutional failures have created fixed entry and other costs that offer advantages to size and reputation. In this scenario, relationships of trust bridge gaps in legal institutions, binding profitable, larger "insider" public and private institutions together, while limiting the entry and growth of "outsiders" who lack access to such privileged relationships.[19] A second scenario, suggested by Rosenn's writing, is that all businesses operate under the handicap of an inefficient system that slows development and puts Brazilian industry at a competitive disadvantage with nations having efficient legal and regulatory systems. Finally, all firms may have found adequate institutional substitutes that allow them to operate about as efficiently as comparable firms in countries with better-functioning formal institutions. In this case, the major question would center around the dynamic effect of reliance on informal mechanisms (issues raised by North), rather than its consequences for static efficiency.

Only a comparison with some other country would allow a clear differentiation between a scenario of generalized inefficiency from formal institutional failure and one of efficiency through effective substitutes. To this end, Chile was chosen as a country where years of conscious reform aimed at improving market efficiency began from a base of a complex legal and regulatory environment comparable to Brazil's. Besides comprehensive macroeconomic reform, Chile has moved to deregulate the economy, attempting to rationalize price, tax, and labor regulation and deregulating and privatizing the financial sector.[20] It is now regarded as having a relatively well-defined property rights system and a liberal economy. In dramatic contrast to the image of Brazil,

---

[19] Peter Evans, *Dependent Development: The Alliance of Multinational, State, and Local Capital in Brazil* (Princeton, N.J.: Princeton University Press, 1979). For a more radical analysis, see Michael Storper, "Who Benefits from Industrial Decentralization? Social Power in the Labor Market, Income Distribution and Spatial Policy in Brazil," *Regional Studies* 18, No. 2 (1984), pp. 143–64. For a less ideological analysis of Brazil's political economy of these interventions, see Barzelay, *The Politicized Market Economy*. Undoubtedly, in many industries, fiscal incentives benefited incumbents and promoted concentration. Frishtak writes: "Through the incentive system, established firms obtained unit cost advantages which have helped them to consolidate their market position. Entrants, competing for increasingly scarce fiscal resources, were at a disadvantage relative to well-informed incumbents that had already demonstrated the ability to fulfill demand requirements." *Industrial Regulatory Policy*, p. iii.

[20] Examples of the reform include a unification of and reduction in tariffs (down from an average of 105% to a level of 11%); a reduction by two-thirds of the number of items with controlled prices; and a replacement of a transactions tax with a value-added tax.

where influence and contacts with bureaucrats have been portrayed as vital to economic success,[21] a recent study finds an environment where entrepreneurs rank "politician and authority contacts" as the least important of seven factors determining their success.[22]

The field surveys

The parallel studies of Brazil and Chile center on the garment industry in the cities of São Paulo and Santiago (and environs). The garment sector was chosen for two reasons. First, unlike many other industrial sectors in Brazil, it was not being specially promoted by the government. A recent evaluation showed the clothing and shoe industry to be low in regulatory and promotional constraints on capital mobility and competition, as well as low in the level of fiscal, credit, and procurement-related incentives relative to all other industrial sectors.[23] Thus, sector-specific interventions were less likely to cloud the impact of economy-wide law and regulation on businesses. Second, the clothing industry has no large, inherent scale economies (hence has small, medium, and large firms competing), enabling the study of problems faced by firms of a variety of sizes. Note, however, that transactions in the garment sector tend to be short-term, limiting our ability to extrapolate from our findings to the impact of the legal system on long-term transactions.

Interviews were conducted with 42 garment firms in each country. The sample was stratified by size of firm. The Brazilian sample comprised 5 large firms (more than 500 employees), 13 medium firms (101 to 500 employees), and 25 small firms (100 or fewer employees). Interviews were also conducted in Brazil with officials of 3 textile firms, with 3 garment subcontractors (not included in the sample), as well as with lawyers, bankers, despachantes, and leaders of industry associations. The Chile sample comprised 7 large firms, 25 medium firms, and 10 small firms.[24] The Chilean sample was stratified to attain ethnic repre-

---

[21] See Barzelay, *The Politicized Market Economy*.

[22] M. Rojas, *Structural Change and Entrepreneurship*, Working Paper, Lund University, Sweden, 1990.

[23] According to Frischtak, "Moderate to high barriers are found in intermediates and capital goods, and somewhat less in consumer durables. Regulatory and promotional regimes have a more marginal impact on consumer non-durable industries populated by a large number of small and medium producers: clothing and shoes, food products (with the exception of flour milling), leather products, beverages and other consumer goods." *Industrial Regulatory Policy*, p. 25.

[24] A definitional difference led one firm of 500 employees in the Chile sample to be classified as "large" and one firm of 100 employees to be classified as "medium." In the Brazil sample, while there are no firms of exactly 500 employees, there is one with 100 that is classified as "small."

sentation proportionate to that in the population of garment industry entrepreneurs, as different groups supply different ends of the market. In both cases, relative to the population of firms, large and medium firms were oversampled. A printed questionnaire, highlighting experiences and obstacles in the four transaction areas discussed below, was verbally administered by one of the authors or an assistant directly to the proprietor or an officer of each firm.[25] The limited area of sampling, the relatively small sample size, and the small number of firms in size categories responding to certain questions severely limit the ability to make valid statistical inferences from the data for the two nations under study, but the results here are highly suggestive of important areas for policy reforms.

3. BUSINESS–GOVERNMENT TRANSACTIONS

Business–government transactions shape the costs of going into and staying in business, as well as the level and certainty of returns to investment. Dealings between business and government are inherently unequal because one party (the government) is making and enforcing the rules that affect the interests of both. Hence, lack of transparency in the regulation of entry and operation may invite opportunistic behavior by officials enforcing the law. Lack of consistency in law and administration increases bureaucratic discretion and may increase opportunities for government officials to seek rents. Institutional failures may impose costs that restrict competition, distort patterns of investment or of sales, and/or divert entrepreneurial attention from economically productive activities to seeking rents. Furthermore, these failings make it hard for businesses to predict the outcome of investment decisions. Yet, as the data will demonstrate, the impact of institutional failings (hence the value of reform) depends on the ability of businesses to find substitutes for inefficient formal institutions.

We examine first the impact of the procedures required to start up a business on entry. Thereafter, we explore the impact on firms of the tax and regulatory requirements associated with business operation. The evidence on the transactions costs of entry and regulation offers surprising insight into the nature of business informality.

Entry: access to formality

Entry is a critical point at which the competitiveness of an economy is determined. Barriers to entry, including large fixed costs, may protect

---

[25] The typical interview took place in an office in the firm itself. A small coffee was inevitably offered, and the authors thank all the respondents for their hospitality.

those firms already in business at the expense of newer firms. If new entrants cannot afford to become formal, they may be doomed to staying small, needing to be invisible to authorities, hence denied access to capital and most associations with formal businesses. If even this route is foreclosed, large incumbent firms will dominate markets.

In 1983 a team from Hernando de Soto's Institute for Liberty and Democracy tried to set up a small garment firm on the outskirts of Lima. In a now-famous experiment, they followed the formal, legal process and found that it took them 289 days to fulfill 11 requirements, $194 in direct costs (including two bribes they had to pay, but not including eight they were asked to pay but avoided), and more than $1,000 in forgone profits. Opening a store was relatively simpler, but more expensive, involving three government departments, requiring 43 days, and costing $590.56, or 15 minimum wages. This high "cost of access" was identified as a major contributor to the large number of informal enterprises in Peru. De Soto's team did not, however, examine the actual costs incurred by garment firms in accessing formal status, only the cost and delays of "going by the book." De Soto suggested that these costs were important explanations of the large number of small, informal firms in Lima.

In Brazil, too, about 11 steps are required for "access to formality" in industry, and we asked businesses about the difficulties they encountered in becoming formal. Contrary to our expectations, they had few complaints. Entry into garment manufacture turns out to be a relatively easy, one-and-a-half-month, one-stop process in practice, though not in law.

In practice, most firms enter with a single payment to an accountant or a despachante. On average, the numerous steps (e.g., with federal, state, and local tax authorities, the Ministries of Industry and Fazenda, the commercial registry, the cadastral authorities, etc.) were completed by the accountant within 6 weeks.[26] The total cost of entry was not insignificant, with estimates varying from as low as $150 to as high as $2,500, averaging around $640 (Table 1). Yet several microenterprise or small limited-liability corporations in our sample had been able to register for less than $500 in about a month,[27] suggesting that the one-time fixed cost of entry is not an overwhelming obstacle to formality.

---

[26] One fact became clear from both the Brazil and Chile surveys: a strong association between age and size. We asked the cost of registering only of firms that had done so in the past ten years (as calculations of cost might be difficult and the regulatory environment substantially different before this). This excluded all of the large firms in the Brazil sample and many medium-sized ones.

[27] Of 16 firms that were asked and responded, 8 registered for $500 or less, with the lowest costing $180. Of 18 firms responding, 10 took one month or less to register.

Table 1. *Time and cost of registration*

	Brazil	Chile
Total cost of registering (U.S. $)	$640 ($n = 15$)	$739 ($n = 15$)
Total time to register (months)	1.6 ($n = 17$)	2.0 ($n = 16$)

Note: Data are based on firms responding. The highest values for both Brazil and Chile were omitted as conspicuous outliers.

When specifically questioned on difficult steps of entry, most firms reported no problems. Accountants (and occasionally despachantes) have provided a simple, clear, effective substitute for the government's complex institutions of business entry.

While $640 and seven weeks may seem high, the Santiago survey provides a surprising comparison: the average cost of registration for all firms was higher, and the average time it took was a bit longer. For small firms the cost was lower than Brazil's, at $500, and the mean time required just over seven weeks. For medium-sized firms, the mean cost reportedly averaged more than four times as much, and it took them more than two months to register. Yet the time it took them may be misleading: in Chile, firms may start operation before the entire registration process is complete.

Overall, the conclusion is that Brazil has neither an overwhelmingly costly nor an overwhelmingly difficult entry process. (In fact, the comparison raises questions about the efficiency of Chile's system.) São Paulo's formal legal requirements would have implied a much more difficult process than the procedure in practice. Only actual measurement reveals the moderate cost of registration in Brazil.

Regulation

Regulation and bureaucratic red tape are often identified as one of the worst products of inefficient government institutions. Excessive regulation may create a generalized drag on all businesses or may favor some kinds of businesses over others, either as an intended consequence of implementation or as a result of the structure of costs imposed by regulation. Poor regulation not only adds to the costs of doing business, but also increases uncertainty about the returns from investments and individual transactions. Finally, if regulation imposes transaction-specific risks or costs, it may encourage companies to integrate vertically into retailing or input production as a way of avoiding market transactions.

At first glance, it would seem impossible for Brazilian firms to contend with the mass of contradictory, rapidly changing, and unknowable law that is the formal reality with which they are confronted. Brazilian garment firms identified the regulations and enforcement practices surrounding federal taxes, the state value-added tax (ICMS), and labor regulations as the most vexing of their regulatory burdens.[28] Entrepreneurs detailed a set of more than 50 federal, state, and municipal taxes they must pay, some of which require monthly contributions. Thus, for taxes alone, firms must comply with over 50 sets of filing and payment requirements with inconsistent record-keeping demands. A typical sale requires the filing of four or more copies of the *nota fiscale*, or sales form. Beyond this, the lack of clarity of and the changeable nature of tax and other law makes compliance difficult and opportunistic manipulation of law by rent-seeking bureaucrats relatively easy. The tax and regulatory burden is said by several entrepreneurs to double the cost of garments sold formally.

Our goal was to learn how firms contended with this complex regulatory system in practice, and at what cost. While it is hard to measure directly the costs that regulation imposes on individual transactions, we collected information (summarized in Figures 1 and 2 and Table 2) on three types of costs to firms associated with regulation: the usage and cost of external accountants; the proportion of proprietors' time spent complying with regulations; and the amount of employees' time devoted to tasks of compliance. This enables us to compare costs between Brazil and Chile, to get a relative sense of the burden on business of Brazil's unreformed system as it exists in practice.

As Table 2 summarizes, small Brazilian firms generally hire an outside accountant to handle their taxes at an average cost of $525 per month, with a range from $91 to more than $2,000. Figure 2 shows us why medium and large firms internalize these functions – once they grow beyond 50 to 60 employees, contracting out becomes too expensive, and a full-time person is needed to focus on the complex requirements of a larger firm (although some firms hire external auditors to assist in compliance with ever-changing regulations). This may be due to tougher

---

[28] Larger firms were inclined to object more to federal tax agencies, while smaller firms concentrated on state tax authorities (ICMS). Complaints about labor regulations were common among all firms. Firms manufacturing garments under license from a foreign company complained about the difficult process of obtaining trademark from the federal agency INPI. Trademark infringement is generally addressed through lawyers and courts; hence, trademark protection can be quite expensive.

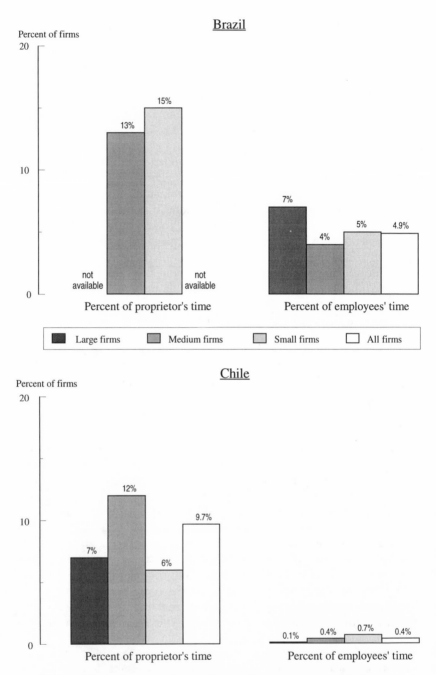

Figure 1. Recurrent costs of compliance with government regulations.

Monthly cost (thousands of US dollars)

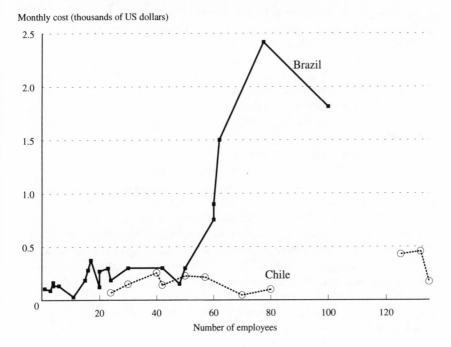

Figure 2. Cost of tax preparation in Brazil and Chile (per month).

Table 2. *Use and cost of external accountants*

	Brazil				Chile			
	Small	Medium	Large	All	Small	Medium	Large	All
% using an accountant	96	15	20	61	70	52	57	57
Monthly cost of accountant (U.S. $)	515	806	n.a.	n.a.	126	409	1,313	400

enforcement by government officials of tax regulations (including pay-roll taxes) against larger firms, as well as to labor regulations that apply to larger firms. In addition, the rewards of scrutiny may be greater for officials in the case of firms with 60 or more employees.

In addition to using outside consultants, Brazilian proprietors of small and medium firms devote an average of nearly 15 percent of their time to regulatory compliance activities. For the largest firms, the function requires whole departments and becomes a specialized management function; hence, an accurate measure of managerial time spent was too complicated for respondents to estimate quickly. In addition to top management's time, between 4 percent (for medium firms) and 7 percent (for large firms) of employees' time (an average of 3.75 full-time employees for small and medium firms) is spent on activities related to compliance with government regulations.

In sharp contrast to Brazil, the most striking feature of Chilean responses was the number of entrepreneurs who had no complaints about the government. The most frequent response to a question about the public agency that created the most difficulties was "none" (22.5 percent of responses, 40 percent for small firms). The common response was, "If you pay your taxes, there is nothing to worry about." Twenty-four percent of respondents said that their proprietors or senior managers spent between zero and 1 percent of their time dealing with bureaucracy. Thirty-one percent of respondents required the equivalent of between zero and one-tenth of one full-time employee to comply with government bureaucracy. While complaints were registered about the Tax Revenue Service, municipal building permits and taxes, and labor regulations, responses indicated a much higher level of contentment. Turning to the specific cost measures, while the majority of Chilean firms use external accounting services, the average cost – $335 per month – is only 63 percent of that of their Brazilian counterparts. In particular, small firms in Chile pay an average of only $111 a month for their accounting services, while Brazilian small firms average a payment of $515 ($428, omitting one outlier). This implies that the minimum fixed accounting-related cost of operation – a necessary burden for all businesses that choose to enter as formal firms – is lower in Chile. In addition, there is a much weaker relationship in Chile between the use of an external accountant and the size of the firm, implying that, other things being equal, there is no size at which government-demanded records become too complex or expensive for an external agent to handle. Fifty-seven percent of large firms use external accountants, paying them an average of $934 per month.

Chilean entrepreneurs spend somewhat less of their own time contending with the requirements of government bureaucracy – 10 percent as compared with 15 percent for their Brazilian counterparts. Furthermore, whereas for Brazil the heaviest burden on proprietors' time falls on small enterprise, the regulatory burden is lightest for the smallest Chilean firms, whose proprietors spend an average of only 6 percent of their time contending with government, again evidencing lower barriers to entry. An even more striking difference lies in the staff time required for compliance: the average Chilean firm requires the equivalent of only two-thirds of one full-time employee to deal with bureaucracy and government requirements, as opposed to an average of over 3.75 full-time equivalents for small and medium Brazilian firms.[29]

In addition to differences in the regulatory costs associated with everyday operation, Brazilian and Chilean firms also differ in the prevalence of disputes with government officials and in the way in which they are resolved. Brazil's complex regulatory environment creates a high level of conflict for medium and larger firms. There was a general feeling among businesses that agents of bureaucracy "could always find something wrong." As Figure 3 (top) shows, two-thirds of the Brazilian firms surveyed have disagreed with a government official and attempted to have a ruling changed, with the proportion highest for large firms. Further, Brazil's medium and large firms are more prone than their smaller counterparts to use formal appeals processes and lawsuits to resolve conflicts with government agencies, with 70 percent of medium firms sampled, and 100 percent of large firms, resorting to formal legal appeal or lawsuit at some time. Legal action defers payment of fines and tax assessments and creates a lengthy period in which a settlement can be negotiated. Furthermore, those who had used formal appeals mechanisms and law suits were not discouraged by them: 81 percent of those who had pursued these means said they would do so again.[30]

In marked contrast to the Brazil response, only 28 percent of the firms in Santiago had taken action regarding a disagreement with a government agency. Unlike their Brazilian counterparts, entrepreneurs made no suggestion that informal payments form a systematic substitute for well-functioning regulatory and conflict resolution mechanisms.[31] As in Brazil, a higher proportion of small firms used informal conflict resolution mechanisms than larger firms (see Figure 3, bottom). Unlike the situation in Brazil, small firms showed no disinclination to use formal appeals processes, compared with larger firms.[32] Yet there was

---

[29] The difference is more dramatic, but the data less sound, if one includes large firms, where one Brazilian firm reported using 510 staff members for bureaucratic compliance requirements and another reported using a third of its 30,000 employees to this end.

[30] This suggests that formal mechanisms may work reasonably well. Perhaps the high level of conflict and the high cost of regulation are more serious problems.

[31] Nonetheless, *propinas* (tips or bribes) and *coimas* (bribes) were not unfamiliar concepts to Chilean entrepreneurs.

[32] This is somewhat hard to interpret, as relatively few small or large firms responded to the question at all. Of those responding who had pursued disagreements, small firms had the highest rate of using both informal contacts with an official and formal procedural conflict resolution mechanisms. Large firms were the most likely to act upon a disagreement (50% vs. 20% for medium and 33% for small), however, and were more inclined to take the issue up with a government agent's superior or to pursue unspecified informal remedies.

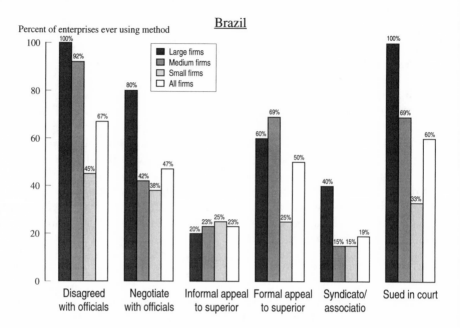

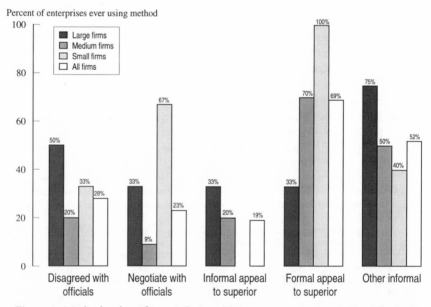

Figure 3. Methods of conflict resolution: business–government. (*Note:* The lack of a bar in the lower graph under "Informal appeal to superior" reflects the fact that no small firms reported using that method of conflict resolution.)

Table 3. *The burden of regulatory constraints by firm size*
(normalized level of difficulty on a zero-to-one scale)

	Firm size			
	Less than 25 employees	25–99 employees	100–499 employees	500 or more employees
Brazil				
Tax bureaucracy	0.50	0.54	0.69	0.65
Labor regulations	0.47	0.66	0.70	0.56
Other bureaucratic procedures	0.28	0.38	0.53	0.40
Chile				
Tax bureaucracy	—[a]	0.28	0.28	0.28
Labor regulations	—[a]	0.28	0.46	0.41
Other bureaucratic procedures	—[a]	0.43	0.31	0.33

[a] Only one firm with fewer than 25 employees was interviewed in Chile; it is included in the 25–99 employee category.

no indication of lawsuits against the government. As in Brazil, it was large firms who were most likely to act upon a disagreement with an agency decision. Overall, Chilean firms clearly bear lower compliance costs and experience less conflict with government officials.

Cumulatively, the effect of regulation in Brazil – but not in Chile – is to create a threshold beyond which firms face sharply increased regulatory costs. Table 3 details the average scores of respondents as to the burden of three types of regulations relative to other constraints on their expansion, with a score of zero for the least binding constraint, and a score of 1 for the most binding. (Section 5 discusses the overall constraint results in more detail.) No systematic variation by firm size is evident for Chilean firms. By contrast, the scores suggest that Brazilian firms confront a "threshold burden":[33] the scores are lowest for the smallest firms, rise as firm size increases, but decline again for the largest group. Consistent with the evidence presented earlier, a plausible explanation for this pattern is that regulatory enforcement is higher for medium firms than for their smaller counterparts.

[33] Brian Levy uses a similar framework to analyze in detail interactions among the threshold burden and the related fiscal and bureaucratic burdens in accounting for regulatory obstacles in Sri Lanka and Tanzania. *Obstacles to the Development of Indigenous Small and Medium Enterprises: An Empirical Assessment*, Policy, Research and External Affairs Working Paper No. 588, World Bank, February 1991.

It follows that firms may rationally limit expansion as a way of remaining below the regulatory threshold. Indeed, in the course of interviews, we commonly encountered the "multiple business card" phenomenon: rather than growing big, entrepreneurs expand into multiple small businesses, each of which can carry on substantial informal activity. Hence, they must fish through their pockets to produce the correct card for the business one is discussing. The sharp increase in regulatory obstacles to medium firms (and the modest decline for large ones) suggests that large incumbents may be somewhat protected from the appearance of new large competitors.

The nature of informality

Taken together, the analyses of entry and regulation point to an interpretation of informality that is rather different from that propounded by Hernando de Soto. Whereas de Soto attributes informality to the high cost of becoming formal, our findings focus attention on the ongoing regulatory and tax-related costs of operating as a formal enterprise. Further, contrary to the picture of a choice between unregistered informality and registered formality, our analysis suggests a more complex reality.

In neither São Paulo nor Santiago did we find unregistered firms. Efforts to track down "informal" firms in São Paulo inevitably led to the discovery of a formally registered firm that conducted a certain amount of informal – "off the books" – activity (although anecdotal evidence suggested that there might well be concentrated pockets of unregistered businesses elsewhere in São Paulo State and near Rio de Janeiro). The overall evidence from the two cities studied indicated that, for those entrepreneurs deciding to start a garment business, the costs of formal legal status do not outweigh its benefits. Hence, informality in garment manufacture is not primarily a phenomenon of unregistered firms. Rather, it is one of registered firms selling a portion of their production informally and of small labor subcontractors evading regulation.[34]

It is virtually the norm for Brazilian small and medium businesses to engage in a considerable amount of informal activity. This activity takes two forms. First, to evade sales-related taxes, goods are sold without

---

[34] One firm we encountered subcontracted to seamstresses in their homes. By avoiding all payroll taxes, benefits, and labor regulations, the firm paid the seamstresses, on a piecework basis, double the prevailing wage, and obtained twice the productivity of its factory workers, saving substantially. One of the seamstresses we interviewed acknowledged that she had none of the health insurance or pension benefits workers are supposed to receive, but questioned the value of these programs to workers as administered by the government.

notas fiscais (government-mandated sales slips) or with *notas* understating their true value. Second, because labor regulations at least double the wage cost of labor, create substantial liabilities with regard to each worker, and prohibit the reward of individual productivity, many firms subcontract for labor on a piecework basis and/or underreport their wage bills.

Irregularities are often discovered by government officials in the record keeping, reporting, or labor and safety conditions in individual firms. Some violations are real, some are artifices of officials' interpretations of Byzantine regulations, and some are the result of direct contradictions between laws of parallel agencies or of different levels of government.[35] Officials have the power to impose stiff fines, and often do. But officials commonly use the fines as a stimulus for a negotiation, in which a settlement of between 5 and 25 percent of the fine is paid to them directly. Like Eskimos with regard to snow, Brazilians have several words for these payments, including *jeitinho, caixinho,* and *cafezinho.*[36] Some 90 percent of small firms, over 70 percent of medium firms, and 60 percent of large firms acknowledged making these payments, a surprisingly large number given most people's obvious reluctance to admit illegal activity. Even so, the declining proportion of acknowledged jeitinhos among larger firms provides additional evidence that, for those who would operate informally, there is a substantial premium on keeping individual operations small.

In sum, manageable entry costs, unmanageable formal regulatory costs, and the ubiquitous jeitinho work together to induce Brazilian firms to register formally, but to operate a portion of their businesses informally. Without regulatory discretion, the jeitinho would lose its role as lubricant of business transactions. But given the complexity of regulations, in the absence of the jeitinho Brazilian firms would be forced to abandon their semiformal practices and choose between operating as purely formal ventures or exiting. Given the quagmire of Brazil's formal regulatory environment, under those circumstances many, perhaps most, would choose to exit.

[35] One (perhaps apocryphal) story related by an entrepreneur illustrates well the lack of consistency among laws and the opportunities it creates for government agents: State and municipal safety codes specify different heights at which fire extinguishers must be mounted. One entrepreneur addressed this problem by having two sets of brackets for each extinguisher. When a state inspector came, the extinguisher would immediately be moved to the appropriate level. The state and municipal inspectors, undaunted by the entrepreneur's ingenuity, conspired to arrive together – so that one was sure to find a violation and elicit a payment.

[36] Meaning "little fix," "collection box," and "small coffee," respectively. *Propina* (tip or bribe) is a blunter word.

4. BUSINESS–BUSINESS TRANSACTIONS

Transactions among businesses also depend on the law and its enforcement. Legal formalism might guide us to an examination of civil law affecting contracts and conflict resolution: transparent law and effective legal conflict resolution mechanisms seem essential for efficient exchange. If laws are unclear and conflict resolution mechanisms slow, expensive, unfair, or unpredictable, it may be harder for businesses to deal with one another. In particular, effective legal institutions would seem to facilitate impersonal transactions: trust or personal ties are not needed if there are sure and swift means to enforce contracts.[37] In this ideal, firms are freed to pursue the most profitable transactions and all competitors are treated equally. Otherwise, firms committing resources to a transaction may be subject to the opportunistic behavior of their trading partners – such as renegotiation of the terms of the exchange or failure to pay after delivery of goods.

Yet, where perfect legal institutions do not exist, and substitutes exist, how do we evaluate the adequacy of these substitutes and the urgency of reform? To provide some initial insights, we apply the NIE approach to two types of transactions: the placing of orders and the provision of credit by the parties to business transactions.

Orders

Producing goods against orders requires either guarantees or trust. A producer must commit time and resources to the production of an order. The more specialized the order, the harder it will be to sell to another customer and the greater will be the loss to the supplier if the orderer cancels or renegotiates once production is complete. If the supplier customizes a good to the needs of a particular customer (imagine, for example, a thousand pink and orange polo shirts with "Rafael's Pizzeria" embroidered on the pocket) without first receiving full payment, the supplier may be left in a disadvantageous position if the order does not constitute an enforceable contract: the product has little value to any other customer. On the other hand, delays in delivery or deviations from product specifications can hurt the retailer or customer (imagine the shop receiving heavy wool suits just in time for spring).

In both Brazil and Chile, orders for garments have no legal status. Yet

---

[37] It is quite another issue as to whether any country has such effective and affordable legal institutions that reputation does not play a substantial role in decisions about partners in business transactions.

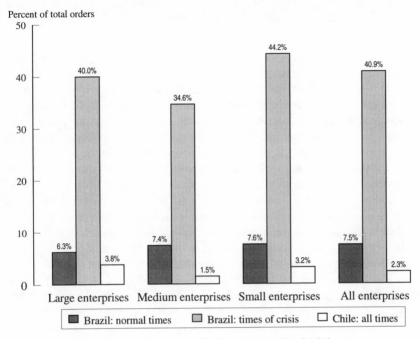

Percent of total orders

Figure 4. Renegotiation of orders in Brazil and Chile.

the consequences are quite different. In Brazil, garment orders are not secure – price and quantity are subject to renegotiation until delivery has been made and signed for. Figure 4 shows that renegotiation is quite common in São Paulo and, in periods of economic crisis, virtually the norm. Whereas in normal economic times (although some respondents denied the premise that such times exist), customers renegotiate between 6 and 8 percent of contracts, in times of crisis (defined by respondents as coinciding with new government economic plans), 35 to 45 percent of orders are renegotiated once the order is ready for delivery. By contrast, in Chile, only about 2 percent of sales are renegotiated, with no reports of recent "crises" or sudden surges in renegotiation.

Where contracts are insecure, firms are less likely to commit large assets to a particular order. They may, instead, adopt alternative sales strategies, such as

• producing noncustomized items and selling from stock and/or accepting orders only for noncustomized items;
• reducing the size of orders (or value of orders) to any one customer to diversify risk; and/or

• vertically integrating – producing for their own shops to avoid the risk of sour transactions (this represents the substitution of a hierarchy for a market).

A look at methods of sales in Brazil and Chile suggests that firms adopt at least the first two of these strategies in response to Brazil's less reliable orders. Brazilian firms in our sample, overall, sell 42 percent of their goods on order from domestic customers, 44 percent from stock, 12 percent directly to retail customers, and 2 percent as exports. By comparison, Chilean retailers sell 50 percent on domestic order, 21 percent from stock, 24 percent directly to retail customers, and 5 percent as exports. If we assume that export sales are on order and that sales to customers are from stock, then São Paulo's garment producers sell 46 percent on order as compared with Chile's 55 percent, a moderate difference. Clearly, trade (and other) policies of the two nations are different, and one cannot conclude a causal link between Brazil's lower reliance on orders and its institutional environment, but the pattern predicted by an inferior contracting environment is there.

Furthermore, in Brazil, many firms have adopted a strategy of accepting only small orders in order to diversify risk. Brazilian firms make an average of 22 percent of their sales to their top three customers, while Chilean firms make 34 percent of their sales to their top trio. More strikingly, Brazilian firms have, on average, more customers than Chilean firms (even more surprising given that there are more small firms in the Brazilian sample): 1,289 for Brazilian firms versus 242 for Chilean firms.[38]

The data provide no support for the proposition that Brazilian firms use vertical integration as an important response to unreliable orders. Specifically, a substantially smaller percentage of Brazilian respondents (39 percent) than Chilean respondents (81 percent) retailed any portion of their product directly to the customer. But we do have reason to suspect that the trend in Brazil is upward: about a fifth of the firms expressed an intention to establish or expand existing retail sales outlets. By contrast, in Chile, there was some indication of a decline in retailing activity among medium and large firms.[39]

One final indicator of a better contracting environment in Chile is the higher level of customization of inputs. Specifically, in São Paulo, gar-

---

[38] This would appear to contradict the "insider–outsider" hypothesis advanced earlier.

[39] Specifically, when asked to compare their current methods of selling their products with their methods before, medium firms said that 25% of their sales were retail sales directly to customers before, while 22% were now retail. Large firms reported a decline from 33% to 29%.

ment firms report that 21 percent of the textiles they purchase are made to their specifications, while in Chile, 33 percent of fabrics are reportedly exclusive to their firms. For large firms in Chile, the figure rises to 45 percent of their inputs.

The unreliable nature of orders in Brazil is the outcome of an unstable economic environment. Clearly, the contracting mechanism used in orders is weak, but it is a weakness mutually consented to by buyer and seller and not a result of a malfunctioning court system. Lawyers informed us that it is perfectly possible to write a binding contract for an order, citing the example of orders for cars. Some garment producers candidly acknowledged that they renegotiate contracts more often than customers, due to unforeseen shifts in the price of their supplies. And older producers recalled that, before the age of extreme inflation, contracts were more secure and renegotiation uncommon. Furthermore, orders are no more legally binding in Chile than in Brazil, yet they are, by comparison, rarely renegotiated.

Figure 4 makes clear that the differences between Brazilian firms of different sizes, or even between Brazilian and Chilean firms, pale in comparison with the differences for all Brazilian firms between periods of intense government economic intervention (including freezing assets and prices) and normal times. Rapid and unstable inflation makes agreement difficult at all times, yet it is sudden shocks in prices and contract values, resulting from government economic policies and the government's direct manipulation of the value of contracts, that appear to have undermined secure contracting.[40] One index of government bond rates used by many firms was recently suppressed by the government to discourage indexation. Furthermore, the government has actively intervened to mandate reindexation of contracted prices. Finally, the government has acted at times to freeze prices and/or assets, undermining agreements and altering values. Some manufacturers lost nearly all their orders when the government froze bank accounts, since their customers simply could not pay them. The government leaves firms with little alternative but to remain as flexible and uncommitted as possible.

Sales with credit

In both Brazil and Chile, there is a sense that the garment trade would grind to a halt without credit. Retailers cannot pay manufacturers until

---

[40] Government inflation control mechanisms have included mandating the reindexation of contracts to conform to government-prescribed inflation adjustment and the freezing of bank accounts. The first type of policy creates uncertainty about the return to assets; the second threatens rights to assets themselves.

clothing is sold; manufacturers cannot pay textile suppliers until they are paid for their product. A formal legal perspective suggests that formal procedures should be developed to facilitate credit transactions and resolve conflicts over debt. Yet, in the garment business, transactions are small and even an efficient formal conflict resolution mechanism is likely to be costly (recall Williamson, above). Where resort to court is expensive and time-consuming,[41] do firms nonetheless extend credit?

The answer in São Paulo's garment sector is yes. Transactions involving sales with credit demonstrate an important institution: an effective information system, which places a premium on an untarnished reputation, largely obviates the need for effective enforcement mechanisms in the case of default. We were, quite frankly, surprised by the readiness of firms to offer credit to new customers and the dominance of supplier credit as a source of working capital. For example, 87 percent of respondents give credit to new customers. Small firms are the most likely to request cash payment on the first transaction, yet only 18 percent of our sample made this their practice. More generally, 85 percent of garment sales in São Paulo are made with credit – including 77 percent of the sales of small firms, 94 percent for medium firms, and 96 percent for large ones. As the following paragraphs detail, the ability of Brazilian firms to give credit with reasonable confidence that they will be repaid arises from an ex ante information system more than from ex post enforcement mechanisms.

Credit is extended in two major ways in Brazil: through *duplicatas* – signed invoices acknowledging receipt of goods – and through postdated checks. Larger businesses accept postdated checks only from retail customers, while smaller businesses may occasionally accept them from retailers as well. The duplicata, the dominant mode of extending credit in this context, is a legally respected document that can be used to obtain credit from banks (although the person who brings the duplicata to a bank for rediscounting, not the issuer, is liable for the loan).

As Figure 5 shows, firms extending credit to new customers check on them in two major ways: through references and through credit agencies. Each has its costs – the time to check oneself or the fee of a credit agency. São Paulo has one major credit agency for checks, Telecheque, and several specialized agencies providing records for other forms of commercial credit. The information is generally up to date and can be obtained nearly instantly by phone or computer terminal.

In normal times, about 8 percent of customers that receive credit fail to pay on time, with the proportion rising to over 27 percent in times of

---

[41] There are relatively few countries where this is not the case.

Public institutions and private transactions

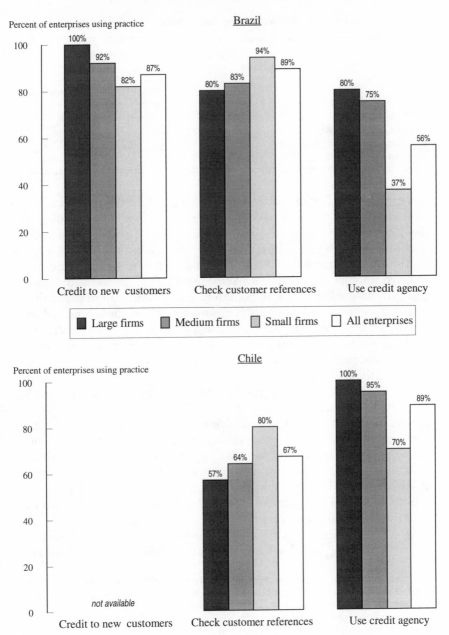

Figure 5. Credit and credit checking in Brazil and Chile.

Table 4. *Resolution of late payment of debt*

	Brazil ("normal" times)	Chile (all times)	
	Duplicatas (%)	Checks (%)	Letras (%)
Pay late	8	4	3
Pay late and reported	4	0.72	0.97
Pay late, reported, and not pay	0.28	0.24	0.13
Total in lawsuit	0.10	0.05	0.02

economic crisis. Patterns of recourse for unpaid debts are similar for duplicatas and for postdated checks; here we describe those relating to the duplicata. If a duplicata is not paid on time, it can either be negotiated and settled between buyer and seller or referred to publicly sanctioned offices *(cartorios)*.[42] About half of the cases of late payment are resolved through negotiation, while the other half go on to the cartorio. The cartorio publishes a list of both those buyers who wait to pay in this office (a common and not very serious offense) and those who fail to pay even then (a relatively serious, though noncriminal, offense). Private credit agencies record and disseminate this information to subscribing firms, allowing them to examine the record of new customers. As Table 4 shows, these collection and information institutions obviate the need for frequent resort to conflict resolution over credit: about 93 percent of those with overdue debts pay in the cartorio (within about 10 days). A retailer with a record of unpaid debts is unlikely to be able to find suppliers, so most pay to preserve their reputation. Among those who fail to pay even the cartorio, negotiation remains the dominant mode of resolution; Table 4 confirms that only a small fraction even of these cases (one-tenth of 1 percent of all transactions involving duplicatas) end up in court. Those that did involved legal proceedings from a low of four months up to three years.[43]

In spite of Brazil's effective alternatives to formal legal resolution of debts, Table 4 suggests that Chile's formal and informal mechanisms are

[42] Cartorios are of two major types: judicial (courts) and extrajudicial (essentially notaries). The extrajudicial cartorios are publicly granted private, highly profitable businesses, oligopolized by a few families for many generations. There are five types of extrajudicial cartorios. In this study, the relevant cartorio is the *tabelionatos de protesto de titulos,* where bad debts and bad checks can be "protested."

[43] Our information on court cases is incomplete and some cases may have been pending for longer than three years. As with other formal legal procedures, large firms are more likely to sue for a bad debt (100% have done so), with medium firms less likely and small firms the least likely (only 27% have ever sued).

superior. Fewer people pay late, and an even smaller percentage go to court. Yet the similarities are more striking than the differences. In Chile, as in Brazil, two mechanisms are used for credit: the postdated check and the *letra* (the equivalent of the Brazilian *duplicata*). In Chile, postdated checks are taken quite seriously. Whereas in Brazil, bad checks may eventually result in the loss of a person's check-writing privileges, in Chile, bad checks will land the writer in jail. Within one to three months, the writer who has not made good her bad check will end up in jail, through a quick criminal law proceeding that requires only the returned check as evidence. Thus postdated checks are widely accepted, accounting for 39 percent of sales for small firms and 30 percent of sales overall.

Letras are employed in some 40 percent of sales. Large firms are the most dependent on letras – which pay for 59 percent of their sales. The penalty for unpaid letras is less severe than for postdated checks, since they are enforceable through civil, not criminal, statutes. Nonetheless, an effective information system – which (as in Brazil) combines both a reporting system on unpaid debts and credit agencies that transmit the information to firms – ensures payment of letras: only 3 percent are paid late, and only 0.02 percent of transactions involving letras wind up in court.

In sum, the comparison of Brazil and Chile suggests that courts are only a small part of the set of institutions that facilitate the flow of short-term credit. Brazilian legal processes have the reputation of being expensive, slow, and unpredictable, whereas Chile's courts are reputed to be relatively swift and consistent in their judgments. Consistent with these differences, problems associated with repayment of debt are somewhat fewer in Chile than Brazil. Yet, with 85 percent of garment sales made on credit, Brazil's cumbersome legal system can hardly be described as a deterrent to the provision of short-term financing among firms. For this type of financing, formal conflict resolution mechanisms do not appear to be the most relevant institutions. A full understanding requires attention to institutions that are not part of the formal legal system: the informational and reputational system that allows firms to extend credit.

5. OBSTACLES TO GROWTH: WHAT ARE THE BINDING CONSTRAINTS?

Both Brazilian and Chilean garment firms reported that they intend to grow substantially during the next two years, and it is important to their economies and to employment (given the high labor intensity of the industry) that they do so. In an economy and society like Brazil's, the agenda for economic reform is broad and far exceeds the government's capacity to address in the short term. How, then, should we rank possible legal and regulatory reforms against other reforms that may consume the time, energy, and political capital of a reform-minded government? Which constraints are binding, which merely a nuisance?

Here, looking at formal law gives us little guidance. Clearly, many laws, enforcement practices, and conflict resolution mechanisms can stand improvement, but what guidance does the Law and Development approach give us about where to start? An NIE approach, however, directs us to the actual experiences and priorities of businesses.[44]

To this end, we asked Brazilian garment entrepreneurs to rate various obstacles to growth and future operation on a scale of 1 to 5. In doing so, they revealed a clear and sobering picture of their most serious obstacles to growth, particularly sobering to those who would target legal reform. Figure 6 presents the average, normalized (on a scale of 0 to 1) evaluation by entrepreneurs of a list of obstacles to future operation and growth that we offered them. The obstacles they find the most serious are not those directly related to legal and regulatory institutional reform, but rather those pertaining to overall economic management. The three factors seen as the greatest obstacles to reform are policy uncertainty, price instability and inflation, and the high level of taxes. A second tier of obstacles relates to tax bureaucracy and labor regulation. Respondents placed obstacles related to the formal legal system and formal conflict resolution (e.g., renegotiated contracts, payment arrears, and debts owed) at the end of a long list of complaints. Our research makes clear that reform of formal legal systems and formal conflict resolution mechanisms were not priority obstacles for garment firms.

In sharp contrast, Chilean respondents did not identify any group of obstacles with equal unanimity or fervor. Policy-related variables did not stand out – the single greatest obstacle identified was the lack of competent workers. Political uncertainty did rank second, most likely due to the recent transition to a democratic government. While rankings, like personal utilities, cannot be compared across nations, it was striking that Chileans systematically chose lower average rankings than Brazilians (even after normalization, due to the high number of zero rankings). Chilean responses are more clustered, implying that no great common problem elicits a consensus response. Only Brazilian entrepreneurs, motivated by common frustration with government policy, lay out a distinct and clear sequence for reform.

[44] Levy, *Obstacles*, discusses in detail the methodology used here.

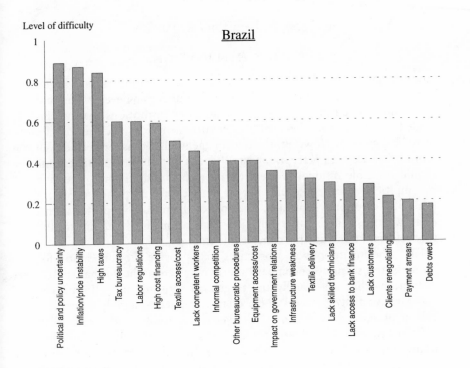

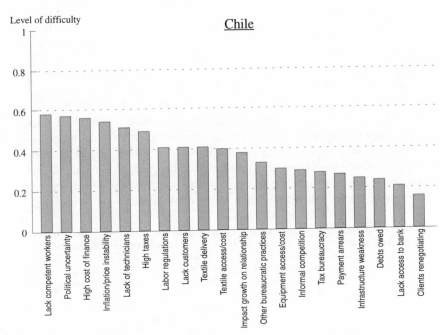

Figure 6. Obstacles to enterprise growth (normalized).

6. POLICY IMPLICATIONS

Since the late 1980s development analysts and practitioners have begun to turn their attention to the institutions that underpin development and have initiated reforms of legal and regulatory institutions that are intended to strengthen the enabling environment for efficient, private sector-led growth. However, the reform agenda has thus far been driven more by an ex ante perception that efficient institutional arrangements should resemble rational Western norms of law and jurisprudence than by empirical assessments of what in practice are the costs to private firms of institutional shortfalls. The goal of the research reported in this essay was to strengthen the empirical foundations for legal and regulatory reform. Four principal conclusions emerge.

First, the institutions and practices that provide the foundation for business transactions encompass much more than the formal, public institutions that are usually the targets of scrutiny and reform. The comparative analysis reveals a Brazilian system considerably more difficult in practice than that of Chile, yet considerably less difficult than written law and formal procedure would imply. Brazilian firms have found surprisingly effective substitutes for the lack of efficient regulation and inexpensive formal conflict resolution – a pattern consistent with Alexander Gerschenkron's classic proposition that developing countries invent institutional substitutes for arrangements prevailing in developed countries.[45] Thus, São Paulo's multistaged, complex formal process of entry (much like the one described for Lima by Hernando de Soto) turned out in practice to be a one-stop, simple process for the average new business, one in which the work of accountants and despachantes in large part substitutes for (the absence of) an efficient formal system of entry. Similarly, credit information and the need to maintain one's reputation to stay in business act as reasonable substitutes for quick and cheap formal conflict resolution mechanisms. Further, in the garment industry, firms have been able to adopt flexible production and marketing strategies – producing noncustomized items and diversifying risk by having many customers, each with small orders – to address the

---

[45] In examining the prerequisites of "modern industrialization," Gerschenkron notes the "great elasticity and variability in the industrialization processes that are known from historical experience." He finds that "it is useful indeed to think of industrial development in terms of graduated patterns of substitution for missing prerequisites." *Economic Backwardness in Historical Perspective: A Book of Essays* (Cambridge, Mass.: Harvard University Press, 1962), pp. 50–51. Albert O. Hirschman echoes this point in describing his principle of the "hiding hands," suggesting that a "prerequisite" may "come into existence *after* the event to which it is supposed to be the prerequisite." *Development Projects Observed* (Washington, D.C.: Brookings Institution, 1967), p. 26.

unpredictable environment for contracting. In this sense, entrepreneurial flexibility substitutes for formal mechanisms by which buyers and producers could commit themselves to firm orders at a preagreed price. As the comparison with Chile confirms, institutional substitutes do not fully compensate for the difficult legal and regulatory environment for business transactions. But they do allow a surprisingly vibrant and competitive industry to operate – albeit one where a substantial fraction of transactions take place outside the formal economy.

Second, the results strongly suggest that, at least in Brazil, legal institutional reform, while ultimately important for attaining the full potential of the economy, can wait for the resolution of more urgent and binding constraints to private-sector development. One clear result of our survey is that, above all, São Paulo's garment entrepreneurs seek a more stable political economy and lower taxes. Indeed, responses highlighted the cost of macro instability to micro efficiency and the security of property rights.

Third, even though institutional substitutes help smooth over the rough edges of Brazil's cumbersome formal institutions, and even though macroeconomic policy clearly emerges as the most binding constraint on enterprises, our research has nonetheless identified an urgent agenda for regulatory reform. To be sure, not all regulation weighs equally on garment firms: the burden of red tape at entry, for example, appears small, as does the burden imposed by cumbersome formal legal institutions. Rather, the two areas that appear most important to Brazilian firms are those regulations relating to taxes and labor. The laws are complex, hard to know, expensive to comply with, and sometimes arbitrarily enforced. Nor does the burden of these regulations fall equally on all firms: the evidence suggests that large incumbents, while not protected from the entry of competitors, may be modestly protected from these competitors' becoming large by the substantial threshold burden imposed by tax and labor regulation as firms grow. This "insider–outsider" pattern limits the potential of new entrepreneurial talent to contribute to the development of the Brazilian economy.

Finally, the research implicitly suggests that proponents of legal reform could strengthen their case by identifying more precisely which business activities are most heavily burdened by a weak formal legal system. Our research suggests that Brazil's legal system and complementary institutional arrangements were adequate for spot transactions and transactions that required short-term commitments, and those that did not involve transaction-specific investments. What is less clear – and what we could not learn from the garment industry (where transaction-specific investments are relatively unimportant) – is whether Brazil's institutional arrangements are adequate for firms to commit assets to production specific to another firm; any inability to commit resources to long-term interfirm relationships could undermine the dynamism of private-sector development. In São Paulo, the ability to commit clearly suffered from the unpredictable rate of inflation. But even with a stable macroeconomy, Brazil's legal system might well turn out to be inadequate for long-term commitments. This implies a need for research of sectors where technology is more specialized.

4

The evolution of modern institutions of growth

THE SOVEREIGN'S DILEMMA

Consider an absolute ruler who controls a country with the aim of maximizing her wealth while protecting her own security. The picture may be a simplification, but it bears resemblance to the behavior of many rulers in history. The ruler faces a dilemma:

1. She can collect the subjects' resources beyond their basic subsistence needs and maximize her wealth in the short run; or
2. she can extend her horizon, lower the rate of taxation, leave resources with the subjects, and take measures to encourage private investments that expand the economy and thus increase her tax base. In future years a larger tax base will yield greater revenue.

Whether alternative 1 or 2 will maximize the *present value* of the ruler's expected flow of income in future years depends on a host of factors, which are summarized in the subjective interest rate that she uses to discount the future. For instance, if the ruler is old and has no heirs or favored successors, she may not be interested in future revenues and may heavily discount future income. Similarly, the ruler may fear that giving her subjects freedom and control of resources beyond bare necessities may lead them to rebel rather than to invest. Also, if attacks from neighboring states are imminent, the ruler's maximization calculations may suggest that her best alternative is to plunder the economy, particularly if she does not have access to effective capital markets.[1] In a

---

[1] In history rapid changes in military technology and large investments in armaments by rival states are frequent causes of fiscal distress and predatory public finance (see Douglass C. North, *Structure and Change in Economic History* [New York: Norton, 1981]). In modern times these issues appear to have contributed to the demise of the Soviet Union. However, a case can also be made that an appropriate degree of rivalry among states may put pressure on the sovereign to decentralize power and provide political foundations for secure markets in order to enlarge the tax base and the future military capabilities of the system.

The evolution of modern institutions of growth

sense, the sovereign's dilemma is the dilemma of an investor faced with great uncertainty.

This model suggests that a stable and rational sovereign who has set up an orderly system of succession will select alternative 2 and select institutional arrangements that expand the economy and the tax base.[2] In the model, the evolution of modern institutions of growth depends on the sovereign's success in pacifying her region and on the absence of internal and external threats to her rule. Institutions do not play an independent role in the evolution; they are instruments at the ruler's disposal.

INSTITUTIONS OF GROWTH

Economic growth depends on specialization, market exchange, and the stock of human and physical capital. When economic activity – investment, production, and exchange – is primarily in the hands of private individuals, these individuals must believe that they have reasonable control over their assets before they will risk them in exchanges across time and space. Economic development requires reasonably secure private and communal property rights. The expectation of arbitrary confiscation, either by the state or by fellow citizens, shortens the individual actor's time horizon, increases the subjective discount rate, and creates disincentives for investment, specialization, and exchange.

For various reasons, the sovereign or the state is in a unique position to provide economic actors with the political foundation of secure markets and property rights for economic growth, but the power of the state can also be used to alter property rights in order to confiscate wealth arbitrarily. The dual nature of state power is not a new discovery; it is an issue that political theorists have discussed for centuries. Hobbes and Locke come to mind, and in 1835 de Tocqueville saw the problem clearly:

It is clear that despotism ruins individuals by preventing them from producing wealth much more than by depriving them of what they had already produced; . . . Freedom, on the contrary, produces far more goods than it destroys, and the nations who are favored by free institutions invariably find that their resources increase even more rapidly than their taxes.[3]

---

[2] For an elaboration of such a model, see Yoram Barzel, "Property Rights and the Evolution of the State," working paper, University of Washington, Department of Economics (1992).

[3] See Alex de Tocqueville, *Democracy in America* (New York: Random House, 1943), Vol. 1, p. 220. Cited by Peter Bernholtz, "Constitutions as Governance Structures: The Political Foundations of Secure Markets – Comment," *Journal of Institutional and Theoretical Economics* 149, No. 1 (1993), 314.

CREDIBLE COMMITMENT

In the following essay, Douglass North and Barry Weingast note, "Rules the sovereign can readily revise differ significantly in their implications for performance from exactly the same rules when not subject to revision." An absolute ruler can set laws that safeguard individual human and physical property, but she has the power also to change these laws, to control the judiciary, and rewrite her contracts ex post. How does an absolute ruler make a credible commitment to her subjects that she will honor her own rules and contracts? Can she be trusted?

There are two answers to these questions.[4] First, the ruler can establish a reputation for fair play. A reputation is a credible commitment if the subjects are convinced that the sovereign would be a net loser if she reneged on her promises and thus destroyed her reputation. A reputation of fair play would become increasingly valuable to a sovereign if it encouraged trust in investors and expanded the national tax base and the ruler's ratings in the credit market. However, a reputation equilibrium is likely to be unstable as various future emergencies and random events shrink the sovereign's time horizon and make predatory public finance the most favorable course of action. Also, an absolute ruler with few constraints may eventually become reckless, irresponsible, or irrational due to mental instability or old age.

Second, the ruler can voluntarily constrain her power by handing some of it over to other parties – thereby partly disabling herself – in the spirit of Homer's Ulysses, who had himself tied to the mast lest he be tempted by the song of the Sirens. Note that the power of an absolute ruler can also be constrained *involuntarily* by her rivals in a struggle for power. For instance, an important group of wealth holders may form an association (e.g., a parliament), challenge the ruler, and take away her power to tax and/or some other functions. The basic notion here is familiar; Montesquieu stated it in 1748: "To prevent this abuse [of power] it is necessary from the very nature of things that power should be a check to power."[5] The notion of a balance of power was also a fundamental concept guiding the authors of the Constitution of the United States.

However, constraining the sovereign is not a plain issue with predict-

---

[4] See Kenneth A. Shepsle, "Discretion, Institutions and the Problem of Government Commitment," in Pierre Bourdrieu and James Coleman (eds.), *Social Theory for a Changing Society* (Boulder, Colo.: Western Press, 1991), pp. 245–66.

[5] See Montesquieu, "The Spirit of the Laws," partly reprinted in M. Curtis (ed.), *The Great Political Theories* (New York: Discus/Avon Books, 1970), p. 397; cited in Bernholtz, "Constitutions as Governance Structures," p. 313.

able results. The new seats of power may for their part abuse power. For instance, a parliament can use the power of taxation to introduce arbitrary and debilitating taxation on groups that do not have a majority in the assembly. In general, decisions made by voting in parliaments need not at all give rise to secure property rights supportive of economic growth. Another consideration relates to the dynamics of the transfer of power from the sovereign to various social groups. In most instances, the decentralization of power cannot be modeled in terms of a maximization calculus of a single ruler bent on maximizing the national tax base. Rather, it is more appropriate to analyze such developments within the framework of game theory and picture them as strategic behavior by various players in a repeated game. In such games, as Weingast has demonstrated, theory tells us that a wide range of outcomes can qualify as equilibrium, including outcomes that are of the prisoner's dilemma variety – where alternative outcomes would make all the players better off.[6]

CONSTITUTIONS AND CREDIBLE COMMITMENT

The fundamental rules for constraining the behavior of those who hold state power are contained in constitutions. If constitutions are to create stability and lay the political foundations of secure markets, they must be enforced and also hard to change. It is important to realize that a powerful player, such as a sovereign or a parliament, need not formally change the constitutional rules. The player can simply decide to play by new rules – which raises an important question: Is it possible to design constitutions specifying the legitimate boundaries of state action that are self-enforced in the sense that all the major players have an incentive to play by the rules, even when they are motivated only by narrow self-interest? Weingast and North answer in the negative.[7] Weingast sees constitutions as a coordination device that must be complemented by shared attitudes of the citizens: "Our approach argues that the foundation for institutional restriction fundamentally rests on the attitudes of citizens."[8] North emphasizes the critical importance of the actors' mental models and the intellectual traditions which they reflect.[9]

---

[6] See Barry R. Weingast, "Constitutions as Governance Structures: The Political Foundations of Secure Markets," *Journal of Institutional and Theoretical Economics* 149, No. 1 (1993), 296–301.
[7] Ibid.; Douglass C. North, "Institutions and Credible Commitment," *Journal of Institutional and Theoretical Economics* 149 (1993), 11–23.
[8] Weingast, "Constitutions as Governance Structures," p. 305.
[9] North, "Institutions and Credible Commitment." See also North's epilogue to this volume.

The evolution of modern institutions of growth

What, then, is the status of the theory of the institutional foundations of secure markets? In short, we still lack a general theory, although the new institutionalism has taken a big step forward by providing valuable insights and identifying a new research agenda. Particularly little is known about the emergence, maintenance, and decay of ideologies and mental models, but these important research issues are at the frontier of research.

WHAT TO LOOK FOR IN THE ESSAY

North and Weingast seek to explain why political rules limiting the power of the Crown emerged in England in the seventeenth century, and they also relate the new rules to structure and performance in the economic spheres. The reader is encouraged to pay attention to how early in the century the growing revenue problems of the Stuarts pushed them to raise revenues using measures that discouraged private economic actors and retarded growth. Study these measures carefully and consider their long-run implications. Pay special attention to the motivational forces behind the coalition that was formed to oppose the Crown.

Consider carefully how the power to affect property rights was divided between the Crown and Parliament after the Glorious Revolution of 1688–89. Be clear about the mechanisms that the Crown used before instituting the reforms for confiscating resources by altering the structure of property rights, and how the new institutional arrangements limited such behavior.

Finally, examine the authors' arguments as to how new political arrangements brought about a fiscal revolution, had strong implications for private capital markets, and affected the relative strength of Britain among other nations. In that context evaluate the following argument: the new rules of the game produced by the Glorious Revolution were seen by Parliament and the Crown as exogenous and, therefore, both parties had an incentive to turn from rent seeking to policies that supported economic growth.

Constitutions and commitment: the evolution of institutions governing public choice in seventeenth-century England

DOUGLASS C. NORTH AND BARRY R. WEINGAST

This article focuses on the political factors underpinning economic growth and the development of markets – not simply the rules governing economic exchange, but also the institutions governing how these rules are enforced and how they may be changed. A critical political factor is the degree to which the regime or sovereign is committed to or bound by these rules. Rules the sovereign can readily revise differ significantly in their implications for performance from exactly the same rules when not subject to revision. The more likely it is that the sovereign will alter property rights for his or her own benefit, the lower the expected returns from investment and the lower in turn the incentive to invest. For economic growth to occur the sovereign or government must not merely establish the relevant set of rights, but must make a credible commitment to them.

A ruler can establish such commitment in two ways. One is by setting a precedent of "responsible behavior," appearing to be committed to a set of rules that he or she will consistently enforce. The second is by being constrained to obey a set of rules that do not permit leeway for violating commitments. We have very seldom observed the former, in good part because the pressures and continual strain of fiscal necessity eventually led rulers to "irresponsible behavior" and the violation of agreements. The latter story is, however, the one we tell.

We attempt to explain the evolution of political institutions in

This essay first appeared in *The Journal of Economic History*, Vol. 49, No. 4 (December 1989). © The Economic History Association. All rights reserved. ISSN 0022-0507.

The authors gratefully acknowledge the helpful comments of Robert Bates, Gary Cox, Paul David, Aaron Director, John Ferejohn, Jack Goldstone, Max Hartwell, Derek Hirst, Leonard Hochberg, Paul Milgrom, Glenn Nichols, Roger Noll, Alvin Rabushka, Thomas Sargent, Kenneth Shepsle, Gordon Tullock, and David Weir. They also thank Elisabeth Case for her editorial assistance. Barry Weingast thanks the National Science Foundation (Grant SES-8617516) for partial support.

seventeenth-century England, focusing on the fundamental institutions of representative government emerging out of the Glorious Revolution of 1688 – a Parliament with a central role alongside the Crown and a judiciary independent of the Crown. In the early seventeenth century fiscal needs led to increased levels of "arbitrary" government, that is, to expropriation of wealth through redefinition of rights in the sovereign's favor. This led, ultimately, to civil war. Several failed experiments with alternative political institutions in turn ushered in the restoration of the monarchy in 1660. This too failed, resulting in the Glorious Revolution of 1688 and its fundamental redesign of the fiscal and governmental institutions.

To explain the changes following the Glorious Revolution we first characterize the problem that the designers of the new institutions sought to solve, namely, control over the exercise of arbitrary and confiscatory power by the Crown.[1] We then show how, given the means, motives, and behavior of the king during this century, the institutional changes altered the incentives of governmental actors in a manner desired by the winners of the Revolution. These changes reflected an explicit attempt to make credible the government's ability to honor its commitments. Explicit limits on the Crown's ability *unilaterally* to alter the terms of its agreements played a key role here, for after the Glorious Revolution the Crown had to obtain parliamentary assent to changes in its agreements. As Parliament represented wealth holders, its increased role markedly reduced the king's ability to renege. Moreover, the institutional structure that evolved after 1688 did not provide incentives for Parliament to replace the Crown and itself engage in similar "irresponsible" behavior. As a consequence the new institutions produced a marked increase in the security of private rights.

As evidence in favor of our thesis, we study the remarkable changes in capital markets over this period. After the first few years of the Stuarts' reign, the Crown was not able systematically to raise funds. By the second decade of the seventeenth century, under mounting fiscal pressure, the Crown resorted to a series of "forced loans," indicating that it could not raise funds at rates it was willing to pay. Following the Glorious Revolution, however, not only did the government become financially solvent, but it gained access to an unprecedented level of funds. In just nine years (from 1688 to 1697), government borrowing increased by more than an order of magnitude. This sharp change in the willingness of lenders to supply funds must reflect a substantial increase

---

[1] Our discussion of the events prior to the Glorious Revolution (1603 to 1688) simply characterizes this period; it does not model or explain it. Moreover, since our history emphasizes the problems the winners (the Whigs) sought to solve, it necessarily contains strong elements of "Whig" history.

in the perceived commitment by the government to honor its agreements. The evidence shows that these expectations were borne out, and that this pattern extends well into the next century.

Since we focus on the evolution and impact of the political institutions, of necessity we slight the larger economic and religious context, even though in many specific instances these larger religious and economic issues were proximate sources of actions and policies that we describe. Indeed, no history of the seventeenth century is complete that does not describe both the growing markets and the evolving organizations that accompanied economic expansion as well as the persistent religious tensions, particularly between Catholic and Protestant. A more thorough study, one far too big for this essay, would attempt to integrate the change in opportunity costs of both the economic and *religious* actors as they intermingled with the immediate political issues on which we concentrate. But having said that, it is important to stress that our central thesis is a key part of the whole process by which an institutional framework evolved in England. We contend that while the English economy had been expanding and its markets growing, in order for economic development to continue the constraints described below had to be altered.

This essay proceeds as follows. Section 1 develops the importance of political institutions and the constitution and their relevance for the sections that follow. Sections 2 and 3 develop the narrative of the period, focusing respectively on England under the Stuarts and on the evolution of new institutions and secure rights following the Glorious Revolution. Section 4 contains the central part of our analysis and reveals why these institutions made *credible* the government's commitment to honoring its agreements. Sections 5 and 6 present our evidence from public and private capital markets.

1. THE ROLE OF POLITICAL INSTITUTIONS AND THE CONSTITUTION

The control of coercive power by the state for social ends has been a central dilemma throughout history. A critical role of the constitution and other political institutions is to place restrictions on the state or sovereign. These institutions in part determine whether the state produces rules and regulations that benefit a small elite and so provide little prospect for long-run growth, or whether it produces rules that foster long-term growth. Put simply, successful long-run economic performance requires appropriate incentives not only for economic actors but for political actors as well.

Because the state has a comparative advantage in coercion, what

Constitutions and commitment

prevents it from using violence to extract all the surplus?[2] Clearly it is not always in the ruler's interests to use power arbitrarily or indiscriminately; by striking a bargain with constituents that provides them some security, the state can often increase its revenue. But this alone is insufficient to guarantee consistent behavior on the part of the ruler.

The literature on transactions costs and institutions emphasizes that while parties may have strong incentives to strike a bargain, their incentives after the fact are not always compatible with maintaining the agreement: compliance is always a potential problem. This literature also notes that when ex post problems are anticipated ex ante, parties will attempt to alter incentives, devising institutions or constitutions that promote compliance with bargains after the fact. Oliver Williamson says:

Transactions that are subject to ex post opportunism will benefit if appropriate actions can be devised ex ante. Rather than reply to opportunism in kind, the wise [bargaining party] is one who seeks both to give and receive "credible commitments." Incentives may be realigned and/or superior governance structures within which to organize transactions may be devised.[3]

Problems of compliance can be reduced or eliminated when the institutions are carefully chosen so as to match the anticipated incentive problems. Under these circumstances, parties are more likely to enter into and maintain complex bargains that prevent abuse of political control by the state.

To succeed in this role, a constitution must arise from the bargaining context between the state and constituents such that its provisions carefully match the potential enforcement problems among the relevant parties. The constitution must be *self-enforcing* in the sense that the major parties to the bargain must have an incentive to abide by the bargain after it is made.[4]

Consider a loan to a sovereign in which the ruler promises to return

---

[2] Throughout late medieval and early modern times, if rulers did not maintain a comparative advantage in coercion, they soon failed to be rulers. See William McNeill, *Pursuit of Power* (Chicago, 1983); Douglass North, *Structure and Change in Economic History* (New York, 1981); and Gordon Tullock, *Autocracy* (Dordrecht, 1987).

[3] Oliver Williamson, *Economic Institutions of Capitalism* (New York, 1985), pp. 48–49.

[4] Our formulation of the problem draws on the "new economics of organization." Application of this approach to political problems – and especially to the problem of providing institutions to enforce bargains over time – is just beginning. See, however, Barry R. Weingast and William Marshall, "The Industrial Organization of Congress; or Why Legislatures, Like Firms, Are Not Organized as Markets," *Journal of Political Economy*, 96 (Feb. 1988), pp. 132–63; and Terry Moe, "The New Economics of Organization," *American Journal of Political Science*, 28 (Aug. 1984), pp. 739–77.

the principal along with interest at a specified date. What prevents the sovereign from simply ignoring the agreement and keeping the money? Reputation has long been noted as an important factor in limiting a sovereign's incentive to renege, and this approach has recently been formalized in the elegant models of modern game theory. The "long arm of the future" provides incentives to honor the loan agreement today so as to retain the opportunity for funds tomorrow. In many of the simple repeated games studied in the literature, this incentive alone is sufficient to prevent reneging.

Yet it is also well known that there are circumstances where this mechanism alone fails to prevent reneging.[5] In the context of current Third World debt, Jeremy Bullow and Kenneth Rogoff show that repeat play alone is insufficient to police reneging, and the more complex institutional arrangements are necessary. Similarly, in the medieval context, John Veitch has recently shown that medieval states had strong but not unambiguous incentives to develop reputations for honoring debt commitments, and that by and large they did so. Nonetheless, a series of major repudiations occurred when a second and typically more plentiful source of funds emerged. Edward I confiscated the wealth of the Jews in the late thirteenth century once the Italian merchants began operating on a larger scale; Phillip IV confiscated the wealth of the Templars under similar circumstances.

One important context in which repeat play alone is insufficient to police repudiation concerns variations in the sovereign's time preference or discount rate. States in early modern Europe were frequently at war. Since wars became increasingly expensive over the period, putting increasingly larger fiscal demands on the sovereign, the survival of the sovereign and regime was placed at risk. When survival was at stake, the sovereign would heavily discount the future, making the one-time gain of reneging more attractive relative to the future opportunities forgone. Indeed, there is a long history of reneging under the fiscal strain accompanying major wars.[6]

---

[5] Paul R. Milgrom, Douglass C. North, and Barry R. Weingast, "The Role of Institutions in the Revival of Trade, Part I: The Medieval Law Merchant," Mimeo., Hoover Institution, Stanford University, 1989. Jeremy Bullow and Kenneth Rogoff, "A Constant Recontracting Model of Sovereign Debt," *Journal of Political Economy*, 97 (Feb. 1989), pp. 155–78; John M. Veitch, "Repudiations and Confiscations by the Medieval State," *Journal of Economic History*, 46 (Mar. 1986), pp. 31–36.

[6] Joseph Schumpeter, "Fiscal Crises and the Tax State," in Richard A. Musgrave and Alan T. Peacock, eds., *Classics in the Theory of Public Finance* (London, 1962); John Hicks, *A Theory of Economic History* (Oxford, 1969); North, *Structure and Change;* and Veitch, "Repudiations and Confiscations." This is not to say that the sovereign will *never* honor commitments, only that he will not *always* do so.

Constitutions and commitment

The insufficiency of repeat play and reputation to prevent reneging provides for the role of political institutions. If the problem of variable discount rates is sufficiently important, individuals have an incentive to devise institutions to protect against reneging. It is important to observe that these institutions do not substitute for reputation-building and associated punishment strategies, but complement them.[7] Appropriately chosen institutions can improve the efficacy of the reputation mechanism by acting as a constraint in precisely those circumstances where reputation alone is insufficient to prevent reneging. The literature on the theory of the firm is replete with illustrations of how specific institutional features of the firm are necessary to mitigate an incentive problem that is insufficiently policed by reputation.[8]

This view provides an endogenous role for political institutions. Restrictions on the ex post behavior of the state improve the state's ability to maintain its part of bargains with constituents, for example, not to expropriate their wealth.[9] As we show below, this logic can be used to interpret the institutional changes at the time of the Glorious Revolution.

Our view also implies that the development of free markets must be accompanied by some credible restrictions on the state's ability to manipulate economic rules to the advantage of itself and its constituents. Successful economic performance, therefore, must be accompanied by institutions that limit economic intervention and allow private rights and markets to prevail in large segments of the economy. Put another way, because constitutional restrictions must be self-enforcing, they must serve to establish a credible commitment by the state to abide by them. Absolutist states which faced no such constraint, such as early modern Spain, created economic conditions that retarded long-run economic growth.

The ability of a government to commit to private rights and exchange is thus an essential condition for growth. It is also, as we shall see, a central issue in the constitutional debate in seventeenth-century England.

---

[7] Weingast and Marshall, "Industrial Organization of Congress"; Milgrom, North, and Weingast, "The Role of Institutions."

[8] Vertical integration is the standard example: because of potential transactions problems due to "asset specificity" or "appropriable quasi-rents," firms that internalize the problem via vertical integration outperform those which do not. See Williamson, *Economic Institutions*.

[9] In this sense our argument parallels that of James Buchanan and Geoffrey Brennan, who argue that the "recognition of the temporal dimensionality of choice provides one 'reason for rules' – rules that will impose binding constraints on choice options after the rules themselves have been established." James Buchanan and Geoffrey Brennan, *Reason of Rules* (Cambridge, 1981), p. 67.

Douglass C. North and Barry R. Weingast

2. ENGLAND UNDER THE STUARTS: LIMITED CREDIBLE COMMITMENT TO RIGHTS

After the Crown passed from the Tudors to the Stuarts in 1603, revenue problems and their consequences became increasingly important (Table 1). At this time the king was expected to "live on his own," that is, to fund the government in the manner of an extended household. The execution of public laws and expenditures was not subject to a public budgetary process, and Parliament played only a small role in the decisions over expenditure and investment. The Crown therefore had considerable discretionary power over how and on what the money was spent. Parliament's main source of influence over policy resulted from its power to provide the Crown with tax revenue, typically for extraordinary purposes such as various wars. Parliament was also responsible for granting the Crown its revenue from other sources, such as customs, but in practice, the Stuarts, particularly Charles I, continued to collect the revenue without parliamentary consent.

Throughout the Stuart period revenue from traditional sources did not match expenditures. While figures for government expenditures during the Stuart period have not been collected as systematically as for the period following the Glorious Revolution, the following picture emerges. At the beginning of the Stuarts' reign, Crown lands produced roughly half the annual revenue. To make up annual shortfalls, the Crown regularly resorted to sale of these lands.[10] Following the war with Spain in 1588, Elizabeth had sold 25 percent of the lands, raising £750,000. Still, James I inherited sizable debts from Elizabeth's war. Over his reign (1603–1624), another 25 percent of Crown lands were sold, and the remainder went during the reign of his son, Charles I (1625–1641). Sale of a major portion of a revenue-producing asset for annual expenses indicates the revenue problem was endemic. It also implies that over time the revenue problem had to get worse, for with every sale the expected future revenue declined. And, indeed, as Table 1 shows, for the year 1617 total revenue did not match expenditures, leaving a deficit of £36,000 or of just under 10 percent of expenditures.

Under the Stuarts, therefore, the search for new sources of revenue became a major priority. An important new source which produced conflict between the Crown and Parliament was the raising of customs revenues through new "impositions." Indeed, in the 1630s such increases almost brought financial solvency, and with it the ability of the Crown to survive without calling Parliament.

[10]See, for example, Derek Hirst, *Authority and Conflict: England, 1603–1658* (Cambridge, MA, 1986), chap. 4, and Lawrence Stone, *The Crisis of the Aristocracy, 1558–1641* (Oxford, 1965).

Table 1. *Revenue sources and expenditure levels, 1617*

Revenue source	Amount (£/year)
Crown lands	£80,000
Customs and "new impositions"	190,000
Wards and so forth (besides purveyance)	180,000
Total revenue	450,000
Total expenditures	486,000
Deficit	36,000

Source: David Hume, *The History of England* (Indianapolis, 1983), appendix to "The Reign of James I."

Another method used by the Crown to raise revenue was to demand loans. The Crown did not, however, develop a systematic, regular relationship with moneyed interests, negotiating a series of loans in which it honored today's agreements because it wanted to avail itself of future loan opportunities. Indeed, just the opposite occurred. The Stuarts secured most of their loans under threat; hence they are known as "forced loans," of which more later. Repayment was highly unpredictable and never on the terms of the original agreement. In the forced loan of 1604/5 the Crown borrowed £111,891, nominally for one year; "although ... ultimately repaid, £20,363 ... was still due as late as December 1609."[11] The forced loan of 1617 (just under £100,000) was not repaid until 1628. The Crown behaved similarly on loans from 1611 and 1625. As time went on, such loans came to look more and more like taxes, but because these were nominally loans the Crown did not need parliamentary assent.[12]

The Crown's inability to honor its contractual agreements for borrowed funds is a visible indicator of its readiness to alter the rights of private parties in its own favor. Despite the significant incentive provided by the desire to raise funds in the future, the Crown followed its short-run interests, reneging on the terms to which it had agreed. As noted above, this type of behavior was not unique to England.

[11] Robert Ashton, *The Crown and the Money Market, 1603–1640* (Oxford, 1960), p. 35.
[12] Ashton, *Crown and the Money Market,* p. 36. Richard Cust, in his recent study of the 1626 forced loan, provides several instances of sanctions imposed on individuals refusing to provide funds: leading refusers were "either committed to prison or pressed in readiness for service abroad." Richard Cust, *The Forced Loans and English Politics* (Oxford, 1987), p. 3.

A second revenue-raising method was the sale of monopolies. While not the most important source of new revenue, it is particularly instructive because of its economic consequences.[13] In order to raise revenue in this manner, the Crown used patents in a new way. Originally designed to protect and promote the invention of new processes, patents came to be used to "reduce settled industries to monopolies under cover of technical improvements."[14] From a revenue standpoint, the best sources of new monopoly rights involved an economic activity that was profitable and whose participants were not part of the king's constituency. This led to a systematic search for and expropriation of quasi-rents in the economy. Moreover, as we will see in the next section, the Crown utilized a different system for enforcing these grants than that used for the older mercantilist controls, and one that was considerably more responsive to the Crown's interests. The system involved circumventing existing rights and the institutions designed to protect these rights.

Grants of monopoly clearly disrupted both existing economic interests in the targeted activity and those who depended on it (for example, suppliers and consumers). Monopoly grants thus acted as a tax that, since it expropriated the value of existing investment as well as future profits, was considerably greater at the margin than a 100 percent tax on profits. This risk lowered the rewards from all such new investments and hence discouraged their undertaking.

Beyond grants of monopoly, James, and especially Charles, used a variety of other, more subtle forms of expropriation of wealth. Because so many dimensions of public policy were involved, the political risk to citizens increased substantially over previous times. One important example was expansion of the peerage by the Crown, again in exchange for revenue.[15] While this expansion had broad social, cultural, and ideological implications, it also had significantly negative effects on existing peers. Expansion of the size of the House of Lords altered the value of an existing seat since it limited the ability of existing lords to protect themselves against the Crown.[16] Between the coronation of

[13] Robert B. Ekelund and Robert D. Tollison, *Mercantilism as a Rent-Seeking Society* (College Station, 1981).

[14] W. Price, *English Patents of Monopoly* (Boston, 1906). Examples include soap, tobacco, and starch.

[15] F. W. Maitland, *Constitutional History of England* (Cambridge, 1908); Wallace Notestein, *The Winning of the Initiative by the House of Commons* (London, 1924); and Stone, *Crisis of the Aristocracy*.

[16] There were two separate reasons for this: the total number of voters was increasing, and the expansion added new members whose views systematically differed from those of existing nobles. The exchange that brought new nobles to the Lords undoubtedly entailed a commitment of support for the king.

James I and the outbreak of the Civil War, the Stuarts' sale of peerages doubled the number of lay peers.

Governmental power was used in other ways to raise revenue. Employing the ancient power of purveyance, agents of the Crown seized various goods for "public purposes," paying prices well below market. Purveyance brought in an annual "unvoted" tax of £40,000 in the 1620s.[17] James also put hereditary titles up for sale: for example, offering to sell the title of baronet for £1,095 and promising that only a fixed number would be sold. This brought in £90,000 by 1614. But James soon reneged on this, lowering the price and selling more than the promised number. By 1622 the price had fallen to £220.[18] Through the court of wards, the Crown managed the estates which had passed to minors. These were often openly run for the advantage of the Crown, not infrequently extracting the full value of the estate.[19] The Crown put "dispensations" up for sale, that is, the use of its powers to allow specific individuals to dispense with a specific law or restriction. "Sale" of this power was often used in conjunction with the enforcement or threat of enforcement of regulations that had not been enforced for years. At times the Crown simply seized the property of citizens. An especially egregious example occurred in 1640 when "the government seized £130,000 of bullion which private merchants had placed in the Tower for safety, causing numerous bankruptcies."[20]

This clash of interests between the king on the one hand and wealth holders and tax payers on the other was a major reason why the Crown failed to obtain grants from Parliament. In exchange for grants, Parliament demanded conditions and limits on the king's power that he was unwilling to accept. Parliamentary interests thereby exacerbated the problem they were attempting to eliminate. Withholding funds worsened the Crown's fiscal problems and intensified its search for alternative sources of revenue.

Institutional basis of Stuart policymaking

Both Parliament and the common law courts fought the Crown's use of monopolies and other changes in rights in its search for revenue. Parliament regularly presented the king with "grievances," lists of problems

---

[17] Hirst, *Authority and Conflict*, p. 103; and C. Hill, *Century of Revolution, 1603–1714* (2nd edn., New York, 1980), chap. 4. See also John Kenyon, *Stuart England* (2nd edn., New York, 1985).
[18] Hirst, *Authority and Conflict*, pp. 113–14.
[19] Ibid., p. 103.
[20] C. Hill, *Century of Revolution*, p. 103.

caused by the king that it wanted addressed.[21] Grievances were part of a larger bargaining process in which Parliament attempted, in exchange for revenue, to limit the Crown's power and its use of policymaking to expropriate wealth. Because of ever-present revenue problems, the Stuarts often called on Parliament for additional revenue. Parliamentary interests regularly demanded that in exchange for revenue the Crown respect traditional property rights and institutions: for example, that it cease declaring new monopolies. The Crown, in turn, was evidently unwilling to accept these restrictions and hence Parliament was often dissolved without having come to an agreement with the Crown.[22]

Attempts were also made to prevent the Crown's using the law to further its objectives. In 1624 Parliament passed the much-noted Statute of Monopolies prohibiting the use of patents to grant monopolies to existing businesses in exchange for revenue. In this manner it attempted to assert the traditional rights of secure property. In addition common law courts handed down the famous "Case of Monopolies" in 1601, making the Crown's use of monopolies illegal in common law. The Crown, however, was able to evade these restrictions. While these evasions often took forms of questionable legality, so long as the Crown did not depend on Parliament for revenue, it was able to use them in practice.

Understanding the subsequent institutional reaction to these royal policies requires that we study the institutional means by which the Crown ran the government. For our purposes three elements of the royal powers and institutions were central to the Crown's success. First, a major source of power for the Crown was the royal prerogative, by which the Crown issued proclamations or royal ordinances. By this means it could issue new rules; that is, it had quasi-legislative powers without recourse to Parliament. Crown rules were enforced, not through the common law court system, but through the prerogative courts and included the power to suspend laws and to dispense with laws for specific individuals.[23]

Second, the Star Chamber, combining legislative, executive, and judi-

[21] For details, see Notestein, *The Winning of the Initiative.*

[22] Part of the Crown's motivation appears to have been a desire to move toward the absolutism prevalent on the continent, notably in France and Spain. As Kenyon observes, at the onset of the seventeenth century, "any further adjustments [in the balance of power between Parliament and the Crown] were likely to be at the expense of Parliament" (Kenyon, *Stuart England,* p. 43). It almost succeeded. Hirst describes debates in Parliament in which the participants were explicitly concerned with this possibility (Hirst, *Authority and Conflict,* chap. 3).

[23] Dispensations for individuals, like most powers under the Stuarts, were put up for sale (Maitland, *Constitutional History,* pt. IV).

cial powers, played a key role. On issues concerning prerogative, the Star Chamber had come to have final say, and could in certain circumstances reverse judgments against the Crown.[24]

Finally, since the Crown was personally responsible for day-to-day government operations, it paid the judges, who served at its pleasure. Increasingly the Stuarts used their power over judges to influence their judgments. Judges – Chief Justices Coke (1616/17) and Crew (1627) – were openly fired for ruling against the Crown. Ultimately this tactic produced judges who by and large supported the Crown.[25]

The effect of these institutions was to combine in the Crown executive, legislative, and judicial powers, limiting external institutional checks. While royal proclamations did not have the same legal status as an act of Parliament, they were enforced directly through the common law courts. While these courts did not have to go along with the king – and often did not – ultimately he won through the higher court, the Star Chamber. Thus, while the common law was often against the king, the king could alter the jurisdiction of a dispute by issuing proclamations. The expanded use of the Star Chamber and the successful running of the government for substantial periods without Parliament limited the ability of traditional institutions to constrain the Crown. Effective possession of legislative and judicial powers also gave the Crown the ability to alter economic and political rights when it was convenient to do so. In comparison with the previous century, the rights that Parliament and other institutions were designed to protect were considerably less secure.

In response, a coalition formed against the Crown, seeking to preserve personal liberties, rights, and wealth. This raised the stakes of the political game to the various economic interests – in particular the value of opposing the king rose. Moreover, because the Crown attempted to extract from its own constituents a major portion of the advantages it had bestowed on them, the value of supporting the king declined. It is clear, however, that the opposition would have been unlikely to succeed, had the English Crown, like its French or Spanish counterpart, had a standing army with which to quell the initial uprising.

---

[24] The Star Chamber, in which the most egregious examples of arbitrary power occurred, became a regular feature of Stuart England. See Maitland, *Constitutional History*, and Friedrich A. Hayek, *Constitution of Liberty* (Chicago, 1960), chap. 11.

[25] Coke's dismissal, "the first of a judge in over thirty years, ushered in a period of increasing royal pressure on the bench: in Charles's reign two other chief justices, Crew and Heath, and one chief baron of the exchequer court, Walter, were to follow Coke" (Hirst, *Authority and Conflict*, p. 121). See also Hayek's excellent and extensive discussion, in *Constitution of Liberty*, chap. 11.

Douglass C. North and Barry R. Weingast

Civil War to Glorious Revolution

Eventually the opposition openly challenged the king, leading the country into civil war. But the ultimate opposition victory was not inevitable.

After seizing power, the opposition modified the institutions underpinning the Crown's most egregious behavior. Not surprisingly, the Star Chamber was abolished in 1641 by an act requiring that all cases involving property be tried at common law, thus adding another milestone along the route toward supremacy of the common law, so favorable to property rights. Restrictions against monopolies were now enforced. In an attempt to prevent the Crown from ruling for substantial periods without calling a Parliament, Parliament passed the Triennial legislation, which called for regular standing of the Parliament. The royal administrative apparatus was dismantled, and with it the royal ability to impose regulatory restrictions on the economy in conflict with the rights enforced by the common law courts.

Important changes reduced restrictions on labor mobility. Land tenure modifications simultaneously favored the development of private rights and markets and reduced the Crown's political hold over this once-important part of its constituency.[26] New and profitable opportunities resulted from lifting restrictions on land use and improving markets.

After the Civil War a number of political innovations occurred, including the abolition of the monarchy and the House of Lords. Their failure led to pressure to bring back the king. With the Restoration of the monarchy in 1660, England was once again ruled by the Stuarts. It is critical for understanding the next series of events to notice a striking limitation of the institutional changes prior to the Restoration. While the details differ considerably, the next twenty-five years repeated the events of the earlier Stuarts' reign in one important respect. Political struggle with constituents resulted in the king's arbitrary encroachment. By far the most important instance of this – indeed, the one resulting in a nation united against the Crown – concerned the rechartering of local governments and political power. Rechartering came in reaction to the Whig-led "Exclusion Crisis"; it allowed the Crown to disenfranchise much of the opposition and thereby reduce impediments to its exercise of power. Of the 104 members of Parliament returned in the mid-1680s by the boroughs receiving new charters, only one Whig was elected. This

---

[26] See H. J. Perkins, "The Social Causes of the British Industrial Revolution," *Transactions of the Royal Historical Society,* 18 (1968). Hill, discussing the 1660 Act confirming the abolition of feudal tenures, notes that in the eighteenth century Blackstone called this Act a greater boon to property owners than the Magna Carta itself (*Century of Revolution,* p. 127).

converted "what had been a formidable, aggressive and highly organized opposition party into an impotent collection of a few individuals."[27]

Had the Crown succeeded in this political maneuver, there would be few checks on its powers, because it allowed the Crown to disenfranchise *any* opposition. But between 1686 and 1688, James II, having disenfranchised the Whig opposition, turned on his own supporters, causing his own constituents to join the opposition to remove him in the Glorious Revolution of 1688.

3. INSTITUTIONAL CHANGES FOLLOWING THE GLORIOUS REVOLUTION

At the same time it extended the Crown to William and Mary, Parliament restructured the society's political institutions in the Revolution Settlement. To understand the new institutions it is necessary to see clearly the problem the parliamentary interests sought to solve. The early Stuarts' use of the Star Chamber and the rechartering of the later Stuarts threatened the liberties and wealth of citizens, leaving them with little protection against Crown attempts to appropriate their wealth. But experience showed that simply removing the powers underpinning arbitrary behavior was insufficient to prevent abuse. Controlling Crown behavior required the solving of financial problems as well as appropriate constraints on the Crown. So the Glorious Revolution also ushered in a fiscal revolution.[28] The main features of the institutional revolution are as follows.

First and foremost, the Revolution initiated the era of parliamentary "supremacy." This settled for the near future the issue of sovereignty: it was now the "king in Parliament," not the king alone.[29] No longer would the Crown, arguing the "divine rights of kings," claim to be above the law. Parliamentary supremacy established a permanent role for Parliament in the ongoing management of the government and hence placed a direct check on the Crown. The Crown no longer called or disbanded Parliament at its discretion alone.

Parliament also gained a central role in financial matters. Its exclusive authority to raise new taxes was firmly reestablished; at the same time the Crown's independent sources of revenue were also limited. For the

[27] Jones, *Revolution of 1688*, pp. 47, 50. As B. W. Hill observes, James's efforts to repack the constituencies "came near to success in every respect but one: they alarmed landed society, Tory as well as Whig." See B. W. Hill, *The Growth of Parliamentary Parties: 1689–1742* (Hamden, 1976).

[28] P. G. M. Dickson, *The Financial Revolution in England* (New York, 1967).

[29] See, for example, Maitland, *Constitutional History*, pp. 298–301, or David Keir, *The Constitutional History of Modern Britain Since 1485* (London, 1966).

Crown to achieve its own goals this meant it had to establish successful relations with Parliament. Shortly thereafter, Parliament gained the never-before-held right to audit how the government had expended its funds. Parliamentary veto over expenditures, combined with the right to monitor how the funds they had voted were spent, placed important constraints over the Crown.

Another important institutional change focused on the royal prerogative powers. These were substantially curtailed and subordinated to common law, and the prerogative courts (which allowed the Crown to enforce its proclamations) were abolished. At the same time the independence of the judiciary from the Crown was assured. Judges now served subject to good behavior (they could only be removed if convicted for a criminal offense or by action of both houses of Parliament) instead of at the king's pleasure. The supremacy of the common law courts, so favorable to private rights, was thereby assured.

Because the Stuarts had violated the personal liberties of their opponents (excessive bail, no writ of Habeas Corpus) as a means of raising the cost of opposition, reducing the arbitrary powers of the Crown resulted not only in more secure economic liberties and property rights, but in political liberties and rights as well. Political rights were seen as a key element of protection against arbitrary violations of economic rights.

Two final points are worth emphasizing. First, part of the glue that held these institutional changes together was the successful dethroning of Charles I and, later, James II. This established a credible threat to the Crown regarding future irresponsible behavior. The conditions which would "trigger" this threat were laid out in the Revolution Settlement, and shortly thereafter in the Declaration of Rights. Second, although parliamentary supremacy meant that Parliament dictated the form of the new political institutions, it did not assume the sole position of power within the government, as it did after the Civil War or in the nineteenth century. While substantial constraints were placed on the king, these did not reduce him to a figurehead.

4. THE GLORIOUS REVOLUTION AND ENGLAND'S CREDIBLE COMMITMENT TO SECURE RIGHTS

The institutional innovations increased dramatically the control of wealth holders over the government. Since fiscal crises inevitably produced pressure on the Crown to break its agreements, eliminating unilateral control by the Crown over key decisions was a necessary component of the new institutions. As previously described, this occurred in two ways. First, by requiring Parliament's assent to major changes in policies (such as changing the terms of loans or taxes), the representatives of wealth holders could veto such moves unless they were also in their interest. This allowed action in times of crisis but eliminated the Crown's unilateral action. Second, several other ways for the Crown to renege on promises were eliminated, notably its ability to legislate unilaterally (through the prerogative), to bypass Parliament (because it had an independent source of funds), or to fire judges who did not conform to Crown desires.

Two factors made the new arrangements self-enforcing. First, the credible threat of removal limited the Crown's ability to ignore the new arrangements. Second, in exchange for the greater say in government, parliamentary interests agreed to put the government on a sound financial footing, that is, they agreed to provide sufficient tax revenue. Not only did this remove a major motive underlying the exercise of arbitrary power, but for the new King William it meant he could launch a major war against France. The arrangement proved so satisfactory for the king that a host of precedents were set putting the new division of powers on a solid footing. As a consequence of these institutional changes, private rights became fundamentally more secure.[30]

Institutional and political constraints on Parliament

The triumph of Parliament raises the issue of why it would not then proceed to act just like the king? Its motives were no more lofty than those of the Crown. But the institutional outcome effectively deterred Parliament from similar behavior. Robert Ekelund and Robert Tollison provide the following general analysis:

Higher costs due to uncertainty and growing private returns reduced industry demands for regulation and control in England. All this strengthened the emergent constitutional democracy, which created conditions making rent-seeking activity on the part of both monarch and merchants more costly. When the locus of power to rent-seeking shifted from the monarch to Parliament . . . the costs of supply of regulation through legislative enactment rose.[31]

They suggest that the natural diversity of views in a legislature raises the cost of supplying private benefits in the form of favorable regulation.

The framework of institutional evolution we have described complements their story. The embedding of economic and political freedoms in the law, the interests of principals (for example, merchants) in a greater

---

[30] Jones, on p. 6 of the *Revolution of 1688,* concludes: "None of its architects could have predicted its effectiveness in securing the liberties, religion, property and independence of the nation after so many previous attempts had failed."
[31] Ekelund and Tollison, *Mercantilism,* p. 149.

measure of freedom, and the ideological considerations that swept England in the late seventeenth century combined to play a role in institutional change. The new constitutional settlement endowed several actors with veto power, and thus created the beginnings of a division or separation of powers.[32] Supplying private benefits at public expense now required the cooperation of the Crown, Parliament, and the courts. Only the Crown could propose an expenditure, but only Parliament could authorize and appropriate funds for the proposal, and it could do so solely for purposes proposed by the Crown. Erskin May summed up this procedure as, "The crown demands, the Commons grants, and the Lords assent to the grant." A balance of power between the Crown and Parliament significantly limited publicly supplied private benefits.[33]

Three other political factors help explain why the new era of parliamentary supremacy did not simply transfer power from the Crown to Parliament. In 1641 the centralized administrative apparatus which enforced royal attempts to alter rights and property was destroyed. The absence of such a structure prevented either the Crown or Parliament from similar encroachment. Because a new apparatus – even one that was initially quite limited – would allow its future expansion, many interests could be counted upon to oppose its initiation.

Second, the commercially minded ruling Whig coalition preferred limited government and especially limited political interference with the common law courts. Parliament was thus *politically* constrained from intervention in the courts. As R. Braun observes:

the Whig oligarchy was anxious to avoid encroachment upon the privacy of the business of those groups from which it drew its support. Not only the constitutional and institutional framework, but also the prevailing ideological basis of the [Whigs and their constituents] prevented the central administrative apparatus of the British government from developing [a major regulatory and control function].[34]

Widespread regulation of markets by Parliament along the line of Colbert in France (or the Stuarts) would have led to a clash with the

---

[32] We emphasize, however, that this division of powers was not a clear-cut system of checks and balances. Nor can it be considered a true separation of powers. The designers of the new institutions were far more worried about constraints on the Crown than on protecting the Crown from encroachments by Parliament. Thus in the latter half of the eighteenth century, the power of the Crown diminished, and with it the constraints (or checks) on Parliament. See A. F. Pollard, *The Evolution of Parliament* (London, 1926).

[33] Erskin May, *Parliamentary Practice* (17th edn., London, 1966; 1st edn., 1844). Further investigation of the procedures devised at this time is called for.

[34] R. Braun, "Taxation, Sociopolitical Structure, and State-Building: Great Britain and Brandenburg-Prussia," in Charles Tilly, ed., *Formation of Nation States in Western Europe* (Princeton, 1975).

common law courts. Thus the political independence of the courts limited potential abuses by Parliament. Combined with the explicit institutional limits on Crown intervention, this assured the courts important and unchallenged authority in large areas of economic activity.

Third, the creation of a politically independent judiciary greatly expanded the government's ability credibly to promise to honor its agreements, that is, to bond itself. By limiting the ability of the government to renege on its agreements, the courts played a central role in assuring a commitment to secure rights. As we will see, this commitment substantially improved the government's ability to raise money through loans.

Thus the institutional and political changes accompanying the Glorious Revolution significantly raised the predictability of the government. By putting the government on a sound financial basis and regularizing taxation, it removed the random component of expropriation associated with royal attempts to garner revenue. Any interest group seeking private gain had now to get approval from both the Crown and the Parliament.

5. THE FISCAL REVOLUTION

To see the profound effects of the Glorious Revolution, we focus on one important element of public finance, government borrowing. Since capital markets are especially sensitive to the security of property rights, they provide a unique and highly visible indicator of the economic and political revolution that took place. Indeed, they are one of the few means for empirically evaluating the effects of the Glorious Revolution.

Prior to the Glorious Revolution, payments on loans were subject to manipulation by the Crown; rescheduling and delays in payments were common. As indicated in Table 2, money was raised through forced loans in 1604/5, 1611/2, 1617, and 1625. In each instance the Crown did not honor its terms. In the loan of 1617, for example, James I raised £100,000 in London at 10 percent for the period of one year. At the end of the year, although James paid the interest, he refused to repay the principal and demanded that the loan be renewed. No interest was paid over the next several years, and each year another renewal was "agreed" to. In 1624 Charles I lowered the interest rate to 8 percent; however, he did not pay any interest, nor did he repay the principal until 1628. Such behavior was hardly designed to gain the confidence of potential sources of loans. As Robert Ashton concludes, the "cavalier treatment which the Crown meted out to its creditors, and more especially to those most unwilling lenders who made more or less compulsory contributions through the medium of the Corporation of London," helps explain why

Table 2. *Forced loans by the early Stuarts, 1603–1625*

Year	Amount (£)	Rate (percent per year)	Repayment (£)
1604/5	111,891	10	20,362 unpaid as of Dec. 1609
1611/2	116,381	10	112,000 unpaid as of Jul. 1616
1617[a]	96,466	10[b]	Unpaid until 1628
1625[c]	60,000	8	Unpaid until 1628

[a]Extension in 1624 secured by Crown lands.
[b]Unilaterally lowered by Charles I in 1624 to 8%.
[c]Secured by Crown lands.
Source: Robert Ashton, *The Crown and the Money Market, 1603–1640* (Oxford, 1960), chaps. 2 and 5.

London and the money interests supported the parliamentary cause.[35] Nor did the Stuarts attempt to develop a major international source of loans.[36]

Several financial innovations occurred under the late Stuarts, including some that were to play a key role in the "financial revolution" after 1688, for example, making notes "assignable," thus allowing them to be sold. The recent work of Glenn Nichols suggests that financial arrangements under the late Stuarts were far superior to those under the early Stuarts. Nonetheless, fiscal stress pressed the system to its limits, and led to a partial repudiation in the famous "stop the exchequer" in 1672. The debt in question, over a million pounds, shows that the late Stuarts – until that time, at least – could raise substantial sums.[37]

Institutional innovations

A series of institutional innovations during the war with France (1689–1697) changed the way the government sought credit, facilitating the regularization of public finance. First, the government began as a regular

---

[35]Ashton, *Crown and the Money Market*, p. 113.
[36]Ashton reports only two such loans, the second of which (£58,400 in 1616) was still outstanding in 1636. Here too the Stuarts failed to develop a reputation for honoring agreements. By the 1630s the Crown was unable to borrow at all from either international sources or London.
[37]See Glenn O. Nichols, "English Government Borrowing Before the Financial Revolution," manuscript, Anderson College, 1988. For details about the stop of the exchequer, see Dickson, *Financial Revolution*. In exchange for its short-term notes, the Crown gave new long-term loans. Much of the interest from the latter was still unpaid at the time of the Glorious Revolution, however.

practice to earmark new taxes, authorized by statute for each new loan issue, to pay the interest on all new long-term loans. By earmarking taxes beforehand, parliamentary interests limited the king's discretion each year over whether to pay bondholders their interest.

Second, the first large, long-term loan (£1,000,000) secured by new taxes took place in 1693. By 1694, however, these funds were exhausted. When the government sought a new large loan, it invited the subscribers to incorporate as the Bank of England. The Bank was responsible for handling the loan accounts of the government and for assuring the continuity of promised distributions. Certain restrictions were also imposed: the Bank could not lend the Crown money or purchase any Crown lands without the explicit consent of Parliament. As Macaulay observed over a century ago, this created a strong instrument of the Whig party (and hence of commercial interests). Since loans to the Crown went through the Bank, "it must have instantly stopped payment if it had ceased to receive the interest on the sum which it had advanced to the government."[38] The government had thus created an additional, private constraint on its future behavior by making it difficult to utilize funds of a current loan if it failed to honor its previous obligations.

Two other changes are worth noting. In 1698 the government created a separate fund to make up deficiencies in the event that the revenue earmarked for specific loans was insufficient to cover the required distributions (as was the case for several loans). This explicitly removed the component of risk associated with each loan due to its ties to a specific tax.[39] Second, during this period the milling of coins began, reducing the debasement of the currency due to shaving of coins.

Government loans, 1688–1740

Thus were the institutional foundations of modern capital markets laid in England. These institutional changes were more successful than their originators had hoped. The original subscription to the Bank of England, for instance, was expected to be slow and possibly unsuccessful. In actuality, one-third of the loan was subscribed on the first day and another third during the next two days. Ten days later the loan was fully subscribed.

[38] Lord Macaulay, *The History of England* (London, 1914), vol. V, p. 2438.
[39] As David Ogg explains: "Thenceforth, the investor knew that, in lending money on a specified tax, he had parliamentary guarantee for the security of this investment, based not only on the particular fund, but on the whole of the national revenue." David Ogg, *England in the Reigns of James II and William III* (Oxford, 1955), p. 413. Regarding the second, see pp. 422–25.

Douglass C. North and Barry R. Weingast

Table 3. Growth of government debt, 1618–1740 (£ million)

Year	Governmental expenditure[1]	Debt[2]	Prices[3] (1701 = 100)
Stuart England			
1618[4]	0.5	0.8	—
Mid-1630s[5]	1.0	1.0	—
1680[6]	1.4	—	113
1688[6]	1.8	1.0[7]	99
Post Glorious Revolution			
1695	6.2	8.4	116
1697	7.9	16.7	122
1700	3.2	14.2	115
1710	9.8	21.4	122
1714	6.2	36.2	103
1720	6.0	54.0	102
1730	5.6	51.4	95
1740	6.2	47.4	100
1750	7.2	78.0	95

Note: Because these figures are obtained from a variety of sources, they are intended solely to provide an indication of underlying trends. Figures for expenditures and debt after the Glorious Revolution are most reliable.
Sources: 1. Government expenditure, post-1688: B. R. Mitchell, *British Historical Statistics* (Cambridge, 1988), chap. 11, table 2. 2. Debt, post-1688: Mitchell, *British Historical Statistics,* chap. 11, table 7. 3. Prices: Mitchell, *British Historical Statistics,* chap. 14: 1680–97, table 1, part A, "consumer goods"; 1697–1750, part B, "consumer goods." 4. Government expenditure and debt, 1618: David Hume, *The History of England* (Indianapolis, 1983), "Appendix to the Reign of James I." 5. Government expenditure and debt, mid-1630s: Derek Hirst, *Authority and Conflict: England, 1603–1658* (Cambridge, MA, 1986), p. 174. 6. Government expenditure, 1680 and 1688: C. D. Chandaman, *The English Public Revenue, 1660–1688* (Oxford, 1975), appendix 2, table 7, "Total Available for Ordinary Purposes." 7. Debt, 1688: H. Fisk, *English Public Finance* (New York, 1920), p. 93.

To see the dramatic results of the fiscal revolution, we turn to the public finances during this period. Table 3 provides information on governmental expenditures and debt. On the eve of the Revolution governmental expenditures were about £1.8 million, reflecting a slow but steady increase over two decades.[40] Government debt was limited to about £1 million, or between 2 and 3 percent of GNP (estimated to be £41 million). Moreover, at a time when Holland was borrowing £5 million long term at 4 percent per year, the English Crown could only

[40] C. D. Chandaman, *The English Public Revenue: 1660–88* (Oxford, 1975).

154

borrow small amounts at short term, paying between 6 and 30 percent per year.[41]

The Revolution radically altered this pattern. In 1697, just nine years later, governmental expenditures had grown fourfold, to £7.9 million. The immediate reason for the rise was the new war with France. But importantly, the government's ability to tap the resources of society increased. This is evidenced by the increase in the size of government debt, which grew during the nine years of war from £1 million to nearly £17 million. This level of debt – approximately 40 percent of GNP – was previously unattainable. Moreover, the ability of the new government to finance a war at unprecedented levels played a critical role in defeating France. To put these figures in modern perspective, a trillion-dollar economy would have begun the period with $25 billion of debt, which in just nine years would grow to almost $400 billion.

Following the war, both government expenditures and the amount financed through debt were substantially higher than previous levels. By 1720 government debt was over fifty times the 1688 level and on the order of GNP. Financing wars by borrowing had another remarkable benefit. Previous instances of unexpected large wars were nearly always accompanied by large fiscal demands, the search for sources of revenue, and consequently unfavorable demands on wealth holders. Such demands were virtually eliminated by the new methods of finance. Another evidence of the new regime's increased predictability is indicated by the series of price changes. Despite sustained deficits resulting in the enormous increase in debt, government policy did not result in inflationary finance.[42]

At the same time that the scope of governmental borrowing increased, however, the market rate charged the government fell. Its initial long-

---

[41] For figures on government debt and GNP estimates, see B. R. Mitchell, *British Historical Statistics* (Cambridge, 1988). On interest rates, see Sidney Homer, *A History of Interest Rates* (New Brunswick, 1963), p. 149.

[42] Prices rose a little over 20 percent between 1690 and 1710 (and then fell again between 1710 and 1730). But the enormous increase in debt during this period suggests that the government did not attempt to meet its debt obligations through inflationary finance. The modern view of inflation suggests two further inferences (see, for example, Thomas Sargent, *Rational Expectations and Inflation* [New York, 1986]). Since inflation in part reflects expectations about future governmental finance of deficits, the lack of major increases in prices suggests that the market did not expect inflationary finance. Since this pattern was maintained for several decades, it indicates that these expectations were "confirmed" in the sense that new information about current governmental behavior did not change expectations. Robert Barro provides evidence that budget deficits had almost no effect on prices from 1700 until the Napoleonic campaigns. Robert Barro, "Government Spending, Interest Rates, Prices, and Budget Deficits in the UK, 1701–1918," *Journal of Monetary Economics*, 20 (Sept. 1987), pp. 221–48.

Table 4. *Government long-term borrowing: interest rates, 1693–1739*
(selected loans)

Date[a]	Amount (£)	Interest (%)	How funded
Jan. 1693	723,394	14.0	Additional excise
Mar. 1694	1,000,000	14.0	Duties on imports
Mar. 1694	1,200,000	8.0	Additional customs and duties
Apr. 1697	1,400,000	6.3	Excise and duties
Jul. 1698	2,000,000	8.0	Additional excise duties
Mar. 1707	1,155,000	6.25	Surplus from funds of five loans from 1690s; duties
Jul. 1721	500,000	5.0	Hereditary revenue of Crown
Mar. 1728	1,750,000	4.0	Coal duties
May 1731	800,000	3.0	Duties
Jun. 1739	300,000	3.0	Sinking fund

[a] Date of royal assent to loan act.
Source: P. G. M. Dickson, *The Financial Revolution in England* (New York, 1967), tables 2, 3, and 22.

term loans in the early 1690s were at 14 percent (see Table 4). By the end of the 1690s the rate was about half, between 6 and 8 percent. The rate continued to fall over the next two decades so that, by the 1730s, interest rates were 3 percent.

These numbers are impressive in two ways. First, the amount of wealth now available for use by others increased tremendously. Second, at the same time as governmental borrowing increased, the interest rate fell. Sharp increases in demand accompanied by decline in rates indicate that the overall risk associated with governmental behavior decreased considerably despite the enormous increase in the size of the debt. As the society gained experience with its new institutions, particularly their predictability and commitment to secure rights, expectations over future actions began to reflect the new order.

These changing expectations were directly reflected in the capital market response. The new institutional underpinnings of public finance provided a clear and dramatic credible commitment that the government would honor its promises and maintain the existing pattern of rights. While underlying economic conditions were surely an important component of the large increase in debt, they alone can not explain the *suddenness* with which the debt increased, nor its magnitude. Even though the later Stuarts were more financially successful than their predecessors, nothing that came before the Glorious Revolution suggests the dramatic change in capital markets that it unleashed.

6. IMPLICATIONS FOR PRIVATE CAPITAL MARKETS

Our thesis is that the credible commitment by the government to honor its financial agreements was part of a larger commitment to secure private rights. The latter was clearly a major factor for the institutional changes at the time of the Glorious Revolution. Data on general economic activity are sparse, so we cannot perform a major test of our thesis, but we can provide some support. As evidence we turn to the development of private capital markets and the necessary evolution of the financial foundation of long-run economic success.

While it is clear that the institutions underlying private capital markets go back at least several centuries, it is widely agreed among economic historians that private capital markets date from the early eighteenth century.[43] The rise of banks and an increasingly differentiated set of securities, providing a relatively secure means of saving, brought individual savings into the financial system. Ashton reports that this "meant that men were less concerned than their fathers . . . to keep quantities of coin, bullion, and plate locked up in safes or buried in their orchards and gardens."[44]

The institutions leading to the growth of a stable market for public debt provided a large and positive externality for the parallel development of a market for private debt. Shortly after its formation for intermediating public debt, the Bank of England began private operations. Numerous other banks also began operations at this time. This development provided the institutional structure for pooling the savings of many individuals and for intermediation between borrowers and lenders. A wide range of securities and negotiable instruments emerged in the early eighteenth century and these were used to finance a large range of activities.[45]

Phyllis Deane summarizes the development of private capital markets alongside that for public capital:

---

[43] This section summarizes the conclusions of the literature on the early eighteenth century. See, for example, T. S. Ashton, *An Economic History of England* (London, 1955); John Clapham, *The Bank of England* (New York, 1945); Phyllis Deane, *The First Industrial Revolution* (2nd edn., Cambridge, 1979); Dickson, *Financial Revolution*; Peter Mathias, *The First Industrial Nation* (2nd edn., London, 1983); and E. Powell, *The Evolution of the Money Market: 1385–1915* (London, 1966).

[44] Ashton, *Economic History*, p. 178.

[45] "The essence of the financial revolution of the early 18th century was the development of a wide range of securities in which new mercantile and financial companies – the chartered trading companies, the partnership banks, the insurance companies, etc. – could flexibly and safely invest and disinvest" (Deane, *Industrial Revolution*, p. 185).

Douglass C. North and Barry R. Weingast

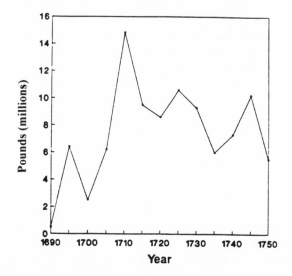

Figure 1. Growth of the stock market: 1690–1750. *Source:* P. G. M. Dickson, *The Financial Revolution in England* (London, 1967), Appendix C.

The secondary effects of the Bank's financial transactions on behalf of the government stemmed from the new financial instruments which were thus created . . . and because [the instruments] issued by a credit-worthy borrower are themselves readily saleable, the effect was further to lubricate the channels linking savings and investment by creating a large stock of negotiable paper assets which new savers could buy. Similarly, the deposits from private sources could also be used as a basis for further credit to the private sector.[46]

As a consequence, private capital markets flourished.

Several sources of evidence support our claims. First, research on interest rates for various forms of private credit reveals that these roughly parallel rates on public credit.[47] Falling private rates increased the range of projects and enterprises that were economically feasible, thus promoting the accumulation of capital. As L. S. Pressnell concludes, the "accumulation of capital in the 18th century, which the declining trend of interest rates . . . clearly indicates, appears in this light as a major social and economic achievement."[48] Unfortunately the data from

[46] Ibid., pp. 184–85.
[47] Clapham, *Bank of England;* L. S. Pressnell, "The Rate of Interest in the 18th Century," in L. S. Pressnell, ed., *Studies in the Industrial Revolution* (London, 1960), p. 181; and Homer, *A History of Interest Rates.*
[48] Pressnell, "Rate of Interest," p. 181.

158

the first half of the eighteenth century, in contrast to those from the second half, are sketchy, and for the period prior to the Glorious Revolution, almost nonexistent.

Second, large-scale trading in private securities dates from this period.[49] Figure 1 shows the growth of one component of the market, short-dated securities. In the early 1690s the volume of these securities averaged £300,000 per year. Ten years later, volume averaged £3,400,000 per year, and by the early 1710s, £11,000,000 per year. While growth trailed off after the collapse of the South Sea Bubble, the market from 1715 to 1750 was far larger than that prior to the Revolution.

Third, the period saw the growth and development of banks. The Bank of England was followed shortly by numerous other banks in London. By the 1720s these numbered about 25. By 1750 there were 30; by 1770, 50; and by 1800, 70. While banks in areas outside London began to appear in large numbers only after 1750, Ashton argues that many of these areas were integrated into a national capital market much earlier.[50] "Inland bills and promissory notes played a considerable part in the trade of all parts of England and Wales. But nowhere had their use extended so far as in the north-west. The ubiquity of the bill was probably the reason why in this area formal banking made its appearance relatively late."[51]

The final set of evidence centers on the Bank of England's private activities in three areas.

1. Discounted bills. Systematic data on the Bank's discounting operations apparently do not survive. Nonetheless, sporadic reports are available and indicate a considerable growth of activity during the

---

[49] As Dickson notes, "The development of a market in securities in London in the period 1688–1756 was one of the more important aspects of the Financial Revolution." Dickson, *Financial Revolution*, p. 457.

[50] See Charles P. Kindleberger, *Financial History of Western Europe* (London, 1984), p. 74; and Mathias, *Industrialized Nation*. The earliest provincial bank cited by Mathias was in Bristol (1716), and there were not more than a dozen in 1750. By 1784, however, there were 120, and by 1800, 370 (Mathias, p. 151).

[51] Ashton, *Economic History*, p. 185. Ashton's claim is also supported by the study of credit instruments other than those provided by banks. B. L. Anderson, discussing the rise of inland bills, notes that their legal status was markedly improved in the first years of the eighteenth century. "This recognition of the bill as a transferable means of payment was a decisive turning point in the development of the English credit system. . . . [The] English practice made it an instrument of credit in a system of accommodation paper that was highly responsive to the community's demand for money." B. L. Anderson, "Money and the Structure of Credit in the 18th Century," *Business History*, 85 (No. 1, 1970), p. 90.

Douglass C. North and Barry R. Weingast

first few decades of the Bank's operations. For 1699 data reveal the following volume of notes discounted: 13–31 June, £8,534; 27 June–4 July, £14,000. By 1730 the *median* day's volume was over £10,000, and by 1760 days over £100,000 were common.[52]

2. Notes in circulation. During the eighteenth century the Bank's notes became a major medium of exchange, first in London, and then throughout England.[53] In the first two years of the Bank's operations the volume of notes grew to about £760,000 (see Table 5). By 1720 they numbered £2,900,000, and they were above £4,500,000 by 1730 and for the next few decades.

3. Drawing accounts. This early form of demand deposit seems to have become systematized about twenty years after the Bank's founding.[54] As shown in Table 5, drawing accounts were quite modest in the late 1690s. By 1720 they numbered more than a million pounds, growing to over two million by 1730. To summarize, the Bank expanded operations over several types of private credit. By 1720, a little over 25 years after the Bank's establishment, these sums reached substantial levels, showing the steady growth in financial services for private economic activity.

Thus it appears that the growth of private capital markets paralleled that of public capital markets. This development mobilized the savings of large numbers of individuals and, by mid-century, provided financial services in an integrated, national market. These funds appear to have financed a large variety of business activities and played a necessary role in the economic expansion throughout this century.[55] While these activities have not been studied in detail as they have for the period following 1750, 1688 appears to be a more abrupt break with the past than 1750. Returning to our main thesis, this growth indicates that the attempts to maintain secure private rights were largely successful.

[52] Clapham, *Bank of England,* p. 126.
[53] While other banks issued notes, by far the largest source for most of the period we are studying are those of the Bank of England. Throughout this period, these notes were convertible to gold. See D. M. Joslin, "London Private Bankers, 1720–1785," in E. M. Carus-Wilson, ed., *Essays in Economic History,* vol. 2, pp. 340–59.
[54] The only year before 1720 reported by Clapham is 1698.
[55] An additional piece of evidence concerns investment in transportation infrastructure, which also increased at this time. By 1724 there were over 1,160 miles of river open to navigation, double that of a century earlier. See Ashton, *Economic History,* p. 73; Mathias, *Industrial Nation,* p. 100. While the "canal age" is usually dated at mid-century, it "did not spring to life in 1750" but was the "conclusion of a mounting momentum of effort"; Mathias, *Industrial Nation,* p. 100. Both Ashton and Mathias noted that there were two big booms in improving rivers during this period, one at the turn of the century and one between 1718 and 1720.

Table 5. *The Bank of England's notes and drawing*
accounts, 1698–1750 (£ thousands)

Year	Notes in circulation	Drawing accounts
1698	1,340	100
1720	2,900	1,300
1730	4,700	2,200
1740	4,400	2,900
1750	4,600	1,900

Note: Figures for 1720–1750 are averages for the five-year period beginning with the year listed.
Source: John Clapham, *The Bank of England: A History* (New York, 1945), vol. 1: *1694–1797*.

Although the evidence cannot be used to discern the precise level of security, it shows that it was substantial. A more systematic test awaits future research on these markets.

7. CONCLUSION

In this essay we have provided a brief account of the successful evolution of institutional forms that permitted economic growth to take place in early modern England. It is clear from this discussion of a century of civil war and revolution, however, that these institutional innovations did not arise naturally. Rather they were forced, often violently, upon the Crown. The Crown, however, nearly won the struggle. Had a standing army existed in England, it would have been under the control of the Crown, and the political and economic future of England would very likely have been different, potentially more in keeping with that of France and Spain.

We have shown how the political institutions governing society can be considered endogenously. Fiscal constraints and a revenue-seeking Crown, problems exacerbated by an uncooperative Parliament, created a situation of insecure rights in which the wealth and welfare of individual citizens were at risk. Prior to the Glorious Revolution, institutions such as the Star Chamber enabled the Crown to alter rights in its favor in a manner that parliamentary interests were hard pressed to resist.

Given their means and motives, the triumph of parliamentary interests in the Glorious Revolution led to five significant institutional changes. First, it removed the underlying source of the expediency, an archaic fiscal system and its attendant fiscal crises. Second, by limiting the Crown's legislative and judicial powers, it limited the Crown's ability to alter rules after the fact without parliamentary consent. Third, parliamentary interests reasserted their dominance of taxation issues, removing the ability of the Crown to alter tax levels unilaterally. Fourth, they assured their own role in allocating funds and monitoring their expenditure. The Crown now had to deal with the Parliament on an equal footing – indeed, the latter clearly had the advantage with its now credible threat of dethroning a sovereign who stepped too far out of line. Fifth, by creating a balance between Parliament and the monarchy – rather than eliminating the latter as occurred after the Civil War – parliamentary interests insured limits on their own tendencies toward arbitrary actions. In combination, these changes greatly enhanced the predictability of governmental decisions.

What established the government's commitment to honoring its agreements – notably the promise not to appropriate wealth or repudiate debt – was that the wealth holders gained a say in each of these decisions through their representatives in Parliament. This meant that only if such changes were in their own interests would they be made. Increasing the number of veto players implied that a larger set of constituencies could protect themselves against political assault, thus markedly reducing the circumstances under which opportunistic behavior by the government could take place.

In the story we have told, the emergence of political and civil liberties was inextricably linked with economic freedom. Opportunistic behavior on the part of the Crown was often accompanied by abuse of the opposition's political rights. The Crown had jailed people without charge or for lengthy periods prior to trial, and had required excessive bail to raise the costs of opposition. Hence protection of political liberties emerged as a component of the political protection of economic rights.

The principal lesson of our article is that the fundamental institutions of representative government – an explicit set of multiple veto points along with the primacy of the common law courts over economic affairs – are intimately related to the struggle for control over governmental power. The success of the propertied and commercially minded interests led to institutions that simultaneously mitigated the motive underlying the Crown's drive to find new sources of revenue and also greatly constrained the behavior of the government (now the "king in Parliament" rather than the king alone). Though these institutional innovations failed to anticipate the decline of the power of the Crown and ascendancy of Parliament in the latter half of the eighteenth century, the system successfully balanced power for well over sixty years. In

comparison with the previous century or with the absolutist governments of the continent, England's institutional commitment to secure
rights was far stronger. Evidence from capital markets provides a striking indication of this.

Recent research that has significantly upgraded France's economic
performance before the French Revolution has led to an overhauling of
traditional interpretations of British as well as French economic history.[56] If England and France were almost at parity in economic performance, the clear implication is that institutions per se – and in particular, the institutional changes we have described – were not so
revolutionary after all. Similarly, the elaborate bureaucratic structure
inherited from Louis XIV was not such a hindrance to economic growth.
But that conclusion ignores the consequences that followed. It is clear
that the institutional changes of the Glorious Revolution permitted the
drive toward British hegemony and dominance of the world. England
could not have beaten France without its financial revolution; and the
funds made available by the growth in debt from 1688 to 1697 were
surely a necessary condition for England's success in this war with
France as well as the next one (1703–1714), from which England
emerged the major power in the world.[57]

France, like England, had an ongoing fiscal crisis; and Louis XIV did
come to terms with his constituents to gain more revenue early in
his reign. But his success was temporary, not rooted in fundamental
institutional change, and it was outdistanced by the magnitude of the
English success. France's economy lived on borrowed time, and ultimately the unresolved institutional contradictions resulted in bankruptcy
and revolution.[58]

The comparison of growth rates alone is therefore insufficient to judge
economic parity. While in 1690 France was the major European power,
it declined in power and stature relative to England over the next century. More wars followed those at the turn of the eighteenth century, so
that in 1765 – at the end of the Seven Years' War, in which France

---

[56] See, for example, F. Crouzet, "England and France in the Eighteenth Century,"
in Max Hartwell, ed., *Causes of the Industrial Revolution in England* (London,
1967).
[57] Dickson, *Financial Revolution*.
[58] See David Bien, "Offices, Corps, and a System of State Credit: The Uses of
Privilege under the Ancient Regime," in K. Baker, ed., *The French Revolution and
the Creation of Modern Political Culture* (New York, 1987), vol. 1, pp. 89–114;
Philip Hoffman, "Taxes, Fiscal Crises, and Representative Institutions: The Case of
Early Modern France," manuscript, California Institute of Technology, 1988; and
Hilton Root and Daniel Ingberman, "Tying the King's Hands," manuscript, Univer-
sity of Pennsylvania, 1987.

suffered a humiliating defeat – it had lost its New World colonies (Canada and Louisiana) and was in financial peril from which it did not recover until after the revolution. The contrast between the two economies in mid-century is striking: in 1765 France was on the verge of bankruptcy while England was on the verge of the Industrial Revolution.[59]

It is always tempting to claim too much. Would Britain really have followed the path of continental countries if the Stuarts had won? Would there have been a first Industrial Revolution in England? One could tell a plausible counterfactual story that put more weight on the fundamental strength of English property rights and the common law that had evolved from the Magna Carta and which would have circumscribed royal behavior and ultimately forced "responsible government." One could point to the robust economy (particularly at the local level) that existed in seventeenth-century England despite the uncertainties we have described. There exists neither a definitive theory of economic growth which would define for us the necessary and sufficient conditions nor the evidence to reconstruct the necessary counterfactual story. But we are convinced from the widespread contemporary Third World and historical evidence that *one* necessary condition for the creation of modern economies dependent on specialization and division of labor (and hence impersonal exchange) is the ability to engage in secure contracting across time and space. That entails low transaction costs per exchange. The creation of impersonal capital markets is the single most important piece of evidence that such a necessary condition has been fulfilled. And we have told a story of how these institutions *did* come about in England.

As evidence against the counterfactual thesis, we again point to the financial revolution. A change of this magnitude in such a short period clearly hinged on the underlying constitutional reorganization. Because the financial revolution played a critical role in England's long-run success, the implication is that even if other forces would ultimately have led England to success under the Stuarts, they would have done so more slowly and probably less decisively.

---

[59] Jeffrey Williamson's recent, if controversial, work provides further support for this thesis. It suggests that British growth rates rose substantially once the long series of wars with France, ending with the Napoleonic campaign, were over. If during this period England's growth rates were not substantially larger than France's, its ability to spend more on war without bringing financial peril meant at most lower domestic consumption and investment, and hence came at the expense of growth. France's near bankruptcy shows that, in comparison, it was living on borrowed time. See Jeffrey G. Williamson, "Why Was British Growth so Slow During the Industrial Revolution?" *Journal of Economic History*, 64 (Sept. 1983), pp. 687–712.

We have thus shown how institutions played a necessary role in making possible economic growth and political freedom. Furthermore, it appears from our survey of seventeenth-century England, from the historical performance of other economies, and from performance records of current Third World economies that the circumstances fostering secure rights and hence economic growth are relatively rare and deserve further exploration.

5

Regulation in a dynamic setting

Regulation is an integral part of institutional change. Regulation sets the rules of the economic game and thereby the incentives faced by the actors. There are several general theories of economic regulation, each fraught with difficulties when one examines the life – and rarely death – of any particular regulation. Finding fault with general theories of regulation, Anne Krueger espouses the case study approach, arguing that we could learn more by amassing historical detailed studies of specific regulation and then generalizing from the results.[1]

Until the pioneering article by Stigler, the dominant view among economists was that market failure calls for regulation.[2] Even today, the standard textbook treatment of externalities and monopoly begins by pointing out the inefficiencies associated with market failure and almost naturally leads students to the conclusion that government intervention is warranted. We label this the *public interest paradigm*. As Krueger states in this essay, "Underlying these sets of policy prescriptions is the notion of government as a benevolent guardian hampered only by ignorance of proper economic policy as it seeks disinterestedly to maximize a Benthamite social welfare function."[3]

[1] An implication of Krueger's case study is that one crucial role for empirical work is to inform theory. But before empirical work can be of much use to theorists, scholars need to generate a sufficient number of case studies that we can sort out the general causal factors in regulation from the historically specific factors.

[2] George J. Stigler, "The Theory of Economic Regulation," *Bell's Journal of Economics and Management Science* (Spring 1971), 3–21. There were those who deviated from this general view, most notably Ronald Coase, in "The Problem of Social Cost," *Journal of Law and Economics* 3 (1960), 1–44.

[3] Some economists still conduct policy analysis under this assumption and naturally reach the conclusion that governments might want to intervene. In a recent review of *Reconcilable Differences? United States–Japan Economic Conflict* by Fred C. Bergsten and Marcus Noland, *The Economist* argues that Bergsten and Noland fall into the trap of believing in benign government and therefore reach unwarranted conclusions advocating "managed trade" by government. "That is because through-

Regulation in a dynamic setting

The Stigler view of regulation followed in the footsteps of Olson,[4] positing that special interest groups have lower costs of organizing and demanding regulation in their self-interest. This position has led to the view that special interest groups "capture" the regulators. Taken to its extreme, this view suggests that because special interest groups benefit ultimately from regulation, they must be the ones who are responsible for the origins of the regulation. The action in this model comes not from the government or the supply side of regulation but rather from the demanders of regulation, who are self-interested, rational, and well informed as to the consequences of regulation.

Another view of regulation is that of the public choice school. Here there are two camps: one composed primarily of economists whose views were initially put forward by Buchanan and Tullock and the other composed primarily of political scientists whose intellectual roots can be traced to William Riker. The economists look at regulation as the outcome of a market with demanders and suppliers. The demanders are special interest groups and the suppliers are politicians and bureaucrats who are also acting in their own self-interest. The political scientists focus more on the supply side of regulation, but not on the actors as much as on the constraints that the suppliers face. For example, they might look at how various types of voting rules affect outcomes or how decision making by committees leads to different outcomes than regulation determined by all legislators jointly making decisions.

Krueger does not abandon the insights gained from these theories but nevertheless does not find them sufficient to explain much regulation and they are certainly not the focus of her essay: the history of the regulation of sugar in the United States. Krueger argues that in the case of sugar the dynamics of policy are important and that any one historical snapshot of the program may give a misleading view of the program in another period. For example, she argues that the sugar program cannot be understood by looking at its origins; the design of the program changed numerous times, which could not have been anticipated by its founders. Indeed, the designers of the original sugar program most likely had revenue on their minds rather than protection. Yet, without the tariffs, most likely sugar would not have been produced at all in the

out the book [*Reconcilable Differences? United States–Japan Economic Conflict*] the authors are asking a question which, however interesting, is somewhat beside the point: could an intelligent government use this policy to serve the public good? In the real world the answer to this question is of limited interest. The right question is: would intelligent citizens grant their government discretion to try? The answer to that, on the evidence the book itself presents, is likely to be NO." *The Economist,* June 26–July 2, 1993, p. 75.

[4] Mancur Olson, *The Logic of Collective Action* (Cambridge, Mass.: Harvard University Press, 1965).

Regulation in a dynamic setting

United States during the twentieth century. To use Oliver Williamson's term, "bounded rationality" can lead to unintended consequences.

Clearly, the originators of the sugar program did not anticipate all of its ramifications; no one could foresee that sugar policy would be an integral part of foreign policy with the Philippines, Hawaii, and Cuba.

WHAT TO LOOK FOR IN THE ESSAY

Krueger's analysis of the sugar program does not fit any tidy monocausal explanation, but it does illustrate several issues explored in other essays in this volume. We encourage the reader to reflect on the following:

1. A historical approach is central to understanding institutions and institutional change because path dependence typifies the evolution of many institutions. In the case of sugar, the increasing complexity of the program over time can be understood only by an appreciation of past policies.

2. Once a policy is in place, people within government (the suppliers of policy) and outside government (the demanders of policy) invest in knowledge specific to the program. As a result policies tend to take on a life of their own, making institutional change difficult. As programs become more complex, information becomes a barrier to entry, enhancing the role of technocrats in the policy process.

3. Government is not simply a veil through which the interests of constituents get articulated. Within government certain individuals are positioned such that they have agenda control and veto power: in the case of sugar the chairs of the Senate Finance Committee and the House Agriculture Committee.

4. Markets react to policy to minimize its adverse effects.[5] The sugar program raised the price of sugar significantly and thereby set in motion a search for sugar substitutes that ultimately reduced dramatically the demand for sugar.

[5] This issue is one of the central themes in the essay by Cheung (Chapter 6).

The political economy of controls:
American sugar

ANNE O. KRUEGER

In economic theory, it is relatively straightforward to analyse the impact of government controls over economic activity. Whether the control is over feed-grain prices in Egypt, the quantities of imports of individual items in India, price controls on 'old' oil, or the 'voluntary' reduction in the number of automobiles exported from Japan to the United States, several conclusions follow straightforwardly. First and foremost, those controls (and most others) at best achieve their objectives in a more costly manner than would alternative mechanisms. Second, the presumed beneficiaries of controls are often quite different from those (if any) actually benefiting. Third, the costs of controls seem to be largely ignored or misunderstood in political decision-making, at least in the first instance.

Despite these well-established results, controls seem to persist. A major challenge confronting those concerned with their costs is to attempt to understand the reasons why the political process often generates and perpetuates high-cost solutions to stated objectives. To establish an understanding of the political economy of controls would appear to be a formidable, but important, challenge, if means are to be sought to lower the costs of attaining political objectives.

This essay is reprinted from *Public Policy and Development: Essays in Honour of Ian Little*, edited by Maurice Scott and Deepak Lal (1990), by permission of Oxford University Press. © Maurice Scott and Deepak Lal 1990.

I am heavily indebted to Paul Pecorino for valuable research assistance in preparation of this chapter. Al Reifman was extremely generous with assistance in providing material from the Congressional Research Service. Richard Snape was exceptionally helpful and generous in commenting on several drafts of the entire manuscript and in sharing his extensive knowledge of the international sugar economy. Stanley Engerman and Maurice Scott provided useful comments on the penultimate draft. Helpful comments and suggestions were also made by members of the Political Economy Workshop at Duke University, and the International Economics Workshops at Virginia Polytechnic and State University, the University of North Carolina, Harvard University, and the University of Rochester.

Anne O. Krueger

The purpose of this chapter is to attempt to further our understanding of the political economy of controls. Section 1 provides a survey of existing models of regulation. The remainder of the chapter is then devoted to an examination of how well those models perform in light of the history of one particular set of controls – the American sugar programme. In part, resort to an inductive effort to understand controls better seems logical in light of economists' puzzlement with their prevalence. In part, however, it seems likely that further advances in understanding of the political economy of controls can take place only with the accumulation of insights emanating from analysis of a number of particular cases. It is to be hoped that they will gradually yield 'stylized facts' upon which better theory can be built. Sugar was chosen for scrutiny for a number of reasons: the programme has had a long and chequered history since 1934; given the transparency of the American system, most of the contending interests have been documented to an unusual degree in Senate and House hearings; and good economic analyses of the programme have been undertaken at various times so that focus here can be on economic-political interactions.

Ian Little has been in the forefront of professional economists using their analytical tool-kit to demonstrate the costs of controls in a variety of settings. His work has been instrumental in convincing the vast majority of the economics profession that the economic costs of controls are far greater than were generally thought two or three decades ago. It is therefore appropriate that an essay in his honour should attempt to further understanding of the political economy of economic policy.

1. MODELS OF ECONOMIC POLICY FORMULATION

The absence among economists[1] of a widely accepted model of economic policy formulation is readily illustrated by the divergent implicit and explicit assumptions about the nature of intervention underlying policy analysis in the various sub-fields in economics. In international trade, the tradition was for long to assume that policy-makers were uninformed and that failure to adopt Pareto-optimal policies reflected ignorance on their part. International economists assumed that a benevolent government would, once informed of the benefits of free trade, immedi-

[1] There is a large literature among political scientists focusing on the determinants of policy. I am heavily indebted to Robert Bates for long and useful discussions about this literature. In this section, I focus only on the economics literature on the subject, in part because of my own comparative advantage, but in part because the intent of the chapter is to focus on political-economic interactions, and the role of market forces in affecting the outcomes of policies adopted by politicians, topics largely neglected in both the economics and the political science literature.

The political economy of controls

ately undertake policy reform. Considerable bewilderment then resulted from the many departures from Pareto-optimal policies in circumstances where infant industry and monopoly power in trade did not apply.

Several models of political-economic interaction in policy formulation have been set forth in an effort to understand the persistence of some policies. Brock and Magee (1978) modelled politicians as needing money to win elections but simultaneously losing votes if they support lobbyists' causes too ardently; an equilibrium occurs when the revenue from lobbying at the margin increases votes by the same amount as further support of special interests loses votes. Corden (1974), by contrast, attempted to explain international economic policy as a consequence of a 'conservative social welfare function': in his view, politicians attempt to protect people's income streams, and thus provide assistance to those who are adversely affected by shifts in prices and competitive positions. Finally, Bhagwati and Srinivasan (1980) modelled 'directly unproductive activity', in which lobbyists spend resources in seeking legislation equal in value to the value of the protection to them.

In public economics, there has been a similar tradition: a presentation of economic efficiency conditions for optimality, with the accompanying assertion that non-fulfilment of these conditions – such as the presence of externalities – represented a case of market failure and therefore justified market intervention. Underlying these sets of policy prescriptions is the notion of government as a benevolent guardian, hampered only by ignorance of proper economic policy as it seeks disinterestedly to maximize a Benthamite social welfare function.

In the field of industrial organization, the tradition was similar until the 1960s. It was assumed that government bureaucrats were in fact pursuing the public interest in regulating whatever was regulated – transport, communications, public utilities, and the like. This view was challenged, and largely overthrown, in the 1970s by Stigler (1971), Peltzman (1976), and others, who instead posited full rationality of all actors. In their view, all political agents are rational and use the political process to effect wealth transfers. Thus, the view of the regulatory process changed fundamentally, from being a process fostering the 'common good' to being a rational outcome to private maximization through the political process. Participants were seen to be fully rational and acting in their own self-interest. In this model, policy analysis by economists would serve no useful purpose, as additional information would not change the behaviour of any participant in the regulatory process.

An interesting variant on the Stigler–Peltzman approach has been set forth by Becker (1983), who assumes that political interest groups form in their own self-interest, and that politicians rationally choose policies in response to the competing pressures these groups can exert. With

171

competition among groups, and the assumption that anything which benefits one group must either be financed directly by a tax or indirectly by costing another group (including deadweight losses), Becker concludes that resources are allocated to the political process to maximize the benefits (which are for some groups negative) each group expects to receive.

Yet another approach is that of Olson (1965, 1982). Starting with the 'logic of collective action', in which the 'free-rider' problem prevents the effective collusion of large numbers of small losers, Olson formulated various hypotheses as to which effective pressure groups would emerge and the characteristics of industries and of other economic interest groups that would be likely to be able to organize and effectively represent their interests. These characteristics include both geographic and market concentration. Carrying his analysis further, Olson attempted to explain differentials in growth rates among nations after the Second World War. In Olson's world, interest groups organize to protect their interests as growth progresses. Over time, more and more groups and institutions are in place, and in the process economic efficiency diminishes and growth decelerates. War destroys these groups and interests, at least to some extent, so that war-devastated countries, such as Germany and Japan, are enabled to grow rapidly, freed of many of the resistances to growth that arise over time in a war-free environment.[2]

Olson's model essentially posits that economically inefficient outcomes arise because of free-rider problems: it is rational for individuals not to join groups interested in consumer welfare, etc., because the benefits to them are independent of their own activities. This contrasts significantly with the Stigler–Peltzman–Becker view in two ways: institutional means are not available for large groups of small potential gainers or losers to represent their interests, and interest groups form gradually over time as they learn about their interests (and respond to the gains of other groups).

The final view of the political process is that of Buchanan and public choice theory. Here, the underlying assumption is that individuals behave in their interest in the political, as well as the economic, arena, but that the 'rules of the game' in the political arena may permit choices that, while individually rational, could clearly be improved upon by a different decision rule.

Each of these models doubtless contains elements of truth. None the less, one can ask whether they capture a sufficiently large fraction of it. One could question, for example, the implicit hypothesis underlying the

---

[2] See Mueller (1983) for a series of papers examining the empirical validity of the Olson hypotheses regarding growth rates.

The political economy of controls

views of Becker and Buchanan that all participants understand their own self-interest. An important issue is where the role of knowledge, and of the technocrats who implement controls, enters into such an analysis.

Moreover, almost all the models implicitly or explicitly address controls as if they were a once-and-for-all phenomenon. In many situations, one has more the impression that politicians impose a control with a certain naïveté as to its ramifications; that the market then reacts to minimize the cost of the control; that the politicians in turn find the market solution unacceptable and then alter the control, only to have the market once again react. If this view is correct, a control cannot be analysed as a static, unchanging set of regulations, and must be seen in light of the economic-political forces that it sets in motion to result in continuing evolution of the programme.

As will be seen, the evolution of the American sugar programme contains elements of almost all the models discussed above. Additionally, it is certainly a programme that evolved over time, where market interactions with controls affected not only outcomes, but even the position of various participants with respect to the desirability of controls. Moreover, it is also a programme whose evolution depended, in important ways, on the fact that it was highly complex; complexity in effect created a barrier to entry into the political arena, and thus facilitated the perpetuation of the programme; it also created a vested interest in the perpetuation of the programme on the part of knowledgeable parties. Finally, and perhaps most interestingly, the evolution of the sugar programme is full of 'mistakes', in the sense that various parties on not infrequent occasions took policy stances that turned out, at a later date, to be against their own self-interest.

Background information essential to understanding the sugar economy is presented in Section 2. Thereafter, the origins of the sugar programme are covered in Section 3; the programme during the post-war years from 1948 to 1960 is the subject of Section 4; Section 5 covers the period from 1960 to 1974; Section 6 the period from 1974 to 1981; and Section 7 traces the evolution of the programme on to the present time. Section 8 then assesses the implications of the sugar programme for a richer political economy of controls. The final section draws tentative conclusions.

2. THE SUGAR MARKET

The economic effects of the American sugar programme have been extensively analysed, and are reasonably well known. In this section, the essential characteristics of the sugar industry, and the relation of the American market to the international sugar market, are described. Em-

173

phasis is on those aspects relevant for analysing the political economy of controls, at least as exemplified in the case of sugar.

The production function[3]

Sugar is an unusual commodity. It can be made from either raw cane or sugar-beet, and yet the end-products of the two are perfect substitutes. Cane can grow only in tropical or semi-tropical climates while sugar-beet is grown in temperate climates. Both cane and beet require processing to make sugar. In both cases, initial processing must be undertaken within a very short time after harvest; it must therefore be done close to where the cane or beet is grown.

For beet-sugar, a single-stage refining process has produced refined sugar since the late 1800s. In the case of cane, however, second-stage refining is necessary to make sugar in the crystalline white form used in final consumption; raw sugar (i.e. that processed from cane near the site) can be refined anywhere.[4] While there are a few by-products of cane and of beet, they are not sufficiently valuable to warrant growing the crops in the absence of a demand for their sugar; at any event, the by-products made from cane and beet are similar.

Cane and beet mills and cane refineries are capital-intensive, and apparently have little or no alternative use. No farmer would consider growing cane or sugar-beet without a mill near by, and no mill would be established unless it was anticipated that there would be a proximate source of supply. For this reason, there is a considerable degree of vertical integration in the industry; in Hawaii, for example, most cane is grown in fields owned by the same parties who own the local sugar mill for first-stage refining.

Mills need a fairly steady flow of cane or beet in order to utilize their capacity reasonably steadily over a major part of the year. Arrangements for harvesting sugar-beet and cane therefore include fairly detailed provisions as to the date of delivery of the product to the mill.

One of the interesting political phenomena about the industry, given

---

[3] This section draws heavily on Congressional Research Service (1985). The interested reader can consult that source for considerably greater detail. The facts, however, are in virtually all Congressional *Hearings* pertaining to the sugar programme.

[4] The United States had a tariff on raw imports, and a higher tariff on refined sugar imports, throughout most of the 19th century. At the time, beet-sugar required second-stage refining. The differential in tariffs between raw and refined sugar was high enough to make the effective rate of protection to refining greater than 100%. The best means of determining whether sugar had been refined was the 'Dutch colour test' which graded imports by the extent of brown colouration of the sugar being imported. Among the 19th-century problems with tariff administration was the importation of brown refined sugar. See Taussig (1924), pp. 101 ff., for a description.

The political economy of controls

the evolution of controls, is its relatively small size. It is estimated that, in 1969 (which was the about the peak of sugar production and demand in the United States), there were only 28,000 American farms producing sugar, producing about $1.25 billion of gross output, and employing 150,000 (mostly seasonal and largely immigrant) workers.[5]

The demand for sugar and sweeteners

If it is conventional wisdom that producers are more likely to gain when they are highly concentrated relative to consumers, sugar is an exception. More than 70 per cent of US sugar consumption is by industrial users – bakeries, soft drinks, confectionary, cereals, etc. The remaining 25–30 per cent of consumption goes through distribution directly to consumers (defined as all sugar sold in bags of less than 50 lb.).

Consumption of refined sugar in the United States peaked at about 10.7 million tons in 1972, equivalent to about 102 lb. per capita. At that time, consumption of all caloric sweeteners, including sugar, corn sweeteners, honey, etc. was 13.3 million tons, or 126.7 lb. per capita.[6] By 1986, American consumption of sugar had fallen to 7.4 million tons, or 61.6 lb. per capita, while total caloric sweetener consumption had risen to 15.4 million tons or 131.6 lb. per capita.[7] This decline in sugar consumption resulted from the substitution of high fructose corn syrup (HFCS) for sugar in most of the commercial uses of liquid sugar (soft

[5] See Heston (1975), p. 26. Johnson's estimates (1974) as to the size of the industry are similar.

[6] This contrasts with an estimated consumption per capita of 9 lb. in the United States in 1822 (see Johnson, 1974, p. 5). Here and throughout, the reader should be alert to units; production is often measured in terms of tons (2,000 lb.) of cane or beet; these units (contrast Tables 2 and 3 below) are obviously different from those that measure the weight of refined sugar produced or consumed. Since the yield of cane and beet varies from year to year and place to place, conversion ratios are not constant. However, the conversion factor is close to 10:1 – for example in 1986, 28.743 million tons of cane were produced, which was 3.4 million tons of sugar, raw value. For beet, 25.229 million tons were produced, with 2.989 million tons of sugar, raw value produced. See USDA, *Sugar and Sweetener Situation and Outlook Yearbook,* June 1981. For an amusing discussion of the problems of administering an import quota set in terms of raw value, see House *Hearings* (1974), pp. 95–101.

[7] Consumption of non-caloric sweeteners has also risen; in 1970 it is estimated that they accounted for 5.8 lb. per capita consumption, while by 1987 they were 18.5 lb. per capita. There are many grounds for believing that much of the increase in consumption of non-caloric sweeteners may have represented a shift in tastes, rather than a consequence of relative price changes. For that reason, the evolution of non-caloric sweetener production and consumption will not be further considered in this chapter. Taking it into account would not significantly alter the argument at any stage, as total consumption of non-caloric sweeteners still occupies less than 15% of the entire market for sweeteners.

drinks being the largest) as a result of sugar's high price under the programme. As will be seen, this market response to the high support price for sugar (at approximately 4–5 times the world level) resulted in a major shift in the sugar producers' and sugar refiners' interests in the sugar programme, but simultaneously induced the corn-growers to support perpetuation of the programme in its existing form.

The international sugar economy

There are few countries in the world that do not intervene in their domestic sugar markets. Perhaps this is because both temperate and tropical countries can grow sugar. Regardless of the motives for intervention, the result is that about three-quarters of sugar grown in the world is consumed in the country of production.[8]

For this reason, the international market is somewhat thin, with about 27 million tons out of an estimated total world production of about 100 million tons (sugar equivalent, both cane and beet) entering into international trade (*Sugar and Sweeteners Situation*, June 1987, p. 35) in the 1985/6 crop year. Even out of that total, the existence of a number of preferential arrangements (including the American quota and Cuban–Soviet trade) has meant that the 'free market' price has governed only a small fraction of transactions. American preferences are diminishing in importance, however, as American imports have fallen, for reasons that will become evident below, from 6.2 million tons in 1977 to an estimated 1.5 million tons in 1987.[9]

The price of sugar has always displayed volatility on international markets. Two factors contributed to this. First, there is an 18-month lag between planting of cane and first harvesting. Thereafter, cane is usually cut two more times at approximately six-month intervals before the field is cleared and a new crop planted. Thus, when sugar prices rise, there is a longer time-lag than for annual crops (although not as long as for some tree crops) before additional production reaches the market. When the sugar price falls, it can be an even longer time before the planting response is reflected in reduced sugar output, unless of course the price falls so low that harvesting proves unprofitable. Second, and at least as important, the fact that the international market is a residual has intensified these price swings.

---

[8] One of the many arguments for the sugar programme given by sugar interests has been that sugar is controlled almost everywhere. In most instances, however, it is subsidiary to other arguments put in support of the programme.

[9] In Dec. 1987, the United States Department of Agriculture announced that the permitted level of imports for 1988 would be 750 thousand tons. See *New York Times*, 16 Dec. 1987, p. 29. However, the political reactions to that announcement have not yet been completed. See below, Section 7.

Thus, after Cuba lost her US quota in 1960, world prices rose for several years.[10] Thereafter, new plantings (which took place predominantly in countries which received higher sugar prices because of their increased quotas in the American market) matured, and world sugar supplies rose sharply; the world price fell from a high of 8.50 cents per lb. in 1963 to 1.86 cents per lb. in 1966. That, in turn, apparently discouraged plantings, because by 1969 the sugar price was rising again. However, because of the world-wide commodity boom, the production response was apparently more sluggish and delayed than in earlier periods of high prices. Hence, the price of sugar rose continuously until November 1974, reaching over 40 cents per lb. in that month. There then followed another sharp decline in price as new supplies appeared by 1976, and the price fell for the next two years. By 1980, however, production had once again responded to lower prices, and the price again rose sharply, reaching 29.02 cents per lb. by the end of 1980.

Starting early in 1981, the world price fell and remained depressed for a long period as American imports declined sharply and the European Community increased exports as its production surpluses mounted. It was estimated in 1985 that, if all countries were to adopt free trade in sugar, the world price would be about 12 cents per lb. contrasted with an actual world price of at that time 4 cents per lb. and a US domestic wholesale price of 20.3 cents per lb. (see Table 1).[11] By the end of 1987, the world price had risen substantially, to about 9.5 cents per lb., while the US price was virtually unchanged.

3. ORIGINS OF THE SUGAR PROGRAMME[12]

There have been few years in American history when sugar has not been the object of some degree of intervention. It has always been an importable. Starting in 1796, a tariff on imports was imposed. Until the

---

[10] Cuba's exports and quota constituted the vast majority of sugar imports into the United States prior to 1960. In 1959, for example, Cuba exported 3,437,582 tons to the United States out of total imports of 4,273,000 tons. This contrasted with domestic production of 4,702,619 tons in that year. By 1961, Cuba's exports to the United States were zero. See Senate Finance Committee, *Hearings on Extension of the Sugar Act of 1948*, 1965, p. 11. Cuba's estimated share of the world sugar trade was 28.6% in 1961, and 24.7% in 1984. The Soviet Union replaced the United States as the major market for Cuban sugar in the 1960s. See Tan (1986) for particulars of the Cuban–Soviet sugar trade.

[11] See Leu and Knutson (1987) for one attempt to estimate what the world price would be in the absence of the current US programme. See also Congressional Research Service (1985).

[12] This section draws heavily on Terpstra (1981). Only those aspects of the pre-1934 sugar tariff relevant for later development are discussed here. For a full account, see Taussig (1924), ch. II.

Table 1. *New York and world sugar prices, 1948–1987 (US cents/lb.)*

	Caribbean price (f.o.b.) (1)	New York duty-paid price (2)	Ratio of Col (2) to Col (1) (3)
1948	4.17	5.6	1.34
1949	4.34	5.8	1.34
1950	4.98	5.9	1.18
1951	5.67	6.1	1.08
1952	4.17	6.3	1.51
1953	3.41	6.3	1.85
1954	3.26	6.1	1.87
1955	3.24	6.0	1.85
1956	3.48	6.1	1.75
1957	5.16	6.1	1.18
1958	3.50	6.3	1.80
1959	2.97	6.2	2.09
1960	3.14	6.3	2.01
1961	2.91	6.4	2.20
1962	2.98	6.3	2.11
1963	8.50	8.2	0.96
1964	5.87	6.9	1.18
1965	2.12	6.8	3.21
1966	1.86	7.0	3.76
1967	1.99	7.3	3.67
1968	1.98	7.5	3.79
1969	3.37	7.8	2.31
1970	3.75	8.1	2.16
1971	4.52	8.5	1.88
1972	7.43	9.1	1.22
1973	9.61	10.3	1.07
1974	29.99	29.5	0.98
1975	20.49	22.5	1.10
1976	11.58	13.3	1.15
1977	8.11	11.0	1.36
1978	7.82	13.9	1.78
1979	9.65	15.6	1.61
1980	29.02	30.1	1.04
1981	16.93	19.7	1.16
1982	8.42	19.9	2.36
1983	8.49	22.0	2.59
1984	5.18	21.7	4.19
1985	4.04	20.3	5.02
1986	6.05	21.0	3.47
1987	7.10	21.7	3.06

Source: USDA, *Sugar and Sweeteners Situation,* various issues.

late 1800s, revenue was the major motive for the tariff, as domestic production was less than 10 per cent of consumption and imports supplied more than 90 per cent of US consumption.[13]

Hawaii's relationship to the United States in the 1870s and 1880s was heavily centred around sugar: a free trade agreement with the United States had permitted Hawaiian sugar to be imported without duty, and had encouraged the expansion of Hawaiian cane-growing land. The American Congress then proceeded to rescind the duty on sugar, but to pay a bounty of 2 cents per lb. (about the same as the specific tariff earlier collected and equivalent to 100 per cent nominal protection) to American growers. The desire to have access to the American market at favourable prices seems to have been a major motive behind Hawaiian accession to US jurisdiction, after which the US reverted to tariff protection and Hawaii escaped the sugar tariff. From the 1890s until 1930, American tariff protection continued. Because the Hawaiians were exempt from the tariff (and Cuba also received a 25 per cent reduction in duty),[14] they benefited from protection in the sheltered American market. The Philippine sugar industry also started under the umbrella of American preferential protection.[15]

The Smoot–Hawley tariff in 1930, however, raised the rate of duty faced by Cuba to 2 cents per lb. (compared with a world sugar price of 0.73 cents per lb. in 1932), and the duty on imports from other countries to 2.5 cents per lb. In fact, however, imports from Cuba and the Philippines met US demands, and little sugar was imported from other countries. Indeed, during some periods of the year, the sugar price fell below the world price plus duty as Cuban sugar was more than sufficient to meet demand at that price.

During the Great Depression, sugar prices fell drastically. Among other consequences, the Cuban economy was extremely adversely affected, and, with it, the fortunes of American investors who owned sugar

[13] House Agriculture Committee *Hearings* of 1951; Extension of the Sugar Act of 1948. HR 4521, pp. 34–5. Taussig attributed the expansion of sugar-cane production in Louisiana in the 19th century to the existence of the protective tariff, and documented USDA efforts in the middle and late 19th century that led to the development of sugar-beet production in the United States. See Taussig (1924), chs. IV and VII. According to Taussig, sugar would not have been produced at all in the continental United States had it not been for USDA encouragement. Thus, the sugar programme is an example of an industry whose origins lie in government protective policies, and not of government controls originating because of industry pressure.

[14] Cuban sugar production rose rapidly in the first three decades of the century in response to this partial exemption. Much of the cane was planted, harvested, and processed (first-stage) on American-owned land and sugar-mills. By 1934, it was estimated that Americans owned 70% of Cuban sugar producing capacity (*Hearings* 1934, p. 106). See also House *Hearings* (1952), p. 35.

[15] Again, see Taussig (1924), ch. 6 and US Tariff Commission (1937).

plantations there. Political instability in Cuba was another consequence: a general strike led to pressure from the Roosevelt Administration for a change in leadership, which in turn led to the resignation of President Machado; his successor also could not restore law and order, and an army revolt brought Sergeant Fulgencio Batista to power.[16] Simultaneously, the Roosevelt Administration was introducing parts of its New Deal programme. The Secretary of Commerce, Harold Ickes, reported that, with respect to sugar:

The President is chafing under the present system by which, under the heavy tariff on beet sugar, the whole population is taxed in order to pay a subsidy to the beet sugar growers. . . . If it were not for the political questions involved, the President would put sugar on the free list and pay a subsidy. . . . He has discussed the possibility of wiping out the beet sugar industry over a series of twenty years. (Ickes, 1953, p. 147)

Starting in 1933, the Administration attempted to bring about political stability in Cuba and address the 'sugar situation' by imposing production quotas on US producers, thereby raising prices. The sugar interests opposed this programme so vigorously that several early proposals were withdrawn.[17] In effect, opponents wanted more restriction of imports to increase prices, with no production controls. Finally, in 1934, the Jones–Costigan Act was passed. It provided for a system of production and marketing quotas for domestic producers and import quotas for foreigners (almost exclusively Cuba). The intent of the Jones–Costigan Act seems to have been primarily to shore up the Cuban economy and secondarily to increase American producers' incomes. There was, in addition to production and import restrictions, provision for direct payment to American producers. However, there was also a clear intention to contain the size of the industry. In his message to Congress, President Roosevelt's statement was that:

Steadily increasing sugar production . . . has created a price and marketing situation prejudicial to virtually everyone interested. Farmers in many areas are threatened with low prices for their beets and cane, and Cuban purchases of our goods have dwindled steadily as her shipments of sugar to this country have declined.

There is a school of thought which believes that sugar ought to be on the free list. . . .

I do not at this time recommend placing sugar on the free list. I feel that we ought first to try out a system of quotas with the threefold object of keeping down the price of sugar to consumers, of providing for the retention of beet and

---

[16] Heston (1975), p. 91. Heston says that an ultimatum was delivered that the marines would intervene if Machado did not relinquish power within 48 hours.

[17] See Heston (1975), pp. 102–13 for a description of the political forces opposing and supporting the 1934 sugar programme legislation.

The political economy of controls

cane farming within our continental limits, and also to provide against further expansion of this necessarily expensive industry.[18]

Like much of the New Deal legislation, the Jones–Costigan Act was passed quickly within several days of its introduction and after hearings lasting only a few hours.[19] Although sugar producers were opposed to the Act, their representatives in Congress apparently gave in when threatened with the alternative of a reduced tariff and no programme. Beet-growers were particularly adamant in their opposition as the Act called for a 17 per cent reduction in sugar-beet production from the level of 1933.[20]

Even in the 1934 legislation, sugar refiners sought quotas to restrict imports of refined sugar. They claimed that the 1930 legislation (Smoot–Hawley) left them with a cost disadvantage *vis-à-vis* foreign producers (because Congress had assumed that it took one ton of raw sugar to make a ton of refined, whereas the actual conversion ratio was more like 1.07 to one).[21] So, quotas on imports of refined sugar were imposed to satisfy domestic (second-stage) refining interests; the quota was later

[18] *Sugar Beets and Sugarcane as Basic Agricultural Commodities under the Agricultural Adjustment Act*, HR 7907, 19 February 1934, House *Hearings*, p. 1. The Chief, Section of Sugar and Rice, Agricultural Adjustment Administration, testified that the domestic sugar industry was 'an expensive one from the point of view of the consumer and that lies behind the freezing of sugar beet acreage' (p. 13).

[19] See ibid.

[20] See Heston (1975) and *Hearings* (1934), pp. 84, 118, 121, 132, 145, 148, 152, 167. Because sugar was an import, its regulation should have come under the jurisdiction of the House Ways and Means Committee and the Senate Finance Committee. It did come under the latter. But one of the interesting 'accidents' with important consequences was that when the Jones–Costigan Act was first up for renewal in 1937, the Chairman of the House Agriculture Committee requested, as a favour from his colleague and friend, the Chairman of the Ways and Means Committee, that the House Agriculture Committee handle sugar matters. The Chairman of the House Ways and Means Committee acceded to the request, and the House Agriculture Committee has handled sugar matters ever since. See Price (1971) for an account. Because there is a tax on sugar imports, only the House may initiate legislation. This right of initiation, combined with the fact that sugar is the only agricultural commodity considered by the Senate Finance Committee, has resulted in unusually great power concentrated in the hands of the House Agriculture Committee for dealing with sugar. See the discussion of the 1962 bill below for one instance where the Senate opposed the House decisions but in the end was unable to prevail.

[21] Johnson (1974), p. 30, believes that American refineries had lost their comparative advantage in the 1920s and used the 1.07 to one conversion ratio as an argument for protection which they needed on other grounds. Taussig's documentation, however, suggests that the protection accorded to American sugar refineries as early as the 1870s was more than sufficient to provide needed protection and monopoly profit. See his interesting discussion of the 'Sugar Trust' (Taussig, 1924, ch. VIII). Taussig (1924, p. 104) cites testimony before Congress in 1888 by the head of the American Sugar Refining Company (the Trust) to the effect that 'the mother of all trusts is the customs tariff bill.'

replaced with a prohibition on importing fully refined cane sugar – a necessary condition for preserving the support of the sugar refiners who imported the raw (cane) sugar and refined it in their plants.[22]

As already indicated, the sugar growers opposed the introduction of these quotas in 1934, feeling it was against their interests. When the bill came up for renewal in 1937, however, they had switched sides, and actively supported the sugar programme and production and import quotas (see House *Hearings* (1937), pp. 16–45). Thus, just as the mainland sugar industry originated because of government efforts to encourage it, the 1934 sugar programme was put in place by the government with the opposition of the sugar interests.

Clearly, this sequence of events does not support the Bhagwati–Srinivasan model in which producers expend their resources to attain a programme aimed at supporting their interests. Rather, the USDA in the nineteenth century, and the Roosevelt Administration in 1934, seem to have viewed their roles as benevolent guardians of the social good. Once the programme was in place, however, sugar producers and refiners recognized their interests in its perpetuation, and generally supported it.[23] The major issue in 1937 was the size of the future quotas, and representatives of cane-sugar-producing states urged expansion of their quotas. Florida and Louisiana cane growers particularly pressured for larger quotas. Interestingly, it had been primarily beet producers that had opposed production ceilings in 1934; however, beet producers had not even filled their quotas under the original 1934 Act and did not seek large increases under the 1937 bill (House *Hearings* (1937), p. 145).

Unquestionably, then, the initial opposition of the beet growers had been irrational; they were unconstrained in how much they grew, since the quotas were not binding. Their own later support of the programme demonstrates this. As will be seen, this behaviour of the beet-growing interests is only one of the instances in the history of the sugar programme where it is unquestionable that actors took positions that were clearly against their own interest.[24]

When the sugar programme was up for renewal in 1939, production

---

[22]The precise quotas set forth in the first bill may be found in House *Hearings* (1934), p. 2.

[23]Interestingly, a representative of the United States Sugar Corporation (based in Florida) opposed the 1937 bill on the grounds that Florida could expand production and indicated a preference for unrestricted sugar imports unless Florida's production quota was increased substantially (see House *Hearings* (1937), p. 168).

[24]Puerto Rico and Hawaii had lost out in terms of their production quotas, but gained in terms of a higher sugar price. Both regions in 1937 focused on the prohibition in the 1934 bill which prevented exporting of second-stage refined sugar to the mainland. This provision was, however, not changed. See House *Hearings* (1937), pp. 55, 106.

The political economy of controls

had expanded sufficiently to reach the assigned quotas in most producing regions, and pressures mounted to reduce imports and increase mainland quotas. The Act was renewed, however, with little change in production quotas and in the shares of domestic production and imports in anticipated total consumption. However, with the advent of the Second World War, the entire programme was suspended as the problem became one of increasing output, rather than controlling supply. During the war, Cuban sugar was exported to the United States, even when American prices were below those that could have been realized in other markets.[25]

4. THE 'SUPPORT CUBA' PERIOD, 1948–1960

At the end of the war, commodity prices were high and there was no sugar legislation in effect. It had been put in place as a New Deal programme to deal with low sugar prices and a Cuban political-economic crisis. Sugar producers, who had originally opposed it, had come to support it, but, with the high prices after the war, there was no particular pressure from them for a resumption of the programme.

However, the Sugar Act was reconsidered in 1948. At the time, of course, the world price was high (although the US price was about 30 per cent above it; see Table 1) and the real issue was the percentage of sugar that should be supplied from domestic rather than foreign sources. A major consideration in devising the legislation was the moral debt owed to Cuba, because of Cuban steadfastness in providing sugar to a wartime ally. As passed, the intent of the legislation was to 'protect foreigners' interests in the US market'. This was to be accomplished by continuing to restrict US production to 55 per cent of consumption and allocating the remaining rights to supply the high-price US market to foreign countries, which in practice meant primarily Cuba.[26]

By virtue of the production controls, the US price would be higher than the foreign price by more than the tariff; rights to sell in the US market would therefore be valuable. It was clearly the intent of the Administration that these rights be directed largely toward Cuba. The Cuban share was 98.64 per cent of total import rights and Cuba also received rights to unfilled quotas of other countries. In 1949, for example, the United States imported 3.103 million tons of sugar from Cuba, 525 thousand tons from the Philippines, and 56 thousand tons from all

[25] Sugar Act of 1948, House Agriculture Committee *Hearings* (1947), pp. 42–4. See also Gerber (1976) for a discussion.
[26] House Agriculture Committee *Hearings* (1951), HR 4521. Extension of the Sugar Act of 1948, pp. 34–5. The 55–45 formula had been set in the 1937 Extension of the Jones–Costigan Act.

Anne O. Krueger

other foreign countries (Senate Finance Committee *Hearings* (1965), p. 19).[27]

It is perhaps significant that only one sugar consumer testified in 1948: the American Bakers' Association submitted a short letter indicating its support of a one-year extension of the Sugar Act, and urging a study of the effects of the sugar programme (House *Hearings* (1948), p. 54). This pattern was repeated whenever the programme was up for renewal in the 1950s and right up until 1973. A Sugar Users' Group had formed, and generally testified at hearings, supporting legislation and at most urging minor curtailments in the degree of restrictiveness of the bill.

The sugar programme was changed very little throughout the 1950s. Cuba's share of imports fell somewhat as other countries' production increased, but remained at 3.4 million tons in 1958, contrasted with 980 thousand tons from the Philippines and 291 thousand tons from all other foreign sources. The Sugar Act was renewed in 1951 to continue through 1956, and it was again extended in 1956 to last through 1960. The 1956 extension differed from the earlier ones in that production quotas for US producers were increased along with foreign quotas, and it was decided that quotas would thereafter be established so that American producers would maintain their share in the American market. Thereafter, market growth in excess of 8,350,000 tons was to be shared 55–45 between domestic and foreign producers.[28]

---

[27] The Philippine sugar industry was initially bolstered by the Payne Aldrich Tariff Act of 1909 which gave the Philippines the right to export 300,000 tons duty free to the United States. The duty-free allotment had then been expanded during the First World War. The Philippine production of sugar had expanded greatly in the 1930s. According to the US Tariff Commission, 'the most rapid expansion in both acreage and production occurred in the years 1932–4, when the question of Philippine independence was being debated by Congress. In as much as the several independence bills then under consideration provided for quotas on sugar to be allocated to individual mills and to planters on a production basis, there was an incentive to increase output and hence quota allotments. As a result, Philippine sugar production reached a peak of 1,509,000 short tons in 1934. Since that year it has declined because of the quota provisions of the Jones–Costigan Act and the Independence Act' (US Tariff Commission, 1937, p. 45). After the Second World War, the Philippines were again to be favoured with quotas; initially, however, it was recognized that war damages would prevent their filling their quotas and the unfilled portion was allocated to Cuba.

[28] Data are from US House of Representatives, Committee on Agriculture, *The United States Sugar Program,* 1971, p. 37. As an indication of how complex formulae can become, the 55% additional domestic production quotas were to be distributed as follows: of the first 165,000 tons of increased quota, 51.5 was to go to sugar-beet and 48.5% to mainland cane; the next 20,000 and 2,000 tons were to go to Puerto Rico and the Virgin Islands respectively, and increases in excess of 188,000 tons were to be allocated in proportion to the initial quota allotments (ibid.). For foreign

184

The political economy of controls

During the 1950s, acreages allocated to cane and sugar-beet in the United States remained relatively constant, but production increased somewhat due to rising yields. In 1950, 406,000 acres of cane and 924,000 acres of sugar-beet had been harvested with yields of 34.9 tons and 14.7 tons per acre respectively. By 1960, 406,600 acres of land were devoted to sugar-cane and 897,000 acres were devoted to sugar-beet. Yields had risen respectively to 40.0 and 18.7 tons per acre (USDA, 1985).

5. EXPANDING DOMESTIC PRODUCTION AND ACREAGE, 1960–1974

The battle over the Cuban quota

A major shift occurred after 1959, however, as American relations with Cuba soured. A first step was to amend the earlier legislation to permit the President of the United States to determine the Cuban quota for the period June 1960 to June 1962, and to permit imports from alternative sources not to exceed the amount by which the Cuban quota was reduced. Cuba's quota was thereupon reduced to zero from July 1960.

In so far as a major purpose of the sugar programme from 1948 to 1960 had been to support Cuba, one would have supposed that, at a minimum, country-specific import quotas would have been abandoned in favour of a global quota. Better yet, import quotas might have been replaced with an import duty. Even more preferable would have been a shift to deficiency payments, under which sugar producers would have received compensation to make up the 'deficiency' between a politically determined support price and the actual market price.

Certainly, the sugar producers should not have been interested in country-specific quotas: their interests lay more in increasing the share of domestic production in consumption. None the less, a major political battle over the future of government policy toward sugar then ensued. The original motives for the 1948 Act were no longer valid. Economists in the Administration and outside the government advocated the abandonment of quotas both on domestic production and on imports, and a return to free markets; if not that, at least a global quota (rather than country-specific allocations) would have made sense and was in fact finally supported by the Kennedy Administration. The domestic growers,

countries' 45% additional allocations, 43.2% was to go to Cuba, and 1.8% to other foreign countries in 1956, while in subsequent years Cuba was to receive 29.59% and 15.41% was to go to other foreign countries: the Philippines, however, were not to receive any change in quota. Meanwhile, if any domestic areas failed to fill their quotas, these should be reallocated to other domestic areas and Cuba only.

and especially beet growers, however, seized the opportunity to urge that their production quotas be increased to make up part of the Cuban shortfall, and advocated a continuation of the programme including country-specific quotas.[29]

However, interests of the refiners of raw (i.e. cane) sugar did diverge from those of growers of cane and sugar-beet, and from those of beet and cane millers: reducing the quantity of raw sugar imported and increasing domestic production would necessarily reduce economic activity for raw sugar (cane) refiners. For most of the (second-stage) refiners of cane were located primarily in coastal areas, where imports of raw Cuban sugar (once-processed cane) had once been refined. In so far as domestic beet would substitute for imported cane, new sugar-beet processing capacity would be built near beet-growing areas, and second-stage cane refiners would not receive raw cane-sugar in quantities commensurate with their capacity.

After Cuba lost her quotas, the Chairman of the House Agriculture Committee apparently wanted to reassign a large share of the Cuban quota to the Dominican Republic, at the same time as the State Department was preparing sanctions against the Dominican Republic (under Trujillo). As described by Cater:

> Quite a struggle ensued. For a period, it remained doubtful whose foreign policy would prevail – the US government's or the sugar subgovernment's. Chairman Cooley forced a temporary increase of the Dominican quota, but the US Treasury slapped a special tax on it. With the change of Administrations in 1960, Executive resources were wheeled into the battle, Attorney General Robert Kennedy made it known that he was examining the spending habits of the affluent Dominican lobbyists for evidence of 'improper' efforts at persuasion . . . At long last, Mr Cooley retreated, and soon afterward General Trujillo fell. . . . Despite President Kennedy's desire to move toward a 'global quota' purchased at nonpremium prices, the old arrangement . . . has been preserved largely intact.[30]

---

[29] It should be recalled that the early 1960s were a time of 'surplus production' of agricultural commodities under agricultural price-support programmes. This enabled advocates of expanded sugar-growing areas to argue that enactment would reduce the extent of surpluses of other commodities. For an account of the political force that determined the outcome in 1962, see Berman and Heineman (1963).

[30] Cater (1964), pp. 19–20. The 1962 Congressional Almanac commented that 'Although sugar legislation is not a partisan issue, it has touched off some major Congressional battles in recent years. In general, the Senate has supported the Administration, while the House has followed the lead of its Agriculture Committee, where sugar legislation originates.

'. . . In 1962, the Administration and the House were in accord on increasing domestic quotas, but differed sharply over the foreign quota provisions, with the Administration resisting reassignment of a portion of the reserved Cuban quota to other countries on a permanent basis, and the House supporting such reassignment

The political economy of controls

Although opposition to the bill arose both from those opposing giving something of value to foreigners and from those who wanted to protect domestic growers, the Sugar Act of 1962 none the less passed in a form which enlarged and/or extended quotas to other foreign producers but simultaneously allowed for increases in domestic production.[31] Thus, total acres of cane and beet harvested rose from 1,370,000 in 1960 to 2,065,000 in 1970.[32]

The 1962 amendments to the Sugar Act of 1948 included a provision under which there would be acreage allotments granted to yield 65,000 tons raw value of beet-sugar. Localities were to be selected without regard to earlier producing history, in accordance with the following criteria: 'firmness of capital commitment for construction of factory facilities, need for a cash crop, distance from other producing localities, suitability for sugarbeet production and accessibility to sugar markets. . .'.

157,000 acres were committed to localities in which six new beet mills would be constructed, and another 15,000 acres were allotted in areas where existing mills were thought to have additional capacity (USHR, 1971, p. 39). Over $20 million was invested in additional beet-refining capacity. The designated localities were Mendota, California (1963), Herefore, Texas (1964), Drayton, North Dakota (1965), Montezuma, New York (1965), Easton, Maine (1966), and Chandler, Arizona (1966).[33] This set of provisions appears to defy all of the models of

. . . A controversy arose over the role of lobbyists representing foreign interests, who stood to gain large fees if their clients' countries received quotas . . .' (*Congressional Quarterly Almanac*, 1962, p. 128). I am indebted to Rick Harper for calling this article to my attention.

[31] The version passed in the Senate was considerably more liberal than that passed in the House, but it was the House's version that survived the conference committee. See Berman and Heineman (1963) for an account.

[32] Almost all of this increase took place on the US mainland. Acreage planted in Hawaii rose about 200,000 acres between 1960 and 1970. However, acreage and production in Puerto Rico declined over this period, apparently due to the high costs of production relative to other US sources. It is difficult to determine the reason for Puerto Rico's apparent cost disadvantage. Sugar was grown on small farms in Puerto Rico, and it is probable that scale economies, combined with rising real wages in Puerto Rico, resulted in unprofitability of the crop. There is some discussion of Puerto Rico in the House Agriculture *Hearings* (1974) on the Sugar Act Extension of 1974, p. 293.

[33] Thirty-six Congressmen were on the House Agriculture Committee for the 87th Congress. The Chairman was from North Carolina and the Vice-Chairman from Texas. There was no Congressman from Arizona on the Committee and there were Congressmen from states with more apparent suitability for sugar-beet production than some of those mentioned above. (Committee membership included a representative from Idaho, two from Kansas, two from Iowa, and two from Oklahoma.) There were three Congressmen on the committee from cane-growing states (Hawaii, Louisiana, and Florida). See *Congressional Quarterly Almanac*, 1961, p. 48.

187

control set forth in Section 1. First, it is not obvious why it was in the interests of existing sugar producers that other areas should enter into sugar-beet production. Second, of the six mills that were constructed, only two ever reached full operation: two never started because farmers in the area did not grow enough sugar-beet and two others never reached more than 50 per cent of capacity and went out of business. Thus, even if one were to assert that six additional districts were expected to support the sugar programme in the future, there was serious miscalculation as to the economic benefits to the six areas of beet production.

Cane production and milling capacity were also expanded: during the 1960s, eight new raw-sugar mills were constructed in Florida, so that there were nine large mills in 1970 compared to three in 1960.

Clearly, expanding mainland acreage in sugar did little for existing sugar interests; indeed, second-stage refiners located on the coast and dependent on imported raw sugar were positively hurt. Likewise, maintaining country-specific import quotas did not benefit sugar producers, and cannot be explained in terms of a producer-interest model. Even more interesting is the absence of the sugar users as a vocal and organized group to oppose continuation of the programme; at a minimum, one would have expected strong opposition to further expansion of domestic production capacity. It will be argued below that the chief beneficiaries were those who had learned the intricacies of the sugar programme and that the very existence of the programme, combined with the fact that it was necessarily complex because of market pressures, resulted in a large group of specialists whose human capital would have depreciated sharply had the programme been greatly simplified or eliminated.

Administration of the programme

The Sugar Act of 1962 was renewed, with amendments, until 1974. There were difficulties in both administration and enforcement during these years. For example, sugar tended to be shipped to the United States early in the quota period, leaving US refiners with storage problems. The US Department of Agriculture therefore began restricting the amount of sugar that could be imported under quota in the first part of the year (USHR, 1971).

There was also a problem of how to keep domestic acreage within the desired limits. For some regions, including Hawaii for the entire postwar period and Puerto Rico after 1956, this was not an issue as prices were not sufficiently high to induce increased plantings. For other areas, however, the Secretary of Agriculture was to determine 'proportionate shares' to be allocated to individual farms. These shares were the fraction of a region's allotment that could be produced by the individual farm. These proportionate shares were enforced by a 'conditional payment' granted to farmers staying within their allotments, which constituted an important part of their income. Farmers could feed excess cane or beet to livestock without penalty but could not sell it to the mill; the mill, in turn, could buy it legally but had no incentive to do so because it would not have been able to market it.

This, in turn, caused difficulties in areas where it appeared there would be excess production, because each producer wanted to sell to the mill before the mill's allotment was exhausted. When this happened, 'panic selling' started. To stop this, the Secretary of Agriculture was entitled to impose marketing allotments for individual farms, indicating the proportion of each farmer's crop that could be sold to the mill.

Then, too, criteria had to be established for the allocation of foreign quotas.[34] These included:

1. The governments must be 'friendly' and maintain diplomatic relations with the United States and any country was to be ineligible for a quota which discriminated against American citizens and/or failed to indemnify for any property expropriated.
2. The country must have demonstrated 'dependability as a source of sugar supply as reflected in the country's history in supplying the US market, its maintenance of sugar inventories and its potential for supplying additional sugar upon call during critical periods of short supply' (*US Sugar Program*, p. 49).
3. A country that imported more from the United States, especially agricultural commodities, was to be more favoured.
4. 'Need of the country for a premium priced market . . . including (a) reference to the extent it shares in other premium priced markets,[35] (b) its relative dependence on sugar as a source of foreign exchange, and (c) present stage of and need for economic development' (ibid.).
5. 'Extent to which benefits of participation of this market are shared by factories and larger land owners with farmers and workers together with other socio-economic policies in the quota countries' (ibid.).
6. Location of country, including considerations of how supplies might be affected in case of emergencies.

There were also provisions for the imposition of quotas upon the importation of sugar-containing products in the event it was determined

---

[34] There were even criteria for the allocation of quota deficits, but these were complicated and varied depending on which country was in deficit with respect to its quota, and are not covered here.
[35] This was primarily a reference to sugar exports to the United Kingdom under the Commonwealth Sugar Agreement.

that these would affect the US sugar market and the implementation of the programme.[36] Ironically, administration of the programme was not more complex because sugar prices did not elicit additional production: during most of the 1960s production quotas of mainland producers failed to be filled. This is one of the many pieces of evidence that suggests that the sugar programme resulted in large resource costs and few rents over the longer run, a topic to which attention turns below.

Interest groups

Administrative complications and complexities notwithstanding, the Sugar Act continued to be approved, with amendments, until 1974.[37] Long before that, various groups interested in the sugar programme had organized themselves. As already mentioned, there was (and is) a Sugar Users' Group (consisting of bakers, soft drink bottlers, candy and confectionery manufacturers, etc.) and a Sugar Producers' Group (the growers, millers, and refiners), there were growers' associations in all the main regions, and associations of refiners (of imported raw sugar) and of beet-mill operators.

Foreign lobbyists were also important. Cater, in his Washington exposé of 1964, focused *inter alia* on the 'sugar subgovernment'. As he described it:

since the early 1930s, this agricultural commodity has been subject to a cartel arrangement sponsored by the government. By specific prescription, the sugar market is divided to the last spoonful among domestic cane and beet growers, and foreign suppliers. Ostensibly to insure 'stability' of supply, the US price is

---

[36] There was even quota-exempt sugar importation, for the following situations:
'(1) The first ten short tons, raw value, of sugar or liquid sugar imported from any foreign country, other than Cuba and the Republic of the Philippines;
'(2) the first ten short tons, raw value, of sugar or liquid sugar imported from any foreign country, other than Cuba and the Republic of the Philippines, for religious, sacramental, educational, or experimental purposes;
'(3) liquid sugar, imported from any foreign country, other than Cuba and the Republic of the Philippines, in individual sealed containers of such capacity as determined not in excess of one and one-tenth gallons each; and
'(4) any sugar or liquid sugar imported, brought in, or produced or manufactured in the United States (*a*) for livestock feed or for the production of livestock feed, or (*b*) for the distillation of alcohol (including all polyhydric alcohols), or (*c*) for the production (other than by distillation) of alcohol, including all polyhydric alcohols, but not including any alcohol or resulting by-products for human food consumption, or (*d*) for export as sugar or in sugar-containing products' (*US Sugar Program,* p. 6.4
[37] The Chairman of the House Agriculture Bill introduced one set of amendments to the bill to the House with the introductory statement that the bill was so complex that no one could understand it, and it would be necessary for Congressmen to take his word for it!

pegged at a level considerably above the competitive price in the world market. . . .
Political power within the sugar subgovernment is largely vested in the Chairman of the House Agricultural Committee who works out the schedule of quotas. It is shared by a veteran civil servant . . . who provides the necessary 'expert' advice for such a complex marketing arrangement. Further advice is provided by Washington representatives of the domestic beet and cane sugar growers, the sugar refineries, and the foreign producers. (Cater, 1964, p. 18)

Cater's reference to civil servants once again points to the importance of the technocratic element amongst the sugar interests. Heston (1975) cites the careers of many persons involved in sugar, who went from USDA to become officials of one of the producer groups. That people moved back and forth between administering the programme and lobbying for it should not be surprising: it required considerable knowledge of sugar to do either job. Persons having learned the intricacies of the programme may have had the public welfare at heart, but they had a vested interest in serving the public good through some sort of complex programme.

6. CESSATION OF THE SUGAR ACT, 1974, AND THE ERA OF NO PROGRAMME, 1974–1981

During 1973–4, the price of sugar sky-rocketed, rising from 9.61 cents per lb. on the world market in 1973 to 44.97 cents per lb. at the end of 1974, having reached a high of 57.17 cents in November of that year. The Sugar Act was up for renewal and came to a vote during the period of high prices. At that time, the US price was a little below the world price, so that the quotas to recipient countries were valueless and there was no protection to American producers. Indeed, there was discussion in the hearings as to whether it was 'reasonable' to expect Hawaiians to ship raw sugar to the mainland when they would receive a higher price in Japan. Simultaneously, consumer groups were protesting high retail sugar prices, which reached a dollar a pound at the retail level at about the time the hearings were held (see Council on Wage and Price Stability, 1975).

The National Consumer Congress testified in favour of failing to renew the Sugar Act, eliminating all quotas, and going instead to an income-support basis (deficiency payments) for sugar growers. The consumer group also advocated efforts to reach an international agreement to stabilize sugar prices (House *Hearings* (1974), p. 164).

The Department of Agriculture supported extension of the Sugar Act, but wanted to end domestic quotas and direct payments. It also requested a three-year extension (only) of the programme, with the stated intent of considering ways of bringing the sugar programme under general agricultural legislation. The Sugar Users' Group recommended a two-year extension of the programme, and advocated a wide corridor for the price targets of the Secretary of Agriculture. Simultaneously, it opposed bringing other sweeteners under the programme or controlling them in any way.[38] The National Confectioners' Association also supported extension of the bill, but advocated quotas on imports of confectionary products as an essential part of the legislation.

Thus, support still appeared strong for a sugar programme, but it was less cohesive than had earlier been the case. Cane- and beet-producers' support was somewhat less intense, in part because of the high price of sugar at that time.[39] In particular, raw-sugar refiners' support for the programme had weakened considerably, and the various producer and user groups were more divided than had earlier been the case. In addition, a consumer lobby – protesting against high prices in general but focusing to some extent on sugar – for the first time provided a source of opposition to the bill. The House Agricultural Committee passed a bill, and it was anticipated that the bill would pass both the House and the Senate. However, it was defeated on the House Floor, and the Sugar Act was not renewed.

As a consequence, sugar was without a special programme for the first time since 1948. It still fell under the general provisions applicable to agricultural commodities, however, and thus remained subject to agricultural price supports. In addition there remained a duty on imported sugar.

By the early 1970s, a technology for producing a virtually perfect substitute for sugar in liquid uses from corn (high-fructose corn syrup – HFCS) had been developed. Until the high sugar prices of 1973–4, however, it was uneconomic relative to sugar. With the high prices of 1973–4, however, HFCS came to be produced in increasing quantities and to be used instead of sugar in some commercial uses. As can be seen from Table 2, HFCS constituted less than 1 per cent of sweetener

---

[38] As will be seen below, the emergence of high-fructose corn syrup ultimately curbed the sugar programme; the sugar users were clearly aware of its implications during the 1974 hearings, as is evident from their opposition to extension of the programme. One of the many apparent puzzles confronting the analyst trying to interpret producers' advocacy as rational behaviour is why they did not attempt to control the development of sugar substitutes.

[39] In hearings on each renewal of the Sugar Act, supporter after supporter of the programme testified that one major reason to have the programme was because of price volatility in the sugar market. The failure of the producers to recognize that the 1974 price was temporary is almost incomprehensible, and it is certainly inconsistent with the proposition that they understood their own economic self-interest in the longer term.

The political economy of controls

Table 2. *Sugar and sweetener consumption: USA, 1970–1987*
(millions of tons)

	Refined sugar	HFCS	Total corn	Total sweeteners	Sugar, % of total
1970	10.43	0.07	1.98	12.57	83.0
1971	10.60	0.09	2.16	12.91	82.1
1972	10.74	0.14	2.21	13.11	81.9
1973	10.68	0.22	2.48	13.31	80.2
1974	10.22	0.32	2.68	13.03	78.4
1975	9.63	0.54	2.97	12.75	75.5
1976	10.18	0.78	3.24	13.56	75.0
1977	10.37	1.05	3.44	13.96	74.4
1978	10.18	1.35	3.75	14.10	71.4
1979	10.05	1.67	4.09	14.30	70.2
1980	9.52	2.18	4.58	14.24	64.7
1981	9.13	2.67	5.12	14.39	63.4
1982	8.56	3.10	5.60	14.31	59.8
1983	8.33	3.60	6.12	14.61	57.0
1984	8.01	4.30	6.84	15.01	53.4
1985	7.58	5.39	7.96	15.70	48.2
1986	7.37	5.53	8.12	15.66	47.0
1987	7.44	5.65	8.29	15.89	46.8

Note: Non-caloric sweeteners consumption (in sugar equivalent weight) was 0.59 million tons in 1970 and rose to 2.23 million tons by 1986.
Source: USDA, *Sugar and Sweeteners Situation*, June 1987.

consumption in 1971, but its share began rising sharply thereafter. Indeed, American sugar production peaked in 1972; thereafter, the increment in demand was met by HFCS, and later, HFCS began displacing sugar as a sweetener.

The price of sugar fell much less in real terms after its high of 1974 than it had after earlier downturns. There were repeated pressures, none the less, to reinstate the programme. By 1978, the sugar price had fallen to 7.82 cents and pressures were mounting. Another proposal for a new Sugar Act surfaced. For the first time, however, the sugar refiners testified against it. The representative of the US Cane Sugar Refiners' Association was asked whether the refiners had not earlier supported legislation. The response was: 'Yes and of course that was prior to the new HFCS technology which completely changes it. It is an entirely different ball game . . .' (Senate *Hearings*, p. 140). Simultaneously, the Sugar Users' Group advocated joining the International Sugar Association with deficiency payments to growers if the price fell out of the International Sugar Association range. This would have permitted sugar prices to industrial users and consumers to move with the international price and have supported farmers' incomes. The Sugar Users' Group further opposed quotas, and advocated fees on imports, if necessary, rather than quotas. Thus, by 1978, with the increasing competition from HFCS (see Table 2), the unanimity of interests represented by growers, processors, refiners, and users broke down completely. In these circumstances, the Administration decided to have the United States join the International Sugar Organization as its proposed assistance to domestic sugar interests.[40]

Although action was proposed repeatedly in the mid-1970s as the world price of sugar fell, no bill passed in those years. In 1978 and 1979, price supports were put into effect under general agricultural legislation, but, in the following two years, the world price of sugar (see Table 1) once again soared, rising from 9.65 cents per lb. in 1979 to 41.09 cents per lb. in October 1980, and then falling almost as precipitously to 16.32 cents per lb. by July 1981 (Terpstra, 1981, p. 4).

7. THE SUGAR PROGRAMME OF THE 1980S

It was while the price of sugar was high that a new sugar programme was passed. Unlike earlier measures, however, the sugar programme was treated as part of the overall Agriculture and Food Act of 1981, rather than as a separate piece of legislation. The new programme set domestic price support levels for the period 1982 to 1985, with an interim support level until March 1982 of 16.75 cents per lb.[41] No quotas were set on imports, as it was anticipated that the support price could be maintained

---

[40] The United States did join the International Sugar Organization, which set 13 to 23 cents per lb. raw value as its target price range. As can be seen from Table 1, the ISA was unable to prevent the price from exceeding this range during 1980 and could not prevent its fall below the target range in 1982.

[41] The Administration had not advocated a support price for sugar, but apparently accepted it in return for support for other legislation. It seems likely that the Administration did not anticipate that the world sugar price would fall so drastically or so soon. Just as the producers in 1974 failed to recognize the cyclical nature of the prevailing high prices, the Administration drastically miscalculated the future course of the sugar market after 1981. As will be evident below, less than 6 months elapsed between the passage of the bill and the decline in the price to the point where the Administration was forced to take action under the law it had itself accepted. The Senate had passed a support bill, at an initial price of 16.50 cents a lb.; the House had rejected an amendment that would have made the price 18 cents a lb. for the 1982 crop, and had then voted down the programme. But sugar price supports were passed as part of the 1981 farm programme after the particulars had been worked out in conference committee. Loans until the end of March 1982 were to be made at the rate of 16.75 cents per lb. raw basis and 19.70 cents per lb. of refined beet-sugar. The Secretary of Agriculture was instructed to set the price for the 1982 crop at a level not less than 17 cents per lb., for the 1983 crop at 17.5 cents per lb., at 17.75

The political economy of controls

by altering the tariff and fee applicable to sugar imports (which the President was authorized to do under existing legislation). It was anticipated that the purchase price would not be attractive relative to the world price, and that the domestic price could be adequately supported through import duties and fees (see Terpstra, 1981). One amendment to the bill, adopted, prohibited the financing of the sugar programme from government revenue. Thus, the Commodity Credit Corporation could not buy sugar that would not be repurchased by farmers, for it would have had to take a loss to do so.

Once the law was passed, a number of market reactions ensued. There were unusually large imports at the end of 1981 in anticipation of the higher tariffs that would be imposed (see Terpstra, 1981, p. 8). Also, by late May, the Department of Agriculture had to issue regulations that a sugar processor could not sell more to the government than the minimum he had had on hand over the preceding six-month interval. A *Washington Post* article suggested that sugar processors had deposited more sugar with the CCC than they in fact had with the intent of forcing the government to impose quotas (*Washington Post*, 6 June 1982).

As the sugar price fell on world markets, it became apparent that the Commodity Credit Corporation would end up holding some sugar that it had received from farmers in return for 'loans'. The tariff had already been increased to the maximum extent permissible by law (50 per cent of the world price). As the world price fell (see Table 1), it became evident that maintenance of the support prices mandated by the 1981 law would not be possible without CCC purchases of crops that would not be repurchased by growers unless other action was taken. Since CCC retention was inconsistent with the amendment requiring no budgetary cost from the programme, something had to be done. In May, emergency quarterly import quotas were established on a country-by-country basis to avoid a 'loss to the Treasury'.[42]

---

cents for 1984, and at 18.00 cents for 1985. Growers could get a loan at these prices from the CCC, and decide not to reclaim their produce, which in effect meant that they would repay only if the price rose above the support level. The CCC cannot sell commodities it is holding at less than 1.05 times the purchase price.

[42] One of the precipitating factors blamed by the Administration for its inability to maintain the domestic sugar price at the legally mandated level without CCC purchases was the fact that some sugar was being imported under the Generalized System of Preferences, under which some developing countries were permitted to export to the US at less than normal duty rates. Since most sugar imports came from developing countries, the GSP legislation undermined the effectiveness of the tariff. The Administration also pointed to the European Community sugar policy as a source of excess supply on the world market, and hence of the declining world price. Later on, a similar policy dilemma arose between the Caribbean Basin Initiative and sugar price supports.

This episode is perhaps the one most difficult to explain in terms of any of the political economy models discussed at the outset. First of all, the Administration should have anticipated that the sugar price would not remain at the very high levels of early to mid 1981. But, more importantly, having made that miscalculation, it was not forced to reintroduce country-specific quotas: a global quota would have sufficed! Yet here was an Administration advocating market forces, which had wanted to end the sugar programme but apparently had not had political power to do so (and had 'traded' support of sugar for support of its budget), which then reintroduced the entire, costly, apparatus of country-specific import quotas.

At that time, it was estimated that the 'cost of production' of sugar was about 21–22 cents per lb. in the United States. Production was decreasing in Hawaii and in sugar-beet-growing areas, and mills were in fact closing down. There were no production ceilings on any US source (see Terpstra, 1981, p. 10).

Import quotas were established by the Administration on the basis of average deliveries over the preceding years when entry had been free. This was done to attempt to ensure conformity with the non-discriminatory clauses of GATT pertaining to the imposition of quotas.[43]

As can be seen from the price disparities in Table 1, the divergence between American sugar prices and world prices was now so great that difficulties were bound to ensue. From the raw-sugar (cane) refiners' viewpoint, a major difficulty was that quarterly quotas prevented any futures contracts because of uncertainty as to how much would be importable, and from what source, more than three months hence. They therefore took the government before the US Court of International Trade. The Court, however, ruled in favour of the US Government, so quarterly import quotas persisted (Terpstra, 1981, p. 15).

At least six Presidential proclamations had to be issued between 1982 and 1983 to attempt to contain the side-effects. Among the more interesting were the effects on trade with Canada. Canada had no protection on sugar and imported it at world prices. Some Canadian firms at first added 6 per cent corn syrup to sugar, since anything less than 94 per cent sugar was not 'sugar' from the viewpoint of the regulations. This

---

[43] Until 1974, the US could impose quotas legally under GATT because its agricultural legislation had been in effect from GATT's initiation and had therefore been subject to 'grandfathering'. However, quotas had to be non-discriminatory to qualify when they were reimposed in 1981, as grandfathering no longer applied. When American policy toward Nicaragua shifted, the Administration eliminated the Nicaraguan sugar quota. Nicaragua sued the United States in the International Court of Law and won its case, although the United States failed to provide redress.

was then shipped to northern US points and sold to US producers of sugar-containing products. When these shipments reached 175,000 tons a year, they were banned. Then Canadian firms began producing high-sugar-content cake mixes and other products, which were exported to the United States where, once again, the sugar was extracted. Canadian firms also shipped sugar into the US as 'packets of cocoa and tins of maple syrup and in Aunt Hetty's Patent Pancake Mix' (*The Economist*, 1 June 1985, p. 31). These, too, were banned. However, other countries' exports of sweet products to the US also rose, so that by January 1985 emergency import quotas were placed on all imports of sweetened cocoa, cake mixes, and edible preparations. This latter category was filled by 5 March 1985, meaning that no Korean noodles (0.002 per cent sugar), kosher pizzas, or other products with any sugar could be imported for the remainder of the year (ibid.). Import prohibitions were put on all sugar-containing products after these, and other, responses to the price differential had been felt. Noteworthy were the protests of candy producers, after imports of confectionary products rose from 39,850 tons in 1980 to 95,553 metric tons in 1985: candy producers had been part of the Users' Group which earlier had supported the sugar programme.[44]

Data in Tables 1 to 3 tell the story thereafter. Support prices were set and import quotas established at levels designed to achieve them. However, the substitutability of HFCS was so great that sugar consumption began declining precipitously. All American soft-drink bottlers had shifted entirely to HFCS by 1985. Sugar accounted for less than half of all caloric sweetener consumption by 1985, when its price had risen to five times the world price.

By 1987, US imports had fallen to an estimated 1.48 million tons of raw sugar, down from 5 million tons as recently as 1979 and 1981. Estimates of the total cost of sugar support ranged from $800 million to $2.5 billion, depending on the estimated world price in the absence of the programme, with payments per sugar farm estimated to be $136,000. More than half of all caloric sweetener consumption was now high-fructose corn syrup, and the proportion continued to increase. Moreover, in 1987, it was announced that a technique for making crystalline dry corn sweetener had been discovered.

On existing trends, it is expected that the United States will stop importing sugar in either 1988 or 1989. As earlier mentioned, import

---

[44] See USDA, Foreign Agricultural Circular, *Sugar, Molasses and Honey*, FS 2–86, Nov. 1986, pp. 18–24, for a listing of the 113 significant proclamations, Presidential signatures, notices filed, and USDA announcements pertaining to sugar over the 1982–6 period. See also Council of Economic Advisers, *Economic Report of the President*, 1987, p. 165.

Anne O. Krueger

Table 3. *Sugar: production by area, 1950–1986 crop years*
(1,000 short tons, raw value)

| Crop year | Cane sugar | | | | Total cane | Beet sugar |
	Florida	Louisiana	Hawaii	Puerto Rico		
1950	108	456	961	1,299	2,824	2,015
1951	122	297	996	1,128	2,653	1,541
1952	154	451	1,020	1,372	2,997	1,519
1953	151	481	1,099	1,182	2,913	1,873
1954	132	478	1,077	1,204	2,891	1,999
1955	119	455	1,140	1,166	2,880	1,730
1956	129	432	1,100	1,152	2,813	1,971
1957	136	398	1,085	990	2,609	2,213
1958	136	443	1,158	934	2,278	2,214
1959	175	441	975	1,087	2,678	2,303
1960	160	470	936	1,019	2,585	2,475
1961	208	650	1,092	1,110	3,060	2,431
1962	380	472	1,120	1,009	2,981	2,595
1963	424	759	1,101	989	3,273	3,086
1964	574	573	1,179	989	3,315	3,332
1965	554	550	1,218	897	3,219	2,816
1966	652	562	1,234	883	3,331	2,853
1967	717	740	1,191	818	3,446	2,694
1968	546	669	1,232	645	3,092	3,510
1969	535	537	1,182	483	2,737	n.a.
1970	652	602	1,162	460	2,876	3,401
1971	635	571	1,230	324	2,760	3,552
1972	961	660	1,119	298	3,038	3,624
1973	824	558	1,129	255	2,804	3,200
1974	803	594	1,041	291	2,803	2,916
1975	1,061	640	1,107	303	3,237	4,019
1976	930	650	1,050	312	3,036	3,895
1977	894	668	1,034	267	2,951	3,108
1978	972	550	1,029	204	2,816	3,289
1979	1,047	500	1,060	193	2,893	2,879
1980	1,121	491	1,023	177	2,905	3,149
1981	963	712	1,048	153	2,986	3,388
1982	1,307	675	983	113	3,176	2,737
1983	1,223	603	1,044	100	2,799	2,699
1984	1,412	452	1,062	97	3,002	2,905
1985	1,413	532	2,021	109	3,109	3,000
1986	1,382	650	1,045	95	3,426	3,414

Source: USDA, *Sugar and Sweetener Situation,* Oct. 1986 and June 1987. Figures for beet-sugar, 1950–68, from *Sugar Statistics and Related Data,* Vol. 1 (revised Dec. 1969), Statistical Bulletin no. 293, USDA, Feb. 1970.

quotas for 1988 have been set at 750,000 tons, half the 1987 level. When there are no longer any imports the policy choices available to the politicians will change and their costs will rise. If sugar prices are to be maintained at their present levels, production controls will have to be instituted, stocks will have to mount, or subsidized exports will have to start. If the political process is unwilling to accept any of these three options, price supports will have to be lowered.[45]

8. THE POLITICAL ECONOMY OF THE SUGAR PROGRAMME

No case can ever prove a rule, and the sugar programme is no exception. Like everything else, sugar is unique, and its uniqueness has undoubtedly influenced the evolution of intervention in the sugar market over the years. None the less, one can ask certain questions which pertain to the various models outlined in Section 1, and venture hypotheses as to some missing ingredients.

A first step is to assess the gainers and the losers at various stages of the programme's evolution. Next, some apparent puzzles in the evolution of the sugar programme are discussed. Thereafter, the evolution of the sugar programme is assessed relative to the models of political economy outlined in Section 1. Finally, the phenomena that seem important in analysing the sugar programme, which are absent from these models, are explored.

[45] This section was first written in Dec. 1987. On 7 Jan. 1988, the *New York Times*, under the headline 'Buried in Spending Law', reported that Senator Inouye (Hawaii), with the 'backing of domestic cane and beet sugar growers', had succeeded in getting a little-noticed provision into the $600-billion spending bill to permit an additional 400,000 tons of sugar – in addition to the 750,000 quota – imports into the United States in 1988 'to offset the impact on foreign producers of drastic cuts in American sugar imports in recent years'. The additional 400,000 tons, allocated to the Caribbean and the Philippines, is to be imported at American prices, refined, and may not be sold in the United States, i.e. it must be re-exported at world prices. The 1988 omnibus spending bill further allotted $100 million to cover the financial loss under this programme, equal to 12 cents per lb. Obviously, this additional sugar will increase the capacity utilization rate in domestic sugar refineries. The *New York Times* was silent on the issue of how the additional imported cane would be allocated between refineries. It would therefore appear that the final paragraph of this section was too optimistic: a new instrument has been created under which the US can import raw sugar and re-export it, which will make it relatively straightforward to export domestic surpluses when domestic production exceeds consumption. In March 1988, Secretary of Agriculture Lyng announced that USDA would not import the 400,000 tons because it could not technically do so in a manner consistent with other laws on the books!

Anne O. Krueger

Who gained and who lost?

To a first approximation, the cost to American consumers of the sugar programme is the difference between the domestic price and the world price that would prevail in the absence of the sugar programme: about 10 cents per pound, or a total cost of about $1.5 billion in 1987. Gross income to sugar farms was about $2.06 billion in 1987. Given the costs of purchased inputs, and alternative uses of land, it seems clear that there was great scope for improved resource allocation and compensation of such producers who might have lost from an abandonment of the sugar programme.

All the available evidence suggests that most American land devoted to sugar earns no more than it would in alternative uses. The only possible exception is Hawaii, which will be discussed further below. Even with the relatively high sugar prices of recent years, there has been little expansion of acreage devoted to cane and contraction of acreage devoted to beet.

Moreover, this does not appear to be a new situation. As already mentioned, Taussig believed that there was virtually no rent accruing to land growing sugar because of the high opportunity costs, especially for beet-sugar, in terms of crops in which the United States does have a comparative advantage.[46] When Johnson assessed the system in 1974, he concluded that the sugar programme was an 'evil system, costing between $500 and $730 million, depending on whether the premium per pound was 1.5 or 2.5 cents' (Johnson, 1974, p. 50). This contrasted with gross farm income from sugar at that time of about $870 million.[47]

Johnson estimated that the average income per sugar farm in 1972 was $619,856 in Florida, $312,611 in Hawaii, $75,089 in Louisiana, and above $30,000 in all sugar-producing states except Puerto Rico, Colorado, Montana, Nebraska, Utah, Michigan, and Ohio. There were altogether 175 thousand production workers in 1971, but their average hourly earnings (both in growing and processing) were significantly below the average for persons with comparable training and skills in each state.

Johnson concluded that:

---

[46]This is especially true of beet land in the Upper Midwest where soya beans, wheat, and corn constitute highly viable alternatives.

[47]Johnson, 1974, pp. 54–55. Johnson's estimates excluded Puerto Rican- and Hawaiian-grown sugar. They were based on the assumption of a 2 cents per lb. quota premium in addition to the tariff. Taussig believed that no mainland acreage was profitable for sugar, given alternative uses, and attributed the development of sugar-cane acreage in Louisiana to American protection in the nineteenth century. See Taussig (1924), ch. IV.

the net benefits – the net increase in income going to farm-owned resources – are only a small fraction of the gross benefits. Most of the gross transfers are required because the US is a high-cost producer of sugar. Many resources are used in sugar production that would readily find employment elsewhere. . . . Much of the gross transfer is required to induce these resources to be devoted to sugar production rather than their next best alternative. (Johnson, 1974, p. 58)

Turning to analyse beet and cane separately, Johnson found no evidence that the price of sugar-beet land (near mills) was significantly different from the price of other land in beet-growing areas. He noted that: 'I must admit that these results surprised me. I had expected to find some positive effect. . . . There has been considerable political pressure to establish new sugar beet producing areas, and it seemed reasonable to assume that farmers expected to gain from these efforts' (p. 61).

Of the six new beet-processing plants established after 1962, two (New York and Maine) were 'complete failures' (because they could not obtain enough sugar-beet to operate). The acreage allotted the sugar-beets in Arizona had been only half that anticipated when the plant was built (Johnson, 1974, p. 61). Moreover, the Secretary of Agriculture had not, at that time or since, had to impose 'proportionate allotments' on any producing area since 1966.

As for cane, Puerto Rican production and acreage had been declining for a decade at the time of Johnson's analysis. For Hawaii, most benefits went to the large producers, as noted above, as 25 out of the 705 sugar farms produced 93 per cent of the sugar.[48] In addition, field-worker wages in Hawaii were double the national average and Johnson concluded that 'it is quite possible that some of the economic rent from sugar production in Hawaii has been captured by approximately 5,000 farm workers' (Johnson, 1974, p. 67).[49]

During the 1970s, more beet- and cane-processing plants went bankrupt. USDA data show 58 beet-processing factories operating in 1970, 56 operating in 1975, 43 operating in 1980, and 36 operating in 1986. There were 75 sugar mills processing cane in 1970, and the number fell to 42 by 1986.[50]

Certainly, refiners of imported raw cane-sugar lost from the sugar programme, at least starting with 1970 and the increased inroads of

---

[48] Johnson noted the disappearance of data on size of sugar farms in Hawaii from the Census of Agriculture starting in 1969 (Johnson, 1974, p. 66).

[49] Taussig (1924, ch. 5, p. 65) pointed to immigrant workers as the chief gainers in Hawaii from sugar protection, asserting that native Hawaiians, like native Americans, would not work in cane fields.

[50] See *Sugar and Sweeteners Outlook and Situation*, June 1987, Tables 19 and 20. Total sugar capacity remained approximately constant as those mills still producing were handling larger average volumes.

Anne O. Krueger

HFCS. Some went bankrupt, and the total demand for their product fell sharply as beet and sugar substitutes replaced imported raw cane-sugar. There is little reason to question Johnson's conclusions today. Indeed, subsequent bankruptcies, the failure of the industry to expand despite greater protection and higher real producer sugar prices, all suggest that most of the cost of the sugar programme was absorbed by the excess cost of production. Indeed, even the argument first put forth in 1934 – that the United States should have some domestic production capability in the event that foreign supplies were disrupted – no longer seems compelling in light of the HFCS substitution possibilities.[51]

If there were gainers in the United States, they would have been Hawaiian growers (who are low-cost relative to the mainland). But there, strong unions apparently appropriated most of the rents from higher sugar prices for the plantation workers, who therefore were the chief Hawaiian gainers. Since most workers are immigrants, they should not have a significant political voice.[52] The other identifiable gainers were, at least earlier on, the sugar exporters whose gains under quotas exceeded their losses from the lower world price. Even for them, it is questionable whether the present value of the sugar programme was positive, given that the longer-run effects were to build in a declining total demand for sugar in the United States and a gradual phase-out of American imports of sugar.

The conclusion, then, is that surely in the longer run there were few domestic economic interests that gained from the sugar programme; gains were at best short-term. Even then, it must be asked why the various lobbying groups fought hard for *expansion* of domestic American sugar acreage: increasing the number of mills in 1962 surely did not benefit existing sugar growers. Outside of Hawaii, more than half the acreage under production in 1985 was devoted to other crops as recently as 1960. It is interesting to speculate on the type of political-market model that would yield an outcome in which the chief gainers from controls had no voice in the decisions to adopt those controls.

Some puzzles

One of the fundamental assumptions of economists is that individuals are rational in their own self-interest. Even with individual rationality,

[51]And if concern had genuinely been over the adequacy of foreign supplies, one wonders why distant, landlocked Sub-Saharan African countries should have a quota.
[52]Taussig noted this same apparent anomaly – that immigrant workers were the chief beneficiaries – in his analysis of the sugar programme. At that time, he concluded that the refiners had also gained, at least temporarily, through their formation of the trust.

of course, a group does not necessarily maximize as models of the prisoners' dilemma readily demonstrate. A first question, therefore, is the extent to which individual actors acted in their own self-interest. There are two issues here. First, how well did the representatives of the various interests (cane and beet growers, cane millers, beet refiners, and raw-cane-sugar refiners) know their own interests? Second, was the understanding of economics underlying behaviour approximately correct? Answers to these questions are prerequisites to assessing existing models of political economy and providing clues as to missing elements in those models.

It has already been argued that the long-term gains to sugar producers of the sugar programme have been small indeed: reduced sugar consumption, the availability of alternative uses of the land, and other reactions have resulted in the virtual elimination of any long-term rents that might otherwise have resulted from the sugar programme.

None the less, in the same way that more alternatives are always preferable to fewer, there must have been short-run gains to those already growing sugar, or with the possibility of growing beet or cane, from the sugar programme at most points in time. Even that does not prove that the gains were maximized. Quite aside from the question as to whether pressure for other types of support might not have been more in the interests of sugar producers than the actual programme, the sugar programme could have been altered in ways which would have prevented the emergence of HFCS. For example, had the sugar programme in 1981 been established to provide deficiency payments to farmers (compensating for the difference between the price received by them and a target support price), HFCS could not have made the inroads it did on sweetener consumption.[53]

Moreover, even then, it seems apparent that many of the gains of the sugar programme prior to the 1970s did not go to American interests: many foreign countries were gainers.[54] Certainly there was considerable

---

[53] The only way to reconcile the growers' opposition to deficiency payments is to believe that obscurity was essential to the perpetuation of the programme. There is also a question as to why attempts were not made to prohibit HFCS – the European solution. This, along with other evidence, points to the role of knowledge, and of expertise, in controls. See the next subsection below.

[54] They did not gain by the full amount of the premium times their quota, of course, and some with small quotas into the American market probably lost. For most countries, sugar was sold both to the United States at premium prices and on the residual world market at much lower prices. To the (considerable) extent that the world price would have been higher in the absence of American quotas, only those sugar exporters gained whose quantity exported to the United States times the excess of the premium over the world price in the absence of US quotas exceeded the quantity they exported to the rest of the world times the amount by which the world

political opposition aroused by the activities of foreign lobbyists, especially in 1962 when they were widely blamed for having achieved the 1962 reimposition of country-specific quotas.[55] One might have thought the domestic sugar interests would have dissociated themselves from the foreign interests, yet that does not appear to have happened.

Furthermore, there are several actions that were *not* taken that would have been in the interest of the producers, if one accepts the viewpoint that the overall programme was beneficial to sugar interests.[56] To cite just a few: (i) If large Hawaiian growers really profited from the programme, one would have expected them to support a price ceiling in 1974, rather than to permit the opposition that arose to the very high (and very temporary) price of sugar to defeat the entire programme. (ii) Why did the sugar interests accede to American efforts to support the International Sugar Organization in the late 1970s rather than push for more effective action? (iii) Why in the early 1960s did the sugar interests so adamantly support country-specific quotas, when they could have bargained for a larger domestic fraction of the market with a global quota?

Then, too, there is a list of positive mistakes if one takes a narrow, short-run, self-interest model and accepts that the sugar programme did help American sugar over the short run. There seems little doubt that many of the large growers were among those most adamantly opposed to the programme in 1934, although they did change sides by 1937 (see

price was below its no-sugar-programme level. However, it was not until 1985 that any foreign representative in Washington publicly opposed the programme.

[55] See Berman and Heineman (1963). Since the focus here is on domestic economic-political interactions, many of the irrationalities involved in the allocation of foreign sugar quotas are ignored. Suffice it to note that the Dominican Republic under Trujillo was the big gainer from the 1962 legislation at a time when the Administration was attempting to impose sanctions on the regime. Berman and Heineman's comment was that 'It is not easy to find rational justification for many of the quotas that were recommended by the House Agriculture Committee and included with little change in the final legislation' (p. 425). They proceeded to cite a quota of 15,000 tons for Panama (which had produced only 5,000 tons a year) and several other countries which could not meet their quota, as well as quotas for the Netherlands and Ireland (although a separate provision of the bill prohibited imports from countries that themselves imported sugar as these latter two countries do).

[56] There is abundant evidence world-wide that protection of domestic industries tends to weaken their competitive abilities and thus render them even higher-cost and more uncompetitive in the long run than they are when protection is first introduced. It is certainly conceivable that that has happened to American sugar. While it is unarguable that some sugar land has such good alternatives that it is inherently uncompetitive at any plausible world price of sugar, it is also possible that some lands, such as the Hawaiian, might have been considerably lower-cost producers had they been subject to foreign competition. Some Hawaiian growers opposed quotas initially on the ground that it would weaken their competitive ability. See Krauss and Alexander (1965).

e.g. Krauss and Alexander, 1965, p. 336). There is also the question of why soft-drink bottlers, cake-mix manufacturers, bakers, and confectioners were so willing to support the programme. Indeed, in terms of the interest-group models of controls sketched in Section 1, the failure of the sugar users to oppose the sugar programme is perhaps the major surprise. One can only conjecture that they regarded the demand for their outputs as reasonably price-inelastic, and were therefore not overly concerned about the increased costs of their input under the sugar programme. As experience with competing imports demonstrates,[57] however, that judgement represented an underestimate of the degree of price elasticity. In addition, the support of the sugar refiners was clearly essential for the continuation of the programme and yet was obviously ruinous to them in the long run.

Finally, in the large, there have been several actions which could at best have been very short-term maximization. Given that the United States will shortly stop importing sugar altogether, and that high-fructose corn syrup and crystalline fructose corn can be expected to continue to take an increasing share of the market (along with non-caloric or low-caloric sweeteners which are better able to compete at higher sugar prices) it is interesting to ask whether the sugar programme has even been in the long-run interests of Hawaiian and other low-cost growers.

Moreover, there seems to have been no effort to bring HFCS under regulation to prevent its emergence as a substitute for sugar. Certainly if it was rational to seek a high domestic sugar price, the sugar producers should have sought a ban on high-fructose corn syrup, or if not that, at least a system of deficiency payments rather than price-raising measures. The declining consumption of sugar in the United States and the increasingly competitive position of corn substitutes were clearly not consistent with the longer-term interests of sugar producers, and even less so of refiners. Had sugar growers and refiners been willing to accept a deficiency payment programme in the late 1960s (so that payments to growers would compensate for any divergence between the world price-plus-margins and the domestic support price), much of the HCFS competition would have been avoided.[58]

---

[57] The explanation that belief in price inelasticity accounts for the failure of sugar users to oppose the programme is somewhat less plausible, however, in that testimony before the Council on Wage and Price Stability (1975) indicated that a number of bakers had gone bankrupt in 1973–4 due to the high price of sugar.

[58] The representatives of the corn refiners were at pains to assure Congress that their costs were high, and that 'sugar is still the standard of the sweetener industry'(testimony of Donald E. Nurdlund, Chairman of A. E. Staley Manufacturing Co., representing the corn producers, in House *Hearings* (1978), p. 138).

Anne O. Krueger

At present, the corn producers strongly oppose any switch to deficiency payments on the grounds that they would provide 'unfair competition' to corn in the sweetener market. Indeed, Congressional representatives from corn-producing states now appear to be the strongest supporters of the sugar programme, including import quotas. Whether that support group would have developed had sugar producers correctly estimated the potential competition from corn is an open question. Certainly, to the extent that corn producers are the gainers from the sugar programme, there is no evidence of their apparent support for the programme prior to the 1970s.

The apparent reason for the sugar growers' opposition to deficiency payments seems to have been their concern that a ceiling would be placed on the size of the payment that might be made to any individual farm. This suggests that growers were sensitive to the degree to which benefits were to larger farmers, but it does not indicate why refiners and processers were willing to support import and production quotas. It is not clear whether sensitivity resulted from the concern that, if the size of payments became known, the entire programme would be halted, or whether instead the desire was to protect payments to large growers.[59]

Even beyond that, however, there lies the question – alluded to by Johnson – as to why in the early 1960s it was anticipated that there would be great benefits to expanded beet-sugar production. These do not seem to have been forthcoming, and the evidence strongly suggests that such an expansion was not in the interests of existing producers and did not significantly benefit those in areas where new beet-sugar mills were established.

If one is to believe statements from representatives of the sugar interests, sugar producers have not been happy with the programme. According to *The Economist* after the 1985 bill was passed: 'It might be supposed that the sugar-growers, at least, would be happy with the absurd press for regulations. They are not. They get a government subsidy of 17 cents a pound, but say it costs them 20 cents to produce one. Acreage under sugar cane in Florida, Louisiana and Hawaii, or under sugar beet in the Midwest, continues to contract' (*The Economist*, 1 June 1985, p. 31 of American Survey).

---

[59] For an amusing sidelight to the story, see the testimony of Helen Rohrbach, Head, Quota Section, Special Operations Branch, Office of Operations, US Customs Service. This branch is (or at least was in 1974) in charge of administering all import quotas. Ms Rohrbach explained why her branch could not administer import quotas (which were set in raw value terms) as then currently laid down. Congressman Vigorito, who presided at the hearings, thanked her for her testimony with the statement: 'You have brought to my attention a small group in Customs that I did not know existed . . .' 1974 *Hearings*, p. 97).

The political economy of controls

There is then the curious episode with the International Sugar Association: the ISA could not contain the price of sugar even within a very wide band. In part this was because the EC did not join. However, it is difficult to imagine that, even with EC participation, the target range could have been maintained without resources considerably in excess of those available to the ISA. It is difficult to believe that the ISA was expected to be effective in stabilizing the sugar price: why, then, was support for ISA membership taken as an acceptable substitute by the sugar producers for a sugar programme?

Next, there is an interesting question as to why some arguments are convincing, or are thought convincing, in the political arena. Virtually all witnesses to Congressional hearings on the sugar programme listed as one of its major virtues the fact that 'it costs the taxpayer nothing.'[60]

A second oft-repeated argument pertained to the alleged instability of the international sugar market and the 'need' for price stability for producers. This argument first appeared in Roosevelt's message to Congress in 1934, and was reiterated by almost all witnesses supporting the Sugar Program. Yet the programme was neither designed for 'stability' (since there was no price ceiling) nor were there efforts to set a 'band' within which the price might fluctuate. Whether it was thought that appeals for 'stability' were more convincing than appeals for support prices is open to conjecture, but the inconsistency of rhetoric pertaining to stability with the appeals for higher prices strikes one on even the most casual perusal of Congressional testimony.

Although a large number of other puzzles could be pointed to, it suffices to mention one more: surely in 1974 and again in 1981, it should have been understood that the prevailing price of sugar would not continue indefinitely. Even without any degree of sophisticated understanding of the sugar market domestically and internationally, all testimony before both Houses of Congress had for years emphasized the wide fluctuations in sugar prices as a reason for controls. Yet the Reagan Administration apparently believed that it had a sugar programme which would not require a return to the country-specific quotas that had earlier prevailed.

---

[60] See e.g. the statement contained in the House Agriculture Committee pamphlet on the US Sugar Program (1971): 'The Sugar Act has given us this security of supplies at a reasonable cost to the consumer and at no cost to the taxpayer' (p. 45). Note, however, that the decision to permit the import and re-export of 400,000 tons of sugar in the omnibus spending bill passed by Congress in Dec. 1987 invalidates this argument because there will be a cost to taxpayers, and of course it sets a precedent for subsidies to support exports in future years.

Anne O. Krueger

Conformity with models of political economy

Without doubt, the saga of the American sugar programme over the 1934–87 period contains elements of a number of the models discussed in Section 1. In this section, the 'goodness of fit' of each model is considered in turn.

The 'benevolent guardian' of the public good theory of governmental behaviour seems to conform reasonably well to the motives of the Roosevelt Administration in 1934, and of the Reagan Administration in 1981 in its efforts to bring sugar into general agricultural programmes.

Other than that, however, there is very little of the 'benevolent guardian, social-welfare-maximizing' government in the story, and that model fails to account for the evolution of the programme, and especially for the 1960–2 period, and the resumption of country-specific quotas in 1981.

Turning then to interest-group models, there is no doubt that lobbying groups emerged as a result of the sugar programme. However, the Brock–Magee model fails in that the politicians supporting the sugar programme were from sugar states and, by and large, appear to have gained votes as a consequence of their attainment of the sugar programme. Clearly lobbying was important, as the various components of the sugar industry sought to increase the benefits they perceived as emanating from the bill and foreign lobbyists did the same thing for their clients. Perhaps the Brock–Magee approach suggests that those politicians *not* from sugar-producing regions might have lost votes had the sugar programme become even more costly, but in light of what happened, it is difficult to believe that sugar prices could have been supported at very much higher levels than they in fact were.

An interesting point to note with respect to lobbying models, however, is that they do not fit Olson's prediction that interest groups would form when the group on the opposite side of the market consists of relatively small and fragmented entities. Sugar users were at least as large as sugar producers and none the less joined in the coalition. One would not have forecast the coalition of interests that did emerge because their interests were, at least from an economist's viewpoint, antagonistic. There was ultimately a significant conflict between the interests of domestic and foreign growers, between domestic growers and refiners, and between domestic producers and domestic industrial users. The latter were large, which is not normally anticipated in discussions of lobbying.[61] The

---

[61] There is no doubt that Americans owned some sources of foreign supply. This was especially true in the 1930s. However, even then, only about a third of Cuban sugar was produced under American ownership. For the Philippines, the fraction did

puzzle here is thrown in even sharper relief when it is asked why sugar growers, millers, refiners, and users were all on the same side of the issue when there were clearly some divergent interests among them.

Lobbying, at least by domestic growers, was *not* significant in the inauguration of the sugar programme, however. Growers seem actively to have opposed it initially, and it is certain they did not lobby for it. In that respect, the Bhagwati–Srinivasan revenue-seeking model, in which resources are spent in an effort to obtain a programme of value, does not seem appropriate for the initiation of the sugar programme. Once the programme was in place, however, domestic sugar growers rallied to its support. Likewise, corn producers did not support the programme until after HFCS had become an important sugar substitute: had revenue-seeking taken place, corn producers would have supported the programme sooner.

The conservative social welfare function argument – that the political process attempts to protect incomes of those losing out for whatever reason – reasonably well fits the motive for introduction of the sugar programme in 1934; it does not explain its reintroduction in 1948, its continuation of country-specific quotas after 1960, nor the evolution of the programme thereafter. Certainly, the effort to increase mainland acreage after 1960 was not an effort to protect sugar growers.

The Stigler–Peltzman–Becker view of the political-economic process certainly has elements of truth in it once the sugar programme had been established. Sugar growers must have believed that the programme increased their incomes, and used the political process to attempt to effect a transfer. However, the Stigler–Peltzman–Becker view does not help in explaining the inauguration of the programme in 1934, its reintroduction in 1981, nor why import quotas (and country-specific ones at that) were the instrument of choice, rather than tariffs. Were wealth redistribution among Americans the dominant political logic, foreign governments would not have been the beneficiaries of the sugar premiums.

Ingredients for a fuller model of the political economy of controls

There is no doubt that economic interests and lobbying go part way toward explaining the sugar programme. There are missing elements,

not reach that level until after Philippine preferences were in place, and the mechanism seems to have worked the other way round: the American preference induced American firms to start producing in the Philippines. See US Tariff Commission (1937).

Anne O. Krueger

however, to which attention now turns. First, it is apparent that institutional mechanisms were necessary in order to facilitate the continuation of the programme, and that alternative arrangements might have reduced the economic costs of the programme, even if they would not have eliminated it. Second, it is clear that markets reacted to the various shifts and turns in policy in ways which neither politicians nor sugar interests anticipated. In this sense, there never was 'the' sugar programme; rather, policies evolved over time as politicians reacted to market responses (and exogenous events) and markets reacted to the changes in policy. Finally, any reading of the evolution of sugar policies over time suggests that a number of key issues surrounding transparency, knowledge, and the role of technocrats must be addressed.

Institutional issues. Several institutional issues are noteworthy. First, there is the anomaly (for the American Congress) that sugar legislation was handled by the Senate Finance Committee (because it is an import) and the House Agriculture Committee (by historical accident). Moreover, because it was an import and thus had revenue implications, only the House had the power to initiate legislation. This gave the House Agriculture Committee considerably more power over sugar than it would have had had the counterpart body been the Senate Agriculture Committee, and the House Agriculture Committee had considerably more ability to focus its attention on sugar than would the House Ways and Means Committee.[62]

Second, the sugar programme could not have persisted in anything like the form that it did had sugar not been an import. At a minimum, there would have been a budgetary cost to any programme which raised price. As mentioned above, the 'lack of budgetary cost' was frequently mentioned as an important point by advocates of the programme. Had there needed to be an explicit vote of funds to support the programme, it is evident that political opposition would have increased, as evidenced by the amendment in 1981 which prohibited budgetary expenditures in support of sugar prices. The fact that 'no cost to the government' was so frequently used in testimony before Congress suggests that the argument was appealing.

Likewise, because sugar was an import, the programme provided instruments of foreign policy (the sugar quotas) which would otherwise

[62] Had the House Ways and Means Committee handled the legislation, its attention would have been spread over other issues with the result that it could not have devoted as much time to it as did the House Agriculture Committee. Moreover, membership on the House Ways and Means Committee would have been determined with respect to many more issues and thus could not have been as specialized as was the House Agriculture Committee. For a discussion of these issues, see Price (1971).

The political economy of controls

not have been present. Moreover, had sugar not been an import, it would have been dealt with together with other agricultural commodities: the ability of sugar interests to influence the outcome (for better or worse in their own self-interest) would have been less as other interests would have competed for scarce resources.[63]

Indeed, it is arguable that it was the ability of the sugar interests to distance themselves from other elements of a political situation that was crucial to the continuation of the programme: it was an import, and therefore came before the Senate Finance Committee and was not dealt with as part of other agricultural legislation. While an import, it was agricultural and thus not dealt with in other trade legislation along with other importable commodities.

Third, it took the agreement of all producing interests – beet growers, cane growers, beet refiners, cane millers, and cane refiners – to ensure the continuation of the programme. Indeed, until the mid-1970s, what is remarkable is that the Sugar Users' Group did not oppose the programme. Why they failed to do so is one of the mysteries of the Sugar Program – one can only conjecture that either they believed that an increased input price did not affect them or they believed they were unable to influence the outcome significantly. As already seen, the first possibility seems less than plausible in light of testimony about bankruptcies resulting from high sugar prices, while the latter was manifestly wrong, as all observers believed, and stated, that all parties had to agree to perpetuate the programme.

Fourth, the fact that the interrelationships were complex undoubtedly increased the political influence of those who did understand the economics and politics of the sugar programme: in a sense, the complexity of the issues stood as a barrier to entry of non-specialists.

Interaction of economic and political markets. Examination of the history of the sugar programme strongly suggests that, once created, a policy instrument will: (a) be seized upon by groups who perceive themselves to benefit (regardless of whether they had anything to do with initiating the programme or not); (b) induce economic market reactions which will minimize the costs of the programme; (c) lead to political responses to (b) by the groups formed under (a) to attempt to offset these economic market reactions, which in turn will lead to (d) increasingly complex policy instruments designed both to deal with the compet-

---

[63] The above paragraph was written prior to the passage of the 1987 omnibus spending bill. That bill sets a precedent for expenditures on supporting sugar prices that may ease the way for subsidy payments when sugar is no longer imported. Even so, one might guess that pressures against sugar will mount when the programme has to be financed from the budget.

ing interest groups that form around the policy instrument and simultaneously to subvert the sorts of market responses perceived to be detrimental.

This sequence, which as articulated sounds very straightforward, is perhaps the most obvious, but also the most complex, of conclusions. For it suggests that, once an instrument is in place, a variety of political forces will emerge that will act upon it and try to seize it in ways that are largely unpredictable. In the case of the US Sugar Program, the instrument was initially opposed by the sugar producers, but they very quickly reversed their position and supported its continuation. Likewise, the sugar-exporting countries strongly supported the programme until the mid-1980s, and then reversed their position in response to the market forces set in motion by the price support programme.

Ironically in 1948 it was a perceived obligation to Cuba, rather than any motivation of domestic producers, that led to the reinstatement of the programme. During the years 1948 to 1960, Congressmen dealing with the sugar programme were regarded virtually as foreign agents – their interests appear to have been primarily in allocating import quotas rather than benefiting domestic interests.

There are two interesting mental experiments that can be performed: (i) what would have happened had the Cuban Government not changed, and (ii) what would have happened if there had been no sugar programme prior to 1960 when the Cuban Government changed? In answer to the first, the most reasonable conjecture would appear to be that the US Sugar Program would have continued, much as before, and that there never would have been the expansion of beet acreage and high-cost (and possibly even ill-advised on the part of those who undertook them) expansions of beet-refining capacity that characterized the 1960s. It is hard to imagine the impetus that would have been necessary to increase substantially American acreage at the expense of imports.

With regard to the second question, had there been no sugar programme in 1960 the most likely outcome is that the United States would have continued buying sugar on world markets. It is difficult to imagine a sequence of events under which a changed Cuban Government could have been seized upon as a rationale for the inauguration of a Sugar Program.

In so far as these conjectures are plausible, they strongly suggest that it is much easier to adapt, or seize, an already-existing instrument, than it is to have a new one created. For that reason alone, an existing instrument is very likely to become used for objectives and by groups that may not have been the intended beneficiaries at all when the instrument was first formed.

The political economy of controls

There is then the question of market reaction. Clearly, the market will minimize the cost of any given policy-imposed distortion. In the case of sugar, this entailed two important reactions and several minor ones. The first important reaction was the shift in the location of production (with expansion of Florida land and reduction in beet land). The second was the development of substitutes and, with it, the potential disappearance of sugar as an importable good: that will make the Sugar Program, in its present form (with a legislated mandate to avoid any payments by the US government), infeasible. In the absence of a legal ban on development of all substitutes, it is difficult to see how the political process can further increase the real price of sugar, especially as and if crystalline corn sugar becomes economic. In the longer term, this market reaction to the sugar programme may result in the closure of the entire sugar industry in the United States – thereby doing the very thing that many supporters of the Sugar Program claimed they were trying to avoid.[64]

The minor reactions include: the importation of soft drinks, cake mixes, and other sugar-containing products from Canada and elsewhere; the need for detailed regulation of imports to avoid storage costs for American refiners; the seizure of the programme by sugar refiners as a basis on which to press for a ban on imported raw sugar or of refined beet-sugar; and the diplomatic and other complications arising out of establishing and implementing import quotas for a large number of countries. An interesting reaction, difficult to classify, has been the increased volatility of the international sugar price in response to the smaller and smaller volume of transactions going through the 'free market' (which would more appropriately be termed the 'residual' market).

These market reactions in turn have induced: political responses; bans on imports of cake mixes, and then of processed food products containing sugar; movement from annual to quarterly import quotas; reactions to the high sugar price of the early 1970s (which itself was arguably the outcome of the earlier decision to increase domestic production,

---

[64] HFCS was discovered in the 1960s, but was uneconomic to produce. Estimates are that it was economic at around 14 cents per lb. in the early 1980s, contrasted with a then-estimated world price of sugar of 12 cents per lb. if the US adopted free trade. Once established, of course, HFCS processors were likely to continue producing at a price somewhat below that which induced them to build capacity. Given that cost estimates for US sugar are well in excess of 20 cents per lb. from almost all sources, it seems likely that HFCS can compete for the entire liquid-sugar market. If crystalline corn becomes economic, as is said to be the case, it does not seem possible further to increase the producer price of sugar over the longer term except through direct subsidies (deficiency payments?) to producers. As already stated, the representatives of the corn growers vehemently oppose such a shift in the nature of the programme.

which depressed the world price, leading to amplified fluctuations in plantings and in sugar price cycles) which led to the (temporary) abandonment of the programme, and so on.

In a sense, this 'life of its own' hypothesis is the most disturbing for potential economist-policymakers. If the hypothesis is correct, it says that even if a programme is designed to meet socially desirable objectives in cost-minimizing ways, it will likely be seized upon by groups and in circumstances only remotely related to the initial intent of the programme. Once put in place, a policy may evolve in ways unrelated to the initial purpose.[65]

Role of knowledge and technocrats. Partly because of the interaction of economic and political markets, any ongoing programme is likely to become very complex. While sugar may be especially so, it is at least arguable that price supports, production controls, or deficiency payments to other agricultural commodities, imports subject to quota, health regulations, and most other policy instruments inevitably become highly complex. One important consequence is that a coterie of specialists is called for whose human capital consists of their understanding of the programme, and one hopes, of the economic implications of alternative changes in policies.[66]

Complexity in and of itself provides a significant barrier to participation of non-specialist groups in the decision process. In the case of sugar legislation, it seems evident that there were several efforts to resist changes that might have made the programme more transparent: sugar producers opposed deficiency payments (until it was too late) probably because the size of payment per farm would have been apparent and they feared a ceiling; import quotas were country-specific, rather than global, and there was opposition to any change; import quotas, rather than tariffs, were the chosen instrument for protection; raw-sugar refin-

---

[65] One needs only to point to the complexity of American income tax laws (even after reform) and of the Multi Fibre Arrangement to convince oneself that the phenomenon is not limited to the sugar case.

[66] One indication of the ways in which these interests grow is to examine the length of hearings and the number of witnesses who appeared before the House Agriculture Committee each time the Sugar Act was under consideration. The 1934 *Hearings* were 251 pages long with 33 witnesses; in 1937 *Hearings* were 373 pages long with 47 witnesses. In 1940 *Hearings* were 302 pages with 40 witnesses; the 1948 *Hearings* were short, with 114 pages and 10 witnesses; 1951 *Hearings* were 323 pages with 46 witnesses and submissions; 1955 *Hearings* were 768 pages with 136 witnesses and submissions; 1962 *Hearings* were 552 pages with 81 witnesses and submissions; 1965 *Hearings* were 365 pages with 74 witnesses and submissions; 1971 *Hearings* were 789 pages with 132 witnesses and submissions. Even this understates the increase, as coalitions of supporters (such as the Sugar Users' Group and the Sugar Producers' Group) formed.

ers supported the programme and sought prohibition of imports rather than seeking protection from foreign refiners; and corn producers were adamant in wanting sugar prices supported rather than seeking higher support prices and deficiency payments for corn growers directly.

In addition, however, the specialists in a given policy instrument become a vested interest in the maintenance of *some* policy.[67] Those with understanding of the US Sugar Program could seek employment as lobbyists for foreign governments, or as representatives of domestic groups, as Congressional staff assistants, or with the Department of Agriculture. For any non-specialist to enter the policy dialogue in a meaningful way would require a considerable investment.

All of these phenomena suggest that public discussion of policy options might be significantly improved if means could be found to keep policies transparent and simple. The opposition to deficiency payments and other transparent procedures was surely based at least in part on the belief that they would not have withstood careful scrutiny. Whether means can be found in complex markets of limiting the types of interventions that are permitted is a difficult subject, and one well beyond the scope of this chapter. None the less, it seems highly likely that, had the Sugar Program been transparent and readily comprehensible to an informed citizenry, it could not have persisted in anything like the form it did.

9. SOME TENTATIVE CONCLUSIONS

No case-study can provide the generalizations desirable to form a basis for a theory of political-economic interactions. The US Sugar Program is, none the less, interesting in that it raises some questions that are not readily handled with the use of traditional models. Its evolution demonstrates that a static analysis of the costs and benefits of the programme at a point in time would significantly misstate the programme's impact: clearly account must be taken of the ways in which economic and political responses will alter the programme over time. It is to be hoped that future research will enable the transformation of some of the questions raised here into testable hypotheses.

Several questions clearly call for further research. Among them: (i) To what extent are the economic outcomes of policies reasonably correctly anticipated and to what extent do side-effects render the outcomes unac-

---

[67] It might be argued that they would prefer some changes because that generates more work, but that issue is secondary. The hypothesis here is that the loss of human capital that would be involved in the complete abandonment of a programme is probably so large as to induce specialists to advocate more rational programmes, rather than programme abandonment.

ceptable to the policies' advocates? (ii) Can one find meaningful charac-
terizations of the logic of interaction between political and economic
markets? (iii) Can one classify policy instruments according to criteria
(such as transparency) and then make meaningful predictions as to,
for example, the likely excess cost of policies pursued with each of
these instruments?

At this stage, the conclusions that emerge arise primarily with regard
to the sugar programme itself. First, when it was originally formulated
in 1934, and then when it was reinstated in 1948, the intentions of its
advocates bore little resemblance to the purposes to which it was put
some 20 or 30 years later. Second, it seems highly unlikely that the
electorate would support a programme that provides payments of over
$136,000 per farm were that figure highly publicized. Third, at least
some of the supporters of the sugar programme over the years – the
importers and refiners of raw sugar and the beet-mill owners who went
bankrupt at the very least – would not have been so enthusiastic had
they known the outcome.

At a more general level, two tentative lessons emerge. First, at the very
least, economists advocating government intervention in markets would
be well advised to recognize that the measures they advocate will, once
enacted, have lives – including supporters – of their own. Second, in
choosing between alternative policy instruments, there should be a
strong presumption in favour of simple, transparent instruments: the
likelihood that those instruments can be seized in ways unacceptable to
a comprehending electorate would be reduced.

REFERENCES

Becker, Gary S. (1983), 'A Theory of Competition among Pressure Groups
for Political Influence', *Quarterly Journal of Economics*, 98 (Aug.), pp.
371–400.
Berman, Daniel M., and Heineman, Robert A. (1963), 'Lobbying by Foreign
Governments on the Sugar Act Amendments of 1962', *Law and Contempo-
rary Problems*, 28/2, pp. 416–27.
Bhagwati, Jagdish, and Srinivasan, T. N. (1980), 'Revenue Seeking: A General-
ization of the Theory of Tariffs', *Journal of Political Economy*, 88/6, pp.
1069–87.
Borrell, Brent, Sturgiss, Robert, and Wong, Gordon (1987), 'U.S. Sugar Policy –
Its Effects on the World Sugar Market', paper presented at International
Sweetener Colloquium, California, Feb. 1987.
Brock, W. A., and Magee, S. P. (1978), 'The Economics of Special Interest
Politics: The Case of Tariffs', *American Economic Review*, 68, pp. 246–50.
Buchanan, James M. (1987), 'The Constitution of Economic Policy', *American
Economic Review*, 77 (June), pp. 243–50.

The political economy of controls

Cameron, Laurie A., and Berg, Gerald C. (undated), 'The U.S. Sugar Program, An Historical Overview', mimeo.

Campos, José Edgardo L. (1987), 'A Simple Political Economy Model of Price Supports', Ph.D. dissertation, California Institute of Technology.

Cater, Douglass (1964), Power in Washington (New York: Random House).

Congressional Quarterly Almanac (1962), 'Congress Again Revises Sugar Quotas', CQ Almanac, pp. 127–30.

Congressional Research Service (1985), 'World Sugar Trade and US Sugar Policy', Report no. 85–144, ENR, 12 July.

Corden, W. M. (1974), Trade Policy and Economic Welfare (Oxford: OUP).

Council on Wage and Price Stability (1975), Staff Report on Sugar Prices (May).

Ferguson, Allen R. (undated), 'The Sugar Price Support Program', mimeo.

General Accounting Office (1984), 'US Sweetener/Sugar Issues and Concerns', GAD/RCED 85–19, 15 Nov.

Gerber, David J. (1976), 'The United States Sugar Program: A Study in the Direct Congressional Control of Imports', Journal of Law and Economics, 19/1, pp. 103–47.

Harris, Simon (1985), 'Protectionism in the World Sugar Economy Revisited' (São Paulo), mimeo.

Heston, Thomas J. (1975), 'Sweet Subsidy: The Economic and Diplomatic Effects of the US Sugar Acts – 1934 to 1974', Ph.D. dissertation, Case Western Reserve University, 1975.

Ickes, Harold I. (1953), The Secret Diary of Harold I. Ickes, Vol. 1: The First Thousand Days (New York: Simon & Schuster).

Johnson, D. Gale (1974), The Sugar Program (American Enterprise Institute).

Krauss, Bob, and Alexander, William P. (1965), Grove Farm Plantation: The Biography of a Hawaiian Sugar Plantation (Palo Alto: Pacific Books).

Leu, Gwo-Jiun Mike, and Knutson, Ronald D. (1987), 'U.S. Sugar Policy: Costs, Benefits, Consequences', Paper presented at Western Economic Association, July.

Maskus, Keith E. (1987), 'The International Political Economy of U.S. Sugar Policy in the 1980s', US Department of State, Bureau of Economic and Business Affairs, Planning and Economic Analysis Staff, WP/87/1.

Mueller, Dennis C. (1983), The Political Economy of Growth (New Haven: Yale Univ. Press).

Olson, Mancur (1965), The Logic of Collective Action (Cambridge, Mass.: Harvard Univ. Press).

(1982), The Rise and Decline of Nations: Economic Growth, Stagflation, and Social Rigidities (New Haven: Yale Univ. Press).

Peltzman, Sam (1976), 'Toward a More General Theory of Regulation', Journal of Law and Economics, 19, pp. 211–40.

Price, David E. (1971). 'The Politics of Sugar', Review of Politics, 33 (April), pp. 212–231.

Snape, Richard H. (1963), 'Some Effects of Protection in the World Sugar Industry', Economica, 30 (Feb.), pp. 63–73.

Stigler, George J. (1971), 'The Theory of Economic Regulation', Bell's Journal of Economics and Management Science (Spring), pp. 3–21.

Tan, C. Suan (1986), Cuba–USSR Sugar Trade, Commodity Studies and Projections Division, World Bank, Division Working Paper no. 1986–2 (Washington, DC: World Bank).

Anne O. Krueger

Tarr, David G., and Morkre, Morris E. (1984), *Aggregate Costs to the United States of Tariffs and Quotas on Imports*, Federal Trade Commission (Dec.).

Taussig, Frank William (1924), *Some Aspects of the Tariff Question* (Cambridge, Mass.: Harvard Univ. Press).

(1931), *A Tariff History of the United States* (New York and London: Putnam & Sons).

Terpstra, A. Ellen (1981), 'U.S. Sugar Policy and Proposals Since 1974', Congressional Research Service, HD 9100 (July).

USDA (1985), 'Background to 1985 Sugar Legislation', Economic Research Service (US Dept. of Agriculture).

USHR (1974), Subcommittee on Domestic Marketing and Consumer Relations of the Committee on Agriculture, *Examination of Sugar Marketing Conditions Since Defeat of Sugar Bill*, 9, 10, 11, 12, and 19 Dec. 1974. Serial 93–XXX. Referenced as Sugar Marketing Hearings, 1974 (US House of Representatives).

USHR (various dates), Committee on Agriculture, Hearings on Sugar Program, cited as House *Hearings*, with date indicated (US House of Representatives).

US Tariff Commission (1937), *United States–Philippine Trade*, Report no. 118, 2nd Series (US Government Printing Office).

6

Price controls, property rights, and institutional change

RESTRICTING THE PRICE MECHANISM

Price control changes the structure of property rights and has complex economic consequences that often are unforeseen by economic actors. In a free market, before controls are instituted, prices allocate scarce resources among competing individuals according to the willingness and ability to pay. The question of who gets what is settled on the basis of individual preferences and purchasing power. However, the use of prices to ration the rights to scarce resources frequently conflicts with the self-interest or ideologies of economic and political actors, who may seek to restrict or even abolish the price mechanism, at least in specific areas. The suspension of the price mechanism calls for some alternative method of rationing, such as direct assignment by the state, rationing by waiting, lottery, fistfights, or warfare. The alternative system of rationing can also be based on social norms and custom – which usually is the case, for example, within the family.

It is important to realize that the system used to ration economic resources affects not only the distribution of wealth in a community but also the overall level of wealth. The behavior of investors and producers is influenced by the methods used to reward them and their degree of control over inputs and outputs in production and so is also the supply of goods and services.

The authorities may interfere with the price mechanism either by subsidizing or restricting the demand and/or the supply of commodities or by directly controlling prices. The following essay by Steven Cheung is concerned with the institutional economics of government price controls – the fixing of legitimate prices below market prices.

Price controls, property rights, institutional change

THE MANY CAUSES OF NONEXCLUSIVITY

Consider the case of an apartment in a big city that would rent for $1,000 a month in the absence of rent control, but that the city council allows the landlord to rent for no more than $300.

If the authorities took no measures other than introducing a price ceiling, a value equal to $700 would, in the short run, be left in the public domain. As secure control of the $700 has not been assigned to any particular party, we can also refer to the sum as *nonexclusive income*. Nonexclusivity gives rise to competition among actors to acquire the values in question, and the race for possession uses up scarce resources. The amount that an actor decides to invest in such a race depends on the value to her of the nonexclusive asset. The dissipation of nonexclusive income or resources is not restricted to cases when regulation is used to suppress market price; it is a universal phenomenon. For instance, when the ownership of fishing grounds is nonexclusive, competition among fishermen usually dissipates the resource rent. Similarly, when all seats in a theater are sold at the same price, waiting and other forms of nonprice competition dissipate the unpriced value of the best seats.

It is clear that nonexclusivity can emerge for several reasons. When a profit-oriented firm sets one price for all the seats in its theater, it is likely that the cost of enforcing exclusive rights to premium seats may exceed the benefits to customers. The pricing policy is therefore efficient in the usual sense of economic theory. Nonexclusivity in a fishery may reflect the cost of establishing exclusive rights, special interests, ideologies, or perverse outcomes of the political process.

Efficient deviations from the price mechanism, found even in a highly developed market system, are due to the cost of using the price mechanism, as Coase observed.[1] Often it does not pay to measure and price separately all valuable margins of a complex commodity. Some form of average pricing is frequently the rule, and resources are dissipated in the search for unpriced values.[2]

THE EXAMPLE OF RENT CONTROL

In a landmark paper on the theory of price control, Cheung argued that

(a) Effective price control leaves resources in the public domain, unless alternative institutions either exist or are created to establish clear and secure ownership of the unpriced values.

[1] Ronald H. Coase, "The Nature of the Firm," *Economica* 4 (1937), 386–405.
[2] For an elaboration of these issues, see Yoram Barzel, *Economic Analysis of Property Rights* (Cambridge University Press, 1989).

(b) The use of government regulations to establish clear and secure ownership over these unpriced values (non-exclusive income) is a difficult and costly task, because economic actors frequently undermine the effectiveness of the regulations by making adjustments on any of several margins.

(c) In their competition to possess unpriced values, actors use scarce resources in a non-productive way: they dissipate non-exclusive income.

(d) Under price control, it is in the self-interest of economic actors to find arrangements that minimize the dissipation of non-exclusive income.[3]

We now briefly discuss rent control in the residential housing market to illustrate these issues. Let us assume that the authorities intend to use rent control to transfer wealth from landlords to tenants. If rent control is not effectively supported by additional measures, the attempt is likely to be futile. Setting the rent below the market rate creates shortages in the housing market and encourages competition among tenants, who inevitably will find ways to supplement their rental payments with clandestine transfers to their landlords. High transaction costs make it impractical for the authorities to enforce a ban against such payments.

Next consider a situation in which the authorities both impose rent controls and allocate the unpriced values directly to specific individual tenants, for instance in a lottery. Such a joint measure would strengthen the tenants' rights, but the rights are still insecure unless additional measures are taken. The tenants must be protected against harassment – note Cheung's account in the present essay of irate landlords in Hong Kong of the 1920s who responded to rent control by removing windows from their tenements to drive out the tenants. The landlords can dilute the bundle of services they offer. Residential housing is a complex asset, and in the free market not all valuable margins are priced individually. Tenants pay a composite price, which usually includes a certain level of maintenance. Sometimes custodian and security services, and even water, gas, and electricity, are also included in the rent. When faced with price control, landlords have an incentive to withdraw various valuable margins from the bundle of rights that they formerly transferred to their tenants, unless they are constrained not to do so. Landlords can also try to escape the regulations by transforming their tenements into, for instance, office buildings or hotels.

UNINTENDED SIDE EFFECTS AND
INSTITUTIONAL CHANGE

To continue the example of rent control, consider a situation in which the authorities have managed to close all loopholes by designing myriad

[3] Steven N. S. Cheung, "A Theory of Price Control," *Journal of Law and Economics* 17, No. 1 (1974), 1–22.

regulations and enforcement agencies. As a result, prices in the residential housing market are substantially below the free market rate, and tenants unambiguously enjoy inexpensive housing. In the case of unanticipated rent control, it follows that the return on investment in residential housing is no longer competitive and investors will stay away, thus shrinking the supply of new rental housing. With a growing population, the community will soon have a housing emergency, unless the authorities exclude new housing from rent control, subsidize private investment in new housing, or invest directly in new housing projects, as many communities have done.

Finally, consider Cheung's third point, that it is in the self-interest of economic actors to minimize or limit the dissipation of resources associated with any given regulatory regime. Cheung's point is simple: when choosing among various responses to price control, economic actors have an incentive to select measures that minimize their losses, given the regulatory environment. If the choice is between transforming a tenement into either an unregulated office building or an unregulated warehouse, economic actors will prefer the more valuable of the two alternatives. Similarly, in choosing among alternative methods of making or receiving under-the-counter payments, actors will prefer the form that involves the lowest transaction costs, other things being equal.

A GENERAL THEORY OF PRICE CONTROL?

Can we predict what regulatory path the government will take? Do we have a general theory of price control? The answer is no, as Krueger's essay in Chapter 5 demonstrates eloquently. The unfolding story of price control involves several parts. First, there is the puzzle of what type of price control (or other interference in markets) a particular government will initiate. In each case, the answer depends on goals, constraints, and the specific political processes for decision making. Second, there is the question of how the market will react to the imposition of control. The market reaction will depend on the institutional constraints faced by economic actors, both formal rules and regulations and informal rules such as norms and customs. Third, there is the fact that the market response frequently feeds back to the political sphere, stimulating a new round of regulations, because the initial regulatory measures may have unintended side effects or because they create new interests and new interest groups, which press for action.

Institutional constraints are not general; they have roots in history and are specific to local situations. If we seek to predict how economic actors respond to price controls by substituting on various margins, neither the traditional two-dimensional price–quantity model of economics nor uninformed inclusion of institutional constraints will do. Although we have an analytical apparatus to model behavior, the potential decision points and the institutional constraints in each situation cannot be known in advance; they must be established empirically.

WHAT TO LOOK FOR IN THE ESSAY

Cheung's essay is a study of the market response to price control in a particular situation, the residential housing market of Hong Kong before World War II.[4] It offers an excellent exposition of how to use the analytical tools of institutional economics in a case study and vividly illuminates the role of transaction costs and the complexities of institutional constraints in the real world. Cheung identifies the crucial constraints in the housing market and explains the market response to rent control in terms of constrained optimization. Note that, although providing interesting insights into the political process, Cheung does not attempt to explain the behavior of the Legislative Council.

We suggest that the reader consider the following assertions:

1. In the free market, the fixed monthly rent of two identical tenements can differ substantially at any time owing to a different choice of contracts.
2. Rent controls are ineffective if landlords have an unrestricted right to repossess the leased tenements.
3. Rent control can cause the premature demolition and reconstruction of buildings. Premature reconstruction does not take place when the transaction costs of making *shoe money* contracts are zero.
4. In Hong Kong of the 1920s the transaction costs of making shoe money contracts tended to be greater than the transaction costs of forming *key money* contracts.
5. Specific situations can be identified in which the cost of making shoe money contracts is relatively high.
6. Under rent control, the premature reconstruction of tenements often involves (a) the partial transfer of nonexclusive income to the landlords and (b) the partial dissipation of nonexclusive income.

---

[4] For a study of rent controls in post–World War II Hong Kong, see Steven N. S. Cheung, "Rent Control and Housing Reconstruction: The Postwar Experience of Prewar Premises in Hong Kong," *Journal of Law and Economics* 22, No. 1 (1979), 27–53.

Roofs or stars: the stated intents and actual effects of a rents ordinance

STEVEN N. S. CHEUNG

History must be replete with instances where the stated intentions of legislative actions have diverged from the actual effects. However, for two reasons it is difficult to demonstrate such variance empirically in actual case studies.[1] For one thing, legislators often tend to express their intentions in such vague terms as "to improve welfare." How can one measure by any commonly accepted criteria how well the observable effects attributable to a given piece of legislation fulfill such an intention? Second, before observed effects can even be attributed to a given enactment, it is imperative that implications be derived which can be confirmed or falsified by facts; and this, in turn, demands sufficient information on the relevant constraints.

The rent control in Hong Kong enacted under the Rents Ordinance of 1921 presents an exceptionally useful case. The legislative intents could not have been stated more clearly: rent control was imposed to keep a roof over the heads of the sitting tenants and to encourage the construction of new buildings on vacant lands. And although most of the records were destroyed by the Japanese occupation of the colony during World War II, adequate information is still available to allow derivation of some crucial implications of the control.

1. THE ARGUMENTS FOR THE RENTS ORDINANCE

"The object of the Bill is to protect the tenants, not landlords," declared the Hon. J. H. Kemp, Attorney-General of Hong Kong, on July 18,

This essay originally appeared in *Economic Inquiry*, Vol. 13 (March 1975). Thanks are due to Yoram Barzel, Daniel K. Benjamin, Masanori Hashimoto, Harry Johnson, Levis A. Kochin and William Schworm for their comments, and to the National Science Foundation for supporting my research in the general area of contracts.
[1] For fine performances of this nature, see two papers by Peltzman (1973) and (1974).

1921, in the second reading of the Rents Ordinance Bill which passed the same day.[2] In a period of rising rent prompted by the influx of refugees into the Colony, one reason given was "to keep a roof over the heads of the present occupiers and to protect them from excessive exploitation."[3]

The exploitation argument was nothing new, nor was the implication in the legislative discussion that investment in real property would yield a higher return than in other assets.[4] Judging both from the Legislative Council's reference to English law and from the similarity of the rents Ordinance to the Rent Act in England (1915), the influence of the mother country appears strong.[5] But the chief cause of the Bill seems to have been the Council's recognition that any landlord could evict his tenants at will simply by raising rents.

A group of 31 landlords, represented by Mr. C. G. Alabaster, unsuccessfully protested the Bill.[6] One doubts that even a stronger protest would have carried weight, since sentiment ran high in favor of the tenants. The Bill was hastily prepared, and only 19 days elapsed from its first reading until it became statutory law.[7] Originally designed for only one year, the Ordinance was extended four times before it was allowed to expire in June 1926.[8]

The record of the legislative proceedings would seem to indicate that before the enactment of the Ordinance its effects were hardly analyzed, except for some discussion of the relationship between the restriction on the rents of existing tenements and the construction of new buildings.[9] The argument of the Legislative Council was that since the proposed Bill would control the rents only of the existing rental contracts, not those of newly constructed premises, it would tend to stimulate the construction of new buildings to meet the rising demand for housing:

It is hoped that one subsidiary effect of the Ordinance will be to encourage the erection of new domestic buildings. In the first place, such *new* buildings will be entirely *free* from the restrictions of the Ordinance, and the owners will be

---

[2] *Hong Kong Hansard* (1921, p. 87).
[3] *Ibid.*, p. 85; see also pp. 78–80 and pp. 85–89 for similar statements.
[4] See *ibid.*, pp. 93–94. The belief that investment in land would yield a return at a rate higher than the rate of interest, however, was supported neither by theory nor by facts.
[5] Compare next section with Megarry (1961).
[6] See *Hansard* (1921, pp. 89–92). Mr. Alabaster argued that the control was not in accord with the rules of market, a truism already known to the Legislative Council. Virtually no comment was made on the protest.
[7] See *ibid.*, pp. 78–97. The Governor, in citing a few cases of rising rent, concluded: "I think these cases supply all the comment that is necessary" (*ibid.*, p. 94).
[8] See *Hansard* (1922, p. 52); (1923, p. 57); (1924, p. 23); and (1925, p. 36).
[9] See *Hansard* (1921, pp. 78–79); and esp. *Hansard* (1922, p. 28).

Steven N. S. Cheung

entitled to charge whatever rents they can obtain. In the second place, as tenants cannot be turned out so long as they pay the standard rent, well-to-do immigrants who wish to acquire a residence in Hong Kong will have to build for themselves.[10]

The term "new buildings" may refer either to new construction on vacant lands or to reconstruction of existing premises,[11] but in the cited paragraph the Council obviously meant that the control would encourage new buildings on *vacant* lands. Given only that rent would be held below the free-market level, the information is insufficient to support any definite prediction.[12] A much broader set of constraints relevant for decision-making under the control must be considered. The two prices mentioned by the Council – the controlled rent of an existing premise vis-à-vis the market rent of a new building erected on vacant or marginal land – were not necessarily the relevant alternatives. To the extent that the gains of building on vacant land were unaffected by rent control, its utilization for construction would remain unchanged; and nothing in the Council's argument indicates that the gains of such building would rise as a result of the control. However, the controlled rent of an existing premise as against the market rent obtainable if that premise were reconstructed formed a highly relevant comparison which apparently slipped the minds of the members of the Legislative Council. As we shall see, the Council was right in expecting an increase in construction but badly erred as to its nature.

It is not clear whether the view expressed by the Council – that rent control will encourage housing development in the uncontrolled sector – was a popular view at that time. Certainly it has come into vogue in the postwar period, supported by the more sophisticated arguments of economists typified by the summary statement of Lionel Needleman:

If the price and availability of only part of the housing supply is controlled, then in a period of housing shortage, the excess demand will be channelled into the uncontrolled sector and in that sector, rents and prices will be much higher than if control had never been imposed.[13]

[10] *Hansard* (1921, p. 79). Italics added. Similar statements are found in *ibid.*, pp. 85–86.
[11] Partial renewal, however costly, did not constitute a "new" building exempt from the control. See Ip Yuk Kwong v. Fong Hon Sam [S.J. 990 of 1922], in *Hongkong Law Reports* (1922, pp. 41–47).
[12] See Cheung (1974).
[13] Needleman (1965, p. 163). A similar view is found in Paish (1950, pp. 79–80); Brown and Wiseman (1964, pp. 214–222). This view is partially challenged by J. R. Gould and S. G. B. Henry. For example, under what they have chosen to call the "rationing" assumption, they argued that the price of a substitute in the uncontrolled sector will rise only if both the controlled and the uncontrolled goods have "normal" income effects. See Gould and Henry (1967, pp. 42–49).

226

This "spillover" hypothesis, like any of a large number of hypotheses pertaining to price control, is plausible, because it may be made consistent with economic theory simply by asserting additional constraints to the control in price. The same arbitrary assertion will yield whatever results are desired in any other context where price is controlled. In such cases, however, the predictive power of economic theory flounders if it turns out that the actual constraints differ in essential aspects from those imagined or asserted. It is therefore futile to make any general statement on what particular effect a control in price must bring. Rather, to derive implications to be tested against observations, it is essential to investigate the real-world constraints applicable to the control in question.[14]

2. THE LEGAL CONSTRAINTS OF THE RENTS ORDINANCE INTERPRETED

Although our main concern is to analyze the effects of the Rents Ordinance of 1921 upon housing construction, it is essential that we examine broadly the legal provisions governing decision making under the control. The interrelationship of articles and the effectiveness of the control can be revealed only if the constraints are studied as an integrated whole, which we do in this section. In the following section, the constraints governing housing construction will be drastically simplified to expedite the derivation of implications. Comparison of these two sections will show, however, that the constraints so simplified conform in essential aspects with those in real practice. For clarity of presentation, we here classify the constraints of the Rents Ordinance into several groups.

Fixation of the standard rent

The maximum rent collectable by a landlord was a "standard rent." In the Rents Ordinance, we find:

[1] "Standard rent" ... means ... the rate of rent which was recoverable from the tenant in actual occupation on the 31st of December, 1920; and if ... not actually let on [that date] ... the rate of rent which was recoverable from the tenant in actual occupation on the last occasion before [that date]. ...[15]
[2] Notwithstanding any agreement to the contrary, whether made before or after the commencement of this Ordinance, ... no rent shall be recoverable in respect of any *domestic* tenement, ... in excess of the standard rent. ...[16]

---

[14] This investigation, in turn, requires the dictate of a theory. See Cheung (1974).
[15] *The Ordinances of Hongkong* (1921, pp. 108–109).
[16] *Ibid.*, p. 109. Italics added.

[3] Where the rights of any lessee of any building ... are affected by the operation of this Ordinance, it shall be lawful for such lessee to apply to the court for the revision of the rent payable under the lease, and upon which such application the court may make such order as it shall think fit.[17]

The choice of December 31, 1920, as the date on which rent was recoverable, thus fixing a "standard rent" (see cited Paragraph [1]), was based on administrative convenience.[18] However, the difference between standard rent and the market rent prevailing when the Ordinance took effect in July 1921 is not necessarily the amount by which monthly rent had risen since December 1920.

To illustrate, let R_s be the regulated standard rent (that is, the monthly rent of December 1920), and let R_0 be the market rent of July 1921. Given that rent for succeeding months was expected to rise, that is, $R_0 < R_1 < \cdots < R_n$, a lease contract with a specified duration up to the nth month will yield a constant monthly rent, R_c, such that $V_0 = R_c[(1+\rho)^n - 1]/[\rho(1+\rho)^n]$, and $R_c < R_0$, where ρ is the monthly rate of interest and V_0 is the present value of the rents of n months. That is, for July 1921 R_0 is the relevant market rent if it is subject to monthly revision by the contracting parties, but R_c is the relevant rent if the contract stipulates no rent revision within n months. Similarly, if a law generates an expectation that rent will not be revisable for n months, the would-be monthly market rent as viewed by the contracting parties is R_c, not R_0. Therefore, even if monthly rent had not risen from December 1920 to July 1921, the enforcement of the Ordinance would yield immediate conflict between the landlord and the tenant if future rents were expected to rise.

Thus the relevant comparison of market and standard rents when the Ordinance was enacted was between R_c and R_s, with R_c computed by using the expected time length within which R_s would be effectively enforced. Their difference would be progressively larger (1) the greater the rise in rent since the recoverable date, (2) the greater the expected rise in future rents, and (3) the longer the rent control was expected to extend beyond that time within which the contracting parties had privately agreed not to revise the terms.[19]

It is, of course, possible that the rents of two identical tenements on

---

[17] *Ibid.*, p. 112.

[18] See *Hansard* (1921, p. 78). Earlier dates such as 1914 and 1915 had been suggested.

[19] The reportedly "excessive" rise in rents (numerical data are not available) in the few months prior to the commencement of the Ordinance might be attributable to a general expectation that the Ordinance would come. See *ibid.*, p. 79.

In the absence of government regulations on lease contracts for domestic tenements, the stipulated time within which rent is not revisable is usually quite short. In

the recoverable date differed substantially owing to different choices of contracts. The provision in cited Paragraph [3] indicates that the court had power to equalize such discrepancies, although the available record of court cases of this period is inadequate to permit investigation of such procedures. As seen in cited Paragraph [2], only domestic tenements were subject to control by the Ordinance. The definition of a "domestic tenement" as one used "for human habitation" was sufficiently ambiguous to cause concern that a tenant might convert a warehouse into a domestic building or a landlord might convert a domestic building into a hotel.[20] Arbitrary criteria designed in 1922[21] to counter these possibilities resulted in discrimination: some tenements were controlled and some were free of control.

Restriction on the right to possession

Under a law enforced by judicial proceedings, a restriction on the right to collect rent will be effective only if the right to repossess the leased tenement is also restricted.[22] If a landlord has the right to evict a tenant at will, he may do so and pocket a side payment from a new tenant without issuing any receipt. If a prospective tenant voluntarily chooses to buy a broken chair from the landlord for a thousand dollars, the court is helpless to act.[23] Indeed, the mere threat of eviction by the landlord, if he has such a right, will generate "gifts" from resident tenants.

The Ordinance of 1921 granted the landlord permission to repossess a leased tenement under stipulated conditions including the following:

Notwithstanding any notice to quit, whether given before or after the commencement of this Ordinance, and notwithstanding the terms of any agreement whatsoever, . . . an order or judgment against any tenant in actual occupation for the recovery of possession . . . shall be made or given . . . if:[24]

[a] the lessor *bona fide* requires possession of the domestic tenement in order to pull down such domestic tenement or in order to reconstruct such domestic

renting for production, however, it is more advantageous in certain cases to choose relatively long-term contracts. See Cheung (1969).

[20] See *Ordinances* (1921, pp. 107–108); and *Hansard* (1922, pp. 45–47).

[21] See *Ordinances* (1922, pp. 61–62).

[22] This point, which the Hong Kong Legislative Council seemed never to fully understand, became one main reason for the many amendments which usually followed in the wake of each Ordinance throughout the entire history of rent control in that colony.

[23] Effective prohibition of such a side payment may be carried out to some extent by the use of government agents posing as prospective tenants. In this case, however, "corruption" would emerge.

[24] *Ordinances* (1921, p. 110).

tenement to such an extent as to make such domestic tenement a new building . . . , and shall have given the tenant three months notice to quit.[25]

[b] the domestic tenement is reasonably required by the lessor for occupation as a residence for himself or for his family . . . , and the court is satisfied that alternative accommodation, reasonably equivalent as regards rent and suitability in all respects, is available [for the tenant].[26] Where a lessor has obtained an order . . . for possession . . . for his own occupation, and it is subsequently [shown] that the order was obtained by misrepresentation . . . , the court may order the lessor to pay to the former tenant such sum as appears sufficient as compensation for damage or loss. . . .[27]

The Ordinance also provided for ejection by the landlord of a tenant who failed to pay the standard rent or who created excessive nuisance to adjoining occupiers.[28] However, an outright sale of the tenement to a third party did not constitute sufficient ground for evicting the resident tenant unless the purchaser also *"bona fide* intends forthwith to pull down [the] tenement . . . to reconstruct. . . ."[29]

Provisions for subletting

The intensity of subletting in Hong Kong has been a striking phenomenon attributable to rent control, but we will not here analyze this aspect. In the Ordinance of 1921 and its related amendments, subletting by a tenant was not restricted:

A lessee of any domestic tenement . . . who sublets other portions of such domestic tenement, shall be deemed to be the tenant in actual occupation of such domestic tenement as regards his immediate lessor. A sub-lessee from any such lessee . . . shall be deemed to be the tenant in actual occupation. . . .[30]

The lack of clarity in this paragraph may be explained by the Legislative Council's inexperience in dealing with what subsequently turned out to be highly complex subletting arrangements. It was only when another rent-control program was set up in the postwar period that terms such as "derivative landlords," "principal tenants," "sub-tenants," and "sub-sub-tenants" came into use.

---

[25] *Ibid.*, p. 111. A November 1921 amendment provided that the landlord's intention to reconstruct the tenement must be put in writing. See *ibid.*, p. 163.

[26] *Ibid.*, pp. 110–111. Under rent control in Hong Kong during the postwar period, repossession for owner occupation has been nearly impossible, since the court requires a "proof" that the hardship suffered by the landlord in not evicting the tenant would be greater than that suffered by the tenant evicted.

[27] *Ibid.*, p. 112.

[28] *Ibid.*, p. 110.

[29] Amended in November 1921. See *ibid.*, p. 165.

[30] *Ibid.*, p. 109.

Stated intents and actual effects of a rents ordinance

Not only was subletting permitted by the Rents Ordinance; no restriction was set on the rents to be charged by the lessee to a sublessee. Indeed, one year after the Ordinance became law the Attorney-General had the following to say:

Great complaint has been made by the landlords of the subletting of houses by the tenants at a profit. Many suggestions have been made, but I do not think it is possible to deal with that point at all. One suggestion was that the tenant should never be allowed to collect more from his subtenants than he paid the landlord. . . . That would be *unfair because the tenant takes the risk* of vacancies, and non-payment of rent[,] and it is not fair to restrict him to the same rent that he pays the landlord. . . .[31]

Strangely enough, this double standard went through the Legislative Council unchallenged. In a free market the landlord takes the same risks described here, and it would be equally "unfair" to restrict his rental income in favor of the tenant. If rent is effectively restricted to a low enough level, and if the tenant sublets his entire contract, then a case can be made that it is the original tenant himself who is closer to being a landlord.[32]

Restrictions of side payments

It goes almost without saying that the exaction of side payments by the landlord was prohibited:

No person shall, as a condition or pretended condition of the grant, renewal, or continuance, by himself or by any other person of a tenancy of any domestic tenement, demand payment of any sum of money whatsoever, in addition to the [standard] rent. . . . Every person demanding any payment in contravention of this section shall be liable upon summary conviction to a fine not exceeding one thousand dollars. . . .[33]

As noted earlier, side payments in the form of "gifts" would have been impossible to prohibit under the prevailing method of enforcement. The problem we face, then, is to identify situations where side payments would be voluntary, as opposed to situations where their exaction would yield potential lawsuits. It is not clear whether the quoted paragraph was intended to curb a traditional form of side payment called "shoe money": legend has it that tenants once had to pay for the services of a middleman to obtain a rental contract and, since the go-between had to walk about in searching and negotiating the contract, payment for his

---

[31] *Hansard* (1922, p. 35). Italics added.
[32] During the postwar period, the term "derivative landlord" was appropriately coined for such a contingency.
[33] *Ordinances* (1921, p. 116).

231

Steven N. S. Cheung

help was politely viewed as compensation to repair his shoes. The same convenient term was eventually applied to payments tendered the landlord himself, who was now assumed to do the "searching." In the postwar period, the lump-sum payment of shoe money to obtain a lease-right frequently amounted to many times the monthly rent.

Before the passing of the Bill of 1921, the Attorney-General argued:

It was suggested [by the Council] that the collection of "shoe money" should be prohibited, but we felt that in a Bill already rather exceptional it would be unwise further to disturb existing practices by prohibiting a custom which, bad as it may be, is certainly widespread. While the Bill remains in operation there is no reason why anyone should be forced to pay any excessive "shoe money" . . . if [he] pays the standard rent, [because] as long as the Bill remains in force, [he] cannot be turned out.[34]

The last statement is partially correct. Security of tenancy, plus a law which effectively prohibits the landlord from creating damage to the tenement, will insure that no side payment need be made. But if a threat of eviction is allowed by law, side payment will follow if the costs of negotiating for that payment are less than the associated net gains to the contracting parties. Prior to the formation of a lease contract, the collection of "shoe money" cannot be effectively prohibited by law. With a standard rent below the market rent, a prospective tenant will pay a lump-sum rather than forgo the lease. Similarly, a potential eviction will generate the same payment from a resident tenant provided that the cost of negotiation for that payment is not prohibitive. The court can do nothing to eliminate a "gift," with or without rent control.

We may review the effective constraints of the Rents Ordinance of 1921. The fixation of the standard rent was unambiguous and effective. Provided that (1) rent at the recoverable date was substantiated by evidence and (2) any threat of eviction was absent, a tenant in occupation enjoyed a rent lower than the market rent so long as the Ordinance was in force. However, a tenant's right to the difference between market and standard rents was insecure in two respects. One was uncertainty as to the duration of the Ordinance; another was the incentive to side payments posed in certain cases by the possibility of eviction. Since such a possibility rendered the control ineffective, it is natural that subsequent amendments to the Ordinance were largely aimed toward its correction.

Only three months after the commencement of the Ordinance, for example, it was reported that "certain landlords have gone so far as to remove windows in wet weather and even staircases to drive the tenants out."[35] And within a year tenants asserted in a petition "that in some

[34] *Hansard* (1921, p. 86).
[35] *Ibid.*, p. 144.

232

cases the landlord, in order to get the tenants out, will put in workmen and make the house generally unpleasant. . . ."[36] Perhaps because it was assumed that the common law would protect tenants in these and similar cases no effort was made in the original Rents Ordinance to preclude the chance that landlords might deliberately cause a nuisance for tenants or might "underrepair" or "overrepair" the tenements. Substantial fines against these practices were promptly inserted, and by June 1922 the Ordinance had grown to 27 sections from the original 17.[37]

Lacking the right of arbitrary eviction, the landlord now had only two options to evict the tenants: he could claim the tenement for his own occupancy or he could evict for reconstruction. The first option, however, was feasible only under rare circumstances. As cited earlier, similar accommodations – "reasonably equivalent as regards rent and suitability in all respects" – had to be found for the tenants, and that was difficult under rent control. Furthermore, any *mala fide* repossession for the landlord's own occupancy might prove very costly, since compensation for the tenant might subsequently be demanded by the court. Thus, in *general*, reconstruction was the only alternative to eviction or the threat of eviction; under this second option, the Rents Ordinance required no compensation by the landlord to the tenants.

3. THE EFFECTS ON RECONSTRUCTION AND THE DISSOLUTION OF THE RENTS ORDINANCE

We now turn to analyze the effects of the Rents Ordinance on housing construction or, rather, on *reconstruction*. As the Ordinance was routinely renewed in 1922 and 1923, the general expectation may have been that the control would last indefinitely. For simplicity (only), we assume that in the neighborhood of 1922–1923 the rent control was expected to last to perpetuity, and that all tenements, old and new, would physically last to perpetuity.

In a *free* market, and under our simplifying assumptions, the economic condition for reconstruction can be found in the equation

$$G_f = (R^*/\rho) - (R_c/\rho) - C. \tag{1}$$

In this equation, R^* is the market rent of a newly constructed tenement and R_c is the market rent of the existing structure. Both are measured as weighted monthly averages, or as "annuities," with R^* stretching back to the date when the sitting tenants are vacated for reconstruction. The

---

[36] *Hansard* (1922, p. 35).
[37] Compare No. 13 of 1921 with No. 14 of 1922, in *Ordinances* (1921, pp. 107–117), and *Ordinances* (1922, pp. 61–74).

Steven N. S. Cheung

relevant interest rate is ρ. The present value of all costs associated with demolition and rebuilding is C. Since R^* is stretched back to the date of tenant vacation, the rent forgone during the reconstruction period is no longer part of the reconstruction costs. The present value of the *net* gain, or the gain in site value, of the reconstruction is G_f. In a free market, given the chosen new structure, reconstruction will take place if G_f is positive.

Under the Rents Ordinance, R_c is replaced by the standard rent, R_s. As an approximation, assume that all other variables remain unchanged. Changing R_c to R_s, we obtain

$$G_s = (R^*/\rho) - (R_s/\rho) - C, \qquad (2)$$

where G_s is the net gain from reconstruction with the standard rent. The fact that $R_s < R_c$ makes $G_s > G_f$.

Since the net gain from reconstruction (positive or negative) is necessarily greater under the Rents Ordinance than in the free market, one is tempted to conclude right away that the Rents Ordinance would accelerate and encourage premature reconstruction (that is, reconstruction with $G_f < 0$). One would be inclined to think that reconstruction would take place under the control if and when $G_s > 0$, and that in a substantial number of marginal cases for which in a free market $G_f < 0$ the equation would now yield $G_s > 0$ under the control. This conclusion would be correct except that the tenants of the existing tenement now have incentive to offer a money "gift" to the landlord to dissuade him from reconstructing.

The *maximum* amount the tenants of a tenement (as a group) are willing to pay the landlord to obtain a perpetual lease right with the standard rent will be

$$S = (R_c - R_s)/\rho \qquad (3)$$

where S, a present value, stands for "shoe money." The use of perpetual discounting here is for simplicity in the algebraic expression, in accord with what we assumed for equation (1). With this simplification, however, a contract for the present transaction of shoe money will include the stipulation that the landlord will refund the tenants by the same amount if at some future date the landlord decides to reconstruct. Of course, a shoe-money contract may not take this particular form, but it is a simple way for us to derive some general implications.[38]

[38] Note that the stipulation to refund the shoe money at some future date will not affect the condition that reconstruction will take place when $G_f > 0$. Implied in our present discussion also is that so long as shoe-money transactions – which may take a variety of forms – can be costlessly negotiated and enforced, further restriction on the rent of a reconstructed tenement will not affect the reconstruction date.

Stated intents and actual effects of a rents ordinance

From equations (1) through (3) we obtain

$$G_s - G_f = S. \tag{4}$$

This implies that if all costs of contracting for S are zero, the rent control will never generate premature reconstruction (that is, reconstruction with $G_f < 0$). More specific implications follow. If $G_s < 0$, and if this condition is known to all contracting parties, then reconstruction will not occur even under the rent control and no threat of eviction will yield any payment in S. If $G_f > 0$, then $G_s > S$ – reconstruction will occur with or without rent control. If $G_f < 0$, then $S > G_s$ – the threat of eviction and bargaining for S will occur provided $G_s > 0$ also.

The crucial hypothesis of the above analysis is that if the costs of negotiating and enforcing the shoe-money contract are positive, then premature reconstruction will in general occur for some cases for which $G_f < 0$ and $G_s > 0$. Let T stand for such transaction costs. Under rent control, premature reconstruction will occur only if $(S-T) < G_s > 0 > G_f$. The greater the costs of forming shoe-money contracts, other things equal, the more likely it becomes that reconstruction will occur. Refutable implications can be obtained by identifying situations where the above variables differ and, most crucially, situations where the values of T differ.

In the usual usage of the term, shoe money is the same as key money, a payment offered by a prospective tenant to a landlord to obtain the lease-right of a *vacant* tenement under rent control. Having vacant possession (and under most rent-control laws) the landlord has the right to exclude any prospective tenant he sees fit. Competition among prospective tenants to obtain the lease will thus generate a lump-sum payment to the landlord roughly equal to the present value of the difference between market and controlled rents, and the transaction costs involved will be rather low. This situation, however, is very different from that of our present consideration: the payment of shoe money by resident tenants to dissuade a landlord from reconstructing.

For several reasons shoe-money transactions between landlords and tenants in occupation under the Rents Ordinance involved substantial costs. In the absence of competing offers from prospective tenants, a sitting tenant had less inducement to offer shoe money sufficient to dissuade the landlord from reconstructing. The costs of such a transaction was further complicated by the presence of multiple tenant households in one building. Not only did a Hong Kong building typically have several floors, occupied by different tenants, but each floor might be occupied by several households owing to subletting. Collective decisions are notoriously more costly than individual decisions and involve the "free-rider" problem of transaction costs. On this score, other things equal, our hypothesis indicates that tenements with more tenant households would more frequently be reconstructed than those with fewer households. In addition, since the overall duration of the Rents Ordinance was never clearly specified,[39] different expectations among tenants as to when the Ordinance would end would have raised the cost of forming any shoe-money contract. The implication is that, other things equal, the more specific the duration of the control the fewer reconstructions will take place. Third, the illegality both of any threat of eviction and of the collection of side payments also increased the costs of transactions. A landlord's refusal to issue a receipt for shoe money, for example, could preclude tenants from enforcing their lease rights after payments of a lump sum; thus they would prefer to make more complicated monthly "gifts" to the landlord. The implication here is that the more restrictive legal devices are adopted to curb the threat of eviction, the more landlords will invoke their right to reconstruct.

Available information does not permit the testing of the first implication; different situations as described in the second did not exist; and although more restrictive devices were introduced to curb the threat of eviction,[40] information on tenement reconstruction is insufficient to permit the drawing of any correlation. However, the multiplicity of tenants, the indefinite duration of the Ordinance, and the illegal nature of side payment all clearly imply that the high costs involved in reaching agreement with landlords would lead to premature reconstruction.

Before examining the observed effects of such a regime, let me briefly relate the present analysis of housing reconstruction to some general propositions for price-control analysis offered elsewhere,[41] to see in perspective the economic issues involved. Price or rent control generally gives rise to what I have chosen to call non-exclusive income, or income that has no exclusive claimant. With respect to the Rents Ordinance, the right to the difference between market rent and standard rent of an existing domestic tenement was partially rendered non-exclusive by the absence of a clearly delimited lease period within which a tenant was granted the right to pay only the standard rent: the security of tenure was threatened by the possibility of eviction for reconstruction, particularly when $G_s > 0$. Competition among the contracting parties for this non-exclusive income would tend to lead to its dissipation. But, by the postulate of constrained maximization, each and every party involved

---

[39] The Rents Ordinance stated that it was "lawful for the Legislative Council from time to time by resolution to extend the duration of this Ordinance . . . not exceeding one year at any one time." *Ordinances* (1921, p. 114).
[40] See Ordinances No. 25 of 1921, No. 14 of 1922, and No. 8 of 1923; in *Ordinances* (1921) (1922) and (1923).
[41] Cheung (1974).

will seek to minimize the dissipation. One way to do so is to seek alternative contractual arrangements subject to the constraint of transaction costs, as in our example of a shoe-money contract. In effect, such an agreement aims to define more clearly than is provided by law who has an exclusive right to the difference between market rent and standard rent. Another way to reduce the dissipation is to seek alternative use of the resource. Housing reconstruction, as our particular alternative, will occur prematurely if and when the transaction costs for a shoe-money contract become prohibitive.[42] The transaction costs incurred or the loss caused by premature reconstruction constitute in either case the amount of the dissipation, necessarily a constrained minimum.

We may summarize the alternative results of reconstruction under the Rents Ordinance. In cases when $G_s < 0$ or when $G_f > 0$, and when these values are correctly estimated by all parties concerned, no shoe-money contracts would obtain and there would be little non-exclusive income to dissipate. In the event that $G_s > 0$ and $G_f < 0$, and that the landlord was dissuaded from reconstruction by an illegal shoe-money contract, non-exclusive income would dissipate by the amount of the transaction costs. Finally, in the event that $G_f < 0$ and reconstruction followed unsuccessful or unattempted negotiation, in present value non-exclusive income would dissipate by the absolute value of G_f plus whatever transaction costs were incurred.

We now turn to the recorded evidence. The only available information on tenement reconstruction during the existence of the Rents Ordinance is contained in the legislative proceedings. However persuasive, the evidence does not conclusively demonstrate that many reconstructions were indeed premature. Regardless of the reported age at which an existing tenement was pulled down, much more information is needed to confirm that the demolition was premature.[43] Judgment of the following facts, therefore, rests with the reader.

In February 1923, about 18 months after the inception of the Rents Ordinance, Governor R. E. Stubbs informed the Legislative Council that "the progress of the provision of houses is going on very well. . . ."[44] In no report up to that time had reconstruction been regarded as "exces-

---

[42] We ignore here the possibility that monthly shoe-money payments were made to the landlord for some time but were then discontinued owing to the costs of repeating the illegal contract, and that premature reconstruction was thus temporarily delayed.

[43] In a forthcoming book which investigates various rent controls in Hong Kong (Cheung, in progress), detailed evidence will be presented to confirm that premature reconstructions occurred in some tenements protected by the Landlord and Tenant Ordinance during the postwar period.

[44] *Hansard* (1923, p. 1). No indication was given at this time on whether the "provision of houses" was in the form of reconstructions or constructions on vacant lands.

sive" or "undesirable." Four months later, on June 14, 1923, an alarm was sounded about tenement reconstructions. To support a Bill laid before the Council for discussion, the Hon. Mr. H. E. Pollock read a report of over four thousand words.[45] In this report the variation between standard rents and market rents of comparable (reconstructed) tenements was estimated. As of 1923 (and based on a few examples) market rents were said to be about 50 to 100 per cent higher than standard rents. But the chief message of the report is on housing reconstruction.

Addressing the Governor, Mr. Pollock observed:

Thousands of tenants who are perfectly willing and able to pay the standard rent have been evicted or are being threatened with eviction through no fault of their own. . . .[46]

And as a consequence of a law designed to keep roofs over the heads of resident tenants, some of these tenants were now sleeping out under the stars:

. . . the present situation is that hundreds of persons at the present moment are sleeping in the streets. Well, Sir, I have heard the observation made that it is a nice, healthy thing to sleep out in the open air in the street, but I think that observation hardly applies to weather such as we are experiencing at present.[47]

Pollock pinpointed the cause of the problem:

[One] drawback of [the] reconstruction schemes is that they have the immediate effect – and nobody can help them from having that effect – of reducing the existing housing accommodation and they thereby increase the housing shortage. . . . There can be no doubt, Sir, that this craze for reconstruction has hit the people of all races in the Colony.[48]

The speaker went on to cite a number of examples of reconstruction where, in his opinion and in the opinion of the Building Authority, the tenements had been in sufficiently good condition that reconstruction was not warranted.[49] His factual examples were climaxed by:

Another case, Sir, to which I wish to refer is that of No. 349 Shanghai Street. This house was erected in 1921. The condition of the premises is stated by the Building Ordinance officer as "O.K." . . . Well, Sir, although it may possibly be a praiseworthy thing to rebuild the other houses, I submit it is nothing short of

---

[45] *Ibid.,* pp. 40–48.
[46] *Ibid.,* p. 42.
[47] *Loc. cit.*
[48] *Loc. cit.*
[49] *Ibid.,* pp. 42–44.

criminal in the present state of housing accommodation to sanction any scheme which involves pulling down a house which was erected as recently as the year 1921.[50]

In recommending that the "reconstruction craze" be checked immediately, Mr. Pollock proposed to amend the principal Ordinance to read that "a Committee ... appointed by the Governor ... may, in its absolute discretion, postpone the operation of the notice to quit and also the demolition and reconstruction of domestic tenements. ..."[51]

Before the amendment was put to vote, however, Governor Stubbs had something to say. Although in favor of the rent control in 1921, by June 1922 he had taken the stand to state that the control was "an offense against good economic doctrine. ..."[52] Similarly, on Mr. Pollock's proposal, the Governor commented:

If I had to vote I should vote against it for two reasons. In the first place ... I think it is a mistake to tinker with a temporary Ordinance, and thus lead people to believe it is more likely to be renewed than is the case. The second reason is that ... the adoption of the clause may tend to prevent people [from] reconstructing in cases where it is manifestly desirable that reconstruction should take place.[53]

The amendment was then put to vote, and the Governor, who had no voting right, asserted, "I think the 'No's' have it."[54] Mr. Pollock called for a division. The amendment was defeated, eight to five. Mr. Pollock mumbled something to the effect that it did not amount to free voting, and an unpleasant verbal exchange between the Governor and Mr. Pollock followed.[55]

The reconstruction craze apparently continued, for on February 28, 1924, a Bill was again introduced to check the trend. The Attorney-General stated explicitly that "some landlords used [reconstruction] for the sake of the increased rent they can obtain from the new house. ..."[56] In the second reading of the Bill a week later, Mr. Pollock, now with stronger support from other members of the Council, again cited factual examples to support his earlier position.[57] In the new proposed amendment the Building Authority was authorized to determine whether

[50] *Ibid.*, p. 44.
[51] *Ibid.*, p. 46.
[52] *Hansard* (1922, p. 45).
[53] *Hansard* (1923, p. 55).
[54] *Ibid.*, p. 56.
[55] *Loc. cit.*
[56] *Hansard* (1924, p. 15).
[57] *Ibid.*, pp. 19–21.

reconstruction was necessary. "The simple test," declared Mr. Pollock, "should be whether the houses are in a good structural condition from the habitable point of view."[58] In other words, the market test was to be completely ruled out.

Governor Stubbs was softened:

I confess that where I went wrong was when I credited the landlords with having more public spirit and more refined ideas of common honesty than they appear to possess. I thought a landlord would only pull down his premises to get a substantial improvement. I did not suppose that many were prepared to go to the extreme length of destroying good buildings in order merely to evade the law. I can only express my regret that I took a higher view of humanity than seems to be justified by local circumstances, and that the hon. member took a more correct view than I did.[59]

No record shows that the Governor had ever credited the landlords with "public spirit" and "honesty," and as one who earlier spoke of economic doctrine, the Governor should have known better. The Bill, of course, easily passed.[60]

No mention was made of the reconstruction issue in three meetings of the Legislative Council in May–June 1925, when the Rents Ordinance was up for renewal. Amended to allow for a maximum of 15 per cent raise in rent over the standard rent,[61] the Ordinance was extended to June 1926, and questions were raised as to whether the extension should last longer.[62] The Governor declared that the Ordinance had lasted longer than he expected and that he thought the circumstances which made it necessary would cease to exist in another year.[63] On several earlier occasions the Governor had expressed the same opinion; this time, however, he was right. By June 1926 "there were so many vacant floors throughout the Colony that further renewal of Rents Control was regarded as no longer necessary."[64] The Rents Ordinance was discontinued.

No information is available on the proportion of vacant tenements of this period; nor is there sufficient information to determine why excessive housing supply suddenly occurred, exerting downward pressure on

[58] *Ibid.*, p. 20.
[59] *Ibid.*, p. 21.
[60] The major clause stated that permission "should not be given unless the Building Authority is of the opinion that the condition of the structure . . . is such that to make the intended reconstruction desirable." *Ordinances* (1924, p. 2).
[61] See *Ordinances* (1925, pp. 25–26).
[62] *Hansard* (1925, p. 24).
[63] *Ibid.*, p. 31.
[64] Rent Control Committee (1953, p. 9).

market rent. Excessive anticipation of an influx of refugees from mainland China is one plausible explanation. A better one, perhaps, is that enforcement of the Rents Ordinance had generated misleading information on market rental prices as signals for reconstruction. Interpreted as free market rents, the signals encouraged construction of taller buildings; but such rents were no longer obtainable when a large number of landlords acted simultaneously to increase accommodations. The individual owner was further misled when market rents increased during the temporary decrease in housing while massive reconstruction was taking place. The implication is that only a "smoothly" functioning futures market in house rentals would have made it possible to predict before reconstruction what rents would eventually clear the market. All rental contracts would then have been obtained in advance and subsequently enforced. But the formation of such a market is costly – which is really to say that costs are high in obtaining correct information on future rental prices. Landlords and tenants apparently were not willing to pay that cost.

4. CONCLUDING REMARKS

In a world where information is costly, many decisions will inevitably be based on inadequate knowledge and will prove faulty. Any decision maker will therefore seek ways to reduce the frequency and magnitude of his errors. In the absence of private property rights constraining legislative decision making, we naturally expect that behavior of legislators towards the avoidance of errors to be different than that of individuals in the market place. But whereas the constraints governing individual decisions in the market are familiar to us, those governing legislative decisions are not and may vary from place to place. We are therefore unable to conclude on theoretical grounds whether legislative decisions are more error prone. Certainly such a conclusion is not reached in this paper.

Confining our observations to the enactments covering rent control in Hong Kong, we note some general differences in legislative behavior as contrasted with market behavior. One feature common to all the ordinances was that the control was imposed over the entire colony's tenements of a given class, thus affecting in one stroke resources of enormous total value. Such drastic action would be difficult to find in the market. Granted, there are firms of immense size, chain stores or franchises that spread nationally or internationally; yet, whether these enterprises are owned jointly or solely, they have attained their status through gradual expansion, and for each successful growth a multitude of relatively small attempts may have failed. Learning from past errors is frequently the least costly way to avoid decision errors, and cost minimization would require that the lesson be learned on the smallest possible scale.

Given the comprehensive scope of the rent-control ordinances in Hong Kong, the most feasible protection against massive error lay in making each enactment a temporary or "emergency" measure, subject to consideration for discontinuance after a year or two. Yet the effectiveness of this provision appears to be nullified by the fact that the Rents Ordinance of 1921 was the only one ever to be permanently discontinued by legislative action.[65] It cannot be held that the other ordinances generated no divergence between their expressed intents and actual effects: they all did, in varying degree. However, the course routinely chosen was to amend the principal ordinances, often in the process generating additional unintended side effects.

It is sometimes noted that one way to correct an error in decision is to admit its occurrence. For an individual constrained by private property rights, however, no admission of error can mitigate his punishment. The market penalizes his every mistake, and he will survive any venture only if he takes proper corrective action.

The constraints subject to which a legislator will survive, on the other hand, are beyond the scope of this inquiry. One may speculate whether the admission of error would serve any better purpose in the context of legislative decision making than in the private sector. Here, again, facts point to a negative answer. The Hong Kong legislative proceedings for 1921–1972 indicate that Governor Stubbs stood alone in openly admitting a decision error. A man who verbally admits his fault faces the cost of potential decline in his human capital, and except for some uncommon constraints there is usually little to gain. Such uncommon constraints were apparently not governing the behavior of the members of the Hong Kong Legislative Council.

---

[65] The Prevention of Eviction Ordinance, enacted in 1938, was terminated by the Japanese occupation of the colony in 1941. The Landlord and Tenant Ordinance, enacted in 1947 to control the rents of all prewar tenements, still survives today. The Rent Increases (Domestic Premises) Control Ordinance – enacted in 1963, discontinued in 1965 and reintroduced in 1970 – survives today. This ordinance controls the rents of domestic premises built in the postwar period which have estimated rental values below a certain amount. Three other less significant ordinances are related to rent control – the Tenancy (Prolonged Duration) Ordinance (1952), the Tenancy (Notice of Termination) Ordinance (1962), and the Demolished Buildings (Re-development of Sites) Ordinance (1962); they all survive today.

It is important to note that both the dissolution of the Rents Ordinance in 1926 and the discontinuation of the Rent Increases Ordinance in 1965 occurred in periods when market rents had fallen to a point that rendered the controls largely ineffective. The former experience, as we have seen, was attributed to the "reconstruction craze," the latter was due to a banking crisis in the colony in 1964.

REFERENCES

Brown, E. H. Phelps, and Wiseman, J., *A Course in Applied Economics*, 2nd ed., London 1964.

Cheung, Steven N. S., "Transaction Costs, Risk Aversion, and the Choice of Contractual Arrangements," *Journal of Law and Economics* (April 1969), *12*, pp. 23–42.

"A Theory of Price Control," *Journal of Law and Economics* (April 1974), *17*, pp. 53–71.

The Squatters Above and the Tenants Below: An Economic Investigation of the Hong Kong Rent Controls (in progress).

Gould, J. R., and Henry, S. G. B., "The Effects of Price Control on a Related Market," *Economica* (February 1967), pp. 42–49.

Megarry, R. E., *The Rent Acts*, 9th ed., London 1961.

Needleman, Lionel, *The Economics of Housing*, London 1965.

Paish, P. W., *The Post-War Financial Problem and Other Essays*, London 1950.

Peltzman, Sam, "An Evaluation of Consumer Protection Legislation: The 1962 Drug Amendments," *Journal of Political Economy* (September/October 1973), *81*, pp. 1049–1091.

"The Effects of Automobile Safety Regulation" (unpublished manuscript, 1974).

Hong Kong Government, *Hongkong Law Reports – 1922*, Hong Kong 1922.

The Ordinances of Hong Kong – 1921, Hong Kong 1921.

The Ordinances of Hong Kong – 1922, Hong Kong 1922.

The Ordinances of Hong Kong – 1923, Hong Kong 1923.

The Ordinances of Hong Kong – 1924, Hong Kong 1924.

The Ordinances of Hong Kong – 1925, Hong Kong 1925.

Hong Kong Legislative Council, *Hong Kong Hansard – 1921*, Hong Kong 1921.

Hong Kong Hansard – 1922, Hong Kong 1922.

Hong Kong Hansard – 1923, Hong Kong 1923.

Hong Kong Hansard – 1924, Hong Kong 1924.

Hong Kong Hansard – 1925, Hong Kong 1925.

Rent Control Committee (John McNeill, Chairman), *Rent Control*, Hong Kong 1953.

7

Regulating natural resources: the evolution of perverse property rights

In most societies individual private ownership of natural resources such as minerals, forests, and fisheries is rare. Unless regulated, open-access conditions will result in overuse of a resource relative to what would prevail under private ownership. Regulation of the commons faces two challenges: (1) the prevention of overuse and (2) exploitation of the resource in the least costly manner. The following essay by Robert Higgs analyzes the causes and consequences of the regulations restricting the catch of salmon in the Pacific Northwest. For the most part the focus is on the costs of regulation rather than on the issue of preventing overuse.[1] Higgs argues that because of the anadromous nature of salmon, the least costly means of catch is the use of upstream techniques or traps at the mouths of rivers, yet legislators have generally outlawed the highly successful catch techniques. The result of the regulations, according to Higgs, is technical regress; we now harvest fewer salmon with more inputs than we did before the regulations were instituted.

Higgs's essay is rich in historical detail. As in the essay by Krueger (Chapter 5), without such historical knowledge the dynamics of regulation would be difficult to understand. For example, sport fishermen today are among the important players in the policy arena and were not a potent force when the original legislation was put in place. It is not reasonable to assume that the original designers could have foreseen the future role of sport fishermen.

The historical detail does not imply that more general lessons cannot

---

[1] Regulation of the commons has been the focus of much of the work of Elinor Ostrom. She suggests that decentralized regulation by users leads to better use of resources than regulation by central governments. Local knowledge and homogeneous interests may explain this result. See her *Governing the Commons* (Cambridge University Press, 1990).

be gleaned from the account.[2] Central to the concerns of this volume are the conditions under which institutional change is more likely to favor economic growth or redistribution at the expense of economic growth. In the case of the Pacific salmon fishery, regulation resulted in redistribution. Redistributive policies as opposed to those encouraging growth appear more likely when the competing interests are heterogeneous, because heterogeneity increases the costs of making side payments such that all parties can benefit. Instead, one party can gain at the expense of another. If all parties had the same stake in an issue, the economic growth solution would be more likely.[3] In the case of the fishery, those employing upstream techniques tended to be wealthy and few in number, while the more numerous downstream fishermen tended to be men of small means. The more numerous fishermen were able to outlaw the more productive techniques, thus leading to technical regress. This is in contrast to the general presumption that more concentrated interest groups tend to win out over more numerous and dispersed interest groups.

Voter sympathy with the small guys as opposed to the fat cats may be general in the regulation of natural resources. Gary Libecap has argued that the numerous small-scale oil drillers in Texas have been able to block legislation favoring early unitization of oil fields.[4] The absence of early unitization has resulted in redistribution away from the fewer large-scale producers and a rate of exploitation that has raised the total costs of extraction. Voter sympathy for the small guys or envy of the rich may also explain the strong rights of squatters in most Latin American countries.

In the regulation of natural resources, perceptions of fairness seem particularly important; if a resource is owned in common, wealth should not be a barrier to entry. Such thinking is used to justify the subsidization of U.S. national parks, even though low-income people are infrequent users of park facilities.[5] Further augmenting the likelihood of legislation against the wealthy in cases of natural resources is the belief that the supply of natural resources is fixed. If the supply is fixed, giving

---

[2] Indeed, we believe that the best way now to improve the current state of our theoretical knowledge is to generalize from a sufficient number of historically rich case studies such as the one by Higgs.

[3] This is why homogeneous local groups tend to regulate the commons more effectively.

[4] Gary Libecap, *Contracting for Property Rights* (Cambridge University Press, 1989).

[5] Again we stress that legislators act on perceptions of reality. Information is a costly resource.

to one group over another does not appear to involve a net loss, as long as the rate of exploitation is limited. Yet, as Higgs ably demonstrates, the costs of extraction of the same catch can vary dramatically and affect the productivity of a society.

An important element in the regulation story told by Higgs is the role of crises.[6] Especially important was the Great Depression, when a high premium was placed on the employment of labor per se. Higgs argues that crises give politicians more scope for change and that in times of crisis constituents want politicians to do something. In economic crises – regulation of the fishery was labeled a crisis – constituents frequently ask: Is the present situation fair? If deemed unfair, politicians will redistribute.

Higgs does not argue that technical regress was the goal of legislators. It was an unintended consequence. Conservation of natural resources was the ostensible goal of regulation, but redistribution was most likely the central concern of the fishermen. We doubt that much thought was ever given to the long-run effects on technical regress.

WHAT TO LOOK FOR IN THE ESSAY

We encourage the reader to reflect on the following questions:

1. Are there some problems inherent in using the political process to regulate other natural resources, such as forests, minerals, and grazing land?
2. What other regulations have led to technical regress?
3. In general, for environmental legislation, is crisis a sufficient and necessary condition for institutional change?

---

[6] Higgs argues elsewhere that crisis situations throughout the twentieth century allowed the federal government to expand its control over the private economy. See Robert Higgs, *Crisis and Leviathan* (New York: Oxford University Press, 1987).

Legally induced technical regress in the Washington salmon fishery

ROBERT HIGGS

The history of the Washington salmon fishery is a legal and economic horror story. When the whites first encountered the flourishing aboriginal fishery, they failed to recognize the virtues of its technical and, in a certain sense, legal organization. Determined to transform into private wealth an immensely valuable natural resource, they rushed to appropriate the salmon fishery and threatened its survival. The state's voters, legislators, and appointed managers of the fishery, where the salmon ostensibly "belonged" to all the citizens of Washington collectively, would not permit outright destruction of the resource. But their response to the threat of overfishing was neither to limit entry into the fishery nor to create and enforce a private property right in it, something the Indians had approximated before the advent of the whites. Rather, the state's solution was to limit the harvest by penalizing or prohibiting the more productive harvesting techniques. In the Washington fishery today fewer than 10,000 commercial fishermen, aided by many millions of dollars' worth of fishing gear, harvest about 6 million salmon annually. Before World War I a similar number of men, working with much less than the modern amount of capital, normally harvested three to four times more salmon each year. Thus, commercial fishing productivity is now only a small fraction of what it was 70 years ago. This technical regress did not have to happen; in no sense was it inexorable. Those who created and enforced the legal rules of the fishery – voters, legislators, and state officials – made it happen. My story deals with how and why they did so and some of the economic consequences.

This essay originally appeared in *Research in Economic History*, Vol. 7 (1982), pp. 55–86. Copyright © 1982 by JAI Press Inc.

Robert Higgs

1. RUDIMENTS OF THE FISHERY

Five species of Pacific salmon – chinook, coho, sockeye, pink, and chum – and the steelhead trout are native to the waters of Washington. Although they differ in various respects, these species all follow an anadromous life course. They spawn in the gravel beds of shallow, clear, fast-running mountain streams. After a period of early growth in fresh water, the juvenile fish migrate downstream and enter the salt water of Puget Sound or the Pacific Ocean. Eventually, most of those in the sound continue through the Strait of Juan de Fuca to the Pacific. In the ocean, they feed, attempt to elude numerous predators, and – with luck – grow to maturity. While at sea, the several races of salmon disperse and intermingle with each other. At the age of 2 to 6 years, depending on the species, they migrate back to their places of origin. Each race moves homeward at a characteristic time – most sockeye from the Fraser River system, for example, pass eastward through the strait in late July and August. Many runs overlap, as the sockeye and the pink do in the northern sound, but each varies little from year to year in its return migration schedule. (Pink salmon in Puget Sound have the unique peculiarity that they run only in odd-numbered years.) As a run approaches its spawning site, its members become increasingly concentrated and separated from other runs. When they reenter fresh water, the salmon – but not the steelhead – cease feeding. For the remainder of their journey, which in some cases is more than a thousand miles, they consume their own body fat as a source of energy. Finally arriving at their places of origin, they dig nests in the gravel, deposit and fertilize their eggs, and die. The steelhead, again an exception, may live to migrate and spawn again, some passing through as many as three or four cycles.

For present purposes, two aspects of the life course of these fish are especially important to note:

First, their migration paths take them through long, narrow passages, in most cases either the Columbia River or the Strait of Juan de Fuca and Puget Sound, where *successive fisheries* can be placed (see Figure 1). Of course, everyone knows exactly where the adult fish ultimately will arrive, and therefore, from a societal point of view, it is wasteful to employ resources in attempts to locate and capture them prior to their arrival at their spawning streams.[1] However, in the absence of legal rules and enforcement to preclude it, prior interception may be economically

---

[1] A qualification which the modern troll fishermen espouse to justify their occupation is that salmon caught in the ocean command a price premium for superior quality. In the modern fishery this quality differential exists mainly because the trollers clean and ice their catch immediately, whereas the net fishermen of the "inside" fisheries do not; also, some fish are bruised by rough treatment in the

248

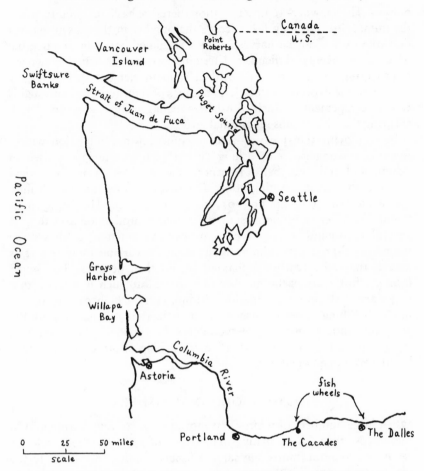

Figure 1. Landmarks and waters of the Washington salmon fishery.

attractive from a private point of view. The narrow passages through which the runs must pass facilitate such premature interception.

Second, in long-run equilibrium there exists a relation between the number of spawners and the number of subsequently returning fish. This relation is not monotonically increasing, because too many spawners can overload the capacity of a spawning area: there is neither sufficient space for building nests and depositing eggs nor enough nutrients available to sustain the overnumerous offspring; a congestion externality

nets. However, in the absence of a troll fishery, high-quality fish with undamaged flesh certainly could be taken by fish traps at the river mouths, if it were legal to do so.

249

obtains. The spawner–returner relation therefore has a maximum. When the number of returning fish exceeds the number in the parent generation, the excess can be harvested on a sustained basis. In practice the harvestable excess is difficult to determine, because the actual spawner–returner relation is stochastic with a random element that is largely relative to the expected values. The number of returners not harvested is called "escapement." Much of fisheries management is concerned with ensuring that this attains an optimal level.

By employing the spawner–returner function in conjunction with a function relating catch to fishing "effort" (composite inputs used in fishing) and to the number of returners, one can derive a sustained-yield function that relates fishing effort and catch in long-run equilibrium. (See Anderson, 1977, pp. 99–101, for the derivation.) This is the counterpart in fisheries economics of the familiar production function in general economics. Like a typical production function, it shows the output (catch) rising at a diminishing rate as the variable input (effort) is added; the catch reaches a maximum and then declines. Too much fishing effort reduces the number of spawners to such low levels that they cannot sustain a population yielding current high catches indefinitely. If fishing effort is pushed far enough, runs can be virtually destroyed, although normally it would not be economically rewarding, from a private point of view, to carry fishing effort to such drastic lengths even in an open-access fishery.

2. THE ABORIGINAL FISHERY

When large numbers of whites first moved into western Washington in the 1850s, they found many small tribes of Indians whose cultures revolved around a flourishing salmon fishery. Suiting their tools to the occasion, the aborigines employed a variety of fishing gear, including traps, weirs, baskets, dip nets, spears, hooks and lines, gaffs, and assorted entangling nets and seines, to capture salmon. The diversity of their gear notwithstanding, they clearly placed major reliance on fixed appliances operated at strategic positions along the rivers (*United States v. Washington*, 1974, pp. 352–381; American Friends Service Committee, 1970, pp. 61, 64, 176). As Anthony Netboy (1958, p. 11) has observed, "The red man had studied carefully the habits and movements of the salmon and knew that the places to trap them were at the mouths of the tributaries and churning cascades and waterfalls."

The Indians also appreciated the importance of spawning escapement: "when the Indians had obtained enough fish they would remove the weirs from the river in order that the fish they did not need could go upstream and lay their eggs so that there would be a supply of fish for future years" (Sextas Ward, a Quileute Indian born about 1852, quoted in American Friends Service Committee, 1970, p. 176). That the Indians had maintained the salmon fishery for centuries without destroying or markedly diminishing it testifies to their intelligence as fishery managers. Of course, their small populations – fewer than 10,000 in the 1850s – and primitive techniques for preserving and transporting their catch combined to render them less threatening to the resource than the more numerous and technically advanced whites subsequently would prove to be. Nevertheless, the Indians' conscious regulation of the fishery played an important role in maintaining its yield over time.

Indian regulation of the fishery, though varying from tribe to tribe, rested on the enforcement of clearly understood property rights. In some cases these rights resided in the tribe as a whole; in other cases in families or individuals; sometimes in a mixture of the two. Judge George Boldt, in the findings of fact for a landmark court decision (*United States v. Washington*, 1974, pp. 352, 353), described these rights as follows:

Generally, individual Indians had primary use rights in the territory where they resided and permissive use rights in the natal territory (if this was different) or in territories where they had consanguineal kin. Subject to such individual claims, most groups claimed autumn fishing use rights in the waters near to their winter villages. Spring and summer fishing areas were often more distantly located and often were shared with other groups from other villages. . . . Control and use patterns of fishing gear varied according to the nature of the gear. Certain types required cooperative effort in their construction and/or handling. Weirs were classed as cooperative property but the component fishing stations on the weir were individually controlled.

In some instances – for example, the fishing stands at the great Celilo Falls of the Columbia, and the reef net locations of the Lummi tribe in northern Puget Sound – fishing rights were heritable individual properties passed down from father to son (Netboy, 1958, p. 16; *United States v. Washington*, 1974, p. 361).

In sum, as Russel Barsh (1977, pp. 22–23) has emphasized, the Indians possessed a well-developed property system in the fishery, and the crucial right recognized and protected under this system was "their exclusive right to take [salmon] by fixed gear" *in or near the rivers* where the fish returned to spawn. As already noted, this is a socially efficient assignment of property rights because it encourages the taking of salmon in the least costly manner. It cannot be stressed too much that what the Indians owned was *not* simply a claim on certain quantities of fish. Rather, the Indians' property rights ensured them the opportunity to take the salmon normally returning – that is, returning without human interception – to certain riparian fishing stations, using any gear whatever but allowing for adequate escapement. The state of Washington would subsequently permit extreme attenuation of these aboriginal property rights, substituting, in Barsh's words, "a law that is economically inferior to the property system originally established by the tribes." For more than one reason, it was unfortunate that the development of the fishery by white men doomed the Indians to a marginal status as fishermen and wholly destroyed the technical and legal apparatus they had employed for centuries.

3. INTERCEPTION EXTERNALITY: A SIMPLE MODEL

The aboriginal salmon fishery was efficient because it was, with unimportant exceptions, a riparian fishery free from marine interceptions of returning adult fish. The salmon fishery developed by the whites would turn out to be *increasingly* inefficient because it allowed the attenuation of riparian fishing rights through the unobstructed establishment of intercepting marine fisheries and because, in important instances, an outright prohibition of highly productive gear was enforced. New forms of gear kept "getting in front of" the established gear. This progressive "robbery," which inexorably pushed the focus of fishing activities toward the open sea, continued because the state's property system condoned it, nay, actually encouraged and promoted it. The result was a fishery employing mixed gear: some terminal, some intercepting. The intercepting gear, itself relatively unproductive because it required higher costs to search for and capture more dispersed salmon stocks, also rendered the terminal gear less productive by reducing the size of and dispersing the runs arriving at the terminal gear sites.

A convenient apparatus for showing the workings of the *interception externality* is Figure 2. In the short term, the run size is exogenously determined and independent of the amount or mix of fishing gear. Assume that two fixed-coefficient techniques are available: (1) the more capital-intensive technique represented by the expansion ray OT (mnemonic for traps), and (2) the more labor-intensive technique represented by the expansion ray OS (mnemonic for seines). If fishing effort were increased along OT, that is, using traps alone, the catch would after some point increase at a diminishing rate because of the fixed run size; similarly along OS. Therefore, the isoquants differing by a unit of catch are increasingly far apart as inputs are added along either activity ray.

At low levels of fishing effort, techniques can be combined without noticeable external effects. Thus, the catch obtained by traps alone operated at point A or by seines alone operated at point B can also be obtained by a linear combination of the two techniques. The straight line segment AB is the isoquant representing the locus of input combinations that hold the catch constant for various mixes of the two techniques. Here the diagram displays only an elementary proposition of activity analysis (Lancaster, 1969, pp. 64–66).

The twist appears at higher levels of fishing effort. Consider, for example, moving from point C (all traps) to point D (all seines), two points that represent the same catch level. Without interception externality, the interconnecting isoquant would be the straight line segment CED. With such high levels of fishing effort, however, the substitution of seines for traps will significantly "rob" the remaining traps in the technical mix and require more effort (inputs of labor and capital) simply to compensate for the loss through interception. The interconnecting isoquant will bow out, away from the origin, as shown by line segment $CE'D$. At higher levels of fishing effort the concavity of the mixed-technique isoquants becomes more and more pronounced, reflecting the growing severity of the interception externality as more gear is used with a fixed run size.

If a single wealth-maximizing owner operated the fishery, or if the terminal gear operators possessed enforceable property rights in runs headed for their trapping areas, mixed gear would *never* be used. Depending on the relative physical productivities of the two gear types (in isolation) and the relative input prices, either traps alone or seines alone would be cheaper than mixed gear for capturing a given catch. Consider, for example, the factor cost ratio represented by the lines K_1L_1 and K_2L_2. At those relative factor prices, the catch level represented by the isoquant FHG would be taken most cheaply by traps alone at point F. If a lack of property rights permits operation of the fishery with the mixed gear represented by point H, then the total costs of taking the catch will be increased. The excess cost can be measured either by the cost of acquiring the amount of labor L_2-L_1 or by the cost of acquiring the amount of capital K_2-K_1. At higher levels of fishing effort, the social waste caused by the interception externality grows proportionately larger. (Note that the operators of each gear type recover their full private opportunity costs of inputs. The social inefficiency reflects the dissipation of the potential rent of the fishery, not a private operating inefficiency of any sort.)

The model portrayed in Figure 2 can be generalized to cover more than two inputs, substitutable-input production technologies, and more than two successively intercepting gear types. The substantive conclusions remain the same. Interception imposes socially unnecessary costs on the fishery. The larger the total fishing effort, *ceteris paribus*, the greater is the social waste of a mixed gear fishery for anadromous stocks. Fishery managers concerned about social efficiency would attempt to discourage mixed gear; given a choice, they would favor gear in proportion to its "terminality" and strive to obstruct new modes of intercep-

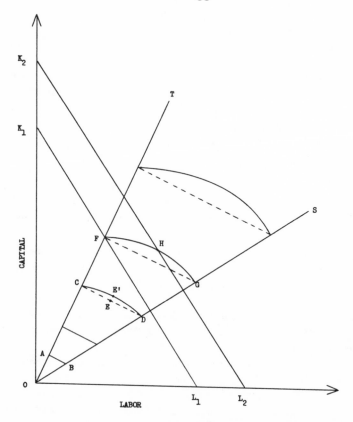

Figure 2. Fishing techniques and interception externality.

tion. If the fishery managers do not behave in this way, it is either because they do not consider social efficiency at all or because they place higher priority on other objectives with which social efficiency conflicts. Historically, the ruling motives involved both sources of inefficient management.

4. THE COLUMBIA RIVER FISHERY TO 1934

Washington's modern salmon industry originated in the 1860s on the Columbia River, set in motion by technical improvements in the art of canning. The first salmon cannery on the Columbia began operation at Eagle Cliff, about 40 miles east of Astoria, in 1866; it quickly proved successful. The Columbia salmon pack increased rapidly, from 4,000 cases in 1866 to 100,000 cases in 1869 to 200,000 cases in 1871. (A standard case contains 48 one-pound cans.) By the early 1880s, when

Technical regress in the Washington salmon fishery

the Columbia industry was nearing its all-time peak, about three dozen canneries were operating. In 1883 and 1884, the peak years, they packed more than 600,000 cases annually (Cobb, 1930, p. 562). As the packers established new markets, improved their canning techniques, and accelerated their rate of output, they created a booming demand for fish.

At first the fishermen had little difficulty keeping up with the growing demand. The river teemed with salmon, and even unsophisticated gear could harvest them in huge numbers at little cost. Small beach seines, traps, and drift gillnets comprised the initial gear on the Columbia.[2] One packer reported in 1871 that his cannery had packed 25,000 cases in 90 days, the fish being caught by four small gillnets, each 125 fathoms long and 25–30 meshes deep. According to the Portland *Oregonian,* the average catch per gillnet boat on the Columbia in 1876 was 3,850 fish (Carstensen, 1971, pp. 66, 76).

The amount of gear on the river soon increased greatly. Surveying the Columbia in 1888, the Corps of Engineers discovered 1,600 drift gillnets averaging 300 fathoms each (all together, 545 miles of gillnet!), 136 fish traps, an undisclosed number of beach seines, and seven fish wheels. Small wonder that the average catch per gillnetter in 1887 had fallen to 600 fish (Carstensen, 1971, pp. 66, 76). Already the productivity decline characteristic of a developing open-access fishery was obvious. The potential rent of the fishery was being dissipated by socially unnecessary payments to fishermen and the owners of fishing gear. With nothing to limit further entry, the situation continued to deteriorate. In 1892 the Washington State Fish Commissioner (Washington State, Fishery *Reports,* 3, 1892, p. 18) reported that "at least twenty-five hundred gill nets, five hundred traps, seventy-five fish wheels and twenty-five seines are employed every season in taking salmon, and it is a fortunate fish that reaches the spawning grounds." Of course, the catch per unit of gear declined even further.

Declining productivity created intense hostilities among the operators of various types of gear. Although the problem clearly arose from the growing excess of total gear, each group blamed the overfishing and its consequences on other groups and sought to curtail the fishing privileges of its rivals. From time to time, smoldering hostilities flamed into violent conflicts, some of which resulted in loss of life (Smith, 1974, p. 2).

The gillnetters, most of whom operated along the lower river near Astoria, seldom failed to play a central role in these conflicts. In the late nineteenth and early twentieth centuries, before the adoption of gasoline engines, gillnetting was hard and dangerous work. Most of the gillnet-

[2] Readers unfamiliar with the gear commonly used to harvest Pacific salmon can find brief descriptions in the Appendix.

ters were itinerant, unmarried immigrant men who came from San Francisco to work on the Columbia during the summer fishing season. Among them were many Italians, Greeks, Slavs, Portuguese, Spaniards, and Scandinavians. Carefully deleting the Scandinavians, who were considered "Americans," the Seattle *Post-Intelligencer* once described the remaining fishermen as "piratical dagoes" (Carstensen, 1971, p. 67). Over the years, many lost their lives, being swept out to sea and drowned by the sudden gales that frequent the mouth of the Columbia.

Men accustomed to danger, the gillnetters sometimes freely assumed other risks. Not uncommonly, they tried to steal fish from the traps on the river's north shore across from Astoria at Baker's Bay. An old trap fisherman (Jackson, 1977, p. 203) recently recalled that "during the heavy fish runs in summer it was necessary to lift the traps at low water night and day as gillnetters would, if given the chance, lay alongside the pots and cut them open, taking whatever fish they could reach." Gillnetters and trap men sometimes exchanged gunfire, and many casualties resulted from these infamous "salmon wars." On one occasion, when the gillnetters were striking against the canneries for higher prices in 1896,

Some of the most radical of the strikers attempted by threats and violence to deter any one from fishing for less than the rate established by the union, and numerous attacks were made by strikers upon those who attempted to deliver salmon at less than five cents per pound. This was especially the case with regard to the pound net fishermen of Baker's bay, and the sheriff of Pacific county [Washington] being called upon by the owners of these pound nets for protection, concluded that with the means at his demand [*sic*] it would be impossible for him to afford the protection necessary, and after consulting with the prosecuting attorney of that county, he informed the governor of the serious nature of the trouble on the river, and asked for assistance in seeing that the law was upheld and the pound net fishermen protected. Acting upon the representations made to him by the sheriff and prosecuting attorney, the governor ordered a company of militia to the scene of disturbance, and from their arrival at Ilwaco no more trouble was experienced by the pound net operators. The situation became so serious on the other side of the river that the governor of Oregon was also obliged to send milita to maintain order. (Washington State, Fishery *Reports*, 7, 1896, p. 5; note that "pound net" is simply another name for a fish trap)

The gillnetters also despised the operators of the fish wheels farther upriver. It galled them to witness fish being dumped rhythmically into huge piles without so much as an erg of human effort being exerted. The wheels, with their enormously visible productivity, seemed capable of destroying the salmon runs and with them the livelihood of the gillnetters. The lower river men were reluctant to recognize publicly that the gillnets, being so numerous, captured many times more salmon than the small number of productive wheels (Washington State, Fishery *Reports*, 36–37, 1927, p. 14). The interception externality created by the gillnetters was clearly demonstrated in July 1896. When the gillnetters went on strike against the fish buyers at Astoria, leaving the lower river unobstructed by nets, the sockeye came upriver " 'like smelt' so thickly that all one [wheel operator] could see below the wheel was their backs sticking out of the water. They swarmed into the scoops of the wheel in such numbers that it was necessary for [the operator of this wheel] to raise the dips above the water to prevent foundering and disaster" (Donaldson and Cramer, 1971, pp. 63–64). Although many fish wheels failed even to cover their costs, their productivity being highly site specific and the number of good sites limited, they provoked "many years of perennial fish fights between Seufert Brothers Company [the principal owner of wheels at the Dalles] and the fishermen of the lower Columbia" (Donaldson and Cramer, 1971, pp. 20, 91).

The legislatures of Washington and Oregon began regulating the commercial fishing seasons and gear on the Columbia during the 1870s (Wendler, 1966; Oregon State Planning Board, 1938, pp. 38–39). Although the laws passed and regulations issued were ostensibly conservation measures, their discriminating terms can be understood only in the context of the competition between the operators of different fishing gear. Increasingly, the operators of fixed gear, who constituted a small minority of the total fishing labor force, suffered disproportionately from restrictions and taxes.

In 1893 the Washington legislature passed an act "To Regulate and License the Catching of Salmon" (Washington State, *Session Laws*, 1893, pp. 15–18). The act imposed restrictions on and required licenses for fixed gear only. It restricted the mesh size, lead length, and spacing of fixed appliances, limited each licensee to three licenses, and set the fee at $10 per license. No restrictions were placed on nor were licenses required of gillnetters or other operators of mobile gear.

The Washington legislature in 1897 repealed the act of 1893 and replaced it with an act "Regulating the Catching of Salmon" (Washington State, *Session Laws*, 1897, pp. 214–220). This act retained the physical restrictions previously imposed on fixed appliances. It required for the first time a license for gillnetting. The license fees it established, however, placed a relatively light burden on gillnetters:

For each drag seine not exceeding 250 feet in length	$2.50
For each drag seine more than 250 feet and less than 500 feet in length	10.00
For each drag seine upwards of 500 feet in length	15.00
For each purse seine	25.00
For each gill net or drift net	2.50

For each set net	1.00
For each pound net, trap or weir on the Columbia River	15.00
For each pound net, trap or weir on Willapa harbor	10.00
For each pound net, trap or weir (except on the Columbia river or on Willapa harbor)	25.00
For each scow fish wheel	15.00

Stationery [*sic*] fish wheels shall pay $25.00 for first class wheels, and $15.00 for second class wheels; the classification to be determined by the fish commissioner. (Washington State, *Session Laws*, 1897, p. 218)

As usual, the legislature placed a concluding section in the act to declare that "an emergency exists."

An act of 1899 "Relating to Food Fishes" (Washington State, *Session Laws*, 1899, pp. 194–206) modified and made slightly more detailed the structure of the license fees. It also imposed a discriminatory tax on the catch of traps and wheels: $1.00 for each 1,000 fish taken. For the most productive traps in Puget Sound, this tax amounted to several hundred dollars per season. No catch tax was levied on the operators of nets.

When the Washington legislature, in an attempt to systematize its fishery laws, enacted a "Fisheries Code" in 1915 (Washington State, *Session Laws*, 1915, pp. 67 ff.), the license fees were set as follows (pp. 85–86): double-ended traps on Puget Sound, $100; single-ended traps on Puget sound, $50; first-class traps on the Columbia, $25; second-class traps on the Columbia, $15 (a trap's classification as first or second class depended on whether it caught more or less than $1,000 worth of salmon during the preceding season); traps on Willapa Bay and Grays Harbor, $15; stationary fish wheels, $35; scow fish wheels, $25; purse seines, $25 (purse seines over 1,800 feet were prohibited); gillnets on Puget Sound, $5 plus one cent per foot for every foot over 600 of length (gillnets over 3,000 feet were prohibited on Puget Sound); gillnets on other Washington waters, $7.50; beach seines, 3 cents per foot of length; set nets, $3.75.

A more important discrimination than the license fees was the catch tax from which gillnetters were explicitly exempted: $3.00 per 1,000 chinook or steelhead ($5.00 per 1,000 chinook on the Columbia before August 26); $1.50 per 1,000 sockeye; $1.00 per 1,000 coho or chum; $0.50 per 1,000 pink (Washington State, *Session Laws*, 1915, pp. 89–90). The State Fish Commissioner observed in 1919 (Washington State, *Fishery Reports*, 28–29, 1920, p. 23) that "the seemingly insignificant exemption from the catch tax of fish taken in gill nets and set nets permits fully seventy-five percent of the fish taken in the waters of the Columbia river to escape without the payment of any catch tax." In addition, the Fisheries Code of 1915 (pp. 97–98) required that "the owner or operator of the fish trap or pound net shall constantly main-

258

tain, during the weekly closed season, a watchman, whose duty, among other things, it shall be to cause such pound net or trap to be closed" in a manner stipulated in detail by the act. This requirement entailed a substantial additional cost of labor for trap operators. As the Fish Commissioner plainly recognized, "the law at the present time favors certain classes of the industry as against other classes" (Washington State, Fishery *Reports*, 28–29, p. 24).

Although the operators of fixed gear suffered increasingly from discriminatory license fees, operational restrictions, and catch taxes, they were not, prior to 1927, forbidden to operate on the Columbia. In 1926, however, an important political battle took place in Oregon, a struggle whose outcome foreshadowed a similar but even more sweeping political decision in Washington 8 years later.

The Oregon contest pitted the old enemies, gillnetters and wheel operators (Donaldson and Cramer, 1971, pp. 111–113; Smith, 1974, pp. 4–5). The gillnetters placed on the ballot in 1926 an initiative proposal to outlaw all fish wheels in Oregon waters and all beach seines and traps on the Oregon side of the Columbia above the Cascades. The Oregon State Grange, the Oregon Federation of Labor, the Oregon Fish Commission, and most sportmen's groups endorsed the initiative. Opposing it were the owners of the threatened gear, their employees, upriver business interests, and the Astoria cannery operators. The affirmative argument printed in the official voters' pamphlet maintained "that two families (Seufert and Warren) took 85 percent of the fish caught above tidewater and employed relatively few men in their operations, and that a few fishwheels took as many fish in 24 hours as the average gill-net fisherman took in 4 years of labor. . . . The negative position [asked] . . . by what American principle of fair dealing could the takers of 88 percent of the fish demand confiscation of the large investments in equipment, factories, and labor of those who took less than 7 percent of the fish" (Donaldson and Cramer, 1971, p. 112).

When the voters went to the Oregon polls in 1926, more than 102,000 favored outlawing the wheels; only 73,000 wished to uphold the long-established private property rights under attack and to sustain the highly productive fixed gear for harvesting salmon (Smith, 1974, p. 3). Wheel owners subsequently failed in their attempts to have the initiative law declared unconstitutional by the courts. In Oregon, the fish wheel era had, after a half-century filled with strife, finally come to an end. In 1927, Frank A. Seufert, still fuming over his heavy capital losses, painted in large letters on the roof of a barn near his upriver cannery: TO BUILD THIS BUSINESS IT TOOK 47 YEARS. THE INITIATIVE LAW OF OREGON DESTROYED IT IN ONE DAY (photograph in Donaldson and Cramer, 1971, p. 112). Outlawing the Oregon wheels had little if any effect on the total harvest of salmon in the Columbia. Probably few people really cared about that. "The long-drawn-out 'fishwheel fight' on the Columbia was actually not fought for conservation, as depicted. Rather, the compelling reasons were economic, each side striving to catch as many fish as possible, with the low-cost production on the Upper river being particularly irritating to the lower-river operators" (Donaldson and Cramer, 1971, p. 113). This was by no means the first time that the political process had favored "equity" at the expense of productivity; nor, in the Pacific salmon fishery, would it be the last.

5. THE PUGET SOUND FISHERY TO 1934

The Puget Sound district lagged behind the Columbia River district in the development of the modern salmon industry, but once it had gained momentum it far exceeded the scale of its precursor. The first cannery began operation at Mukilteo, about 20 miles north of Seattle, in 1877. It packed only 5,000 cases. For the next 15 years the Puget Sound pack of canned salmon fluctuated erratically, never exceeding 27,000 cases. Then, in the mid-1890s, it began to grow explosively: from 90,000 cases in 1893, the pack increased to 180,000 cases in 1895, to 494,000 cases in 1897, and to 1,381,000 cases in 1901 (Cobb, 1930, p. 557).[3] By this time the Puget Sound industry had far outstripped its counterpart on the Columbia. Puget Sound canneries experienced their golden age between the turn of the century and 1919, the peak year being 1913, when 2,583,000 cases were packed. After 1919, the pack settled on a fluctuating plateau less than half as high as that sustained during the golden age. In 1917, 45 canneries operated on Puget Sound. After 1919, never more than 23, and in several years only 10–14, operated. The estimated value of the pack, which reached a high of more than $16 million in 1917, never exceeded $10 million between 1920 and 1934 (*Pacific Fisherman Yearbook*, 1935, p. 80). Between 1909 and 1934, approximately nine-tenths of the salmon caught by commercial fishermen in Washington waters came from Puget Sound. During those years – after the Columbia fishery had peaked but before the development of a huge ocean fishery – the sound and the salmon fishery were almost synonymous.

[3] The reader will notice that the catch data cited in this section always pertain to odd-numbered years. This practice is necessary to preserve comparability between years. The pink salmon of Puget Sound run only in odd-numbered years. The sockeye, though they run annually, exhibited in the early twentieth century a pronounced quadrennial cycle, the "big years" being 1901, 1905, 1909, and 1913. Because of a rockslide that almost completely blocked the Fraser River at Hell's Gate in 1913, the sockeye run was decimated and the amplitude of its cycle became less pronounced subsequently.

Technical regress in the Washington salmon fishery

During the incipient period of the fishery, 1877–1892, a few units of simple gear could easily harvest the salmon packed on Puget Sound. The State Fish Commissioner reported in 1892 that the gear consisted of 19 beach seines, 19 purse seines, and 10 gillnets (Washington State, Fishery Reports, 3, 1892, p. 14). Several experimental fish traps were constructed on the sound during the 1880s, but apparently none was successful.

The point of inflection in the growth of the Puget Sound salmon industry occurred in 1891, when the first successful traps were constructed near Point Roberts, just below the Canadian border. This area is propitiously situated on the migration path of the sockeye and pink salmon that spawn in British Columbia's Fraser River system. During the later 1890s, a great trap fishery developed in Washington waters stretching from Point Roberts through the San Juan Islands and southward along the west coasts of Fidalgo and Whidbey Islands (Rounsefell and Kelez, 1935, pp. 3, 6; Cobb, 1930, pp. 424, 483). These traps, much larger, more elaborate, and more expensive than their counterparts on the Columbia, proved to be the most awesomely productive appliances ever devised for capturing salmon. As such, they provoked the hostilities of sportsmen and fishermen operating less productive forms of gear and became the focus of a "salmon war" that spanned four decades. They also made a few people quite rich – which is not unrelated to the hostilities they provoked.

To obtain exclusive private property rights over a trap site, one had to obtain a trap license (the license fee was $50 in Puget Sound after 1898), then file the initial claim to a location marked by at least three substantial piles, upon which the license number was posted. After filing a location map with the proper state authority, the licensed claimant possessed "the exclusive right to hold, occupy and fish such location, to renew the license therefor, and to mortgage, sell and transfer the same." Licenses had to be renewed annually, but Puget Sound trap sites could be legally retained by actually constructing the trap only once every 4 years (Washington State, Session Laws, 1915, pp. 76–79). To construct a Puget Sound trap cost between $5,000 and $14,000, depending on the physical conditions of the site and the size and design of the trap (Darwin, 1916, p. 4; Cobb, 1930, p. 483). Prospectors who had filed claims on good locations in the 1890s were well placed to reap large capital gains when the Puget Sound salmon fishery began to grow explosively at the end of the century.

In 1899, Roland Onffroy organized the Pacific American Fisheries Company, a syndicate funded by Chicago investors. Onffroy was said to have brought from Chicago "a million dollars to buy up the available traps, fleets, and canneries" (Teck, 1903, p. 186). Whether or not he

Robert Higgs

had a million to spend, he certainly had more than anyone had ever before spent on trap sites. Many owners sold their sites to Pacific American and to competing canneries at prices between $20,000 and $90,000 each (Teck, 1903, pp. 186–187; Cobb, 1930, p. 483); others scrambled to stake new claims. This was the high-water mark when, as a contemporary writer expressed it, "Onffroy made princes of our fish trap barons" and transported them "from the strenuous struggle to the lap of ease by the fish trap route" (Teck, 1903, p. 186). Many claims proved unremunerative and were abandoned: from 454 Puget Sound trap sites licensed in 1900, the number fell to 305 in 1902; thereafter, more than 300 licenses were issued only in 1912 and 1913, and the number was usually between 200 and 300. License holders actually constructed traps on only about two-thirds of their sites in any given year; more traps were built in odd-numbered years to take advantage of the pink runs. Trap sites varied enormously in value. While pointing out in 1917 that "some fish trap locations in Puget Sound are worth many times more than other locations," the Washington Fish Commissioner (Washington State, Fishery *Reports*, 26–27, 1917, pp. 26, 35) referred in passing to "fishing locations worth in some instances hundreds of thousands of dollars."

It was significant that the canneries acquired ownership rights over most of the traps early in the development of the Puget Sound salmon industry. Perhaps, as the Fish Commissioner remarked in 1919 (Washington State, Fishery *Reports*, 28–29, 1919, p. 10), "because of [the traps'] greater ability to take fish, prejudice had naturally been aroused against them." But their tremendous catching power would not have provoked such intense and widespread hostility if they had been independently owned and operated. The canneries were "big business"; their operators were "barons" and "millionaires." The traps, in the eyes of that large segment of the public inclined toward leveling, gave an "unfair" advantage to persons whose wealth already placed them in enviably advantaged positions. As most of the net fishermen were men of small means, many of them immigrants, it was easy for the public to sympathize with the "little men" in their struggle to capture a larger share of the salmon and obtain higher prices from the canneries for the fish they caught.

While the traps dominated the fishery in the first decade of the twentieth century, the little men's day was dawning. As elsewhere in the American economy of that era, the critical innovation was the gasoline engine. Installed in the purse seine vessel – virtually the entire fleet adopted it during the years 1903–1906 – it transformed that type of harvesting gear and made if for the first time a serious competitor of the fish trap (Rounsefell and Kelez, 1935, pp. 3–5; Washington State Fish-

262

ery *Reports,* 28–29, 1919, p. 10). In 1908, only 69 purse seiners were licensed in Puget Sound. Their numbers then increased rapidly to 252 in 1913 and 420, an all-time peak, in 1917. Their share of the catch increased with their numbers. In 1913, when comprehensive catch data were first collected, purse seiners caught only about a third of the total catch; the traps caught 61 percent, and miscellaneous gear, mostly gillnets, took the small residual share. Two years later, 110 additional purse seiners having been licensed in the interim, the seiners took 57 percent of the catch. They continued to outfish the traps during 1916–1917 and 1919. In the 1920s the traps recovered some of their former share, but even then the purse seiners outfished them in some years. After 1929 the seiners always caught more than the traps (Washington State Fishery *Reports,* 46–49, 1939, pp. 69–73). "Use of the purse seine," said the State Fish Commissioner (Washington State, Fishery *Reports,* 28–29, 1919, p. 10), "stole upon us like a thing in the night. Their greatly increasing use occurred during the world war and for that reason did not attract the notice or excite the comment they would have under ordinary conditions."

Although it cost about $7,000 and required a crew of seven to nine men, and hence was relatively expensive to operate, the gasoline-powered purse seiner did possess "deadly effectiveness . . . as a catcher of fish" (Washington State, Fishery *Reports,* 28–29, 1919, p. 10; Darwin, 1916, p. 4). Its most valuable attribute was mobility. Seiners could meet the returning salmon in June on the Swiftsure Bank southwest of Vancouver Island, follow them through the Strait of Juan de Fuca, northward through the San Juan Islands to the Canadian border or southward through Admiralty Inlet into inner Puget Sound (Rounsefell and Kelez, 1935, p. 5). Observed the *Pacific Fisherman* (July 1936, p. 28), "where there is a congregation of fish, there will be a congregation of purse seiners."

The purse seine catch, however, was by no means all a net addition to the total. Many of the fish the seiners caught, if allowed to proceed, would have entered the traps. By placing themselves "in front of" the traps – sometimes the seiners flagrantly set their nets immediately adjacent to the traps, where the trap leads had concentrated schools of fish – the seiners created a classic interception externality. The Fish Commissioner recognized this as early as 1913 (Washington State, *Fishery Reports,* 22–23, 1913, p. 33), when he observed that

there has undoubtedly been an increase in number and efficiency of purse seines during the last few years. But it is also a fact that the increase in the number and efficiency of purse seines reduces the efficiency of the pound nets and traps in the taking of fish, for the reason – among others – that the prevalence of purse seines in the vicinity of fish traps scatters and diverts the schools of fish and causes them to pass out into deep water beyond the traps, and we think that it can be safely asserted that while the total number of appliances and gear may have been increased in recent years, the efficiency in the catching of fish has not been much, if any, increased.

Attempts to intercept salmon became frantic during World War I. "During the five-year period from 1913 to 1917 more fishing gear was employed than in any year before or since"; the year 1917 witnessed the most intensive effort of all (Rounsefell and Kelez, 1935, pp. 13, 15). The price of salmon rose to undreamed of heights: from an average paid to fishermen of 12.8 cents per fish in 1913, the price jumped to 53.9 cents in 1917 and 71.2 cents in 1918 (Washington State, Fishery *Reports*, 28–29, 1919, p. 36). "Stimulated by the high prices which they received for their catch, the fishermen [were] building larger boats *so as to enable them to go farther out to sea,* making use of larger nets, while the ranks of the fishermen [were] steadily augmented by persons attracted from other occupations" (Washington State, Fishery *Reports*, 28–29, 1919, pp. 35–36; emphasis added).

Close in the wake of the purse seiners came other "little men." Trollers, intent on intercepting fish before they reached the existing interceptors, emerged in huge numbers during the war. Said the Fish Commissioner in 1919 (Washington State, Fishery *Reports*, 28–29, 1919, p. 9):

One of the most amazing developments of the fishing industry of this state during the last four years has been fishing for our salmon with hook and line. . . . [T]his period of time witnessed the building up of the great fleets for operation off our Pacific Coast line from the Columbia river to Cape Flattery. . . . It was the hook and line fisherman or the troller who first started the intensive offshore fishing for immature salmon. Because of his presence in much greater numbers, it is possible that in the course of a year the hook and line fishers take more salmon than are taken by any of the other appliances off the mouth of the Columbia river.

While most of them fished off the mouth of the Columbia, several hundred operated west of the Strait of Juan de Fuca, in the open sea, beyond the jurisdiction of the Washington authorities (Washington State, Fishery *Reports*, 30– 31, 1921, pp. 42–43,78). The purse seiners then began to taste the same bitter medicine they had administered in such large doses to the trap men during the past decade.

With the depression of 1921 and the decline of fish prices from their wartime peaks, the Puget Sound fishery experienced a period of retrenchment in the early 1920s. "The drop in the run of fish, and greatly increased cost of operating due to the war, together with the low selling value of the fish, made the industry unprofitable for the purse seiners, and many of them removed to California or Alaska with their vessels" (Washington State, Fishery *Reports*, 32–33, 1923, p. 10). Recovery after 1923 was slow but steady. The number of purse seiners licensed in Puget Sound rose from 133 in 1923 to 251 in 1931. The seiners and the trap men, as if they had declared a truce, took about equal shares of the total catch during the 1920s. The truce, however, was more apparent than real. The seiners, not satisfied with their large share of the catch, longed to banish the trap men from the fishery altogether. The Great Depression – and some unexpectedly powerful new allies – would create favorable conditions for the realization of their objective.

6. THE POLITICAL ECONOMY OF INITIATIVE NO. 77

The Great Depression promoted a multifaceted transformation of American opinions and values. Perhaps the most obvious shift was the high premium that came to be placed on the employment of labor per se. Given an opportunity to choose politically between labor-saving and labor-intensive techniques of production, most people favored the latter more strongly than ever before. Overlapping the heightened preference for labor-intensive, employment-creating techniques was a shift of sympathies toward helping the poor and disadvantaged. The other side of this coin was a more intense hostility toward the rich and advantaged. Especially suspect were the "monopolists" and "big businessmen," those who had vainly claimed responsibility for the New Prosperity of the 1920s and now stood vulnerable to an unwelcome attribution of responsibility for the Great Depression. Another significant characteristic of public opinion in the 1930s was a renewed concern for the conservation of natural resources, a concern strongly embraced and articulated by Franklin Roosevelt's administration (Graham, 1976, pp. 36–43; Gunderson, 1976, pp. 443–446).

Each of these elements played a part in reshaping the political context within which the electorate and the legislature of Washington regulated the salmon fishery. In particular, the proposal to conserve the salmon runs by outlawing the highly productive but labor-saving trap technique promised simultaneously to conserve a valuable natural resource, to expand employment opportunities, to reward the poor and disadvantaged (the net fishermen), and to punish big business (the canneries, which owned most of the traps). Thus, the prevailing public opinions of the 1930s created a much more conducive environment for the net fishermen's assault on the trap men.

Probably no important change would have occurred, however, without the arrival on the political stage of a significant new actor: the sport fisherman. People had caught salmon for sport since the late nineteenth

Robert Higgs

century, but with the increase of personal income, the decline of the work week, and the wide diffusion of the automobile in the 1920s the ranks of the sport fishermen began to increase rapidly. The Director of the Department of Fisheries (Washington State, Fishery *Reports*, 40–41, 1931, p. 7) referred in 1930 to "sport fishing activities in salt water areas [that were] growing by leaps and bounds." In 1937, a Seattle journalist proclaimed that "a new industry has sprung up in the past 10 years, that of sports fishing in Puget Sound, providing *employment* to thousands and *enjoyment* to thousands more. That industry is entitled to protection and encouragement" (quoted in "No Fish Traps," 1937, p. 6; emphasis in original). Here was a political force to be reckoned with. Tens of thousands of resident sport fishermen, along with all those interested in supplying and transporting them or otherwise catering to their demands, formed a potential bloc of voters numerous enough to overwhelm any commercial fishing group if the bloc could only be inspired and organized for political action.

The inspiration was the easy part; it arose from the mere sight of the traps. Sportsmen cruising the waters of Puget Sound could always see the traps. They could also see the cannery tenders hauling scows piled full of salmon, tens of thousands of them in a single load, taken from the traps. To see so many salmon in one load confirmed their worst fears about the imminent destruction of the runs. The gillnetters, who fished at night, and the purse seiners, who often operated far from shore, were less visible and hence less immediately threatening. As usual, the limited and biased evidence of immediate experience received more weight than the systematic data available, which showed that the purse seiners caught most of the salmon (Washington State, Fishery *Reports*, 46–49, 1939, pp. 71–73).

In retrospect, one can see that the sportsmen's proposal to conserve the salmon by abolishing the traps was both ill-considered and misrepresented. On the one hand, they failed to recognize that a fish caught is a fish caught: conservation would not be promoted if other types of gear remained free to take fish previously taken by the traps. Also, they failed to recognize that they actually competed more directly with the trollers and the seiners than with the traps. The former types of gear intercepted many chinook and coho – the only species of interest to sportsmen, the others being not readily caught by hook and line – before they reached the Puget Sound areas then frequented by the sportsmen. In the fishing areas adjacent to the trap sites, the sportsmen themselves could intercept the salmon before they reached the traps. Further, the traps relied heavily on catches of sockeye, pink, and chum species of no interest to sportsmen. Finally, of course, the sportsmen's crusade against trap fishing was scarcely a true conservation scheme at all. Rather, like most

266

proclaimed conservation measures (Maass, 1968, pp. 271–279), it was an attempt to take from "them" and give to "us," a simple transfer of wealth disguised in the trappings of an abstract policy prescription held in high regard by the general public and the electorate. Although they liked to think of themselves as noble and public-spirited citizens campaigning against greed and the destruction of nature's bounty, the sportsmen were simply a special interest group, as grasping as the next.

Direct appeals to the state legislature met with no success. In 1933, a bill was introduced in the House to prohibit fish traps, but it died in committee (McLeod, 1937, p. 15). The issue was too hot for the timid legislators to handle. The sportsmen and the operators of mobile commercial gear needed a more coherent and organized effort to achieve their objective. Frustrated by their rebuff in the legislative session of 1933, they resolved to carry their appeal directly to the people.

They decided to circulate an initiative petition. Over the years, this device had been attempted on five different occasions by Washington fishery interests, but each time the sponsors had been unable to secure enough signatures to place their proposal on the ballot (Washington Secretary of State, 1966). Oregon groups, however, had placed more than a dozen fishery initiatives on their state's ballots; and in 1926, as previously noted, the Oregon voters had approved an initiative outlawing fish wheels and restricting the areas where beach seines and fish traps could operate on the Oregon side of the Columbia (Smith, 1974, p. 3). An initiative petition allowed the antitrap forces to circumvent the legislature and its intricacies of committees, procedural hurdles, and strategic vote trading, and to present the issue directly to the voters.

To publicize the issue and perform the political leg work, the antitrap groups put aside their differences and entered into a formal coalition. Early in 1934 they formed the Salmon Conservation League. Described by its founders as "an expedient combination of both commercial and sports interests" (*Washington Sportsman*, 2, Feb.–Mar. 1936, p. 4), the league brought together the Washington State Sportsmen's Council, which claimed to represent 120 sportsmen's clubs with some 40,000 members (*Washington Sportsman*, 2, Apr.–May 1936, p. 15), the Purse Seine Fishermen's Association, the Puget Sound Gill Netters' Association, and the Trolling Vessel Owners' Association. The commercial fishermen's associations provided the money, and the sportsmen's groups supplied the manpower (*Washington Sportsman*, 2, Feb.–Mar. 1936, p. 4).

On February 1, 1934, the Salmon Conservation League filed Initiative Measure No. 77 with the Secretary of State and began to circulate petitions to collect the voter signatures required to place it on the November ballot (Washington Secretary of State, 1966; *Pacific Fisherman*,

March 1934, p. 12). A counterinitiative, No. 82, was filed on March 10, 1934 (Washington Secretary of State, 1966; *Pacific Fisherman,* April 1934, p. 17). Initiative 82 proposed new restrictions on the net size, vessel length, and operating areas of purse seiners. The backers of No. 82 failed to secure enough signatures to place their measure on the ballot. The Salmon Conservation League, on the other hand, did validate its petitions. In November 1934, the voters of Washington would have their first direct opportunity to choose whether a sweeping reorganization of the state's salmon fishery should take place.

Initiative No. 77 contained several substantive provisions. It divided Puget Sound into two areas separated by a line running easterly from Angeles Point on the Olympic Peninsula to Penn Cove on the east side of Whidbey Island, thence northerly to Sinclair Island, thence irregularly northward along Lummi Island and to the mainland, enclosing Lummi Bay. Within the Washington waters east and south of the line, it was made unlawful to fish for salmon with any gear other than hook and line, *except* that other mobile gear could fish there between October 5 and November 20 at any time other than the weekend closed period (4:00 P.M. Friday to 4:00 A.M. Sunday). Puget Sound gillnet licenses were made personal and nontransferable and issuable only to those who had held such licenses during either 1932 or 1933. Gillnets on the Columbia were limited to 250 fathoms in length. Beach seines on the Washington side of the Columbia were made unlawful. Most importantly, the initiative made it "unlawful to construct, install, use, operate, or maintain, within any of the waters of the State of Washington, any pound net, fish trap, fish wheel, scow fish wheel, set net, weir, or any fixed appliance for the purpose of catching salmon, salmon trout, or steel head, or to take salmon, salmon trout, or steel head by any such means" (Washington State, *Session Laws,* 1935, pp. 3–8).

Initiative No. 77 promised substantial benefits to each of its sponsors. Most important to all of them, of course, was getting rid of the traps and other fixed gear. In addition, the gillnetters of Puget Sound protected themselves against new entry into their gear group. The purse seiners gained much and lost little or nothing. Although commercial purse seine fishing was allowed inside the line only between October 5 and November 20, this period turned out to be the prime season for the seiners to enter that area in any event. During July through September, they normally concentrated on the runs of sockeye and pink salmon passing through the Strait of Juan de Fuca and the San Juans on their way back to spawn in the Fraser River. In October and November, when the coho and chum runs arrived in inner Puget Sound, the seiners would still be free to pursue them (*Pacific Fisherman,* July 1936, p. 28). The sportsmen found their alliance with the seiners a congenial one. Sportsmen value the chinook, or king, salmon above all others. At maturity, these fish reach an average weight of 20–25 pounds; the largest range up to 100 pounds. Sport fishermen dream of catching a huge chinook as a trophy. As it happened, "the purse seine catch of Chinooks" – fish that run more individually and less in schools than other salmon – was "purely incidental to fishing for other species; at no time [did] the fleet fish principally for Chinooks" (*Pacific Fisherman*, July 1936, p. 28). Therefore, the sportsmen felt themselves little threatened by the seiners, even though the incidental catch of chinooks was substantial and the purse seines captured huge numbers of coho, the other (but smaller) species of interest to sportsmen.

The campaign was hard fought. While the Salmon Conservation League hammered away at the conservation theme, the trap men fought back with advertisements that proclaimed the initiative would (*Pacific Fisherman*, October 1934, p. 32; emphasis in original):

- increase taxes
- throw thousands of men and women out of work
- confiscate the property of hundreds of small fishermen and deny them the right of earning a living
- deprive the farmer, the manufacturer, and the merchant of hundreds of thousands of dollars now spent with them annually by the salmon industry
- create an absolute monopoly. Read Section 8, of Initiative No. 77 in the pamphlet sent you by the Secretary of State. By making it unlawful to use any other type of fishing gear, it leaves the purse seiners, trollers and gill netters with a complete monopoly. They demand the exclusive privilege of catching the salmon which belong to all the people of the state. No wonder their slogan is, "Save OUR Salmon." Under present conditions they are YOUR salmon, fully protected by rigid state regulations. It is the only instance where the people have been asked to turn over a natural resource to an absolute monopoly. . . . *Then watch the price of salmon go up.*

Most voters chose to ignore these dire, and partly spurious, warnings. In addition, the Democratic Party of Washington helped to promote Initiative No. 77 by making it a part of the party's platform in 1934 (McLeod, 1936–1937, p. 22). When the votes were finally counted, there were 275,507 in favor and only 153,811 opposed (Washington Secretary of State, 1934, p. 3).

The trap interests refused to accept defeat without a struggle. Both in the courts and in the legislature, they retaliated against those who had backed Initiative No. 77. During the legislative session of 1935, "a number of rather important fishery measures were killed by the legislature, among them being one designed to increase the license fee on purse seiners" (*Pacific Fisherman*, April 1935, p. 14).

The legislature of 1935 also had to act on an Initiative to the Legislature, No. 5, which had been filed on October 20, 1934 (Washington Secretary of State, 1966). Under state law, this type of initiative measure goes first to the legislature; if defeated there, it must be presented to the electorate at the next general election. The initiative was filed by William K. Fisher, who was identified as president of the Cowlitz County Sportsmen's Association, and its sponsors represented it as a sportsmen's proposal (*Pacific Fisherman*, Dec. 1934, p. 13; Drumheller, 1935, p. 19). This was a ruse. Ken McLeod, who served as the secretary of both the Sportsmen's Council and the Salmon Conservation League, declared that the Cowlitz County Sportsmen's Association was, in fact, "dormant" and that "Initiative No. 5 was plainly filed as a reprisal against the purse seine fishermen for having supported No. 77. It was financed by several individuals who were prominent in the fight against 77. . . . [T]he hope of the sponsors [was] that if they could wipe out the commercial salmon fishery on Puget Sound, they might have their fish traps reinstated when a readjustment was made" (McLeod, 1936–1937, p. 22).

Initiative No. 5 proposed to prohibit "the use of purse seines and the owning, using or maintaining of any boat or other appliance in connection therewith used in fishing for salmon" (Washington State, Secretary of State, 1936).

After the legislature failed to pass Initiative No. 5 at its session of 1935, the sportsmen turned their attention toward defeating it at the general election in 1936. At the August, 1936, meeting of the Sportsmen's Council, L. W. Whitlow, president of the Salmon Conservation League, argued vigorously against Initiative No. 5. Denouncing it as a retaliatory measure against Initiative No. 77, he argued that No. 5, if passed, would serve as an entering wedge for reestablishment of the trap fishery. He requested that the assembled delegates urge their memberships to vote against the measure (*Washington Sportsman*, 2, Oct.–Nov. 1936, p. 19).

The voters never had an opportunity to decide the fate of Initiative No. 5. On October 1, 1936, the State Supreme Court ordered the initiative struck from the ballot because a sufficient number of signatures on the petitions had not been checked by the Secretary of State to validate the measure. McLeod, exultant over this latest "crushing defeat suffered by the adversaries of Initiative No. 77," proclaimed October 1 "another red letter day for the sportsmen" (McLeod, 1936–1937, p. 22).

Still, the trap interests did not give up, and during the legislative session of 1937 the battle raged furiously. Several proposals to alter Initiative No. 77 were debated. One proposed to reestablish trap fishing only in certain areas. Another, advocated by the State Department of

Fisheries, sought greater flexibility in the use of purse seines and gillnets inside the line fixed by No. 77 at the discretion of the Director of Fisheries (*Pacific Fisherman*, Feb. 1937, p. 28). Ultimately, the disputes focused on Senate Bill No. 29, introduced by Senator T. C. Bloomer, which sought to repeal Initiative No. 77 outright.

The battle over Bloomer's bill took a familiar shape. "There is a tie-up between certain purse-seiners and certain sportsmen's leaders," said Bloomer, "with the purse-seiners providing the money to defeat any measure to modify No. 77." Whitlow, addressing a meeting of the Sportsmen's Council on January 31, 1937, declared that "this is a fight of manpower and principle against greed and money" ("No Fish Traps," 1937, p. 5). Ben Paris, the operator of a restaurant and sporting-goods store in Seattle and a leader of the fight for No. 77, placed an advertisement in the *Washington Sportsman* (March 1937, p. 12; emphasis in original) that exhorted the magazine's readers to

FIGHT FOR INITIATIVE 77! If you appreciate the wonderful sport of salmon fishing, *join in the fight* to protect our salmon against the destructive fish traps! Write your Senator and Representatives in the Legislature – *make yourself heard* in behalf of conservation and against the repeal of Initiative 77!

The same issue of the *Sportsman* contained a lengthy article under the headline "NO FISH TRAPS! Sportsmen United in Opposition to Return of Destructive Gear; Rally to Defend Initiative 77." A cartoon printed with the article shows a bulbous speaker addressing a crowd with the words, "We might compromise with four or five traps in the Columbia River;" offstage, two Daddy Warbucks types labeled "trap operators" are listening, diamond stickpins aglow, and one is saying, "O Boy! If we can get four or five traps on the Washington side of the Columbia, we'll get 'em all back!"

In January 1937, Paris had sent a letter to all members of the legislature soliciting their stand on Initiative No. 77. Almost all of the 27 respondents expressed a commitment to resist any changes. Senator Mary Farquharson added to her expressed assurances the statement that "it is necessary for the government to step in and take control of our natural resources." Representative Robert W. Ginnett wrote, "I am deeply aware of the destruction of the fishing industry by the trap men when they were given full leeway and I feel that we should now all work together for the conservation of this natural resource." Only one legislator, Senator Edmund J. Miller, had the intelligence and courage to say: "I have never had any valid reason as to why Initiative 77 should be considered a conservation measure. Neither has anyone ever shown me where the purse seiner is not as great a detriment as any other type of fisherman. . . . Do not misunderstand me. I am for the conservation

Robert Higgs

of our natural resources, but I have yet to be shown that Initiative 77 accomplishes this" (quoted in "No Fish Traps," 1937, pp. 6, 15).

On March 6, 1937, the Senate overwhelmingly defeated the Bloomer bill, thereby preserving Initiative No. 77 (*Washington Sportsman*, 3, Apr. 1937, p. 3). Proposals for more limited changes similarly met defeat.

Challenges to the constitutionality of No. 77 had, with one minor exception, already failed (*Pacific Fisherman*, Aug. 1935, p. 16). In *Campbell v. Case* (182 Wash. 334), the State Supreme Court on July 2, 1935, upheld the initiative as it applied to a Puget Sound trap fisherman. In *Gile v. Huse* (183 Wash. 560), the high court on September 18, 1935, ruled that a Columbia River trap fisherman challenging No. 77 on different grounds could not escape the fate to which the initiative had consigned him. In *Bacich v. Huse* (187 Wash. 75), the court on August 4, 1936, ruled that the initiative's restriction of Puget Sound gillnet licenses was unconstitutional. This was a small setback for the Salmon Conservation League; it hardly marred the sweeping triumph.

Although the sportsmen continued to fret about a few Indians permitted to maintain fish traps on their reservations (*Washington v. Edwards*, 188 Wash. 467; *Washington Sportsman*, 3, Aug. 1937, p. 9), the fight was really finished. Finally resigned to a reliance on purse seiners for their fish, the canneries gave up their resistance to Initiative No. 77 and concentrated on gaining control over seine vessels to assure themselves a supply of raw materials. The sportsmen and the purse seiners had effected "the most radical change that has taken place in the fisheries of this state" (*Pacific Fisherman*, Jan. 1935, p. 57), and, for the moment at least, they were happy.

7. SOME ECONOMIC EFFECTS OF INITIATIVE NO. 77

Initiative No. 77 had several important economic effects. Perhaps the most obvious was the confiscation of private property: the virtually complete destruction of the owners' investments in stationary fishing gear and the total destruction of the value of their fishing sites. According to reports made to the Department of Fisheries for 1933 (Washington State, Fishery *Reports*, 42–45, 1936, p. 119), the value of gear alone was as follows: trap gear, $1,211,635; Columbia River beach seines, $284,900; fish wheels, $89,837; total, $1,586,372. No comprehensive data are available on the value of trap sites. It is suggestive that Pacific American Fisheries, while awaiting a court decision on the constitutionality of Initiative No. 77 in 1935, still carried on its corporate books an asset valuation of $275,100 for an undisclosed number of Puget Sound trap sites (Drumheller, 1935, Auditors' Note 5). In 1933,

272

Technical regress in the Washington salmon fishery

Washington owners held 686 separate licenses – and presumably an equal number of sites – for the operation of fixed fishing appliances later outlawed by No. 77 (Washington State, Fishery Reports, 42–45, 1936, p. 119). If the average site was worth only $1,000, which seems far too low even under the conditions prevailing in 1933, then the total value of the sites was $686,000. Adding this to the value of the outlawed gear, one obtains a total loss of $2,272,372. I suspect strongly that this estimate is short of the truth. My own guess is at least $3 million. In any event, the loss was far from trivial. Of course, no compensation whatever was paid by the state. So much for the sanctity of private property rights.

The social loss occasioned by Initiative No. 77 was another, and far more important, matter. This loss, an ongoing suppression of economic productivity, arose from the superior resource productivity of the traps relative to the legal gear. Of course, interception externality had greatly reduced the productivity of the traps, beach seines, and wheels long before No. 77 abolished them outright. To see just how far Washington had strayed from its production possibility frontier in the harvesting of salmon, one must perform some calculations pertaining to a hypothetical alternative.

To establish an empirical benchmark, consider first that in 1913 the state's 629 traps, 26 wheels, and 25 Columbia River beach seines – 680 units of fixed gear in all – captured approximately 25 million fish (Washington State, Fishery Reports, 46–49, 1939, p. 85). These totals imply an average catch of almost 37,000 fish per unit of fixed gear. This establishes what fixed gear demonstrably could do, even under the physical restrictions enforced by the law in 1913.[4] Next consider that during 1937, the legal mobile gear, which included 1,111 gillnets, 213 purse seines, 395 troll units, 49 reef nets, and an assortment of minor gear, caught about 7.6 million salmon inside Washington's jurisdiction (Washington State, Fishery Reports, 46–49, 1939, pp. 67, 90). If fixed gear had been permitted and mobile gear eliminated in 1937, then, assuming only an average harvest of 37,000 fish per unit of fixed gear, 205 units of fixed gear could have taken the same number of fish that were actually taken by the assorted mobile gear.

To operate the mobile gear of 1937 required at least 3,400 men plus

[4]The most important restrictions were that traps could not be located within 3 miles of a river mouth nor in water deeper than 65 feet at low tide; minimum allowable mesh size was 3 inches stretch measure; leads could not exceed 2,500 feet in length in Puget Sound, 800 feet elsewhere; an end passageway at least 600 feet and a lateral passageway at least 2,400 feet had to be maintained between all fixed appliances in Puget Sound, 30 and 900 feet, respectively, elsewhere (Washington State, Session Laws, 1899, pp. 194–197).

Robert Higgs

1,100 gillnet boats, 213 purse seine vessels, and 395 troll vessels. Let us eliminate the trollers on the grounds that their catch occurred mostly outside Washington's jurisdiction and hence was not included in the total catch figure. Allowing a minimum capital and operating cost per year of about $300 per gillnet boat and $2,000 per purse seine vessel, one finds the total to be $756,000. Allowing a minimum average labor cost of $400 per season (Washington State, Fishery *Reports*, 42–45, 1936, p. 120), one obtains a total labor cost of $1,200,000. The total costs of capital and labor for the mobile gear of 1937 were therefore *at least* $1,956,000 – say, $2 million as a round, lower-limit estimate.

To operate 205 units of fixed gear would have cost, *at most*, $732,000; that is, the sum of $400,000 for capital services and $332,000 for labor. By this (admittedly rough but still adequately illustrative) calculation, society could have saved about two-thirds of the total costs of the salmon harvest of 1937 by the simple expedient of outlawing the relatively *un*productive rather than the relatively productive gear.

Actually, the situation was even worse than illustrated by the hypothetical calculations above. There is little doubt that any post-1934 salmon harvest could have been accomplished by no more than 100 traps *if* those devices had been placed in the river mouths, free of design restrictions, and protected from intercepting gear. This means that something in the neighborhood of five-sixths of the resources expended in harvesting salmon since 1934 could have been saved and allocated to alternative employments of value to society. At only $2 million per year (in the purchasing power of 1937), *every* year since 1934, the total social waste is staggering.

Sad to say, the loss has been even greater. Under the regulatory policies embraced during the past 40 years, erratic time and area closures have been the principal policy tools used to preserve the salmon runs by allowing escapement for spawning. This kind of regulation has failed to obstruct either further entry into the mobile commercial fleets or the effective exertion of additional effort by existing operators. The social resource waste has therefore grown steadily larger over time. Today, from a comprehensive point of view, the Washington salmon fishery almost certainly makes a negative contribution to net national product. The opportunity costs of the *socially unnecessary* resources employed there, plus the *socially unnecessary* costs of governmental research, management, and regulation, are greater than the *total* value added by all the labor and capital employed in the fishery (Royce et al., 1963, pp. 37–52; Crutchfield and Pontecorvo, 1969, p. 166; Barsh, 1977, pp. 23–30; Higgs, 1978, pp. 34–39).

What a difference it would have made if Initiative No. 77 could only

274

have been stood on its head, abolishing the mobile intercepting gear and sustaining the fixed appliances. But given the political realities in Washington's history, one must be a dreamer to imagine that outcome. In an open political contest between productivity and perceived "equity," the realistic bettors will place their wagers on equity.

APPENDIX: SALMON FISHING GEAR

To appreciate fully the discussion of this paper, one must know something about the principal forms of gear used in harvesting salmon. This appendix provides brief descriptions.

Drift gillnets are long rectangular nets designed, as their name suggests, to entangle fish by the gills. The upper edge of the net is kept afloat by corks while the lower edge is pulled down by lead weights; the net therefore forms a vertical wall with which the fish collide and become entangled. Mesh sizes vary according to the species sought. Columbia chinook nets, for example, commonly had a stretch mesh of about 9 inches at the turn of the century. At that time, drift gillnets averaged about 300 fathoms in length and 45 meshes in depth. To set the net, the fisherman first attaches a buoy to one end of it, then pays out about two-thirds of its length as the boat moves perpendicular to the current. The boat is then turned downstream and the remainder of the net paid out. The boat and gear drift with the current from about an hour before to about an hour after the turn of the tide. The fisherman then retraces his way along the net, hauling it in over a roller at the stern of the boat, removing any fish caught in the meshes and throwing them into the bottom of the boat. Gillnetters usually operate at night, when the fish are less able to see and evade the net. Before the first decade of the twentieth century, the boats employed oars and sails and carried a two-man crew. Afterward, with the introduction of gasoline engines, they were usually operated by a single man.

Set nets are gillnets held in position by stakes or anchors, often with one end secured to the shore. They are generally much shorter than drift gillnets, seldom exceeding 100 fathoms; some are as short as 10 fathoms. They can be operated most effectively in the narrower upper reaches of the rivers.

Beach (or haul or drag) seines are 100 to 400 fathoms long and vary from about 35 meshes in depth at the shallow end to as much as 400 meshes at the deep end. Starting from offshore, a dory attached to the shallow end heads for the beach while a larger seine boat pays out the net in a large semicircle against the current. As soon as the net is fully paid out, a line attached to the offshore (deep) end is brought ashore, where several horses aid in pulling the entire net onto the beach as rapidly as possible to prevent the escape of encircled salmon. Beach seines operated mostly along the shallow bars and beaches near the mouth of the Columbia River.

Purse seines, 200–300 fathoms long with a depth of 20–25 fathoms and a 4-inch stretch mesh, are encircling nets designed to prevent the encircled fish from escaping by sounding while the net is being hauled in. To set the seine, one end is attached to a skiff. The larger purse seine vessel pays out the net in a wide circle, returning to the skiff to join the two ends of the net and haul it onboard. As the net is hauled in, a line running through rings at the bottom edge of the seine is hauled in faster than the cork line at the upper edge. This action closes the bottom of the net in the same way that a drawstring closes a purse; hence the name. When most of the net has been hauled onboard, the fish within it are forced into the bunt remaining alongside the vessel; they are easily scooped out with a dip net. The great advantage of the purse seine is its mobility. Until the introduction of the power block in the 1950s, its great disadvantage was that it required a crew of 7–10 men.

The *traps (or pound nets)* of the lower Columbia River and Puget Sound were carefully shaped arrangements of netting or wire mesh secured to driven piles, usually placed not far from shore along demonstrated migration paths of returning salmon. The "lead" was a straight fence of netting, often several hundred feet long, extending from the bottom to the high water level and running in a direction approximately perpendicular to the shoreline. After encountering the lead, the salmon swam along it toward the shore into the "outer heart," a V-shaped, semienclosed arrangement of netting; proceeding through the outer heart toward the shore, they squeezed into the "inner heart," another V-shaped enclosure from which the only avenue of escape was the narrow passage through which they had entered. (Some traps had no inner heart.) From the inner heart, the determined salmon, whose instinctual reluctance to turn in their own wake makes the traps so effective, proceeded through a narrowing tunnel into the "pot," a shallow holding area from which almost no fish could escape. Some traps had a "spiller" adjacent to the pot, and connected with it by another tunnel, to facilitate emptying the captured fish into a scow. A few traps, so-called double-headers, had hearts and pots at both ends of the lead.

Fish wheels were used at two areas with rapid currents along the Columbia River: the Cascades, 34–42 river miles east of Portland; and the Dalles, 187–201 river miles east of Portland. One type of fish wheel was stationary, positioned within a sturdy framework of heavy timbers and stone or concrete constructed near the bank; another type was mobile (though stationary while operating), mounted at the end of a large scow. Both types utilized the same principles: the river's rapid current turned the wheel, which consisted of three large, wire-mesh dip nets radiating from the axle; as the wheel revolved, fish scooped up in the nets slid toward the axle, down a chute, and into a holding box. Leads of piling and planks extending diagonally in a downstream direction were often used to direct the fish toward the wheel channel. Wheels ranged from 9 to 32 feet in diameter and from 5 to 15 feet in width.

Trolling gear is nothing more than an elaborate arrangement of hooks and lines. Some trollers use as many as six lines, three on each side of the boat. The lines are held away from the hull by a pole extending perpendicular to the fore-and-aft line. Each line holds about half a dozen leaders with baited hooks or artificial lures. The lines can be set to troll at varying depths. Modern trollers use a power winch ("gurdy") to haul in the lines. Modern lines are made of stainless steel and weighted by heavy lead cannonball sinkers.

For more detailed discussions, diagrams, and photographs of the gear discussed above, see Cobb (1930, pp. 477–490); Browning (1974, pp. 117–249); and Donaldson and Cramer (1971, *passim*).

REFERENCES

American Friends Service Committee (1970), *Uncommon Controversy: Fishing Rights of the Muckleshoot, Puyallup, and Nisqually Indians*. Seattle: University of Washington Press.

Anderson, Lee G. (1977), *The Economics of Fisheries Management*. Baltimore: Johns Hopkins University Press.

Bacich v. Huse (1936), 187 Wash. 75.

Barsh, Russel L. (1977), *The Washington Fishing Rights Controversy: An Economic Critique*. Seattle: University of Washington Graduate School of Business Administration.

Browning, Robert J. (1974), *Fisheries of the North Pacific: History, Species, Gear, and Processes*. Anchorage: Alaska Northwest Publ.

Campbell v. Case (1935), 182 Wash. 334.

Carstensen, Vernon (1971), "The Fisherman's Frontier on the Pacific Coast: The Rise of the Salmon-Canning Industry," In John G. Clark (ed.), *The Frontier Challenge: Responses to the Trans-Mississippi West*. Lawrence, Kans.: University Press of Kansas.

Cobb, John N. (1930), *Pacific Salmon Fisheries*. Washington, D.C.: U.S. Department of Commerce, Bureau of Fisheries, Doc. No. 1092.

Crutchfield, James A., and Giulio Pontecorvo (1969), *The Pacific Salmon Fisheries: A Study of Irrational Conservation*. Baltimore: Johns Hopkins University Press.

Darwin, L. H. (1916), *The Fisheries of the State of Washington*. Olympia, Wash.: Washington State Bureau of Statistics and Immigration.

Donaldson, Ivan J., and Frederick K. Cramer (1971), *Fishwheels of the Columbia*. Portland, Oreg.: Binfords & Mort.

Drumheller, Ehrlichman, and White (1935), *A Review of the Salmon Industry*. Seattle: privately printed.

Robert Higgs

Gile v. Huse (1935), 183 Wash. 560.

Graham, Otis L., Jr. (1976), *Toward a Planned Society*. New York: Oxford University Press.

Gunderson, Gerald (1976), *A New Economic History of America*. New York: McGraw-Hill.

Higgs, Robert (1978), "Preliminary Report on the Probable Socio-Economic Effects of a Moratorium on the Issuance of New Vessel Licenses in the Pacific Ocean Commercial Salmon Fishery." Prepared under PFMC Contract No. 78-18 for the Pacific Fishery Management Council.

Jackson, Laurence D. (1977), "Fish Trap Art." *Oregon Historical Quarterly* 78: 197–206.

Lancaster, Kelvin (1969), *Introduction to Modern Microeconomics*. Chicago: Rand McNally.

Maass, Arthur (1968), "Conservation: I. Political and Social Aspects." *International Encyclopedia of the Social Sciences* 3: 271–279.

McLeod, Ken (1936), "Salmon Treaty Developments." *Washington Sportsman* 2 (Feb.–Mar.): 3–4.

McLeod, Ken (1936–1937), "Sponsors of '77' Again Victorious." *Washington Sportsman* 2 (Dec.–Jan.): 22.

McLeod, Ken (1937), "Initiative 77 Withstands Legislative Attacks; Who Was For and Who *Against?*" *Washington Sportsman* 3 (April): 14–15.

Netboy, Anthony (1958), *Salmon of the Pacific Northwest: Fish vs. Dams*. Portland, Oreg.: Binfords & Mort.

"No Fish Traps!" (1937), *Washington Sportsman* 3 (March): 5–6, 15.

Oregon State, Planning Board (1938), *A Study of Commercial Fishing Operations on the Columbia River*. Portland, Oreg.: State Planning Board.

Pacific Fisherman (various years). Seattle.

Rounsefell, George A., and George B. Kelez (1935), "Abundance and Seasonal Occurrence of the Salmon in the Puget Sound Region and the Development of the Fishery," *Special Report*. Washington, D.C.: U.S. Department of Commerce, Bureau of Fisheries.

Royce, William F., and others (1963), *Salmon Gear Limitations in Northern Washington Waters*. Seattle: University of Washington Publications in Fisheries, New Series.

Smith, Courtland L. (1974), "Oregon Fish Fights." Oregon State University, Corvallis, Sea Grant College Program, Publ. No. ORESU-T-74-004.

Teck, Frank C. (1903), "How Onffroy Made Princes of Our Fish Trap Barons; or, From the Strenuous Struggle to the Lap of Ease by the Fish Trap Route." An unidentified newspaper clipping in the C. B. Bagley Scrapbook No. 1, pp. 186–187. University of Washington Library, Northwest Collection.

United States v. Washington (1974), 384 F. Supp. 312.

Washington Sportsman (various years). Seattle.

Washington State, Fishery *Reports* (various years). Olympia, Wash.: State Printer. Reports 1–31 (1890–1921) are *Annual Reports of the State Fish Commissioner;* Reports 32–35 (1922–1925) are *Annual Reports of the State Supervisor of Fisheries;* Reports 36–41 (1926–1931) are *Annual Reports of the State Department of Fisheries and Game, Division of Fisheries;* Reports 42–88 (1932–1978) are *Annual Reports of the State Department of Fisheries.*

Washington State, Secretary of State (1934), *Abstract of Votes polled in the*

State of Washington at the General Election held November 6, 1934. Olympia, Wash.: State Printer.

Washington State, Secretary of State (1936), *Official Voters' Pamphlet*. Olympia, Wash.: State Printer.

Washington State, Secretary of State (1966), *History of State Initiative and Referendum Measures*. Olympia, Wash.: State Printer.

Washington State, *Session Laws* (various years). Olympia, Wash.: State Printer.

Washington v. Edwards (1936), 188 Wash. 467.

Wendler, Henry O. (1966), "Regulation of Commercial Fishing Gear and Seasons in the Columbia River from 1859 to 1963." Washington Department of Fisheries, *Fisheries Research Papers* 2: 19–31.

8

The politics of institutional change in a representative democracy

THE ECONOMIC SPHERE AND THE RULE-MAKING SPHERE

The following essay by William Riker and Itai Sened analyzes a fascinating case of institutional change: the evolution of property rights in time slots (the rights to land and to take off) at four heavily used U.S. airports. In these airports, the structure of rights in slots changed in 1969 from open access and queuing on a first-come, first-served basis to communal property governed by the established carriers. In 1985 the structure changed again, to exclusive salable property rights.

Riker and Sened take their analysis beyond the naive model of property rights, which examines the behavior of only economic actors and organizations (the demand side of institutional change), and strongly emphasize the role of political actors and organizations (the supply side). In other words, the study analyzes the behavior of actors in both the economic sphere and the rule-making or public-choice sphere, but not in the constitutional sphere, since the institutional change in question did not involve new procedures for public choice.

In society, the design of formal rules for granting property rights is ultimately the domain of the actors who control the state, because they (usually) have the resources and the will to determine the basic structure of property rights in their territory. Riker and Sened assume that these political actors act rationally and grant property rights in order to promote their own welfare, broadly defined to include individual wealth, power, and social ideals.[1] However, political actors are constrained by their physical and social environment and do not have unlimited capac-

---

[1] Note that the sets of economic and political actors intersect, with some individuals acting in both roles. The size of the resulting subset is variable from one political system to another; for instance, it was particularly large in the former Soviet Union.

ity to structure property rights. In particular, the constraint of maintaining their position and authority is of fundamental importance for political actors.

THE PARTITIONING OF RIGHTS IN THE RULE-MAKING SPHERE

The economics of property rights has given much attention to the partitioning of property rights in the economic sphere, and scholars have analyzed the logic and consequences of divided rights. For instance, Alchian introduces the issue by discussing how rights in land are frequently divided among unrelated categories of users, such as cultivators, pedestrians, hunters, and aviators.[2] As the following essay well illustrates, the rights of political actors in the rule-making sphere are also partitioned among various individuals and organizations that are related both vertically and horizontally in the political power structure. The specific partitioning of rule-making rights has important implications for institutional change and is a major defining characteristic of political systems.

WHAT TO LOOK FOR IN THE ESSAY

Riker and Sened carefully lay out the partitioning of rights among the various sets of political actors who control the property rights environment of economic organizations and individuals who value and have conflicting claims on the resources used by the four airports. The authors also discuss various relevant groups in the economic sphere but focus on domestic commercial carriers. The reader is encouraged to note the main players on both the supply and the demand side and to attempt to reconstruct their apparent goals, constraints, and conflicts of interest.

The study demonstrates how divisions among the chief economic and political actors tend to influence institutional change. On the economic side, disagreement over the desired structure of property rights arises not only among different kinds of users (owners of commercial aircraft vs. owners of other aircraft, or aircraft owners vs. airport neighbors) but also among individuals who share comparable uses for the resources (domestic commercial carriers). It is obvious that the costs of bargaining may paralyze either or both sides, the demanders and the suppliers, and render them incapable of collectively reacting to changes in their environment (the introduction of jet aircraft, increased demand for air

---

[2] A. A. Alchian, "Some Economics of Property Rights" (1961), reprinted in idem, *Economic Forces at Work* (Indianapolis: Liberty Press, 1977).

travel) with institutional change appropriate for maximizing the wealth of the community. The Riker–Sened study clearly illustrates that the optimistic prediction of the naive model, that institutions are adjusted efficiently to changing circumstances, is a special case rather than a general rule. Yet their story has a happy ending in that property rights in air slots were adjusted to changing circumstances in a fairly efficient manner. One intriguing aspect of their account is that pressure for efficient change in institutions came not from the relevant economic organizations but from a subgroup of political actors. We suggest that the reader contemplate why these particular political actors pressed for efficient property rights in time slots and, in general, consider the relative role in institutional change of narrow self-interest and intellectual fashions, as well as how the costs and benefits to political actors of acting in step with certain intellectual currents are affected by the distribution and general popularity of these ideas.

A political theory of the origin of property rights: airport slots

WILLIAM H. RIKER AND ITAI SENED

Property rights enable private persons or groups to control resources that might otherwise be controlled politically. That these rights (to use, sell, rent, profit from, and exclude others from) exist and are recognized means that rulers allow persons other than themselves to exercise control over valuables. In the abstract this is a puzzling fact. Why should rulers, with their supposed monopoly of force, leave great treasure in hands other than their own? Yet they do, and, presumably, they have good reason to do so. To identify their reason is to provide a partial explanation, at least, of the origin of property rights.

Traditional justifications of property rights ordinarily include some reference to origins. Unfortunately, many descriptions of origins devised for justificatory purposes are not historically or scientifically convincing and thereby weaken the justifications. To remedy this weakness, we set forth a positive explanation of rulers' motivations to grant property rights and citizens' motivations to petition for them and to respect them. We illustrate our theory with a contemporary example so that it, unlike most other discussions of origins, can be checked against easily available detail.

But first a caveat. Our purpose is not to debate the philosophical justification of rights. We recognize, of course, that despite our self-

This essay originally appeared in the *American Journal of Political Science*, Vol. 35, No. 4 (November 1991), pp. 951–69. © 1991 by the University of Texas Press, P.O. Box 7819, Austin, TX 78713. Reprinted with the permission of the University of Wisconsin Press.

We thank the John M. Olin Foundation, which supported our research; Charles Plott, who gave us data he had collected; Christopher DeMuth, Lynn Helms, Randall Malin, Nestor Pylypec, Richard Yates, and many people in the government and the airline industry who helped us understand the issues; and academic critics who saved us from errors: David Austen-Smith, Larry Bartels, Randall Calvert, Henry Manne, David Meiselman, William Thomson, David Weimer, and Carl Wellman.

imposed restrictions, our theory may have implications for these justifications that depend crucially on incomplete descriptions of origins. But we do not explore this complicated possibility because we wish merely to describe the origin of property rights by placing one concrete instance in an analytical context.

1. ALTERNATIVE EXPLANATIONS

Our procedure thus differs from previous discussions that have lacked both concrete detail and a descriptive theory to organize the study of origins. We do not blame our predecessors for these lacunae because we know that detail about origins is elusive. Rights to trade goods apparently antedate written history, and for Europe at least, rights to land developed from feudal holdings in a process obscured in casually reported case law and unrecorded economic circumstances (Denman 1958). Recently, some detail on other creations of rights have, however, become available (Eggertsson 1990; Libecap 1989; Umbeck 1981).

In the previous absence of detailed knowledge, therefore, philosophers have depicted alternative origins with a broad brush. Theorists of natural rights have used the broadest brush of all, finessing the question of origins by positing that rights inhere in humans. This implies that rights always and necessarily exist, at least potentially. This postulate is vulnerable philosophically and historically. Against assertions that property is unnatural, proponents of natural rights can only appeal to authority, which is indecisive when authorities dispute. And if property rights "should" exist but, historically, do not, the claim that existence is potential begs the question because it offers no explanation of what realizes the potentiality. In contrast, our research concerns exactly what natural rights theorists evade, namely, the historical origins of the social embodiment of rights; and we have nothing to say about their moral bases.

Social contract theorists, for another example, explain the origin of property rights in a contract drawn between the people and the government or among the people severally (Buchanan and Tullock 1962; Umbeck 1981). Despite the analytical value of these theories for study of the consequences of rights or their normative value to justify enforcement, they are manifestly incorrect as descriptions of events. Governments have existed throughout recorded history, and all primitive societies today display at least a judicial system enforcing a customary law. Since, in known history, government of some sort has always existed, social contracts cannot have created governments and thus rights. In fact, as we shall show, the causal relation probably runs the other way: rulers themselves (legislatures, executives, judges) have generated property rights, hoping to encourage efficiency and, doubtless also, to increase tax income. We recognize, of course, that economists (e.g., Buchanan and Tullock 1962) and philosophers (e.g., Rawls 1971) have usefully inferred moral and legal principles from the social contract as an abstract ideal, wholly and properly unhistorical. This rhetorical device admits analytical interpretation while bypassing historical errors. Nevertheless, whether normatively useful or restrictive, the social contract explanation of the origin of rights distorts description, and we want to eliminate that distortion.

Demsetz (1964, 1967) has, more convincingly, identified economic conditions under which property rights come to have value: scarcity and the need to internalize externalities. He pointed out that, when it is too costly to price them, goods may have a zero market price. But technological, demographic, or social change may bring about positive prices. Property rights then effectively allocate goods to avoid their misuse (as in pollution) or their overuse (as in the tragedy of the commons, Hardin 1968). Market allocations thus replace allocations by command or by initial possession.

Demsetz's explanation of "the emergence of property rights" is a considerable step forward, but it suffers from the typical defect of neoclassical political economy of specifying the conditions for and properties of an equilibrium, without specifying how those conditions occur in the real world. This defect is here clearly visible. Sometimes Demsetz's conditions are met, but property rights do not emerge, as we learn from frequent historical periods of protracted economic inefficiency (North 1981). This indicates that Demsetz's conditions are at best necessary, but not sufficient. Alchian and Demsetz (1973, 17, 23–27) have recognized this weakness and, therefore, have recommended further investigation of the emergence of property rights.

This failure of the neoclassical approach rests on its complete exclusion of political structures (Riker 1988). As Demsetz himself explained, he deliberately excluded politics in order to understand the economic features of perfect competition. But if, in that model, "the legal system and government [are] relegated to the distant background by the simple device of stating the resources [are] 'privately owned' " (Demsetz 1982, 7), it follows that the model can say very little about the excluded political features. In real economic activity, which is embedded in political activity, law and government have much to do with the origin of property rights. We simply cannot avoid politics. Following North, we think that property rights influence the operation of an economy as much as technology, demography, and competition (North 1981, 1). Therefore, we wish to study the origin of rights in a more realistic context than the neoclassical model permits.

2. A POLITICAL MODEL

We begin with an interpretation of rights. Following Hohfeld (1919), we think of rights as a combination of duties and claims, of which the content is what a right-holder can claim and what a duty-bearer should respect. When a right (say, land ownership) exists, the bearer owes a duty (e.g., not to trespass) to the holder, and the holder has a claim on the bearer to perform the duty owed. In order to locate these first-order relations of duties and claims within the social system, there are second-order relations that serve as operations on the first-order relations. These second-order relations are power, which concerns the ability to change the rules about duties and claims, and immunity, which the right-holder possesses if the first-order relations are unalterable (Sumner 1987). With this vocabulary we restate our initial question: Under what circumstances does a power-holder grant a right-holder a claim on duty-bearers to respect the granted right?

The first-order relations can characterize right-holders' claims coming from any source – nature, custom, "social contract." Potential holders may claim rights and duty-bearers may customarily respect them for reciprocal gain. But claims enforced only by reputational incentives are at best contingent rights, which may be ignored if duty-bearers perceive an advantage in doing so. Hence follows the importance of the second-order relations of enforcement and immunity. These relations are political, so at some point, whatever their justifications, property rights are politically determined. Our question is, then: at what point?

To answer we set up a model with testable hypotheses. The actors are potential right-holders who desire property rights, officials who make rules about them, and duty-bearers who respect them. The postulates for the model are

POSTULATE 1: Political actors maximize utility.

This postulate subsumes the usual axioms of rationality and covers officials, right-holders, and duty-bearers. Rulers maximize toward some goals, which include the possession of resources, tax income, the authority and emoluments of office, and even sometimes benevolent public service. To achieve their goals, they need popular support, which they acquire by ideological appeals and by various forms of grants including (1) money (e.g., subsidies, welfare, pork barrel); (2) chances for rents (e.g., monopolies, regulation); and (3) property rights. Our concern here is with the third category.

For right-holders, postulate 1 implies that scarcity is necessary for the emergence of rights. If goods are free, rational holders forgo ownership, if possible. But when goods, like land or liberty of speech, are scarce and hence worth possessing, holders seek rights over them. For duty-bearers, the postulate means that they respect the right if the net benefit of respecting, if any, is greater than the net benefit (including the cost from punishment) of not respecting it.

POSTULATE 2: Public officials have more resources (military, acknowledged legitimacy) than other actors.

Government is said to have a monopoly of force – an exaggeration. Still, either government can defeat challengers or challengers can become the government. Postulate 2 means that, as the strongest (and legitimate) force, public officials can obtain any scarce goods, provided they have not chosen to acknowledge the immunity of other right-holders.

Given these assumptions, what are the necessary conditions for the emergence of a right? We have already inferred one condition.

CONDITION 1: Scarcity. The content of the right is scarce, driving its value above enforcement costs. Without such value, control is pointless.

Further necessary conditions are that private property is to actors' advantage.

CONDITION 2: Right-holders desire the right. If this condition is not satisfied, holders do not seek the right; hence, it does not emerge.

CONDITION 3: Rule makers desire to recognize the right. This condition is necessary because a right unproclaimed by enforcers is not ultimately enforceable.

Since rule makers are (by postulate 2) the enforcers, they must wish to establish and maintain the right to obtain their net benefits of enforcement (i.e., tax income and the gratitude of right-holders and others who consciously gain from efficiency, less the costs of enforcement). Condition 3 is crucial to differentiate our theory from a strictly economic one like Demsetz's, in which scarcity is sufficient. According to our theory, even with scarcity, rights do not emerge unless officials are advantaged by them.

CONDITION 4: Duty-bearers respect the right. This is a necessary, but often unnoticed, condition.

William H. Riker and Itai Sened

In one sense it is not logically independent but merely a qualification to condition 3. Rule makers cannot successfully proclaim rights if duty-bearers do not respect them. Thus, duty-bearers are merely a cost of enforcement. Since this cost is often negligible, many analysts neglect this condition. Yet in a deeper sense, this condition is indeed logically independent. Rights require the acquiescence of most participants, which may be extremely costly if duty-bearers must be militarily coerced. So one must distinguish between the will of the officials to grant the rights and the will of the duty-bearers to respect them.

We summarize our model by stating explicitly our theory of the emergence of rights: rights originate in a historical event. As such there are identifiable actors with identifiable motives, who create rights. Rule makers grant a right to grantees, the Hohfeldian right-holders. By so doing they guarantee the right-holders a permanent claim over the content of the right, and they impose on the duty-bearers the duty to respect the holders' claim. Since the grantor thereby commits itself to police continually, it undertakes this obligation only if the gain from tax income and gratitude exceeds the cost of enforcement. Similarly, right-holders value the right only if the benefit from the enforced right exceeds the cost in taxes and gratitude. And duty-bearers respect the right only if enforcement eliminates the marginal benefits of not respecting it.

We acknowledge, of course, that this explanation of the origin of rights has a long history. Thomas More expressed it (for liberty of speech) as early as 1523 (Riker 1990; Roper 1935); and even in the heyday of natural rights, Blackstone (1765) effectively reiterated it (for land). In the United States, we find it in Hamilton's remark (*Federalist* no. 84): "... bills of rights are ... stipulations between kings and their subjects, abridgements of prerogative in favor of privilege." But while the grantor–grantee explanation is perhaps the oldest one, it has not been carefully formulated, which is our task here.

3. PROPERTY IN SLOTS

We now examine an illustrative instance: the creation of property in time slots at four heavily used airports. Slots are rights to land or take off during a well-defined time period, typically one-half hour.[1] Slots are not a widely held property, and technically they are limited by reservations; nor is their survival as property assured. But they are a real

---

[1] For example, between 8:45 and 9:15 A.M., 20 slots might be defined. We discuss only the rights to instrument operations for domestic trunk carriers, excluding visual operations, slots for commuter, business, and recreational aircraft, and slots for foreign trunk carriers, all of which are regulated differently.

right and a recent creation, so we can investigate them. Our program, organized around the four conditions, is to show that scarcity led government and potential right-holders to create common property, which turned out to be highly inefficient. After considerable internal dispute, government, with little help from potential right-holders, then created what amounts to private property in slots.

Scarcity, first phase

Prior to the invention of the airplane, no one claimed property in airspace. But in the Air Commerce Act of 1926, the United States claimed its airspace, which became a kind of common asset, for which over the next 50 years, an allocation procedure developed. As traffic increased, Congress passed the Civil Aeronautics Act of 1938 (revised 1940, 1958, and partially negated in 1978), which assigned control of airspace to the Civil Aeronautics Authority, later Board (CAB). The purpose was to promote the industry by regulating routes, airports, prices, oligopolies, and safety. Air traffic took a quantum leap forward in the early 1960s with jet motors; airlines became quite profitable (James 1982, 186, 192); and signs of scarcity appeared: congested airports, especially LaGuardia, Kennedy, O'Hare, Washington National, and Newark. The congestion hurt airline profits (*Aviation Week*, 4 January 1970). In 1968 the industry, encouraged by the CAB, which gave carriers immunity from antitrust laws, established "scheduling committees" to allocate slots in congested airports. The Federal Aviation Authority (FAA), as supervisors of air traffic, subjected (3 December 1968) these airports to a High Density Rule (HDR) that limited the number of landings and takeoffs allowed (i.e., defined the number of slots to be allocated) under instrument flight rules for four airports (LaGuardia, Kennedy, O'Hare, and National). Airports operated under this arrangement from 1969 to 1985, each with a scheduling committee that semiannually adjusted slot allocations. Two "general aviation" groups opposed this settlement: the National Business Aircraft Association and the Aircraft Owners and Pilots Association. Both sued, arguing correctly that the HDR allowed scheduled carriers privileged use of federally funded facilities. But the court dismissed the owners' suit holding that the FAA had exercised its discretion properly.[2]

This allocation procedure was the first large step toward private property. Previously the United States, the communal owner, controlled us-

---

[2] *Aviation Week and Space Technology*, 27 January 1969; *Aircraft Owners and Pilots Association* vs. *Volpe*, U.S. Dist. Ct., D.C., 14 May 1969 civil action no. 927-69.

age by "open skies," which meant a queue: first come, first served. The HDR permanently reserved for scheduled carriers (the Hohfeldian right-holders) a right over the slots (the Hohfeldian content) and required other aircraft owners (Hohfeldian duty-bearers) to respect the reservations. Thereby slots became quasi-permanent rights, almost private property.[3]

The property was incompletely private because the slots were not salable; but the carriers had permanent possession, short of bankruptcy or the FAA's technically necessary seizure. This is analogous to the intermediate stage between feudal tenure and land ownership. Initially, the lord granted fiefs to military subordinates for the period of their service. Gradually the fiefs became heritable, then alienable, so feudal tenure became ownership (Palmer 1985). The scheduling committee system amounted to inheritance, substituting the corporation for the family. Salability, the remaining step, was taken in 1985.

This first response to scarcity satisfied the three rationality conditions. Condition 2: the carriers (potential right-holders) clearly desired to relieve congestion and cooperated to do so. Condition 3: the rule-making FAA and CAB clearly desired to improve their stewardship; so they granted carriers immunity from antitrust and promptly promulgated the HDR. Condition 4: the other users (duty-bearers), while clearly opposed, nevertheless acquiesced, which illustrates both our postulate about governmental resources and the trivial way in which condition 4 is usually satisfied.

Scarcity, second phase

The scheduling committees worked smoothly, though probably inefficiently (Grether, Isaac, and Plott 1981a, 1981b), as long as the CAB cartelized the industry. But in the 1970s, public and politicians alike lost confidence in regulatory cartels. On a theoretical level, a revived appreciation of competition replaced enthusiasm for a managed economy. On a practical level, intrastate carriers in California and Texas (i.e., outside the national oligopoly) showed that competition generated a mass market at low prices. Consequently, Congress required the CAB to phase out both itself and the cartel.

Within the CAB cartel, airlines could compete only on services, which increased average costs. Furthermore, the CAB provided "fair returns to

---

[3] Against Braniff's claim that slots were property distributable in bankruptcy, the fifth circuit held (*In re: Braniff Airways*, 1983, 700 F 2d 935) that they merely restricted airline usage. Still, the court approved the FAA's promise to return them to Braniff if it recovered.

investment," which generated an upward price spiral. Once the CAB ceased to regulate prices and allocate routes, intense price competition led carriers to adopt the efficient "hub and spoke" system, which concentrated passengers at the hubs (James 1982, 81). Since the high density airports were also hubs, scarcity in slots increased.

This second round of scarcity might have been alleviated by several expedients, but none were attempted.

Additional airports. New construction required cooperation among carriers, several levels of government, and airport neighbors. Yet carriers had no incentive to increase competition; governments had no incentive to pay the costs; and neighbors had no incentive to accept noise pollution.

More hubs and better schedules. From 1978 to 1985, the FAA preferred this solution.[4] Under the principle of "open skies" when carriers wait in queues, the rational response is to shift to less dense airports, just as rational herdsmen shift from overgrazed commons to more remote parts. But "open skies" failed. Why? The efficient cause, in Aristotelian terms, was that, under deregulation, air transport turned into mass transit faster than the industry could expand facilities. The formal cause was that "open skies" entailed the "tragedy of the commons," in which users consume a free resource until it is gone – here gridlock.

Scheduling committees. While this system worked well for allocations among cartel members, it collapsed when applied to allocations among competitors, including new entrants. This failure led ultimately to privatization.

At each high density airport, the committee consisted of a representative from each using carrier, a chairman from the Air Transport Association, and regulatory observers. These committees semiannually allocated slots by unanimous decision, usually after much compromise and straw votes on entire allocations until they found one on which all could, perhaps reluctantly, agree. In the abstract, unanimity seems designed to produce deadlock, and ultimately, it did so. But before deregulation (1978), indeed before the controllers' strike (1981), the committees usually agreed. Why so? As Grether, Isaac, and Plott point out (1981b, IV-7), the equilibrium allocation was determined by the airlines' fear of

---

[4]Grether, Isaac, and Plott (1981b) report (n. 2, p. IV-8) that Langhorne Bond, FAA administrator (1976–81), favored this solution. Lynn Helms, FAA administrator (1981–84), told us in 1988 that he liked "open skies." So did Harvey Safeer, the FAA official immediately responsible for policy on slots, 1982–85.

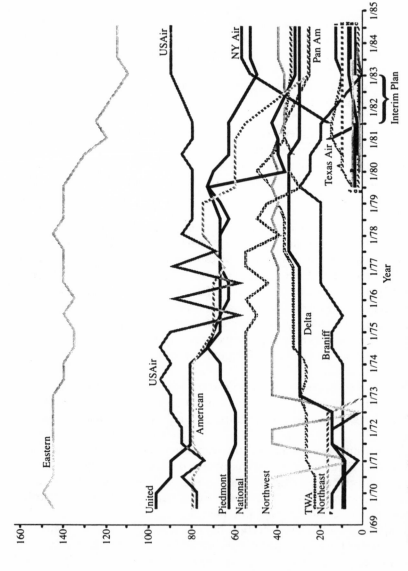

Figure 1. Slot allocation by carrier in Washington National.

default (i.e., the failure to agree). (In this context an equilibrium allocation is an allocation such that, for each carrier, it is at least as good as
default, and perhaps better, and there is no other allocation that is
preferred by all.) Since the FAA never announced a default rule, the
carriers could only speculate among grandfathering (existing allocations), "open skies" (queues), FAA assignment, lotteries, auctions, and
markets. Except for grandfathering, carriers were fearful of all possibilities. "Open skies" and lotteries would take away their slots. Auctions
would make them pay for what was now free. FAA assignment would
be much influenced by Congress and hence unpredictable. Since grandfathering seemed unlikely, the carriers wanted the best agreeable allocation, which is the Grether, Isaac, and Plott equilibrium (1981a).

Unfortunately for the committee system, this equilibrium gradually
approached the worst, until default itself was the best allocation. New
entrants claimed slots that old carriers had to give up. Small carriers
claimed slots from large ones, but failed to get enough to become efficient. While initially committee meetings had been friendly and fast, by
1979 they displayed deadlock, acrimony, and frustration (Grether, Isaac,
and Plott 1981b).

Figure 1 depicts the allocation of slots for Washington National,
1969–85. (Charles Plott gathered these data, and we thank him for
them.) In 1969 there were 11 carriers, leaving nine when Northeast and
Mohawk disappeared in mergers. By 1985 deregulation produced 17
carriers. Ignoring seasonal variations and the constant allocations after
the 1983 deadlock, Figure 1 strikingly depicts large carriers' loss and
small carriers' gain. Eastern went from 147 to 107; United from 96 to
34; American from 82 to 30. Among the large carriers, only USAir,
Piedmont, and Northwest kept their positions. Delta and TWA, neither
large at National, also held constant. After deregulation, 10 small airlines appeared, but only New York Air became large. In general, after
1978, the large carriers either lost or held constant, while entrants,
except for New York Air, did not get enough slots to compete seriously.
So the best outcome for both large and small became default.

Peak load pricing or a market. However economically desirable, these
alternatives were politically infeasible. Peak load pricing, based on airport control of slots, had many enemies: carriers and travelers feared
monopoly prices; general aircraft owners feared exclusion; the FAA
feared losing control of airspace. No wonder that only economists recommended peak load pricing (Levine 1969; Hahn and Kroszner 1988).
As for a market, based on carrier ownership, carriers disliked the loss of
current rents, and the FAA disliked losing control.

Thus, in the second phase of scarcity, there was no acceptable solution. So here at least, Demsetz's conditions (i.e., scarcity and externalities) were perhaps necessary but certainly not sufficient. Extreme scarcity existed, but property did not emerge. But when officials took the lead in granting rights, private property did emerge, which suggests that political conditions are also necessary, and, together with scarcity, are sufficient.

The grantor: staking out ideological positions

While one might expect the carriers to seek property in slots, it seems to us that, in the 1979–85 phase of scarcity, the government initiated ownership. The carriers, who could use but not transfer slots, presumably calculated their expected gain from privatization (i.e., the prospective market value less the loss of the current rent) and found it was negative. So they refused to petition for ownership. When the grantor promised grandfathering, the calculation changed to positive for most carriers, who then petitioned.

The Grether, Isaac, and Plott report (1981b) initially frightened the carriers from seeking ownership. This study, though commissioned by the CAB, was simply a scholarly analysis, not official policy. The carriers feared, however, that its proposal of auctions would sharply increase costs. (During the six-week buy/sell experiment, prices of some slots reached $1,000,000, Bailey 1986, 295.) With about 4,500 slots at the four airports, carriers could reasonably visualize costs of at least $1 billion in an industry with about $9 billion capitalization (James 1982; Brenner, Leet, and Schutt 1985, chap. 5). Consequently, most people in the industry pejoratively characterized the study as academic (Bailey 1986).

So, as the committee system deadlocked, the government rather than the carriers took the initiative. The Department of Transportation (DOT) asked for alternative procedures (45 FR 17236, 10/27/80). Soon thereafter, President Reagan required (Executive Order 12291) that administrative rules be based on cost–benefit analyses and assigned the enforcement to the Office of Information and Regulatory Affairs (OIRA) in the Office of Management and the Budget (OMB). OIRA Administrator Christopher DeMuth and his assistant Wayne Liess firmly believed in privatizing slots.

Before serious discussion, however, the controllers' strike (August 1981) intensified scarcity. While training replacements for the discharged strikers, the FAA sharply reduced operations pro rata. The FAA then adopted a bimonthly lottery of slots that became available as newly trained controllers came on duty. This mechanism was not satisfactory.

New entrants and small carriers failed to win enough slots for successful operation; large existing carriers used all their slots, sometimes even unprofitably, because they feared that they would forfeit unused slots under the "use-or-lose" rule (Bailey 1986, 299; OMB internal memo 08/17/84).

OIRA staff believed that this mechanism violated Executive Order 12291; so they tried to revise it. DeMuth reports their hardest job was internal: David Stockman, chief of OMB, wanted an auction, for income; but DeMuth persuaded him that, ultimately, a prosperous industry would generate more revenue than auctions. Transportation Secretary Drew Lewis, sympathizing both with OIRA goals and with his FAA subordinates, compromised on a "buy/sell experiment" for six weeks, beginning 10 May 1982. This experiment succeeded because, according to CAB member Elizabeth Bailey (1986), the trades "made sense." Still the FAA wanted to retain its politically valuable activity of allocating slots, so it suspended the experiment (47 FR 114, 06/14/82 and 6/24/82, 25508–10) until 1986. It still permitted barters, which provided some market efficiency, but entrants and small airlines had little to trade.

So matters stood until spring 1983, when the FAA had trained enough controllers. It then reactivated the committees, "letting," as Administrator Helms wrote, "the industry participants solve their own problems" (Internal memo, DOT, 05/25/83).

Carriers: the reluctant right-holders and condition 2

Despite Helms's suggestion, the industry did not solve its problems, and from 1983 there was deadlock. When the scheduling committee at National defaulted, the FAA allocated the status quo (1983), which signaled that default was costless. While this pleased the large carriers, they were unwilling as a group to seek rights. Nevertheless, they were individually eager to obtain competitive advantage: by trading slots in many ways and by administrative allocation which, as USAir complained, violated the FAA's own rules (Hearing 99-33, 1985, 310–33). The carriers made no agreement to solve their problems, until brought together by government, because they did not agree on what they wanted. Our condition 2 provides that potential owners petition to privatize only if their expected gain from the asset exceeds the loss of present rent. So the eager lobbyists were committee losers in Figure 1 (like American) or aggressive rent seekers (like NY Air). But committee gainers in rents (like USAir) supported the status quo. Consequently, the carriers did not act jointly. While group lobbying was unlikely because of divisions on the value of the status quo, for most carriers the cost of lobbying on their own probably exceeded immediate benefits.

So deadlock continued, until DeMuth of OIRA mobilized the carriers on an occasion provided by Charles Plott, a professor of economics and the New York Air representative on a committee established to discover mechanisms to break deadlocks. Though he had previously recommended auctions, Plott perceived that carriers, fearing them, would support buy/sell only with grandfathering. So he wrote to DeMuth, pointing out that the industry perceived OMB as favoring periodic auctions for revenue, while the industry itself was strongly opposed to them. He asked DeMuth's opinion of a market wherein carriers would keep their current slots, which would be salable (Plott to DeMuth, 14 April 1983). DeMuth responded (26 May 1983):

... Periodic auctions were first proposed by the Department of Transportation ... on October 21, 1980. This proposal, ... under a previous administration, ... does not reflect this Administration's position. Our dominant interest is efficient allocation of slots, not merely raising revenues. . . .

We are intrigued by your proposal, which has several evident advantages. . . . first, it uses private markets to ensure that the limited existing slots are used most efficiently, eliminating the transaction costs and uncertainty of the scheduling committees as well as the possibility of administrative allocation by the FAA. Second, it would use the price system to allocate any new slots to their highest-valued uses. Third, the grandfathering of current slots, while perhaps continuing short-term inefficiencies, could provide a smooth transition from scheduling committee allocation to market allocation, minimizing the dislocations inherent in an initiating lottery or auction. . . .

This letter was widely publicized and appreciated in the industry, so most carriers came to favor a market. Condition 2 was thus satisfied, but not because the carriers initially sought rights, although one carrier did employ Plott. Rather, some officials wanted the presumed efficiencies and changed the payoff structure to satisfy condition 2.

The grantor: FAA versus OMB

To realize potential rights, by condition 3 government must declare them. In our story so far, however, the administration has been divided. Although officials benefit from declaring rights, the calculation is confused when the manager of the common resource (FAA) and the advocate of privatization (OMB) are different persons. The managers lose jobs and gain nothing, while the advocates lose nothing and gain credit. So to satisfy condition 3, OMB somehow had to disarm FAA, as analyzed in this internal OMB memorandum (5 August 1983):

The [scheduling] committee [of National] collapsed, throwing the allocation to DOT. . . . This memo provides background. . . .

Political theory of the origin of property rights

Nearly all airlines serving National support buy/sell, but there are divisions over the initial allocation mechanism. . . . There is strong support for grandfathering and a slot market in DOT; however, the FAA unconditionally opposes. . . . The Secretary has not spoken yet on buy/sell, but she appears to be leaning against it.

Strategy: . . . Our strategy is simple: [to] get a slot market proposal NPRM [Notice of Proposed Rule-Making] out for comment. The airlines who support it should help carry it from there.

Dr. Charles Plott . . . helped us dispel the airlines' belief that OMB's . . . interest is balancing the budget. . . . [He] circulated our response to the airlines. As a result, their knee jerk rejection of slot markets has been replaced with conditional support. . . .

Secretary Dole. . . . The Scheduling Committee failure may . . . force her to issue an NPRM for slot allocation to which . . . buy/sell [could be attached].

DOT (Policy Office and General Counsel) must draft the NPRM and Final rule . . . and try to win over the Secretary. No NPRM will be forthcoming without the Secretary overruling Helms. [The Policy Office] at DOT must coordinate this effort. They must also pull and cajole the airlines. . . .

The NPRM should elicit support . . . and divide opposition. . . .

OMB must . . . prevent Helms or the airlines from end-running us to the White House. . . .

Inside DOT Secretary Dole, for whom slots were only a minor issue, was cross-pressured. People in the Office of Policy liked buy/sell, while FAA officials opposed it strongly.

Externally, the cross-pressure was even worse: general aviation lobbyists were powerful antagonists because their clients, often politically active, lived in nearly every congressional district and feared that a market would limit their runway access, which the FAA had usually protected. Furthermore, Secretary Dole's husband was senator from Kansas, where Beech and Cessna, two main producers for general aviation, are located. On the other hand, given Executive Order 12291, the secretary could not resolve congestion without the OMB, which insisted on markets.

Thus, cross-pressured, DOT temporized. Nearly a year after deadlocked carriers petitioned for a market (Jenkins, Gomez-Ibanez, and Meyer 1987, 3), the DOT published Notices (84-6, 84-7) of Proposed Rule-Making (49 FR 23788 and 23806, 06/07/84). In response, most carriers, including commuter lines, supported buy/sell (Dockets 24105, 24110). Among large carriers only USAir and Delta opposed.

The main ideological objection concerned grandfathering without auctions, presumably a windfall profit. The practical rejoinder was that auctions would disrupt the system until the carriers could match slots with schedules. The rejoinder in economic theory was that the windfall occurred in 1969, when the slots became carriers' economic capital, through not accounting capital. The 1985 proposal would merely liquefy some illiquid capital (Hearing 99-59, p. 267).

Summarizing the NPRMs for Secretary Dole, Matthew V. Scocozza, assistant secretary for Policy and International Affairs, wrote (20 December 1984): "The options that merit the most serious consideration are (a) the enhanced deadlock breaking mechanism . . . and (b) the buy/ sell. FAA favors the [first] while the Policy Office . . . [the second]." He specifically rejected auctions because of industry opposition and because they would require major legislation.

Thus passed 1984. In 1985 the secretary asked her general counsel, Sam Podberesky, "to convince OMB that the FAA's position was the right position" (Jenkins, Gomez-Ibanez, and Meyer 1987, 10). Of course, this effort was doomed to failure. Congressmen became impatient. The secretary could temporize no more. In February, Representative Shultze (R-PA) introduced HR 984 providing for an aftermarket. In September, Representative Mineta (D-CA), after Hearing 99-33, 1985, urged the secretary to decide. She did, and a buy/sell rule was issued.

4. THE BUY/SELL RULE

The rule (50 FR 52180–52201, 12/20/85) provided at the high density airports for:

1. Allocation of slots to carriers and commuters holding them 12/16/85, the FAA to record the holdings, and sales to begin 04/01/86.
2. Return to the FAA of slots not used 65% of any two-month period ("use-or-lose"), carriers to report on usage.
3. Lottery for new and returned slots, in separate pools for carriers, commuters, and others.
4. Assignment, by lottery, of priority numbers to all slots for recall, if necessary, by the FAA to satisfy needs of Essential Air Service (mainly to small communities), international operations at Kennedy, and operations.

The rule also provided: "Slots do not represent a property right but represent an operating privilege subject to absolute FAA control. Slots may be withdrawn at any time to fulfill the Department's operational needs" (Sec. 93.223). This provision permits, so we are told, the FAA to recall slots without activating the takings clause of the Fifth Amendment. It does not alter the fact that slot owners have excludable, alienable, universal property rights, though with reservations not theoretically different from zoning restrictions on land. In addition, owners can buy protection from recall by exchanging a low priority slot for a high one. We have evidence of trades that apparently were intended to achieve this goal.

The duty-bearers' response

Condition 4 for the emergence of rights is that duty-bearers respect them. Here the duty-bearers are citizens generally, carriers (including nonholders), and general aviation. It is easy to overlook duty-bearers, yet their acquiescence is necessary, especially those in general aviation. One of the forces that killed "open skies" was the resistance of duty-bearers, namely, airport neighbors who feared noise and accidents. When (by NPRM 83-2, 48 FR 13434, 03/31/83) the FAA proposed "open skies," O'Hare neighbors sued to stop it. They lost (FAA Docket 22471), but their intervention discouraged the FAA.

Following the buy/sell rule, duty-bearers again objected. S. 1966, rescinding the rule, was reported in the Senate (13 March 1986, Specter 1986a, 1986b); on 9 April it was attached, by 82-12, to S.1017, transferring National and Dulles from DOT ownership to a regional authority; and on 11 April S. 1017 passed, by 62–28. The House Subcommittee on Aviation, however, ignored S.1017 and inserted the airport transfer into an appropriations bill (Hearing 99-59, 1986) because, committee staffers tell us, members simply could not devise an alternative to buy/sell. Rumblings continued, led by Senator Kassenbaum, who, like Secretary Dole's husband, represented Kansas (Hearing 99-746, 1986; 99-299, 1986). But the dispute now seems quiet, especially as airport ownership and landing fees have become an issue; so we believe property in slots will survive at the four airports.

5. DISCUSSION

In this event all four of our conditions are satisfied. Furthermore, we confirmed some nonobvious inferences from these conditions. Thus, one of our main claims was that grantors must desire the right, implying that when grantors are bureaucratically divided, with some gaining and others losing, grantors dispute and delay the grant, as here the FAA and OMB disputed. Another example is our claim that potential rightholders must perceive an advantage, implying that those who perceive it lobby for the right and those who do not perceive it either do nothing or oppose, as here committee losers lobbied for and committee gainers against. So the detail of this event supports detailed inferences from the theory. We recognize, of course, that one event is limited evidence, and we look forward to similar tests in the future.

By way of conclusion, we compare our work with existing studies of the origin of rights. As against Demsetz, our most surprising and perhaps counterintuitive observation is the pervasive role of government officials in creating rights. Most prospective right-holders waited passively for officials to thrust rights on them. This role for government surprised us until we reflected on the ways of politics. The generic method for politicians to obtain support is to give supporters valuable things, such as money, rents, and rights. Here the dominance of government is clear because the configuration of rights granted satisfied the grantor's interest (i.e., the OMB's interest after it defeated the FAA) rather more than that of the holders, most of whom were content to keep their rents and to avoid FAA's possibly arbitrary allocation. Furthermore, the creation of rights over slots necessarily partially deprived general aviation, without compensation, of customary privileges, which emphasizes that full government guarantees rather than merely customary trade practices are necessary for enforcement. Politicians have a special motive to create property rights. Unlike money transfers (subsidies, entitlements) and the deadweight losses of pork barrel and regulatory cartels, property rights increase efficiency by encouraging owners to use assets most productively. Efficiency makes for prosperity, which rebounds to politicians' credit. Hence, we expect ambitious and clever politicians to give bureaucrats career incentives to create rights. President Reagan did this with OIRA, and the new rulers of formerly Marxist lands are now creating property rights on a grand scale.

Neoclassical economic theory obscures the role of politics, appropriately so in a theory intended exclusively to explain economics. Nevertheless, politics do matter, and so we corrected Demsetz's reliance on an unseen hand.[5] As against the Lockean theory, the surprising and counterintuitive feature of our observations is the primacy of scarcity. Scarcity preceded possession. Carriers "mixed their labor" with slots, from the moment air travel began. They acquired rights, however, not because they had invested, but rather because of the political response to scarcity, the high density rule. So in our account, as in Demsetz's, scarcity, not investment, sets the scene for property rights. Locke's description is, in fact, exactly backward. He argued that possessors create government to protect their assets. Conversely, our theory, supported by our evidence, as well as, for example, evidence from the history of

---

[5] In Demsetz's running illustration, property in land among Quebec Indians, rights emerge by common consent to conserve beaver. But Demsetz's sources flatly contradict the unseen hand theory. The Hudson Bay Company and later the government of Canada pressured for conservation by individual land occupancy (Leacock 1951). The Indians did not have private property, merely private occupancy, because their land was not salable (Witt 1987).

Political theory of the origin of property rights

English land law (North 1981), holds that governments create rights to solve problems of scarcity. Locke, like many classical and neoclassical economists, believed that men in the agora force men on the acropolis to protect traders' interests. Conversely, we believe that men on the acropolis offer protection to men in the agora in return for support.

Thus, Demsetz ignored conditions 3 and 4, and Locke ignored conditions 1 and 3. Adequate description, however, requires all four, and omission of any one distorts the theory. While we have limited ourselves to a positive theory of the origin of property rights, we recognize that our description may put limits on possible justifications. Consequently, we hope that further investigation of comprehensive descriptions may improve moral reasoning. But positive investigation of the origin of property rights should continue, independently of moral considerations, for the sake of studying the operation of rights institutions. For example, such studies should help us to understand why governments sometimes abolish particular rights and place reservations on others. But most of all, positive investigation should improve our understanding of the role of government in the maintenance of the rights institutions on which our economic and social system depends.

REFERENCES

Alchian, Armen A., and Harold Demsetz. 1973. "The Property Rights Paradigms." *Journal of Economic History* 33: 16–27.
Bailey, E. Elizabeth. 1986. "Economic Models and Policy Reality: Lessons from Airport Access." In *Price Competition and Equilibrium*, ed. Maurice Peston and Richard E. Quant. Oxford: Philip Allan.
Blackstone, Sir William. 1765. *Commentaries on the Laws of England.*
Brenner, Melvin A., James O. Leet, and Elihu Schutt. 1985. *Airline Deregulation.* Westport, CT: ENO Foundation.
Buchanan, James, and Gordon Tullock. 1962. *The Calculus of Consent.* Ann Arbor: University of Michigan Press.
Demsetz, Harold. 1964. "The Exchange and Enforcement of Property Rights." *Journal of Law and Economics* 7: 11–26.
    1967. "Toward a Theory of Property Rights." *American Economic Review* 57: 347–59.
    1982. *Economic, Legal, and Political Dimensions of Competition.* Amsterdam: North Holland.
Denman, Donald R. 1958. *Origin of Ownership.* London: Ruskin House.
Eggertsson, Thráinn. 1990. *Economic Behavior and Institutions.* Cambridge: Cambridge University Press.
Grether, David M., R. Mark Isaac, and Charles R. Plott. 1981a. "The Allocation of Landing Rights among Competitors." *American Economic Association Papers and Proceedings* 71.2: 166–71.
    1981b. *Alternative Methods of Allocating Airport Slots: Performance and Evaluation.* Pasadena: Polinomics Research Laboratories; reissued as *The Allocation of Scarce Resources: Experimental Economics and the Problems of Allocating Airport Slots.* Boulder, CO: Westview, 1989.

Hahn, Robert W., and Randall S. Kroszner. 1988. "The Mismanagement of Air Transport: A Supply-Side Perspective." Working Paper, Council of Economic Advisors.

Hardin, Garrett. 1968. "The Tragedy of the Commons." *Science* 162: 1243–48.

Hohfeld, Wesley Newcomb. 1919. *Fundamental Legal Conceptions.* New Haven: Yale University Press.

James, William George, ed. 1982. *Airline Economics.* Lexington, MA: Lexington Books.

Jenkins, Vlad, A. Gomez-Ibanez, and John Meyer. 1987. "The Department of Transportation and Airport Landing Slots." Case Study N. C16-87-7810.0 of the Case Program of the Kennedy School of Government, Harvard University.

Leacock, Eleanor. 1954. *The Montagnis "Hunting Territory" and the Fur Trade.* AAA Memoir 78. Washington, DC: American Anthropological Association.

Levine, Michael. 1969. "Landing Fees and the Airport Congestion Problem." *Journal of Law and Economics* 12: 79–108.

Libecap, Gary D. 1989. *Contracting for Property Rights.* Cambridge: Cambridge University Press.

North, Douglass C. 1981. *Structure and Change in Economic History.* New York: Norton.

Palmer, Robert C. 1985. "The Origin of Property in England." *Law and History Review* 3: 1–50.

Rawls, John. 1971. *A Theory of Justice.* Cambridge: Harvard University Press.

Riker, William H. 1988. "The Place of Political Science in Public Choice." *Public Choice* 57: 247–57.

1990. "Civil Rights and Property Rights." In *Liberty, Property, and the Future of Constitutional Development,* ed. Ellen Paul and Howard Dickman. Albany: State University of New York Press.

Roper, William. 1935 (1626). *Lyfe of Sir Thomas More,* ed. Elsie V. Hitchcock. London: Oxford University Press.

Simpson, A. W. B. 1986. *A History of the Land Law.* 2d ed. Oxford: Oxford University Press.

Specter, Michael. 1986a. "Rule Allowing Sale of Landing Slots of Airports Attacked." *Washington Post,* 31 March, 883, col. 1.

1986b. "Soft Landing." *New Republic,* April 1986, 10–11.

Sumner, L. W. 1987. *The Moral Foundation of Rights.* Oxford: Oxford University Press.

Umbeck, John R. 1981. *A Theory of Property Rights with Applications to the California Gold Rush.* Ames: Iowa State University Press.

Witt, Ulrich. 1987. "The Demsetz Hypothesis on the Emergence of Property Rights Reconsidered." In *Efficiency, Institutions, and Economic Policy,* ed. Richard Pethig and Ulrich Schlieper. Heidelberg: Springer-Verlag.

Government Documents:

Hearings 98-63. 1983. "Report of the Airport Access Task Force." Before the Sub-Committee of Investigation and Oversight/Committee on Public Works and Transportation, House of Representatives. 17 May.

Hearings 99-33. 1985. "Government Policies on the Transfer of Operating Rights. . . ." Before the Sub-Committee on Aviation/Committee on Public Works and Transportation, House of Representatives. 10, 19 September; 22 October.

Hearings 99-746. 1986. "Buying and Selling Airport Operating Rights." Before the Sub-Committee on Aviation/Committee on Commerce, Science, and Transportation, U.S. Senate. 6 February.

Hearings 99-59. 1986. "Allocation of Slots at High Density Airports." Before the Sub-Committee on Aviation/Committee on Public Works and Transportation, House of Representatives. Second Session. 12 June.

Report 99-299. 1986. "Operating Rights at Congested Domestic Airports." Submitted by Senator Danforth, Committee on Commerce, Science, and Transportation, U.S. Senate. 14 May.

9

The economics and politics of institutional change

Institutional change takes place within an institutional framework. In short, not everything is up for grabs all at once. In the following essay, Lee Alston and Joseph Ferrie are careful to specify which institutions are constraints to everyone and which institutions are choice variables to some actors and constraints to others. Alston and Ferrie argue that the institution of social control in the U.S. South – the laws and customs in the South that resulted in a lack of civil rights and condonement of violence – increased the value to agricultural workers of having a protector/employer. Augmenting the value of a protector was the absence of a federal welfare system that would have substituted for some of the value of a paternalistic employer. The reader should note that in the Alston–Ferrie framework social control and the absence of a federal welfare system placed constraints on agricultural labor but also served as choice variables for the very people who were protectors – the politically powerful agricultural elite. The federal welfare net ultimately expanded as a result of technological changes that changed the economic incentives faced by the Southern elite; it no longer paid the South to block the demands of Northern liberal politicians. The essay highlights how institutions give rise to incentives in contracts and also how the dynamics of an economic system can lead to institutional changes. It tells a complicated story and points out the need to wed economic theories of contracting with the positive political theory of political institutions in order to understand the dynamics of institutional change.

Institutional change can arise from either a change in the demands of constituents or a change in the power of the suppliers of institutions – that is, government actors. The demands of constituents could change for a variety of reasons. For example, if technological change leads to an increase in the value of land we would expect greater pressure on politicians from land claimants to define the rights to land more precisely in

The economics and politics of institutional change

order to prevent dissipation of rents. Alternatively, institutional change could arise from changes in the supply side. As the result of a new election, existing politicians could lose political power to another group, inducing changes in the institutional structure; or existing politicians who represent some constituency could face different incentives as a result of changes in the demands of their constituents.

An important point to keep in mind is that economic growth will change the relative costs and benefits of existing institutions. But this does not imply that institutions will necessarily evolve in ways that encourage economic growth. Institutions act as constraints and are slow to change. Moreover, individuals and groups invest in knowledge specific to particular institutions and as such have much to lose if institutions change, even if in the aggregate society would be better off; how else can one explain the resistance to change in the former Soviet Union? Even if parties recognize the benefits of institutional change in the aggregate and the ability of a minority to block change, the beliefs in a society may prevent the majority from engineering side payments to those with veto power. This holds not just for former communist countries but also for democracies. For example, Alston and Ferrie chronicle the ability of committee chairpersons in the U.S. Congress to block legislation that a majority of members of Congress might favor.

Part of the problem associated with the rigidity of institutions that are inappropriate for economic growth is the lack of explicit property rights in formal institutions. This raises the transaction costs for institutional change. For example, suppose that the auto industry, consumers, and politicians would all be better off if we eliminated all tariffs and quotas on imported cars; part of the savings generated by the reduced prices of cars could be transferred to the auto producers and another part to politicians. This will not happen, however, not just because consumers would find such transfers abhorrent but also because no one has an explicit right over the existing restrictions such that we could buy them out.

WHAT TO LOOK FOR IN THE ESSAY

We encourage the reader to think about the following questions and issues while reading this essay:

1. Alston and Ferrie maintain that social control was a choice variable for the rural elite in the South. How would their story change if social control were an exogenous constraint?
2. Technological change is taken as exogenous to paternalism. Is it likely that paternalism delayed the advent of mechanization in the South?

3. Technology eroded the advantages of using paternalism. Is it likely that it also eroded the system of social control?
4. The authors argue that economic incentives eroded the political incentive to block federal welfare programs. Did ideology play an independent role in shaping federal welfare programs?

Paternalism in agricultural labor contracts in the U.S. South: implications for the growth of the welfare state

LEE J. ALSTON AND JOSEPH P. FERRIE

Economists generally treat institutions as exogenous and examine their impact on the economy. But institutions, which define the "rules of the game" in an economy and the payoffs to pursuing different strategies, can change over time. Understanding the forces that prompt changes in institutions and how the payoffs to strategies change in response to institutional changes is important for understanding the developmental pattern of societies.[1] For example, explicit contracts may be the most efficient means of structuring transactions under one institutional regime, but less formal agreements with entirely different enforcement mechanisms may be most efficient under another. Different ways of structuring transactions may lead to different growth paths.

In this paper we examine the rise and decline of paternalism in Southern labor relations. By "paternalism" we mean an implicit contract whereby workers exchange dependable labor services for a variety of

This essay originally appeared in the *American Economic Review*, Vol. 83, No. 4 (September 1993). © The American Economic Association.

We are especially grateful to Robert Higgs and Larry Neal for their advice and their careful reading of this manuscript. For comments on earlier drafts, we thank George Akerlof, Jeremy Atack, Leonard Carlson, Gary Cox, Stefano Fenoaltea, Victor Goldberg, Avner Greif, James Heckman, Jon Hughes, Marvin McInnis, David Montgomery, Joel Mokyr, Pablo Spiller, the participants at the CERES/Fulbright Conference on Institutions and Economic Development (Montevideo, Uruguay, June 11–13, 1990). Roger Ransom and participants at the Economic History Association Meetings (Montreal, Canada, September 13–16, 1990), seminar participants at Queens University, Brigham Young University, the University of Alberta, the University of Western Ontario, the University of Chicago, Yale Law School, and Washington University, and three anonymous referees. For research assistance, we are grateful to Roxana Barrantes and Bernardo Mueller.

[1] In the 1980's, scholars devoted increasing attention to the importance of institutions. Douglass C. North (1981, 1990) and Oliver Williamson (1985) sparked this revival. Their predecessors included Ronald H. Coase (1937, 1960) and Joseph Schumpeter (1950).

goods and services. "Dependable" implies a long-term commitment to an employer that transcends the textbook notion of spot-market exchange. In return, workers receive such goods and services as credit, housing, medical and old-age assistance, and most importantly, protection from acts of violence. Paternalism, we argue, emerged along with a particular institution – the system of social control that emerged in the late 19th century and characterized the American South during the first half of the 20th century. The South's system of social control, we have suggested elsewhere (Alston and Ferrie, 1989 pp. 133–4), comprised

a variety of laws and practices, the effect of which was the dependence of blacks and poor whites on the white rural elite. Examples include low levels of expenditure on education, old-age security, and welfare, the exclusion of blacks and many poor whites from the electoral process, a pronounced lack of civil rights, and the tolerance of violence.

A large body of circumstantial evidence is consistent with the view that technological forces caused paternalism to be adopted as a means to secure labor in the climate fostered by the institution of social control, while technological changes and the erosion of social control in the 1950's and 1960's combined to lead the South to abandon paternalism.[2] This change, we argue, in turn allowed for the expansion of the American welfare state in the 1960's. Central to our argument is the role played by the political power of Southern congressmen and their principals, the Southern rural elite.

1. SOME HISTORICAL BACKGROUND ON PATERNALISM IN THE SOUTH[3]

The system of paternalism in place in the 1930's was not a simple extension of the antebellum master–slave relationship into the postbellum Southern economy. It was instead the product of the dislocation occasioned by the Civil War and the actions of planters trying to secure an adequate labor supply in these circumstances.

The initial response of planters to the difficulties of keeping laborers in the immediate postwar period was to offer former slaves a variety of nonmonetary inducements to remain at least through the harvest of the present crop. The rise of virulent racism in the post-Reconstruction

---

[2] By examining both the rise and the fall of paternalism in Southern agricultural contracts, we are less open to the criticisms that plague functionalist explanations: much work in the applied analysis of contracting suffers from explaining the existence of a contract solely by an appeal to its functions.

[3] We are grateful to Robert Higgs for providing much of the primary source material on which this section is based.

period presented planters with an opportunity to offer to their workers protection from racist violence and the capricious judgments of a racist legal system, in exchange for continued dependable service in the planters' fields. Their role as protector of the physical safety of their workers evolved in the 20th century into a more general role as protector of workers in commercial and legal transactions and in many dealings with the world outside the plantation. That role ensured the opposition of planters to federal interference in Southern labor and race relations in the first half of the 20th century.

After the Civil War, Southern agriculture faced enormous difficulties. The abolition of slavery, the coercive system which had organized labor relations before the war, was clearly the greatest problem. Though the South suffered tremendous physical destruction, including the loss of livestock, fences, and barns, and though many of its fields had been neglected throughout the war, what most concerned planters was the lack of a system to assure an adequate supply of labor (N. B. Cloud, 1867; U.S. Department of Agriculture, 1867). Fields could be rehabilitated and new workstock and animals purchased after a season or two of hardship – farmers had often been forced to do so in the past after natural disasters – but replacing slavery with a new system was a more daunting task. Some former masters, those "who had dealt honorably and humanely towards their slaves," were able to retain many of their former fieldhands (U.S. Congress, 1866 p. 125).[4] Most planters, though, particularly those who were not so highly regarded by their former slaves, had great difficulty in satisfying their demand for labor (see Freedmen's Bureau, 1866 p. 95).[5]

Into this chaos stepped the Freedmen's Bureau as an intermediary, at least for a short time. The Bureau, an agency of the federal government, initially enjoyed the trust of the freedmen. As a repository of their trust, it could "disabuse them of any extravagant notions and expectations . . . [and] administer them good advice and be voluntarily obeyed" (Carl

---

[4] Most of those hiring large numbers of hands after the war were the same planters who had controlled the largest plantations before the war. For evidence on the lack of turnover in the "plantation elite" as a result of the war, see Jay R. Mandle (1973), Jonathan M. Wiener (1978), and Michael Wayne (1983). After Reconstruction, it was the planter elite rather than the petty merchants who retained the greatest political and economic power in the rural South. For example, crop lien laws gave planters rather than merchants first claim on the output of sharecroppers indebted to both (Harold D. Woodman, 1979 p. 328). Woodman has also shown that laws relegated sharecroppers to the legal status of wage workers, enhancing the power of landlords (Woodman, 1979 pp. 324–6).
[5] See Leon F. Litwack (1979) and Gerald D. Jaynes (1986 pp. 207–23) for a discussion of the disorder in agricultural labor markets immediately following the Civil War.

Lee J. Alston and Joseph P. Ferrie

Schurz, 1866 p. 40). The Bureau had the power to compel the observance of labor contracts and for this earned the early respect of planters. The Freedmen's Bureau had done nothing to change the fact that the abolition of slavery had raised the cost of labor.[6] During the period of excess demand for labor which existed until the adjustment to this new, higher equilibrium wage, some planters raided their competitors for labor and bitterly complained as their own work forces were raided.

By 1869, the Bureau had ceased to function as a go-between and guarantor. Both planters and freedmen seem to have seen less need for the offices of the agency after only three years' experience with it, perhaps because of a desire for greater flexibility than the Bureau-approved contracts allowed (Ralph Shlomowitz, 1978 p. 35). The Bureau had attempted to stabilize the agricultural labor market in the first confused years after emancipation.[7] The demise of the Freedmen's Bureau left planters and freedmen to contract among themselves directly. Writing in 1872, one observer noted conditions much like those in the immediate aftermath of the war: workers were being hired away by competing employers, leaving planters with insufficient labor to bring in the crop, and employers were failing to fulfill the terms of their contracts with their workers (Charles Stearns, 1872 pp. 107–8). Securing adequate labor was described as "a matter of grave uncertainty and deep anxiety" for every planter (Southerner, 1871 p. 329).

In these circumstances, some planters chose a new course, turning to honesty, fair-dealing, and a host of nonwage aspects of their relationship with their workers as additional margins for competition (see Phillip A. Bruce, 1889 pp. 180–1; H. C. Taylor, 1925 p. 329).[8] The amenities which employers offered their workers included improved housing, garden plots, firewood, and plantation schools and churches (J. R. Godwin,

---

[6] Roger L. Ransom and Richard Sutch (1978) argue that emancipation decreased the labor supply of former slaves, who in effect bought greater leisure. Robert W. Fogel (1989) suggests that planters increased their demand for labor after emancipation, because more workers were needed to do the work that had previously been done under the onerous gang system. In either case, the result would have been an increase in the price of labor.

[7] The Bureau's legacy was its intermediation – the first by any federal agency and the last for a long time – in the South's evolving system of labor relations. Though such intervention was attempted again by the Resettlement Administration and the Farm Security Administration in the 1930's, the context had changed considerably by then, and the results were altogether different (see Alston and Ferrie, 1985b).

[8] Jaynes (1986 pp. 78–9, 104–6, 121) describes the introduction of such arrangements between planters and their wage workers in the immediate antebellum period, even before the demise of the Freedmen's Bureau. He does not explore the persistence of these relationships into the post-Reconstruction period or into the 20th century as we have elsewhere (Alston and Ferrie, 1989). Jaynes views "market paternalism" – his term for these arrangements – and tenancy and share contracts as substitutes

Paternalism in agricultural labor contracts

1900 p. 476; U.S. Industrial Commission, 1901 p. 778; Alfred Holt Stone, 1902 p. 250; W. E. B. DuBois, 1906 p. 514; Taylor, 1925 p. 337; C. W. Tebeau, 1936 p. 138; T. J. Woofter, 1938). These perquisites were seldom explicitly stipulated; planters continued to prefer verbal rather than written leases (U.S. Industrial Commission, 1900–1902 pp. 437–8; E. V. Wilcox, 1918 pp. 2–4; Harold Hoffsommer, 1950 p. 389).

By the end of the 19th century, another role, in addition to that of provider of these amenities, had been assumed by large planters: that of protector of their workers. As early as the 1880's, landlords were willing to offer their advice to their workers and to protect them from exploitation at the hands of the local merchants (U.S. Senate, 1885 p. 164). By the turn of the century, the role of protector expanded to include protection from violence.

White hostility toward freed blacks had been evident since the end of the war but had to some extent been kept in check by the Reconstruction governments (Benjamin C. Truman, 1866 p. 10; Schurz, 1866 pp. 47–105; Stearns, 1872 p. 103). The end of Reconstruction saw such hostilities emerge into the open (Tebeau, 1936 p. 139).[9] For example, "white-capping," driving blacks from their homes and forcing them off the lands owned by the largest landowners and merchants, was reported in several Mississippi counties in the early 1890's (Charles H. Otken, 1894 pp. 86–8; William F. Holmes, 1969 pp. 166–9). With disfranchisement, the entire machinery of the state became an instrument with which to coerce blacks. For example, the South's judicial system displayed a clear bias, meting out sentences to blacks in the South far more severe than those given for corresponding crimes in the North (Woofter, 1920 p. 143).

---

used by planters for reducing monitoring costs. We believe that such paternalistic arrangements were not only complementary to tenancy and share contracts in reducing monitoring costs, but were actually *more* likely to be given to tenants and croppers than to wage workers. A long-term relationship like that between planters and their tenants and croppers made such arrangements more effective as monitoring devices. Such arrangements were also increasingly important as wage workers in gangs were replaced by geographically dispersed tenants and croppers. The assignment of tenants and croppers to specific plots created an incentive for planters to reduce turnover and prevent the departure of tenants and croppers in possession of location-specific farming knowledge. The literature on paternalism in the late 19th and early 20th centuries (cited in Alston and Ferrie [1989]) is the basis for our view that these arrangements continued with the transition away from an exclusive reliance on wage labor, and that these arrangements were in fact of even greater value to planters when they employed tenants and croppers than they had been when only wage workers were employed.

[9] For a more general view of the experience of blacks in the post-emancipation Southern economy, see Robert Higgs (1977).

Lee J. Alston and Joseph P. Ferrie

The disfranchisement of blacks and poor whites that helped create the South's regime of social control could not have occurred without the cooperation of the white rural elite. Indeed, J. Morgan Kousser (1974 p. 238) argues convincingly that the new political structure in the South was shaped by Black Belt socioeconomic elites:

The new political structure was not the product of accident or other impersonal forces, nor of decisions demanded by the masses, nor even the white masses. The system which insured the absolute control of predominantly black counties by upper-class whites, the elimination in most areas of parties as a means of organized competition between politicians, and, in general, the nonrepresentation of lower class interests in political decision-making was shaped by those who stood to benefit most from it – Democrats, usually from the Black Belt and always socioeconomically privileged.

This is the sense in which we view the institution of social control in the South as "endogenous": it was the product of decisions made by the white rural elite.[10] The rise of the institution of social control led in turn to the increased use of protection in paternalistic contracts. Planters increasingly offered protection to their faithful black workers as the social and legal environment became more hostile toward blacks – a hostility which, over several decades, the white rural elite was instrumental in creating.

Thus, to limit the departure of their own workers from the South, many planters came to serve as the protectors for their workers as well as the providers of many of their material needs. Planters had posted bond for their workers and accompanied them to court before, but with the pronounced change in the political, legal, and social climate at the turn of the century, such practices took on added importance.[11]

In the following years, the scope of planters' paternalism expanded,

[10]Gavin Wright (1986 p. 122) argues that disfranchisement "was a by-product of the agrarian movement," a movement which he describes as a result of weak world cotton demand in the 1890's. Kousser (1974 pp. 6–8) provides a similar explanation for the disfranchisement of both blacks and poor whites, though one that does not rely on the impact of world cotton demand. Blacks were excluded from the electoral process by the Black Belt elites because "The end of Negro voting would solidify their control over their tenants and free them from having to deal with elected or appointed black officials, a type of contact almost all Southern whites found distasteful" (p. 7). The elites excluded poor, up-country whites to prevent conflict over issues such as taxes and, more generally, to achieve political hegemony in state politics.

[11]See examples from the 1870's in the Phillip H. Pitts papers. C. Vann Woodward (1951 p. 218) also notes the use of paternalism as a protective device for blacks. "Another considerable Negro element saw nothing better than to take refuge under the paternalism of the old masters, who offered some protection against the extreme race doctrines of the upland whites. . . . [The publication] *The Nation* . . . rejoiced that 'Thousands of them' had discovered 'that their interests are bound up with the interest of their old masters.' "

until planters had come to act as intermediaries between their workers and much of the outside world. Planters exercised control over the credit extended to their workers, but they were also willing to "stand good" for their workers' debts with local merchants.[12] Planters reported significant outlays for the payment of doctors' bills, the establishment and maintenance of schools and churches, and various unspecified forms of entertainment (Woofter, 1936 table 14-A); and planters commonly paid legal fines incurred by workers and served as parole sponsors for their workers (Woofter, 1936 table 14-B).

The result was a system of thorough paternalism in which planters looked after most aspects of their workers' lives, and workers responded by offering their loyalty to their patron. Planters had to some degree solved the labor-supply problem they had faced at emancipation: provision of paternalism allowed them to tie black workers to the land in a world of free contracting, though not as firmly as the law had bound black workers under slavery, because coercion was no longer as viable, and exit was an option. They were able to reduce the cost of monitoring labor by providing workers with valuable services which they would forfeit if they were caught shirking. They offered both black and white workers a wide array of nonwage benefits, as well as assistance in commercial and legal transactions, and in addition provided their black workers with protection from the power of the state and the racial hostility of many whites.

The ability of planters to keep labor both cheap and dependable required not only that they continue to supply the full range of paternalistic benefits to their workers, but also that the external threat posed by a racist state continue. Furthermore, planters needed to ensure that no other party stepped forward to act as the workers' protector in commercial and legal dealings. In short, planters had an interest in maintaining a racist state and preventing federal interference in race and labor issues.

2. THE ECONOMICS OF PATERNALISM IN AGRICULTURE[13]

Woofter (1936 pp. 31–2) described some of the social and economic aspects of paternalism in the American South in the 1930's:

[12] Half of all Southern landlords surveyed in 1938 said they would routinely "stand good" for their tenants' debts, while only 3 percent of Northern landlords said they would do so. The study's author described this finding as "evidence of the paternalistic side of the landlord-tenant relationship in the South, an aspect which is insignificant in the North . . ." (Edgar A. Schuler, 1938 p. 172).

[13] For an elaboration of the issues in this section, see Alston and Ferrie (1989). Though we discuss paternalism in the U.S. South, it is not unique to America. Similar

[T]he landlord is also often called upon for services of a social nature, for the large plantation is a social as well as an economic organism and the matrix of a number of plantations often constitutes or dominates the larger unit of civil government in the locality.

Among efficient landlords, tenant health is one of the major considerations and doctors' bills are paid by the landlord and charged against the tenant crop. Those tenants who have a landlord who will "stand for" their bills are far more likely to get physicians' services than are the general run of tenants.

Landlords are also expected to "stand for" their tenants in minor difficulties such as may grow out of gambling games, altercations and traffic infractions. This function is, of course, not exercised indiscriminately. A good worker will, in all probability, be "gotten off" and a drone left in the hands of the law. . . . [T]he landlord assumes responsibility for such tenants who are arrested for minor offenses, especially during the busy season.

In the U.S. South, perhaps the most important aspect of paternalism was the protection planters offered from violence perpetrated by the larger community. Protection was important for all agricultural workers, but particularly for black workers, because they lacked civil rights, and society condoned violence. Paternalism was more than shelter from physical threats; it could also involve interceding in commercial transactions, obtaining medical care, providing influence or money to bail a son out of jail, or settling familial disputes.[14] White workers were not for the most part beneficiaries of paternalistic arrangements, both because they had a lower demand for protection from violence and because they were not as likely as blacks to be employed on plantations. Plantation owners were more likely than other employers to supply paternalism, both because of their political power and because of economies of scale in the provision of some aspects of paternalism, such as housing or medical care.

Paternalism is most prevalent in premechanized and non-science-based agriculture. Before the advent of scientific advances that stabilized yields, workers possessed farm-specific knowledge, which gave landlords an incentive to curb the migration of tenants with such knowledge. Before mechanization, monitoring labor effort was costly because workers were spread over a considerable physical distance, and linkage of reward with effort was difficult because there could be considerable

arrangements have existed in nearly all countries at one time or another. Paternalism or patron–client relationships have existed in South America, England, and Asia in the 20th century (see T. W. Hutchinson, 1957; S. L. Barraclough and A. L. Domike, 1966; Allen W. Johnson, 1971; Howard Newby, 1977; Yujiro Hayami and Masao Kikuchi, 1982). Such relationships also existed in feudal Europe (see Marc Bloch, 1961, 1975).

[14]These examples are illustrative rather than exhaustive.

variation in output the cause of which was difficult to determine. Examples abound: Did the mule go lame naturally or did the workers mistreat the mule? Was the shortfall in output due to too little rain or too little work effort? Paternalism reduced these monitoring costs by reducing workers' tendency to shirk, by raising the costs of shirking and by increasing the length of the time horizon over which workers made decisions.[15]

Because paternalism is a long-term contract of sorts, it may induce in workers a sense that they, as well as the landlord, gain from long-run improvements to soil fertility. This is especially true for fixed-rent tenants who are residual claimants of any given year's output. Paternalism may also reduce the taste for shirking if it is viewed by workers not as a market transaction, but rather as benevolence from the patron. Under such conditions workers respond with goodwill gestures (more work intensity) of their own.[16]

More importantly, paternalism may act as an efficiency wage. Because some of the services acquired under paternalism are not available in markets, workers, who value such services, are not indifferent between the present paternalistic work relationship and the casual labor market.[17] The lack of indifference encourages greater work intensity because workers are afraid of losing their paternalistic benefits if caught shirking. For example, in discussing the variety of services provided by a patron, Hayami and Kikuchi (1982 p. 218) remark that "... the discovery of shirking in one operation ... would endanger the whole set of transactions."

Not all employers in pre-mechanized agriculture offered paternalistic employment contracts. The cost of providing paternalism varied inversely with political influence, which in turn was a function of farm size. This is why paternalism in the U.S. South was associated with plantations. For much of the late 19th and early 20th centuries, individual Southern plantation owners had the local political influence to ensure the delivery of protection and, by the turn of the century, the collective political influence at the state level to create a discriminatory socio-legal environment from which they then offered dispensation (see Kousser, 1974). Furthermore, from the end of Reconstruction through the 1960's, plantation owners collectively had the political power at the

---

[15] The mechanisms through which paternalism could reduce monitoring costs in these ways are discussed in greater detail in Alston and Ferrie (1989).

[16] A similar model is described in George A. Akerlof (1982).

[17] Of course, instead of paternalistic goods and services, landlords could pay a higher wage than a worker's opportunity wage. Our argument is that paternalism is cheaper than using cash.

Lee J. Alston and Joseph P. Ferrie

national level to prevent, or at least limit, federal interference in Southern race and labor relations (see William C. Havard, 1972; V. O. Key, 1949; George E. Mowry, 1973; Gary W. Cox and Mathew D. McCubbins, 1993).

3. THE POLITICS OF PATERNALISM

Once the plantation elite had a firm grip on politics within the South, the Black Belt areas no longer had to stuff ballot boxes or engage in intimidation. The various means of disfranchisement ensured political hegemony at the state level for the upper socioeconomic class. Despite their power at the local and state levels, in order to maintain paternalism, the Southern rural elite had to prevent interference from both the federal government and the private sector. Government substitutes for paternalism would have raised the costs of monitoring labor, and outmigration of labor or inmigration of capital would have raised reservation wages. Landowners did not operate directly in politics but, rather, had congressmen as their political agents. After the Civil War and especially after the disfranchisement of blacks and poor whites, Southern Democratic congressmen viewed the rural elite as their constituents. At mid-century, Key (1949 p. 668) described the outcome of this arrangement: "the black belts manage to control almost the entire Southern Congressional delegation in opposition to proposals of external interference."

Given that the Southern delegation did not represent a majority in either house of Congress, how were they able to satisfy the desires of their rural elite constituents? Though never an absolute majority, Southern Democrats represented a substantial and influential percentage of the Democratic party. At present there is a lively debate over whether parties have had much influence over decision-making in Congress in the 20th century.[18] Given that the party leadership is in charge of appointments to committees, it is difficult to deny that party leaders can ultimately influence decision-making. However, because short-run authority over legislation is ceded to committees, the composition of committees, when their members differ in preferences from the party median, can affect the outcome of legislation. This is particularly the case in the House when the Rules, Ways and Means, and Appropriations Committees, the so-called "control" committees, include members with preferences far removed from those of the median member. Nevertheless, whether one believes that power is in the hands of parties and exercised through committees or that committees themselves are the repository of

[18] For a synopsis of the issues in the debate, see Cox and McCubbins, 1993.

Paternalism in agricultural labor contracts

power, the proximate source of power is the committees. For this reason we will focus our attention on committee composition.[19]

Decision-making in Congress is not democratic. Although every member has one vote, Congress has ceded considerable authority to committees.[20] Committees decide what legislation comes up for a vote, and when. In the House, when (and sometimes if) legislation reaches the floor is determined by the Rules Committee. Within their policy jurisdictions, committees have agenda control. Legislation originates in and is shaped by committees with jurisdiction over certain policy areas. For example, only the House and Senate Committees on Agriculture have the authority to submit agricultural legislation to the floor. Out of the infinite number of bills that could pass through Congress, committees can choose the bills that best suit the interests of committee members while still commanding a majority of votes in Congress. If the committee is not interested in an issue, even though the majority of Congress is, it can simply fail to report a bill to the floor.[21]

Even after legislation passes in the House or Senate, committees still exercise disproportionate power. Differences in proposed legislation between the House and Senate are settled in conference between representatives of each chamber who are members of the relevant committees from which the proposed legislation emanated. In addition, after the legislation is law, the committees are the watchdogs over its implementation.

As in Congress as a whole, decision-making within committees is not democratic. Steven S. Smith (1989 p. 13) argues that

---

[19] The amount of authority allowed committees may depend on the cohesiveness of the majority party. When parties are factionalized, as the Democratic party was from the New Deal to approximately 1970, coalitions need to be formed and enforced in order for a party to be effective in policy-making. By allowing committees to exercise agenda control, the Democratic party held together the alliance based on Southern support for the party platform in return for noninterference in Southern labor and race relations.

[20] Ceding control over legislation to committees enables legislators to increase the probability that legislation will not be reversed by future Congresses (see Kenneth A. Shepsle and Barry R. Weingast, 1984; Weingast and William Marshall, 1988).

[21] In the postwar period, the committee structure determined the course of legislation as long as it was a time of "business as usual." If an issue received widespread national attention, the norms of reciprocity that gave committees some of their agenda control no longer functioned. For example, the attention given to the civil-rights movement in the media propelled civil rights to be examined by Congress as a whole – more as we naively think democracies should function – but civil-rights legislation, like the decision to go to war, is a marked exception to the general rule we have described. For most issues in the postwar period, an understanding of the makeup of committees is crucial for achieving an understanding of legislative outcomes.

317

... widely recognized norms of apprenticeship and committee deference served to limit effective participation to a few senior committee members. Moreover, the distribution of resources and parliamentary prerogatives advantaged senior, majority-party, committee chairmen in both chambers.

Chairmen of committees set committee meeting times, made appointments to subcommittees, hired the professional staff, led the floor debate on the legislation reported out of their committees, and served on conference committees to reconcile differences between the two houses of Congress.

The importance of committees is not static, but needs to be viewed in a historical context. Seniority in committees was so important in the period from the end of World War II to the early 1970's because party cohesion was weak. During this period, committees and their senior members dominated the legislative process as a result of regional factionalism in the Democratic party (D. Roderick Kiewiet and McCubbins, 1991; Cox and McCubbins, 1993). Leadership was split, giving more autonomy to senior committee members; but senior committee members still had to satisfy a faction within the Democratic party – Southern conservatives or Northern liberals. It was the growth of the Northern liberal faction of the Democratic party that led to the committee reforms in the early 1970's that diluted the power of committee chairmen. Clearly, the reforms were aimed at senior Southern conservative chairs.

Though the handwriting was on the wall in the early 1960's, except for the removal of the veto power of the Rules Committee for one congress (1963–1964), no important changes occurred in committee structure. However, this need not imply that the behavior of Southern congressmen was not influenced. Foreseeing that structural change was in the works and being guided by Northern liberals, Southerners may have tempered their conservative behavior in an effort to forestall change in the institutional structure of Congress. Naturally, Southerners would have given in on the issues that affected them the least, though it may have been in the interest of any individual congressman not to do so.[22] We maintain that, given the ability of Southern agriculture to mechanize at relatively low cost, to shift into less labor-intensive crops prompted in part by government agricultural programs, and to stabilize yields through scientific advances such as weed control and fertilization, opposition to federal welfare was no longer as important to the Southern elite.

Understanding the importance of seniority in the institutional work-

---

[22] We are grateful to an anonymous referee for suggesting this point.

ings of Congress makes apparent why the South could succeed in blocking federal interference: Southern members had far greater seniority than other members. Relative Southern seniority manifested itself in dominance of committees. For example, in 1933, Southerners chaired 12 of the 17 major House committees and nine of the 14 major Senate committees (Mowry, 1973 pp. 45–6).

Moreover, Southern power in Congress was not latent. Southern legislators in the 1930's, 1940's, and 1950's took steps in Congress to prevent the provision of government substitutes for paternalism and to prevent the migration of labor out of the South, either of which would have reduced the value of planter-supplied paternalism. In earlier work we documented the success of Southern legislators in: (1) defeating or altering the coverage of farm workers under the initial Social Security Act; (2) limiting the appropriations of the Farm Security Administration once its agenda turned toward reforming the South; and (3) originating and maintaining a program for the importation of Mexican farm labor (Alston and Ferrie, 1985a,b, 1993). Nevertheless, paternalism disappeared in the late 1950's and early 1960's. Was this the result of diminished economic incentives occasioned by the rapid mechanization of Southern agriculture? Or did Southern politicians lose the political power to prevent outside interference in labor relations? Or both?

4. MECHANIZATION AND THE DISAPPEARANCE OF PATERNALISM[23]

Mechanization and the accompanying science-based technology reduced the economic incentive to provide paternalism. The advances in science that accompanied mechanization increased and stabilized yields, making the farm-specific knowledge of tenants less valuable. Because labor turnover was no longer as costly, the benefits of supplying paternalism were reduced. Mechanization also directly reduced the costs of labor and generating labor effect. With millions of farm workers displaced, the threat of unemployment was sufficient to generate work intensity. Furthermore, mechanization directly reduced the costs of monitoring labor

---

[23] In this section, and throughout the paper, we focus on the impact that mechanization and its accompanying technology had on paternalism because we maintain that mechanization was the most important causal factor. However, mechanization was not the only factor leading to a decline in paternalism. Government agricultural programs and the declining profitability of cotton relative to other crops led to a shift out of cotton and into other crops and livestock. See Frank Maier (1969) and Charles S. Aiken and Merle Prunty (1972) on the impact of government programs and Gilbert C. Fite (1984 Ch. 9) on the relative profitability of cotton.

by standardizing the production process and reducing the variation in the marginal productivity of labor. Paternalism became an outdated contractual device.[24]

To test this hypothesis, we would ideally like a time series on paternalism that we could correlate with mechanization. None exists. Instead, we will take a different tack and rely on several pieces of circumstantial evidence.[25] The first pieces of evidence are the association between

---

[24] One might think that the mechanization of Southern agriculture that displaced labor prompted changes in the interests of politicians because of changed political constituencies. Then, one could ignore the economic interests of the rural South in explaining the lack of Southern resistance to Great Society welfare programs and look only at the interests of the new urban constituents. Such thinking is erroneous. The displaced workers in the South – many of them black – for the most part did not vote and as such did not form a new constituency, at least not until the Voting Rights Act took effect, and this did not occur until *after* the passage of the Economic Opportunity Act (which we discuss below) – the heart of the modern welfare state. The most influential constituents, the wealthy rural elite, did not disappear. Wright (1986 p. 268), discussing the South's receptivity to Civil Rights legislation in the 1960's, emphasized the importance of the changed attitudes of this elite: he suggests that, though the desire of business interests to market the region to outsiders was important in transforming attitudes toward race, "... it is even more important to recognize the basic contribution of the voices that were *not* heard on the other side, the planters and other protectors of the old isolated low-wage Southern labor market" (italics in original). In examining social-welfare legislation, we believe – as does Wright in the case of civil-rights legislation – that changes in the attitudes of the existing constituency, the white rural elite, were more decisive than the birth of new constituencies. Furthermore, relative seniority in Congress insulated Southern congressmen somewhat from the changes, if any, in constituent interests. Southern congressmen who stayed in office after mechanization were on committees that could serve the interests of the rural South (like the Agriculture Committee) and, as such, most likely continued to cater to the interests of the rural South. Switching committees to serve the interests of a new constituency did not make political sense. Evidence in support of our view that political constituencies did not dramatically change immediately with the onset of mechanization comes from examining the Congressional elections of the 86th through 90th Congresses and the revealed preferences of Southerners for committee assignments. Southern congressmen were not turned out of office wholesale with the onset of mechanization. In the 86th through 90th Congresses, the South elected 32 new Democratic representatives, a rate of turnover lower than that outside the South during the same period. Nor did the new representatives seemingly cater to a new constituency. Of the newly elected Southern Democratic representatives, none whose predecessors were on committees most concerned with social welfare and agriculture requested a different committee assignment from his predecessor. At the very least, even if politicians no longer gave as much weight to the preferences of the rural South, it is nevertheless important to consider how mechanization affected the economic incentives of landlords to provide paternalism as a central part of the remaining agricultural contracts. We are grateful to Kenneth Shepsle for providing data on requests for committee assignments by incoming congressmen.

[25] For a methodological discussion of the role of circumstantial evidence in economic history, see Fogel (1982).

mechanization and tenancy and the association between tenancy and paternalism. If mechanization reduced tenancy because of a decline in monitoring and turnover costs, it is likely that mechanization indirectly prompted a decline in paternalism. The second sort of evidence is a proxy for the extent of social control: perceptions by blacks of race relations. One of the hallmarks of the South's system of social control was a certain form of race relations. Blacks were expected to show deference to whites in general under the system of social control, but in particular to employers who provided paternalistic benefits. If mechanization prompted changes in race relations, these changes would have signaled the erosion of the system of social control. Because paternalism was linked to the system of social control, changes in paternalism would have taken place as a result. The third sort of evidence is the use of Southern political power. If Southern Congressmen retained their stranglehold over committees and yet the welfare state expanded, this implies that Southerners retained their power to defeat welfare measures but resisted them less. Moreover, if paternalism was still important to the South, the welfare programs of the 1960's that Southerners did not block had a paradoxical bias: they encouraged rural outmigration.

Plowing up paternalism

The causal connection between mechanization and the decline in tenancy in the South has been established by a number of scholars. As the adoption of the cotton-picker climbed – 42 percent of upland cotton was harvested mechanically in 1960, 82 percent in 1965, and nearly 100 percent in 1969 – mechanization caused a continuous decline in tenancy (see James H. Street, 1957; Richard H. Day, 1967; Maier, 1969; U.S. Department of Agriculture, 1974; Aiken, 1978; Fite, 1984; Pete Daniel, 1985; Wright, 1986; Jack Temple Kirby, 1987; Warren Whatley, 1987).[26] Tenancy began to fall before complete mechanization. Scholars such as Street (1957) and Day (1967) contend that partial mechanization (i.e., the introduction of the tractor) caused both a decline in the number

---

[26] Tenancy also fell for reasons other than mechanization. The most notable cause was the decline in cotton acreage prompted by government agricultural policy ostensibly aimed at soil conservation but actually proposed to raise farm income (see Aiken and Prunty, 1972; Alston, 1981; Fite, 1984). A notable omission from most historical accounts of mechanization is the role played by the importation of Mexican agricultural workers, popularly known as the Bracero Program. The Bracero Program relieved some of the peak labor demand at harvest, encouraging the adoption of the tractor and eroding paternalism through the same mechanism discussed below. The Bracero Program also appears to have delayed the adoption of the cotton-picker in Texas and Arkansas (see Wayne A. Grove, 1993).

of tenants and a decline in the ratio of tenants to wage workers. Plowing with a tractor resulted in less labor demand throughout the season, as significant amounts of labor were now needed only for weeding and harvesting.

As a result, Day (1967 p. 439) argues, the "maintenance of sharecroppers the year round became uneconomic. Instead, a combination of resident wage labor and labor hired from nearby villages was favored." The logical difficulty with this view is that it sees sharecropping as an inflexible arrangement rather than a contractual form in which several margins can be adjusted. For example, just as the share could be adjusted, so too could in-kind benefits such as housing or medical care. Nevertheless, the observation that tenancy fell with partial mechanization is correct. We contend that the rationale for the decline in tenancy with partial mechanization is the same as the rationale in the case of complete mechanization: monitoring costs fall with standardized techniques and with the increased unemployment or underemployment wrought by a decline in the demand for labor.[27]

Street (1957 pp. 218–27) argues that partial mechanization prompted a variety of changes in contractual arrangements. (1) During the war, when male labor was particularly scarce, females would receive a small sharecrop plot for hoeing and picking, and males, when home from jobs in war industries, would be hired on a part-time wage-labor basis. (2) Some landlords continued to use sharecroppers but charged croppers for tractor operations. (3) The landlord's share increased in recognition of his increased inputs. (4) Finally, the labor force was divided into two parts: enough sharecroppers for weed control and the remainder wage workers.[28]

For the South as a whole, tenancy peaked in 1930 and fell thereafter. Tenants numbered close to 1.8 million in 1930, fell to under one million by 1950, and then plummeted to 360,000 by 1959. In the next decade,

---

[27] Claude O. Brannen (1924) observed the same effect in reverse in the 1920's: planters increased the use of tenant contracts in the face of labor scarcity.

[28] Street argues, as have others, that sharecrop contracts secure labor better than wage contracts. The argument is that sharecroppers stay through the harvest for their share, while wage workers are paid by the day, week, or month. This ignores the fact that some wage workers are contracted for the year. Furthermore, there seems to be no logical reason precluding the withholding of some wages until after harvest – say as a bonus like that some workers receive in ski resorts if they stay for the season. After all, as Woodman (1979) has noted, sharecroppers are legally wage workers paid with a share of the crop. The reason a sharecrop contract holds workers better is because sharecroppers earn more on average than wage workers. Therefore, given that landlords advance subsistence to both wage workers and croppers and withhold the rest until the end of the season, sharecroppers would forfeit more by leaving before the end of the season (Alston, 1981).

the number fell in half again. The most precipitous drop in tenancy came during the 1950's, the period when scholars contend that out-migration from the agricultural South became dominated by push rather than pull factors (see U.S. Bureau of the Census, 1975 p. 465; Wright, 1986 p. 245).[29] Wage labor also declined over the entire period, but not by as much (N. L. LeRay et al., 1960; Aiken and Prunty, 1972; Alston, 1985). Hence there was a relative shift out of tenant contracts and into wage labor.

The decline in tenancy suggests that paternalism fell as well and fell most notably in the 1950's during the period of rapid mechanization.[30] The decline in the number of tenants and in the ratio of tenants to wage workers prompted a reduction in the provision of a variety of in-kind goods and services to workers, most notably food and housing, because of economies of scale (Alston and Ferrie, 1986). Previously, if plantation owners provided their workers with food and shelter, they had more contact with them, became more familiar with them, and could thereby provide paternalism at a lower cost. This is because contact and knowledge allowed them to identify "good" workers more easily and provide them with greater paternalism, reinforcing in the minds of workers the causal link between performance and the receipt of paternalism. When fewer in-kind goods were provided, the reduced contact between employers and workers raised the cost of providing paternalism.[31]

---

[29] The fact that pull factors dominated migration in the 1940's is not evidence that paternalism was a failure in securing labor. We need to know the counterfactual: how much migration would have occurred in the absence of paternalism. We do know that planters responded to the tight labor market of the 1940's by individually offering more paternalistic benefits and by collectively fostering state and local government improvements in schools and other social services. The plantation elite were instrumental in encouraging state governments to provide better schools as a means of discouraging out-migration (see Robert A. Margo, 1991 Ch. 3).

[30] Though both the absolute number of tenants and their number relative to the size of the agricultural labor force peaked in the 1930 Census, there is considerable anecdotal evidence that paternalism was still used in the 1930's and the war years. Paternalism did not begin to decline immediately with the decline in tenancy for several reasons: (1) the unemployment that led to the substitution of wage workers for tenants was not expected to be permanent, and paternalism represented a longer-term contract than tenancy; (2) the Agricultural Adjustment Act (AAA) which led to a reduction in labor demand and thereby a reduction in tenancy was initially an emergency measure whose future life was uncertain, as demonstrated by the Supreme Court's ruling it unconstitutional – we doubt that planters in the face of such uncertainty would have immediately abandoned paternalism as part of labor relations; and (3) the cost of using paternalism was in part subsidized through the funds of the Resettlement Administration, which the local elites controlled.

[31] We are advancing a supply-side story for the decline in paternalism, but there was no doubt a decline in the demand for paternalism caused by rising income and education levels, which would have diminished the value of planter intercession in

At the same time, the onset of mechanization prompting the rapid decline in tenancy in the 1950's ushered in a period of relative labor surplus and with it an increased likelihood of unemployment (Day, 1967 pp. 427–49). As long as workers were not indifferent between unemployment and working, then higher unemployment rates enhanced the monitoring effectiveness of any given wage (see Samuel Bowles, 1985; H. Lorne Carmichael, 1989, 1990). Higher unemployment, by reducing monitoring costs, substituted for tenancy and paternalism, prompting employers to negotiate wage contracts with their remaining laborers. Alston (1985) found a negative relationship between unemployment rates and the ratio of the number of tenants to the dollar value of wage expenditures in a pooled time-series cross-section regression for data from ten Southern cotton-growing states for the years 1930–1960. If the expenditures on wage contracts went up relative to the number of tenants, this suggests that paternalism fell, because wage workers were seldom the beneficiaries of paternalism – paternalism was not necessary, as wage workers were closely monitored by human supervisors, were already monitored by the nature of the technology, or were reluctant to shirk because of the threat of unemployment.

Monitoring costs also fell because mechanization reduced variation in the marginal productivity of labor. Machines by their very nature standardize work output and limit the scope for shirking. For example, plowing or cultivating with a tractor provides less scope for shirking than plowing with a mule or cultivating with a hoe. With the tractor technology, employers could evaluate labor effort after a given task better than they could with the mule technology. The ability to monitor labor effort *ex post* reduced supervision costs and thereby part of the rationale for share contracts and paternalism. This created an additional incentive to negotiate wage contracts with the remaining laborers. Using

many commercial transactions and in legal and social difficulties. However, unless one advocates a threshold model for the impact of education and income on paternalism, the steady climb in these factors would have had only a modest impact on the decline in paternalism because education and income had been rising over the course of the 20th century with little discernible impact on paternalism. An alternative demand explanation for the decline in paternalism is World War II. After seeing how the rest of the world worked, former tenants were reluctant to come back to a system of paternalism which they found demeaning. We suspect that World War II did change tastes for some in a way that made paternalistic arrangements less appealing, but this could not be the whole story because many tenants never had any war experience. The majority of Southern tenants did not leave the farm for work in war-related industries or military service in part due to the efforts of Southerners in limiting out-migration through emigration laws and draft deferments. In addition, returning veterans from World War I had not ushered in a period of diminished paternalistic relations in Southern agriculture.

the ratio of tractors to horses plus mules as a proxy for mechanization and supervision costs, Alston (1985) found that mechanization was negatively correlated over time and across space with the relative use of tenancy contracts in the ten major cotton-producing states in the South.[32] The fact that paternalism and tenancy went hand in hand and that both were driven by supervision costs implies that if mechanization prompted a shift into wage contracts, then it also reduced the use of paternalism.

So far we have discussed the impact of mechanization on the supply of paternalism by white landowners. Mechanization also affected the demand for paternalism by primarily black farm workers in two ways. Paternalism was an implicit contract between workers and employers: in return for "good and faithful" labor, employers offered protection and other services. The timing of the exchange was important. "Good and faithful" labor came first, and then the landlord delivered. This relationship was maintained as long as workers expected planters to uphold their side of the bargain. If, during the 1950's, workers foresaw the incentive of planters to renege as mechanization proceeded, the incentive for them to toil in the present diminished as the demand for labor declined. To stimulate work effort, payment had to be made more coincident with labor effort. Paternalism became less effective.

Mechanization also affected paternalism less directly. To be effective, paternalism required a lack of either well-defined and enforced civil rights or government-supplied social services. In such a world, it made sense for blacks (and for that matter poor whites) to obtain a white protector. With the advent of Great Society programs, poor Southerners would have had a substitute for planter paternalism. Mechanization increased the likelihood of Great Society programs in two ways: one via the supply of legislation (which we discuss in greater detail below) and the other via the demand for legislation. By causing out-migration to Northern urban areas, mechanization increased the size of the Northern black constituency.[33] Northern Democrats seized the opportunity to win the augmented urban black and poor white vote by satisfying their demand for Great Society programs (see Francis Fox Piven and Richard

---

[32] Monitoring costs may have fallen for another reason as well. Unlike mules, tractors or cotton-pickers were seldom owned by workers. When landlords owned the capital equipment, they had an incentive to monitor its use. If they were present for this reason, the marginal costs of monitoring labor fell and so too did the incentive for tenancy and paternalism (see Alston and Higgs, 1982).

[33] See Richard P. Young et al. (1992) for a discussion of the impact of Northern black constituents on the voting behavior of senators on civil-rights bills in the 20th century.

Lee J. Alston and Joseph P. Ferrie

Cloward, 1971). With a new federal safety net in place, black and white workers in the South could do without paternalistic relationships, which may have hastened the demise of paternalism.

Tenancy, deference, and the provision of paternalism

For the 1930's, Charles Johnson (1941) found that the best indicator of social conditions in the South – education and race relations among others – was cotton cultivation. Our analysis suggests the reason. Under paternalism, in addition to providing "good and faithful" labor, agricultural tenants showed deference to their landlords, while the system of social control required that black tenants show deference to whites at large.[34] Employers may have insisted on deference because of its impact on production, even though many tenants detested it: deference may have reinforced the hierarchical relationship between landlords and tenants and increased the effectiveness of authority and supervision.[35] Tenancy facilitated the maintenance of deference and of racial etiquette in general.

Tenants received most of their income in-kind. Most notable was the purchasing power advanced at plantation stores or designated stores in the county or town. Black tenants and croppers frequently did not have discretion over where they shopped. To merchants, they were a guaranteed clientele. This enabled merchants to treat blacks differentially from whites without cost. For example, merchants did not permit blacks to try on clothing and would even stop waiting on a black customer to wait on white customers who subsequently entered the store (Powdermaker, 1978 p. 50).

For black agricultural workers, the decline in tenancy brought with it a rise in cash income relative to kind, both because of a reduction in economies of scale in supplying in-kind goods and because wage workers were generally paid in cash and not given advances. Displaced ten-

---

[34] Deference appears to have been (or still is) part of paternalism in a variety of countries around the globe (see Alston and Ferrie, 1989). Morton Rubin (1951 p. 90) described the deferential behavior of Sam, a black tenant: "By inclining his head, Sam shows the white man that he acknowledges him as superior. He tips his hat to white men and women. He does not look a white women straight in the eye. Sam treats all whites, from the "sorriest" poor white to the wealthiest "high type" white from the plantation, with the same deference. He waits until a white person is disengaged before approaching for conversation. . . . He says "sir" or "ma'am" at all times, punctuating his conversation frequently with these titles of courtesy."

[35] Stefano Fenoaltea (1975) describes a similar functioning of authority in medieval England. For documentation of tenants' dislike of displaying deference, see Allison Davis et al. (1969), Arthur Raper (1974), Theodore Rosengarten (1974), Hortense Powdermaker (1978), and Neil McMillen (1989).

ants, if they found employment, got jobs that paid cash wages. In addition, income levels were rising in general, further increasing discretionary cash income. Now, if treated disrespectfully by a merchant, blacks could take their business elsewhere. Merchants responded by yielding concessions to blacks not only because of economic pressure from blacks who stayed within the South, but also because the out-migration accompanying mechanization was causing a scramble for economic survival.

Receiving better treatment in commercial transactions gave blacks increased self-respect that was continually reinforced. As Raper (1974 p. 177) noted, as early as the 1930's:

[T]he dependent family began to acquire training in personal and family responsibility and in discriminating buying. The family seemed to take on a sense of self-direction: when furnished through a commissary, the head of the house and other members went several times a week to get this or that, each time acknowledging their dependence and usually stressing it in order to get what was wanted. When a cash allowance was given a tenant, he reported to the landlord at the first of the month to get what was his by agreement. With this money he went forth to buy where he thought he was getting the best values for his money, and where he was treated with the most consideration.

As a result, race etiquette and deference to whites at large, which had been enforced in part through tenancy and the absence of cash, were being threatened as tenancy declined.

Better treatment of blacks in commercial transactions prompted demands by blacks for better treatment in society. Payment of cash and fewer personal dealings with employers divorced work and social life. Blacks were not independent economically of whites, but the frequency with which they were required to demonstrate dependence through deferential behavior declined as tenancy declined. If this was true, blacks would have perceived race relations as better where tenancy was lower. And they did.

As part of a study of Southern politics in 1961, Donald R. Matthews and James W. Prothro (1966) collected data on the perception of race relations by blacks in communities across the South. Alston (1986) used these data to test for the influence of tenancy on race relations. In an analysis controlling for other influences (median black income, degree of ruralness, the ratio of black population to total population, education, and exposure to television), Alston found results consistent with the hypothesis that tenancy was correlated with traditional Southern race etiquette: a high level of tenancy was the only variable that was consistently and strongly associated with perceptions of poor race relations. This suggests that, as tenancy rates fell, the institution of social control

327

was weakened. Because paternalism was linked to the system of social control, the use of paternalism would have declined as well. Even before the movement for civil rights at the federal level, then, technological forces were working to undermine the South's traditional system of race relations – what we have called its system of "social control" – and the paternalistic relations that it fostered.

Political ability to resist the "Great Society"

Inspector Gregory: "Is there any point to which you would wish to draw my attention?"
Holmes: "To the curious incident of the dog in the night-time."
Inspector Gregory: "The dog did nothing in the night-time."
Holmes: "That was the curious incident."

(Arthur Conan Doyle, 1930 p. 320)

The point to which we wish to draw attention is the curious behavior of Southern congressmen in the 1960's. They no longer blocked welfare legislation as they had formerly. Two explanations are possible. Either Southerners lost political power or they no longer had as much incentive to thwart the expansion of the welfare state. We argue that Southern politicians did not lose committee power in the 1960's, which suggests that paternalism did not die from an inability to sustain it, but rather from a declining economic incentive to employ it.

Political power in Congress from the 1920's through the 1960's was exercised through committees. Christopher J. Deering and Smith (1984) argue that the period from 1947 to the mid-1960's marked the zenith in power of committee chairmen. Before the reforms of committees in the early 1970's, chairmen could withhold legislation from the floor singlehandedly (Smith, 1989 pp. 8–9). Knowing the power of the committee chairmen, other committee members shaped legislation to meet the approval of chairmen. Similarly, in the House, committee chairmen catered to the chairman of the Rules Committee in order to get legislation to the floor (Bruce J. Dierenfield, 1987 p. 231).

Because of the dominance of the Democratic party in the South, Southern congressmen were more senior on average than congressmen in other regions. Consequently, they disproportionately chaired and occupied the senior seats on committees in the postwar period, the era of strong committee chairs. In Table 1, we present evidence on the dominance of Southern Democratic congressmen on committees in the House and Senate from 1947 to 1970. The committees examined were chosen because of either their importance in overseeing legislation in general or their jurisdiction over agriculture, welfare, labor, or civil rights. We consider three eras, all in the period of strong committee chairmanship:

328

Table 1. Seniority of Southern Democratic Congressmen, 1947–1970

Committee	Years chaired by Southern Democrat			Average number of first five Democratic seats occupied by Southern Democrat		
	1947–1960	1961–1964	1965–1970	1947–1960	1961–1964	1965–1970
A. House Committees						
Rules	6	4	6	3.0	3.0	1.7
Appropriations	0	0	6	2.3	2.0	3.3
Ways and Means	10	4	6	3.4	2.0	2.7
Agriculture	10	4	6	4.7	5.0	5.0
Education/Labor	8	0	4	2.0	2.0	1.0
Judiciary	0	0	0	1.3	1.5	1.0
B. Senate Committees						
Rules	0	2	6	1.0	1.0	1.3
Appropriations	4	0	2	2.7	3.5	4.0
Finance	10	4	6	3.5	3.5	3.3
Agriculture	10	4	6	4.0	5.0	5.0
Labor	6	4	6	1.4	2.0	1.7
Judiciary	4	4	6	2.5	4.7	3.2

Notes: The Democrats were in a majority in the House and Senate over the periods 1949–1952 and 1955–1970. We employed the *Congressional Quarterly* definition of the South: the former Confederate states, plus Kentucky and Oklahoma.
Source: Congressional Directory.

from 1947 through the election of President John Kennedy in 1960; the New Frontier years and the first spate of welfare legislation from 1961 to 1964; and the years 1965–1970, which saw the arrival of more Great Society programs under President Lyndon Johnson and their continuation under President Richard Nixon, by which time cotton cultivation in the South was almost fully mechanized.

In the House, in the first period, a Southerner chaired the Ways and Means and Agriculture Committees every year Democrats enjoyed a majority. In addition, Southerners disproportionately occupied the other senior ranks. Southerners averaged 3.4 of the top five Democratic seats on the Ways and Means Committee and 4.7 of the corresponding seats on the Agriculture Committee. Their dominance did not significantly change on these committees in the second and third periods: most importantly they chaired the committees from 1961 to 1970, while their senior representation increased slightly on the Agriculture Committee and fell on the Ways and Means Committee.[36] On the Education and Labor Committee and the Rules Committee, Southern Democrats controlled the chairmanship from 1955 through the remainder of the first period. They also occupied more than their share of the senior ranks on the Rules Committee and two of the five most senior positions on the Education and Labor Committee. From 1961 to 1964, Southerners continued to dominate the Rules Committee as they had since Congressman Smith (VA) assumed the chairmanship in 1955. After 1953, Congressman Colmer (MS) was the second-ranking Democrat on the Rules Committee, followed Smith to the chairmanship in 1967, and held it through our third period. In the Education and Labor Committee, though their senior representation stayed constant in the early 1960's Southerners lost the chairmanship in 1961 but regained it again in 1967 when Congressman Perkins (KY) took over as chair.

Appropriations and Judiciary were the only committees in the first period on which Southerners were not well represented. Southerners lacked influence on the Appropriations Committee until 1965, when Congressman Mahon (TX) ascended to the chairmanship, Southern Democrats occupied more than three of the top five seats, and Congressman Jones (NC) was the second-ranking Republican from 1965 through the remainder of the decade. On the Judiciary Committee, Southern Democratic representation was weak throughout all three periods and roughly constant. However, from 1959 through 1966, Southern Repub-

---

[36] Though the number of Southern congressmen in the top five Democratic seats on the Ways and Means Committee fell in the early 1960's, representation by the South was still considerable. In the period from 1961 to 1964 Southern Democrats held an average of 5.2 of the top ten seats. Furthermore, in the same period, Representative Baker (R-TN) was either the second- or third-ranking Republican on the committee.

lican Congressmen Poff (VA) and Cramer (FL) held two of the top five minority seats.

In the Senate, as in the House, Southerners had disproportionate power in committees. In the first period, Southerners held sway over the Agriculture and Finance Committees, chairing them every year that the Democrats held a majority. A Southerner chaired the Labor Committee after 1954 and the Judiciary Committee beginning in 1957. In the first period, Southerners were weakly represented as chairmen only on Rules and Appropriations. However, despite not having the chairmanship of the Appropriations Committee, Southerners were well represented in the senior ranks, averaging almost three of the first five senior Democratic positions. In the 1960's Southern senators reigned virtually supreme over the committee hierarchy: they chaired the Agriculture, Labor, Finance, and Judiciary Committees in every year; they chaired the Rules Committee from 1963 to 1970; and although Senator Russell (GA) chaired the Appropriations Committee only in 1969 and 1970, he was the second-ranking Democratic member of the committee after 1953, and because he had been on the committee since 1933, he had considerable influence.

Overall, there is no evidence that Southerners lost their control over committees in Congress in the 1960's. Indeed, as judged by the number of chairmanships, by 1965 Southern agenda control had never been greater. Given the essentially static power position of Southerners in the House and their increased power in the Senate in the 1960's it is extremely unlikely that the welfare programs of the 1960's could have emerged from Congress without the countenance of Southern congressmen. Not only did Southerners have the agenda control which committee power and their importance within the Democratic Party produced, but as we will see below, both Kennedy and Johnson needed the Southern vote in order to pass welfare legislation (John C. Donovan, 1967 p. 20).[37]

---

[37] Arthur M. Schlesinger, Jr. described the dependence of Kennedy on the South: "He (Kennedy) could never escape the political arithmetic. The Democrats lost twenty seats (in the 1960 election). . . . All from the North, nearly all liberal Democrats. . . . Many times in the next two years Kennedy desperately needed these twenty votes. Without them he was more than ever dependent on the South . . ." (quoted in Donovan, 1967 p. 20).

Donovan notes that Johnson faced the same situation as Kennedy. Some scholars have suggested that the Great Society would never have come into being without the application of the particular political skills of Johnson. We do not dispute this view, but rather suggest that perhaps the presence of Johnson was a necessary though not sufficient condition for such legislation to have passed. In the presence of Southern opposition, even Franklin Roosevelt, a president as politically astute and as successful in pushing other aspects of his legislative agenda as any, was unable to pass a Social Security Act which encroached on the South's paternalistic labor relations.

Lee J. Alston and Joseph P. Ferrie

The South's role in shaping the War on Poverty

The Great Society "War on Poverty" was in practice a war aimed at urban ghettos. Piven and Cloward (1971), as well as other scholars, argue that the reason for the urban bias was an effort by the administration to capture the Northern black urban vote, which if successful, would have enabled the Democrats to avoid a close call like the 1960 election. We do not disagree with this assessment of the demand for legislation, but considering that Southerners held agenda control and the necessary marginal votes needed for passage of Great Society welfare programs, a look is warranted at why Southerners supplied programs aimed at alleviating poverty in urban ghettos.

If paternalism was still valuable to the South, Southern legislators would not have allowed welfare programs aimed at alleviating poverty in Northern urban areas, because this would have encouraged out-migration, which in turn would have raised labor costs. Instead of remaining valuable, however, paternalism became burdensome with the advance of mechanization, because plantation owners may have felt a moral obligation to uphold their side of an implicit contract. Even if plantation owners felt no guilt over not caring for displaced workers, as long as the local community felt an obligation to provide some, albeit low, level of welfare assistance to displaced workers, the burden would have been felt most by the local elite in increased taxes. A way to avoid the obligations of paternalism or taxes was to encourage out-migration.[38]

Perhaps more importantly, civil rights were coming to the South whether white Southerners wanted them or not – and many white Southerners vehemently opposed them. By the 1960's, however, the threat of civil rights to the white South was no longer its impact on labor relations. Civil rights were actually beneficial to the business community and were seen by many businessmen as such (Wright, 1986 p. 268; Bruce J. Schulman, 1991 pp. 209–10). Rather, civil rights were a direct assault on white supremacy, a cornerstone of the institution of social control in the South. Given that federal welfare was no longer seen as a threat to labor relations and that civil rights were on the horizon, the white Southern rural elite chose to encourage black out-migration to limit the impact of civil rights.

---

[38] As Jill Quadagno (1988 p. 146), another student of the South's role in the evolution of the Social Security system, has noted, "Step by step, Southern congressmen released welfare for the aged poor from local government, passing control to the federal government as the burden of maintaining aged blacks surpassed their economic value and as the threat that direct cash payments to an older relative would subsidize an entire family became less critical to a changing plantation economy."

Paternalism in agricultural labor contracts

Evidence from the birth and life of the Economic Opportunity Act is consistent with our view that mechanization destroyed the economic motive for supplying paternalism and that Southerners worked to limit the anticipated impact of civil rights in the South by promoting out-migration and assuring that control of new federal programs remained in their hands. The Economic Opportunity Bill was conceived in the White House as the centerpiece of the Johnson Administration's War on Poverty. The bill consisted of six parts, only the first three of which were controversial. Title I dealt with youth unemployment and was essentially a redraft of a bill that had previously stalled in the House Rules Committee, which was chaired by Representative Howard Smith (D-VA). The most radical part of the bill was Title II, which established urban and rural community-action programs. What made the programs radical was that they gave no role to state and local governments. The goal was to involve the poor directly and make an end-run around urban bureaucracies. Because poverty had previously been mostly a local issue, the biggest threat was to mayors of large cities. Title III, rural economic opportunity programs, included grants aimed at land reform, principally Southern land reform, the goal of which was to purchase tracts of land for resale to tenants and sharecroppers.

The important distinction made in Title I was that a new "emphasis [was] placed on large 'urban' training and remedial-education centers rather than on conservation camps" (James Sundquist, 1969 p. 26). In Title II, Southerners ensured that governors were given the right to veto the placement of Job Corps Centers and Community Action Programs in their states.[39] Southerners were also concerned that community-action grants would be disruptive to the Southern way of life. Their concern was that the grants might go to groups not under the control of the local power structure. To limit this threat, Southerners "modified the legislation to require grantee organizations either to be public agencies or, if private nonprofit agencies, to have an established record of concern with the problems of the poor, or else a link to such an established record by being created by an established agency" (Adam Yarmolinsky, 1969 p. 46). It was not that congressmen outside the South favored the administration's attempt at bypassing local control, but rather that Southern congressmen were in a better position to do something about it.[40] Grants for land reform in Title III were struck from the final bill as well.

[39] Donovan (1967 pp. 36–7) argues that the veto was part of the price paid by the administration for Southern support.

[40] Southerners continued to have disproportionate influence over the actions of the Office of Economic Opportunity (OEO). At the behest of Senator John Stennis (D-MS), the Senate Appropriations Committee began an investigation in the autumn of

The House passed the Economic Opportunity Bill by a roll-call vote of 226–185. Sixty Southern Democrats voted for the legislation. In the Senate, the Southern vote was not quite as crucial, with half of the Southern delegation voting in favor of the bill. It is important to remember that the votes were taken after the bills were altered in committee. The Economic Opportunity Bill that emerged was aimed at fighting poverty in Northern ghettos by allowing local communities to bypass local urban bureaucracies. From the South's viewpoint, the bill as amended and passed posed little threat to the Southern way of life. In fact, it seems to have been part of an unsuccessful last-ditch effort to maintain the Southern way of life by encouraging out-migration of blacks. Before mechanization and a shift toward less labor-intensive crops, out-migration would have threatened the Southern way of life because it would have increased labor costs. After mechanization and the demise of paternalism, encouraging out-migration was seen as a way of limiting the anticipated impact of civil rights.[41] The final shape of the Economic Opportunity Act was one more piece of evidence demonstrating the death of paternalism in the South.[42]

Additional evidence on the extent to which Southern votes changed as the economic interests of the rural Southern elite changed comes from an examination of the Bracero and Food Stamp programs. The Bracero Program (Public Law 78) provided for the importation of Mexican farm laborers. In 1953, Southerners supported the program by a margin of 104–3 in the House; by 1963, the margin had fallen to 82–23 (Alston and Ferrie, 1993). The program's effect was to enhance the supply of labor, particularly in the newer cotton-producing states of the Southwest, reducing the incentive of cotton workers from the Deep South to migrate west. The result for Southern planters was lower wages and lower labor costs. Though the Bracero program was not a welfare

---

1965 into a Head Start program grant in Mississippi. As a result of the investigation, the Senate tightened its control over the OEO in November 1965. In 1966, the House Education and Labor Committee placed additional constraints on the OEO.

[41] In fact, black workers displaced by mechanization "were frequently given a bus ticket, a token amount of cash, and the address of the welfare office in New York." Former New York mayor and congressman John Lindsay recalled that ". . . his Southern colleagues would clap him on the back and say, 'John, we're sending 'em right up to you' " (Adam Smith [pseud.], 1985 p. 64).

[42] Schulman (1991 pp. 180–1) argues that Southerners were opposed to welfare programs in general. Southerners, however, were not unanimous in their opposition, while they had been almost unanimous in the past: as we noted earlier, 60 Southern Democrats voted for this legislation in the House, while in the Senate, half the Southern delegation voted in favor of the bill. Schulman's evidence on the opposition to welfare is consistent with our hypothesis that Southerners retained sufficient political power to shape welfare programs to encourage rural out-migration and thereby limit the impact of welfare in the rural South.

program, the voting behavior of Southerners on the program is consistent with the hypothesis that mechanization made labor issues less important.[43]

The birth of the Food Stamp program is also consistent with our hypothesis that, with access to mechanization and with civil rights on the horizon, Southern congressmen encouraged rural out-migration. John A. Ferejohn (1986) documents the legislative history of the program. He shows that, though the bill was clearly a piece of urban welfare legislation, it was actually sent to the floor by the House Agriculture Committee, a stronghold of the rural Southern congressional delegation. In 1963, when the Agriculture Committee reported the Food Stamp Bill, the committee was chaired by Representative Cooley (D-NC) and the seven senior Democrats on the committee were from the South. Though many Southern congressmen voted against the bill on the floor of the House, the votes of those Southerners who favored it were decisive; they provided the bill's margin of passage and continued to do so throughout the program's early life (Ferejohn, 1986 pp. 230–3).

5. CONCLUSION

The 1960's represent a watershed in the history of American social-welfare legislation. Sweeping changes in the scope and scale of the U.S. welfare state were legislated over the decade, and an important part of the story of this period was what went on behind the legislation – how changes in economic relationships led to the evaporation of opposition to much of that legislation. We have focused on what we believe was an important such change: the end of paternalistic relations in Southern agriculture.

For the first half of the 20th century, the South represented a formidable obstacle to the expansion of the welfare state. Following the Civil War, in response to the constraints of technology, planters fostered the institution of social control and adopted a paternalistic system of labor relations that reduced labor costs by reducing the cost of monitoring labor effort and discouraging labor turnover. The importance of South-

---

[43] The Bracero program was the only federal legislation bearing upon agricultural labor relations in the South that was voted upon repeatedly over the 1950's and 1960's and for which roll-call votes were recorded. The overall level of Southern cohesiveness in voting on all legislation over this period, though, is also consistent with a clear change in Southern interests. Havard (1972 pp. 644–5) reports that Southerners in the House attained a 90-percent or higher degree of unity on 41 percent of all roll calls in the 1933–1945 period; by the 1950's, they did so on only 19 percent of all roll calls, while in the 1960's, they achieved such high cohesion on only 6 percent of all roll-call votes.

erners within the Democratic party and the committee structure of Congress ensured that senior Southern congressmen could block legislation that threatened that system.

Before mechanization, social control in the South and the rules of the game in Congress shaped not only the paternalistic relationship between Southern plantation landlords and their workers, but also the developmental pattern of the Federal welfare state. The complete mechanization of Southern agriculture reduced the economic incentive of Southern politicians to oppose uniformly federal welfare programs and made possible the expansion of the welfare state in the 1960's.

REFERENCES

Aiken, Charles S., "The Decline of Sharecropping in the Lower Mississippi River Valley," *Geoscience and Man*, 30 June 1978, *19*, 151–65.

Aiken, Charles S. and Prunty, Merle, "The Demise of the Piedmont Cotton Region," *Association of American Geographers Annals*, June 1972, *62*, 283–306.

Akerlof, George A., "Labor Contracts as a Partial Gift Exchange," *Quarterly Journal of Economics*, November 1982, *97*, 543–69.

Alston, Lee J., "Tenure Choice in Southern Agriculture, 1930–1960," *Explorations in Economic History*, July 1981, *18*, 211–32.

Costs of Contracting and the Decline of Tenancy in the South, 1930–60, New York: Garland, 1985.

"Race Etiquette in the South: The Role of Tenancy," in Paul Uselding, ed., *Research in Economic History*, Vol. 10, Greenwich, CT: JAI Press, 1986, pp. 193–205.

Alston, Lee J. and Ferrie, Joseph P., "Labor Costs, Paternalism, and Loyalty in Southern Agriculture: A Constraint on the Growth of the Welfare State," *Journal of Economic History*, March 1985a, *45*, 95–117.

"Resisting the Welfare State: Southern Opposition to the Farm Security Administration," in Robert Higgs, ed., *Emergence of the Modern Political Economy*, Greenwich, CT: JAI Press, 1985b, pp. 83–120.

"A Model of In-Kind Compensation in Agriculture," Agricultural History Center Working Paper No. 34, University of California-Davis, April 1986.

"Social Control and Labor Relations in the American South Before the Mechanization of the Cotton Harvest in the 1950s," *Journal of Institutional and Theoretical Economics*, March 1989, *145*, 133–57.

"The *Bracero* Program and Farm Labor Legislation in World War Two," in Geoffrey T. Mills and Hugh Rockoff, eds., *The Sinews of War*, Ames: Iowa State University Press, 1993, pp. 129–49.

Alston, Lee J. and Higgs, Robert, "Contractual Mix in Southern Agriculture Since the Civil War: Facts, Hypotheses, and Tests," *Journal of Economic History*, June 1982, *42*, 327–53.

Barraclough, S. L. and Domike, A. L., "Agrarian Structure in Seven Latin American Countries," *Land Economics*, November 1966, *42*, 391–424.

Bloch, Marc, *Feudal Society*, Chicago: University of Chicago Press, 1961.

Slavery and Serfdom in the Middle Ages: Selected Essays, Berkeley: University of California Press, 1975.

Bowles, Samuel, "The Production Process in a Competitive Economy: Walrasian, Neo-Hobbesian, and Marxian Models," *American Economic Review*, March 1985, *75*, 16–36.

Brannen, Claude O., "Relation of Land Tenure to Plantation Organization," U.S. Department of Agriculture (Washington, DC) Bulletin No. 1269, 1924.

Bruce, Phillip A., *The Plantation Negro as a Freeman*, New York: Putnam, 1889.

Carmichael H. Lorne, "Self-Enforcing Contracts, Shirking, and Life-Cycle Incentives," *Journal of Economic Perspectives*, Fall 1989, *3*, 65–83.

"Efficiency Wage Models of Unemployment – One View," *Economic Inquiry*, April 1990, *28*, 269–95.

Cloud, N. B., "Cotton Culture in 1866," in U.S. Department of Agriculture, *Report of the Commissioner of Agriculture for the Year 1866*, Washington, DC: U.S. Government Printing Office, 1867, pp. 190–3.

Coase, Ronald H., "The Nature of the Firm," *Economica*, November 1937, *4*, 386–406.

"The Problem of Social Cost," *Journal of Law and Economics*, October 1960, *3*, 1–44.

Cox, Gary W. and McCubbins, Mathew D., *Legislative Leviathan: Party Government in the House*, Berkeley: University of California Press, 1993.

Daniel, Pete, *Breaking the Land: The Transformation of Cotton, Tobacco, and Rice Culture Since 1880*, Urbana: University of Illinois Press, 1985.

Davis, Allison, Gardner, Burleigh B. and Gardner, Mary R., *Deep South: A Social and Anthropological Study of Caste and Class*, Chicago: University of Chicago Press, 1969.

Day, Richard H., "Technological Change and the Sharecropper," *American Economic Review*, June 1967, *57*, 427–49.

Deering, Christopher J. and Smith, Steven S., *Committees in Congress*, Washington, DC: Congressional Quarterly Press, 1984.

Dierenfield, Bruce J., *Keeper of the Rules: Congressman Howard V. Smith of Virginia*, Charlottesville: University of Virginia Press, 1987.

Donovan, John C., *The Politics of Poverty*, New York: Pegasus, 1967.

Doyle, Arthur Conan, *The Complete Sherlock Holmes*, Garden City, NY: Doubleday, 1930.

DuBois, W. E. B., "The Negro Farmer," in *Twelfth Census of the United States: 1900, Special Reports, Supplementary Analysis and Derivative Tables*, Washington, DC: U.S. Government Printing Office, 1906, pp. 511–79.

Fenoaltea, Stefano, "Authority, Efficiency, and Agricultural Organization in Medieval England and Beyond: A Hypothesis," *Journal of Economic History*, December 1975, *35*, 693–718.

Ferejohn, John A., "Logrolling in an Institutional Context: A Case Study of Food Stamp Legislation," in Gerald C. Wright, Jr., Leroy N. Rieselbach, and Lawrence C. Dodd, eds., *Congress and Policy Change*, New York: Agathon, 1986, pp. 223–53.

Fite, Gilbert C., *Cotton Fields No More: Southern Agriculture, 1865–1980*, Lexington: University Press of Kentucky, 1984.

Fogel, Robert W., "Circumstantial Evidence in 'Scientific' and Traditional History," in David Carr, ed., *Philosophy of History and Contemporary Histori-*

Lee J. Alston and Joseph P. Ferrie

ography, Ottawa, Canada: Editions de l'Université d'Ottawa, 1982, pp. 61–112.

Without Consent or Contact: The Rise and Fall of American Slavery, New York: Norton, 1989.

Godwin, J. R., testimony, in U.S. Industrial Commission, Report X, Washington, DC: U.S. Government Printing Office, 1901.

Grove, Wayne A., "Cotton Economy in Transition, 1950 to 1964: Mechanization, Southern Out-Migration and Foreign Labor," Ph.D. dissertation, University of Illinois, Champaign/Urbana, 1993 (forthcoming).

Havard, William C., ed., The Changing Politics of the South, Baton Rouge: Louisiana State University Press, 1972.

Hayami, Yujiro and Kikuchi, Masao, Asian Village Economy at the Crossroads: An Economic Approach to Institutional Change, Baltimore, MD: Johns Hopkins University Press, 1982.

Higgs, Robert, Competition and Coercion: Blacks in the American Economy, 1865–1914, New York: Cambridge University Press, 1977.

Hoffsommer, Harold, ed., The Social and Economic Significance of Land Tenure in the Southwestern States: A Report on the Regional Land Tenure Research Project, Chapel Hill: University of North Carolina Press, 1950.

Holmes, William F., "Whitecapping: Agrarian Violence in Mississippi, 1902–1906," Journal of Southern History, May 1969, 35, 165–85.

Hutchinson, T. W., Village and Plantation Life in Northeastern Brazil, Seattle: University of Washington Press, 1957.

Jaynes, Gerald D., Branches Without Roots: Genesis of the Black Working Class in the American South, 1862–1882, New York: Oxford University Press, 1986.

Johnson, Allen W., Sharecroppers of the Sertaõ, Stanford, CA: Stanford University Press, 1971.

Johnson, Charles, Statistical Atlas of Southern Counties, Chapel Hill: University of North Carolina Press, 1941.

Key, V. O., Southern Politics in State and Nation, New York: Knopf, 1949.

Kiewiet, D. Roderick and McCubbins, Mathew D., The Logic of Delegation: Congressional Parties and the Appropriations Process, Chicago: University of Chicago Press, 1991.

Kirby, Jack Temple, Rural Worlds Lost: The American South, 1920–1960, Baton Rouge: Louisiana State University Press, 1987.

Kousser, J. Morgan, The Shaping of Southern Politics: Suffrage Restriction and the Establishment of the One-Party South, 1880–1910, New Haven, CT: Yale University Press, 1974.

LeRay, N. L., Wilbur, G. L. and Crowe, G. B., "Plantation Organization and the Resident Labor Force, Delta Area," Mississippi State University Agricultural Experiment Station Bulletin No. 606, 1960.

Litwack, Leon F., Been in the Storm So Long: The Aftermath of Slavery, New York: Knopf, 1979.

Maier, Frank, "An Economic Analysis of the Adoption of the Mechanical Cotton Picker," Ph.D. dissertation, University of Chicago, 1969.

Mandle, Jay R., "The Re-Establishment of the Plantation Economy in the South, 1865–1910," Review of Black Political Economy, Winter 1973, 3, 68–88.

Margo, Robert A., Race and Schooling in the South, 1880–1950, Chicago: University of Chicago Press, 1991.

338

Paternalism in agricultural labor contracts

Matthews, Donald R. and Prothro, James W., *Negroes and the New Southern Politics*, New York: Harcourt, Brace & World, 1966.

McMillen, Neil R., *Dark Journey: Black Mississippians in the Age of Jim Crow*, Urbana: University of Illinois Press, 1989.

Mowry, George E., *Another Look at the Twentieth Century South*, Baton Rouge: Louisiana State University Press, 1973.

Newby, Howard, *The Deferential Worker: A Study of Farm Workers in East Anglia*, London: Allen Lane, 1977.

North, Douglass C., *Structure and Change in Economic History*, New York: Norton, 1981.

Institutions, Institutional Change, and Economic Performance, New York: Cambridge University Press, 1990.

Otken, Charles H., *The Ills of the South, or Related Causes Hostile to the General Prosperity of the Southern People*, New York: Putnam, 1894.

[Pitts, Phillip H.], papers, 4 volumes, Southern Historical Collection, File 602, Chapel Hill, n.d.

Piven, Francis Fox and Cloward, Richard, *Regulating the Poor*, New York: Pantheon, 1971.

Powdermaker, Hortense, *After Freedom: A Cultural Study in the Deep South*, New York: Atheneum, 1978.

Quadagno, Jill, *The Transformation of Old Age Security*, Chicago: University of Chicago Press, 1988.

Ransom, Roger L. and Sutch, Richard, *One Kind of Freedom: The Economic Consequences of Emancipation*, New York: Cambridge University Press, 1978.

Raper, Arthur, *Preface to Peasantry*, Chicago: University of Chicago Press, 1974.

Rosengarten, Theodore, *All God's Dangers: The Life of Nate Shaw*, New York: Knopf, 1974.

Rubin, Morton, *Plantation County*, Chapel Hill: University of North Carolina Press, 1951.

Schuler, Edgar A., "Social Status and Farm Tenure – Attitudes and Social Conditions of Corn Belt and Cotton Belt Farmers," U.S. Department of Agriculture, Farm Security Administration and Bureau of Agricultural Economics, *Social Research Report 4*, Washington, DC: U.S. Government Printing Office, 1938.

Schulman, Bruce J., *From Cotton Belt to Sunbelt: Federal Policy, Economic Development, and the Transformation of the South, 1938–1980*, New York: Oxford University Press, 1991.

Schumpeter, Joseph, *Capitalism, Socialism, and Democracy*, New York: Harper, 1950.

[Schurz, Carl], *Senate Executive Documents*, 39th Congress, 1st Session, No. 2, Washington, DC: U.S. Government Printing Office, 1866.

Shepsle, Kenneth A. and Weingast, Barry R., "Legislative Politics and Budget Outcomes," in Gregory B. Mills and John L. Palmer, eds., *Federal Budget Policy in the 1980's*, Washington, DC: Urban Institute Press, 1984, pp. 343–67.

Shlomowitz, Ralph, "The Freedmen's Bureau," Ph.D. dissertation, University of Chicago, 1978.

Smith, Adam [pseud.], "The City as the OK Corral," *Esquire*, July 1985, 64–7.

Smith, Steven S., *Call to Order: Floor Politics in the House and Senate*, Washington, DC: Brookings Institution, 1989.

Southerner [pseud.], "Agricultural Labor at the South," *Galaxy*, September 1871, 12, 328–40.

Stearns, Charles, *The Black Man of the South, and the Rebels; or, The Characteristics of the Former, and the Recent Outrages of the Latter*, New York: American News Company, 1872; reprinted, New York: Negro Universities Press, 1969.

Stone, Alfred Holt, "The Negro in the Yazoo-Mississippi Delta," *Publications of the American Economic Association*, 3rd Series, February 1902 (*Papers and Proceedings*), 3, 234–72.

Street, James H., *The New Revolution in the Cotton Economy*, Chapel Hill: University of North Carolina Press, 1957.

Sundquist, James, ed., *On Fighting Poverty: Perspectives from Experience*, New York: Basic Books, 1969.

Taylor, H. C., *Outlines of Agricultural Economics*, New York: Macmillan, 1925.

Tebeau, C. W., "Some Aspects of Planter–Freedman Relations, 1865–1880," *Journal of Negro History*, April 1936, 21, 130–50.

[Truman, Benjamin C.], *Senate Executive Documents*, 39th Congress, 1st Session, No. 43, Washington, DC: U.S. Government Printing Office, 1866.

Wayne, Michael, *The Reshaping of Plantation Society: The Natchez District, 1860–1880*, Baton Rouge: Louisiana State University Press, 1983.

Weingast, Barry R. and Marshall, William, "The Industrial Organization of Congress: Or Why Legislatures Like Firms Are Not Organized as Markets," *Journal of Political Economy*, February 1988, 96, 132–63.

Whatley, Warren, "Southern Agrarian Labor Contracts as Impediments to Cotton Mechanization," *Journal of Economic History*, March 1987, 47, 45–70.

Wiener, Jonathan M., *Social Origins of the New South: Alabama, 1860–1885*, Baton Rouge: Louisiana State University Press, 1978.

Wilcox, E. V., "Lease Contracts Used in Renting on Shares," U.S. Department of Agriculture (Washington, DC) Bulletin No. 650, Washington, DC: U.S. Government Printing Office, 1918.

Williamson, Oliver, *The Economic Institutions of Capitalism*, New York: Free Press, 1985.

Woodman, Harold D., "Post-Civil War Southern Agriculture and the Law," *Agricultural History*, January 1979, 53, 319–37.

Woodward, C. Vann, *Origins of the New South*, Baton Rouge: Louisiana State University Press, 1951.

Woofter, T. J., *Negro Migration: Changes in Rural Organization and Population of the Cotton Belt*, New York: Gray, 1920; reprinted, New York: Negro Universities Press, 1969.

"The Plantation Economy," U.S. Department of Agriculture, Farm Security Administration and Works Progress Administration, *Social Research Report* 4, Washington, DC: U.S. Government Printing Office, 1936.

"Landlord and Tenant on the Cotton Plantation," Research Monograph No. 5, Works Progress Administration, Division of Social Research, Washington, DC: U.S. Government Printing Office, 1938.

Wright, Gavin, *Old South, New South: Revolutions in the Southern Economy Since the Civil War*, New York: Basic Books, 1986.

Yarmolinsky, Adam, "The Beginnings of OEO," in James Sundquist, ed., *On Fighting Poverty: Perspectives from Experience*, New York: Basic Books, 1969, pp. 34–51.

Young, Richard P., Burstein, Jerome and Higgs, Robert, "Federalism and the Demise of Prescriptive Racism in the United States," paper presented to the Annual Meetings of the American Political Science Association, Chicago, 1992.

Congressional Directory, Washington, DC: U.S. Government Printing Office, various years.

[Freedmen's Bureau], *Senate Executive Documents*, 39th Congress, 1st Session, No. 27, Washington, DC: U.S. Government Printing Office, 1866.

U.S. Bureau of the Census, *Historical Statistics of the U.S., Colonial Times to 1970*, Washington, DC: U.S. Government Printing Office, 1975.

U.S. Congress, *Report of the Joint Committee on Reconstruction at the First Session Thirty-Ninth Congress*, Washington, DC: U.S. Government Printing Office, 1866.

U.S. Department of Agriculture, *Report of the Commissioner of Agriculture for the Year 1866*, Washington, DC: U.S. Government Printing Office, 1867.

Statistics on Cotton and Related Data, 1920–73, Statistical Bulletin No. 535, Economic Research Service, Washington, DC: U.S. Government Printing Office, 1974.

U.S. Industrial Commission, *Report, X and XI*, Washington, DC: U.S. Government Printing Office, 1901.

U.S. Senate, *Report on Relations between Labor and Capital*, Committee on Education and Labor, Washington, DC: U.S. Government Printing Office, 1885.

Epilogue: economic performance through time

I

Economic history is about the performance of economies through time. The objective of research in the field is not only to shed new light on the economic past but also to contribute to economic theory by providing an analytical framework that will enable us to understand economic change. A theory of economic dynamics comparable in precision to general equilibrium theory would be the ideal tool of analysis. In the absence of such a theory we can describe the characteristics of past economies, examine the performance of economies at various times, and engage in comparative static analysis; but missing is an analytical understanding of the way economies evolve through time.

A theory of economic dynamics is also crucial for the field of economic development. There is no mystery why the field of development has failed to develop during the five decades since the end of the Second World War. Neoclassical theory is simply an inappropriate tool to analyze and prescribe policies that will induce development. It is concerned with the operation of markets, not with how markets develop. How can one prescribe policies when one doesn't understand how economies develop? The very methods employed by neoclassical economists have dictated the subject matter and militated against such a development. That theory, in the pristine form that gave it mathematical precision and elegance, modeled a frictionless and static world. When applied to

Prepared for presentation as the Prize Lecture in Economic Science in memory of Alfred Nobel, December 9, 1993. Copyright © by the Nobel Foundation, 1993.

I am indebted to Robert Bates, Lee and Alexandra Benham, Avner Greif, Margaret Levi, Randy Nielsen, John Nye, Jean-Laurent Rosenthal, Norman Schofield, and Barry Weingast for their comments on an earlier draft and to Elisabeth Case for editing this essay.

economic history and development, it focused on technological development and more recently human capital investment but ignored the
incentive structure embodied in institutions that determined the
extent of societal investment in those factors. In the analysis of economic performance through time it contained two erroneous assumptions: first, that institutions do not matter and, second, that time does
not matter.

This essay is about institutions and time. It does not provide a theory
of economic dynamics comparable to general equilibrium theory. We do
not have such a theory.[1] Rather, it provides the initial scaffolding of an
analytical framework capable of increasing our understanding of the
historical evolution of economies and a necessarily crude guide to policy
in the ongoing task of improving the economic performance of economies. The analytical framework is a modification of neoclassical theory.
What it retains is the fundamental assumption of scarcity and hence
competition and the analytical tools of microeconomic theory. What it
modifies is the rationality assumption. What it adds is the dimension
of time.

Institutions form the incentive structure of a society, and political and
economic institutions, in consequence, are the underlying determinant of
economic performance. Time as it relates to economic and societal
change is the dimension in which the learning process of human beings
shapes the way institutions evolve. That is, the beliefs that individuals,
groups, and societies hold which determine choices are a consequence of
learning through time – not just the span of an individual's life or of a
generation of a society, but the learning embodied in individuals, groups,
and societies that is cumulative through time and passed on intergenerationally by the culture of a society.

The next two sections of this essay summarize the work that I and
others have done on the nature of institutions and the way they affect
economic performance (Section II) and then characterize the nature of
institutional change (Section III).[2] The remaining four sections describe
a cognitive science approach to human learning (Section IV); provide an
institutional/cognitive approach to economic history (Section V); indicate the implications of this approach for improving our understanding
of the past (Section VI); and finally suggest implications for current
development policies (Section VII).

---

[1] In fact, such a theory is unlikely. I refer the reader to Frank Hahn's (1991)
prediction about the future of economic theory.
[2] These two sections briefly summarize material contained in North (1990a).

II

Institutions are the humanly devised constraints that structure human interaction. They are made up of formal constraints (rules, laws, constitutions), informal constraints (norms of behavior, conventions, and self-imposed codes of conduct), and their enforcement characteristics. Together they define the incentive structure of societies and specifically economies.

Institutions and the technology employed determine the transaction and transformation costs that add up to the costs of production. It was Ronald Coase (1960) who made the crucial connection between institutions, transaction costs, and neoclassical theory. The neoclassical result of efficient markets obtains only when it is costless to transact. Only under the conditions of costless bargaining will the actors reach the solution that maximizes aggregate income regardless of the institutional arrangements. When it is costly to transact, then institutions matter. And it is costly to transact. Wallis and North (1986) demonstrated in an empirical study that 45 percent of U.S. GNP was devoted to the transaction sector in 1970. Efficient markets are created in the real world when competition is strong enough via arbitrage and efficient information feedback to approximate the Coase zero transaction cost conditions and the parties can realize the gains from trade inherent in the neoclassical argument.

But the informational and institutional requirements necessary to achieve such efficient markets are stringent. Players must not only have objectives but know the correct way to achieve them. But how do the players know the correct way to achieve their objectives? The instrumental rationality answer is that even though the actors may initially have diverse and erroneous models, the informational feedback process and arbitraging actors will correct initially incorrect models, punish deviant behavior, and lead surviving players to correct models.

An even more stringent implicit requirement of the discipline-of-the-competitive-market model is that when there are significant transaction costs, the consequent institutions of the market will be designed to induce the actors to acquire the essential information that will lead them to correct their models. The implication is not only that institutions are designed to achieve efficient outcomes but that they can be ignored in economic analysis because they play no independent role in economic performance.

These are stringent requirements that are realized only very exceptionally. Individuals typically act on incomplete information and with subjectively derived models that are frequently erroneous; the information feedback is typically insufficient to correct these subjective models. Insti-

344

tutions are not necessarily or even usually created to be socially efficient; rather they, or at least the formal rules, are created to serve the interests of those with the bargaining power to create new rules. In a world of zero transaction costs, bargaining strength does not affect the efficiency of outcomes; but in a world of positive transaction costs, it does.

It is exceptional to find economic markets that approximate the conditions necessary for efficiency. It is impossible to find political markets that do. The reason is straightforward. Transaction costs are the costs of specifying what is being exchanged and of enforcing the consequent agreements. In economic markets what is being specified (measured) is the valuable attributes – the physical and property rights dimensions – of goods and services or the performance of agents. While measurement can frequently be costly, there are some standard criteria: the physical dimensions have objective characteristics (size, weight, color, etc.), and the property rights dimensions are defined in legal terms. Competition also plays a critical role in reducing enforcement costs. The judicial system provides coercive enforcement. Still, economic markets in the past and present are typically imperfect and beset by high transaction costs.

Measuring and enforcing agreements in political markets is far more difficult. What is being exchanged (between constituents and legislators in a democracy) is promises for votes. The voter has little incentive to become informed, because the likelihood that one's vote matters is infinitesimal; further, the complexity of the issues produces genuine uncertainty. Enforcement of political agreements is beset by difficulties. Competition is far less effective than in economic markets. For a variety of simple, easy-to-measure, and important-for-constituent-well-being policies, constituents may be well informed, but beyond such straightforward policy issues ideological stereotyping takes over and (as I shall argue in Section IV) shapes the consequent performance of economies.[3] It is the polity that defines and enforces property rights, and in consequence it is not surprising that efficient economic markets are so exceptional.

III

It is the interaction between institutions and organizations that shapes the institutional evolution of an economy. If institutions are the rules of the game, organizations and their entrepreneurs are the players.

Organizations are made up of groups of individuals bound together

[3] See the author's "A Transactions Cost Theory of Politics" for a transaction cost approach to the relative inefficiency of political markets (North, 1990b).

by some common purpose to achieve certain objectives. Organizations include political bodies (political parties, the Senate, a city council, regulatory bodies), economic bodies (firms, trade unions, family farms, cooperatives), social bodies (churches, clubs, athletic associations), and educational bodies (schools, universities, vocational training centers).

The organizations that come into existence will reflect the opportunities provided by the institutional matrix. That is, if the institutional framework rewards piracy, then piratical organizations will come into existence; and if the institutional framework rewards productive activities, then organizations — firms — will come into existence to engage in productive activities.

Economic change is a ubiquitous, ongoing, incremental process that is a consequence of the choices individual actors and entrepreneurs of organizations make every day. While the vast majority of these decisions are routine (Nelson and Winter, 1982) some involve altering existing "contracts" between individuals and organizations. Sometimes that re-contracting can be accomplished within the existing structure of property rights and political rules, but sometimes new contracting forms require an alteration of the rules. Equally, norms of behavior that guide exchanges will gradually be modified or wither away. In both instances, institutions are altered.

Modifications occur because individuals perceive that they could do better by restructuring exchanges (political or economic). The source of the changed perceptions may be exogenous to the economy — for instance, a change in the price or quality of a competitive product in another economy that alters perceptions of entrepreneurs in the given economy about profitable opportunities. But the most fundamental long-run source of change is learning by individuals and entrepreneurs of organizations.

While idle curiosity will result in learning, the rate of learning will reflect the intensity of competition among organizations. Competition, reflecting ubiquitous scarcity, induces organizations to engage in learning to survive. The degree of competition can and does vary. The greater is the degree of monopoly power, the lower is the incentive to learn.

The speed of economic change is a function of the rate of learning, but the direction of that change is a function of the expected payoffs to acquiring different kinds of knowledge. The mental models that the players develop shape perceptions about the payoffs.

IV

It is necessary to dismantle the rationality assumption underlying economic theory in order to approach constructively the nature of human learning. History demonstrates that ideas, ideologies, myths, dogmas, and prejudices matter, and an understanding of the way they evolve is necessary for further developing a framework to understand societal change. The rational choice framework assumes that individuals know what is in their self-interest and act accordingly. That may be correct for individuals making choices in the highly developed markets of modern economies,[4] but it is patently false for those making choices under conditions of uncertainty – the conditions that have characterized the political and economic choices that shaped (and continue to shape) historical change.

Herbert Simon (1986) has stated the issues succinctly:

If . . . we accept the proposition that both the knowledge and the computational power of the decisionmaker are severely limited, then we must distinguish between the real world and the actor's perception of it and reasoning about it. That is to say we must construct a theory (and test it empirically) of the process of decision. Our theory must include not only the reasoning processes but also the processes that generated the actor's subjective representation of the decision problem, his or her frame. (pp. S210–11)

The analytical framework we must build must originate in an understanding of how human learning takes place. We have a way to go before we can construct such a theory, but cognitive science has made immense strides in recent years – enough strides to suggest a tentative approach that can help us understand decision making under uncertainty.[5]

Learning entails developing a structure by which to interpret the varied signals received by the senses. The initial architecture of the structure is genetic, but the subsequent scaffolding is a result of the experiences of the individual. The experiences can be classified into two kinds – those from the physical environment and those from the sociocultural linguistic environment. The structures consist of categories – classifications that gradually evolve from earliest childhood to organize our perceptions and keep track of our memory of analytic results and experiences. Building on these classifications, we form mental models to explain and interpret the environment – typically in ways relevant to some goal. Both the categories and the mental models will evolve, reflecting the feedback derived from new experiences: feedback that sometimes strengthens our initial categories and models or may lead to modifications – in short, learning. Thus, the mental models may

---

[4] However, see the anomalies even here in the studies by Tversky and Kahneman (1986) and others (Hogarth and Reder, 1986).
[5] See Holland et al. (1986) for an excellent introduction to the cognitive science literature.

be continually redefined with new experiences, including contact with others' ideas.

At this juncture the learning process of human beings diverges from that of other animals (such as the sea slug – a favorite research subject of cognitive scientists) and particularly diverge from the computer analogy that dominated early studies of artificial intelligence. The mind appears to order and reorder the mental models from their special-purpose origins to successively more abstract form so that they become available to process other information. The term used by Andy Clark and Annette Karmiloff-Smith (1993) is "representational redescription." The capacity to generalize from the particular to the general and to use analogy is a part of this redescription process. It is this capacity that is the source not only of creative thinking but also of the ideologies and belief systems that underlie the choices humans make.[6]

A common cultural heritage provides a means of reducing the divergence in the mental models that people in a society have and constitutes the means for the intergenerational transfer of unifying perceptions. In premodern societies cultural learning provided a means of internal communication; it also provided shared explanations for phenomena outside the immediate experiences of the members of society in the form of religions, myths, and dogmas. Such belief structures are not, however, confined to primitive societies but are an essential part of modern societies as well.

Belief structures get transformed into societal and economic structures by institutions – both formal rules and informal norms of behavior. The relationship between mental models and institutions is an intimate one. Mental models are the internal representations that individual cognitive systems create to interpret the environment; institutions are the external (to the mind) mechanisms individuals create to structure and order the environment.

V

There is no guarantee that the beliefs and institutions that evolve through time will produce economic growth. Let me tell a brief institutional/cognitive story of long-run economic/political change in order to pose the issue that time presents us.

As tribes evolved in different physical environments, they developed different languages and, with different experiences, different mental

---

[6] Ideologies are mental models shared by groups of individuals that provide both an interpretation of the environment and a prescription as to how that environment should be ordered.

models to explain the world around them. These languages and mental models formed informal constraints that defined the institutional frameworks of the tribes and were passed down intergenerationally as customs, taboos, and myths that provided cultural continuity.[7]

With growing specialization and division of labor, the tribes evolved into polities and economies; the diversity of experience and learning produced increasingly different societies and civilizations with different degrees of success in solving the fundamental economic problems of scarcity. The reason is that as the complexity of the environment increased while human beings became increasingly interdependent, more complex institutional structures were necessary to capture the potential gains from trade. Such evolution requires that a society develop institutions that will permit anonymous, impersonal exchange across time and space. To the extent that the culture and local experiences of societies had produced diverse institutions and belief systems with respect to the gains from such cooperation, the likelihood of creating the necessary institutions to capture the gains from trade of more complex contracting varied. In fact, most societies throughout history got stuck in an institutional matrix that did not evolve into the impersonal exchange essential for capturing the productivity gains generated by the specialization and division of labor that produced the Wealth of Nations.

The key to the foregoing story is the kind of learning that the individuals in a society acquired through time. Time in this context entails not only current experiences and learning but also the cumulative experience of past generations that is embodied in culture. *Collective learning* – a term used by Hayek – consists of those experiences that have passed the slow test of time and are embodied in our language, institutions, technology, and ways of doing things. It is "the transmission in time of our accumulated stock of knowledge" (Hayek 1960: 27). It is culture that provides the key to *path dependence* – a term used to describe the powerful influence of the past on the present and future. The current learning of any generation takes place in the context of the perceptions derived from collective learning. Learning then is an incremental process filtered by the culture of a society that determines the perceived payoffs, but there is no guarantee that the cumulative past experience of societies will necessarily fit them to solve new problems. Societies that get stuck embody belief systems and institutions that fail to confront and solve new social problems.

We need to understand a great deal more about the cumulative learn-

---

[7] Ronald Heiner (1983) in a path-breaking article not only made the connection between the mental capacities of humans and the external environment but suggested the implications for arresting economic progress.

ing of a society. The learning process appears to be a function of (1) the way in which a given belief structure filters the information derived from experiences and (2) the different experiences confronting individuals and societies at different times. The perceived rate of return (private) may be high to military technology (in medieval Europe), to the pursuit and refinement of religious dogma (Rome during and after Constantine), or to research on an accurate chronometer to determine longitude at sea (for which a substantial reward was offered during the age of exploration).

The incentives to acquire pure knowledge, the essential underpinning of modern economic growth, are affected by monetary rewards and punishments; they are also fundamentally influenced by a society's tolerance of creative developments, to which a long list of creative individuals from Galileo to Darwin would attest. While there is a substantial literature on the origins and development of science, very little of it deals with the links between institutional structure, belief systems, and the incentives and disincentives to acquire pure knowledge. A major factor in the development of Western Europe was the gradual perception of the utility of research in pure science.

Incentives embodied in belief systems as expressed in institutions determine economic performance through time, and however we wish to define economic performance the historical record is clear. Throughout most of history and in most societies of the past and present, economic performance has been anything but satisfactory. Human beings have, by trial and error, learned how to make economies perform better; but not only has this learning taken ten millennia (since the first economic revolution), it has still escaped the grasp of almost half of the world's population. Moreover, the radical improvement in economic performance, even when narrowly defined as material well-being, is a modern phenomenon of the past few centuries and was confined until the past few decades to a small part of the world. Explaining the pace and direction of economic change throughout history presents a major challenge.

Let us represent the human experience to date as a 24-hour clock in which the beginning consists of the time (apparently in Africa between 4 and 5 million years ago) when humans became distinct from other primates. Then the beginning of so-called civilization occurs with the development of agriculture and permanent settlement in about 8000 B.C. in the Fertile Crescent – in the last three or four minutes of the clock. For the other 23 hours and 56 or 57 minutes, humans remain hunters and gatherers and while population grows it does so at a very slow pace.

Now if we make a new 24-hour clock for the time of civilization – the ten thousand years from the development of agriculture to the present –

the pace of change appears to be very slow for the first 12 hours, although our archaeological knowledge is very limited. Historical demographers speculate that the rate of population growth may have doubled as compared with that of the previous era but still was very slow. The pace of change accelerates in the past five thousand years with the rise and then decline of economies and civilizations. Population may have grown from about 300 million at the time of Christ to about 800 million by 1750 – a substantial acceleration over earlier rates of growth. The last 250 years – just 35 minutes on our new 24-hour clock – are the era of modern economic growth accompanied by a population explosion that now puts the world population in excess of 5 billion.

If we focus now on the last 250 years, we see that growth is largely restricted to Western Europe and the overseas extensions of Britain for 200 of those 250 years.

Not only has the pace varied over the ages, the change has not been unidirectional. That is not simply a consequence of the decline of individual civilizations; there have been periods of apparent secular stagnation – the most recent being the long hiatus between the end of the Roman Empire in the West and the revival of Western Europe approximately five hundred years later.

VI

What can an institutional/cognitive approach contribute to our understanding of the economic past? First of all, it should make sense of the very uneven pattern of economic performance described in the preceding section. There is nothing automatic about the evolving of conditions that will permit low-cost transacting in the impersonal markets that are essential to productive economies. Game theory characterizes the issue. Individuals will usually find it worthwhile to cooperate with others in exchange when the play is repeated, when they possess complete information about the other players' past performances, and when there is a small number of players. Cooperation is difficult to sustain when the game is not repeated (or there is an endgame), when information about the other players is lacking, and when there is a large number of players. Creating the institutions that will alter the benefit–cost ratios in favor of cooperation in impersonal exchange is a complex process, because it not only entails the creation of economic institutions but requires that they be undergirded by appropriate political institutions.

We are just beginning to explore the nature of this historical process. The remarkable development of Western Europe from relative backwardness in the tenth century to world economic hegemony by the eighteenth century is a story of a gradually evolving belief system in

Douglass C. North

the context of competition among fragmented political/economic units producing economic institutions and political structures that gave rise to modern economic growth.[8] And even within Western Europe there were successes (the Netherlands and England) and failures (Spain and Portugal), reflecting diverse external environmental experiences.[9]

Second, institutional/cognitive analysis should explain path dependence, one of the remarkable regularities of history. Why do economies, once on a path of growth or stagnation, tend to persist? Pioneering work on this subject is beginning to give us insights into the sources of path dependence (Arthur, 1989; David, 1985). But there is much that we still do not know. The rationality assumption of neoclassical theory would suggest that political entrepreneurs of stagnating economies could simply alter the rules and change the direction of failed economies. It is not that rulers have been unaware of poor performance. Rather, the difficulty of turning economies around is a function of the nature of political markets and, underlying that, the belief systems of the actors. The long decline of Spain, for example, from the glories of the Hapsburg Empire of the sixteenth century to its sorry state under Franco in the twentieth century was characterized by endless self-appraisals and frequently bizarre proposed solutions.[10]

Third, this approach will contribute to our understanding of the complex interplay between institutions, technology, and demography in the overall process of economic change. A complete theory of economic performance would entail such an integrated approach to economic history. We certainly have not put all the pieces together yet. For example, Robert Fogel's path-breaking work on demographic theory[11] and its historical implications for reevaluating past economic performance have yet to be fully integrated into institutional analysis. The same is true for technological change. The important work of Nathan Rosenberg (1976) and Joel Mokyr (1990) exploring the impetus for and consequences of technological change has ongoing implications that must be integrated into institutional analysis. An essay by Wallis and North (1994) marks a beginning in the task of integrating technological and institutional analysis. But integrating these separate strands of research remains a major task of economic history.

[8] See North and Thomas (1973), Jones (1981), and Rosenberg and Birdzell (1986) for accounts of this growth.
[9] See North (1990a), part III, for a brief discussion of the contrasting paths of the Netherlands and England, on the one hand, and Spain, on the other.
[10] DeVries (1976) describes the bizarre remedies proposed by a royal commission to reverse Spain's decline (p. 28).
[11] See Fogel (1994).

Epilogue: economic performance through time

VII

We cannot account for the rise and decline of the Soviet Union and world communism with the tools of neoclassical analysis, but we should be able to with an institutional/cognitive approach to contemporary problems of development. To do so – and to provide an analytical framework for understanding economic change – we must take into account the following implications of this approach:

1. It is the admixture of formal rules, informal norms, and enforcement characteristics that shapes economic performance. While the rules may be changed overnight, the informal norms usually change only gradually. Since it is the norms that provide "legitimacy" to a set of rules, revolutionary change is never as revolutionary as its supporters desire and performance is different from what is anticipated. And economies that adopt the formal rules of another economy will have very different performance characteristics than the first economy because of different informal norms and enforcement. The implication is that transferring the formal political and economic rules of successful Western market economies to Third World and Eastern European economies is not a sufficient condition for good economic performance. Privatization is not a panacea for poor economic performance.
2. Polities significantly shape economic performance because they define and enforce the economic rules. Therefore, an essential part of development policy is the creation of polities that will create and enforce efficient property rights. However, we know very little about how to create such polities, because the new political economy (the new institutional economics applied to politics) has largely focused on the United States and developed polities. A pressing research need is to model Third World and Eastern European polities. However, the foregoing analysis does have some implications:
   a. Political institutions will be stable only if undergirded by organizations with a stake in their perpetuation.
   b. Both institutions and belief systems must change for successful reform, since it is the mental models of the actors that will shape choices.
   c. Developing norms of behavior that will support and legitimize new rules is a lengthy process and in the absence of such reinforcing mechanisms polities will tend to be unstable.
   d. While economic growth can occur in the short run with autocratic regimes, long-run economic growth entails the development of the rule of law.

353

e. Informal constraints (norms, conventions, and codes of conduct) favorable to growth can sometimes produce economic growth even with unstable or adverse political rules. The key is the degree to which such adverse rules are enforced.

3. Adaptive rather than allocative efficiency is the key to long-run growth. Successful political/economic systems have evolved flexible institutional structures that can survive the shocks and changes that are a part of successful evolution. But these systems have been a product of long gestation. We do not know how to create adaptive efficiency in the short run.

We have just set out on the long road to achieving an understanding of economic performance through time. The ongoing research embodying new hypotheses that confront historical evidence will not only create an analytical framework that helps us to understand economic change through time; in the process it will enrich economic theory, enabling it to deal effectively with a wide range of contemporary issues currently beyond its ken. The promise is there. The recognition of that promise by the Nobel Committee should be the essential spur to our movement down that road.

REFERENCES

Arthur, Brian (1989). "Competing Technologies, Increasing Returns, and Lockin by Historical Events." *Economic Journal* 99 (March):116–31.

Clark, Andy, and Annette Karmiloff-Smith (1993). "The Cognizer's Innards: A Psychological and Philosophical Perspective on the Development of Thought." *Mind and Language* 8(4):487–519.

Coase, Ronald (1960). "The Problem of Social Cost." *Journal of Law and Economics* 3(1):1–44.

David, Paul A. (1985). "Clio and the Economics of QWERTY." *American Economic Review* 75(May):332–37.

DeVries, Jan (1976). *The Economy of Europe in an Age of Crises, 1600–1750.* Cambridge University Press.

Fogel, Robert (1994). "Economic Growth, Population Theory, and Physiology: The Bearing of Long-Term Processes on the Making of Economic Policy." *American Economic Review* 84(3):369–95.

Hahn, Frank (1991). "The Next Hundred Years." *Economic Journal* 101(Jan.):47–50.

Hayek, Friedrich A. (1960). *The Constitution of Liberty.* University of Chicago Press.

Heiner, Ronald (1983). "The Origins of Predictable Behavior." *American Economic Review* 73:560–95.

Hogarth, Robin M., and Melvin W. Reder (eds.) (1986). *Rational Choice.* University of Chicago Press.

Holland, John H., Keith J. Holyoak, Richard E. Nisbett, and Paul R. Thagard (1986). *Induction: Processes of Inference, Learning, and Discovery.* Cambridge, Mass.: MIT Press.

Jones, E. L. (1981). *The European Miracle.* Cambridge University Press.
Mokyr, Joel (1990). *The Lever of Riches.* New York: Oxford University Press.
Nelson, Richard, and Sidney G. Winter (1982). *An Evolutionary Theory of Economic Change.* Cambridge, Mass.: Harvard University Press.
North, Douglass C. (1990a). *Institutions, Institutional Change, and Economic Performance.* Cambridge University Press.
   (1990b). "A Transactions Cost Theory of Politics." *Journal of Theoretical Politics* 2(4):355–67.
North, Douglass C., and Robert P. Thomas (1973). *The Rise of the Western World: A New Economic History.* Cambridge University Press.
Rosenberg, Nathan (1976). *Perspectives on Technology.* Cambridge University Press.
Rosenberg, Nathan, and L. E. Birdzell (1986). *How the West Grew Rich: The Economic Transformation of the Industrial World.* New York: Basic Books.
Simon, Herbert (1986). "Rationality in Psychology and Economics." In Robin M. Hogarth and Melvin W. Reder (eds.), *Rational Choice.* University of Chicago Press.
Tversky, Amos, and Daniel Kahneman (1986). "Rational Choice and the Framing of Decisions." In Robin M. Hogarth and Melvin W. Reder (eds.), *Rational Choice.* University of Chicago Press.
Wallis, John J., and Douglass C. North (1986). "Measuring the Transaction Sector in the American Economy." In S. L. Engerman and R. E. Gallman, eds., *Long Term Factors in American Economic Growth.* University of Chicago Press.
Wallis, John J., and Douglass C. North (1994). "Institutional Change and Technical Change in American Economic Growth: A Transactions Costs Approach." *Journal of Institutional and Theoretical Economics* 150(4):609–24.

Author index

357

Subject index

access cost to formal markets, 104–6
agency theory, 61

complexity, 214–15
Comstock lode, 35–6, 39–43, 54–7
congressional committees, 316–19
contracts, 9
credit, 119–23

development policy, 353–4
disfranchisement of blacks and poor
    whites, 312

economic development, 342–3
economic history, 342
English civil war, 146–7
    and government borrowing, 151–6
    institutional changes following, 147–51
    and private capital markets, 157–61
English land law, 300

Freedman's Bureau, 309–10

Gompartz function, 51, 53
Great Depression, 265
Great Society, 328, 332–5

ideology, 73
informality, 114–16
instability, macroeconomic, 96
institutional change, 11–13, 25–30, 35,
    166, 304–5, 307
institutional substitutes, 126–7
institutions
    definition, 92, 344
    economics of, 6–13
    informal, 22, 92
    and organizations, 345–6
    political, 139

law and development, 97–8

market socialism, 59–60
mechanization of agriculture, 319–20
    effect on paternalism, 320–6

neoclassical economics, 1, 6–7, 10, 97,
    342
neoclassical theory and efficiency, 345

organization, definition, 9

Pacific salmon
    aboriginal fishery, 250–2
    aboriginal property rights, 251–2
    evolution of productivity, 273–5
    externality in interception, 252–4
    legislation of catch, 257–60, 267–72
    migration paths, 248–50
paternalism in U.S. agriculture
    as contract, 315–16
    description, 313–15
    historical background, 308–13
policy formulation, models of, 166–8,
    170–3
    conformity with sugar policy, 208–9
    ingredients for fuller model, 209–15
political institutions, 139
power, 14–17
predatory states, 65
price controls, 219–23; see also rents ordi-
    nance of 1921
property rights, 7, 9–11, 75, 280–2, 283–
    4
    in airport slots, 288–9, 298–9
    credible commitment to, 131–4
    definition, 286
    naive model of, 3, 31–3
    over salmon traps, 263, 272

Continued from front of book

Elinor Ostrom, *Governing the Commons: The Evolution of Institutions for Collective Action*

Mark Ramseyer and Frances Rosenbluth, *The Politics of Oligarchy: Institutional Choice in Imperial Japan*

Jean-Laurent Rosenthal, *The Fruits of Revolution: Property Rights, Litigation, and French Agriculture*

Charles Stewart III, *Budget Reform Politics: The Design of the Appropriations Process in the House of Representatives, 1865–1921*

John Waterbury, *Exposed to Innumerable Delusions: Public Enterprise and State Power in Egypt, India, Mexico, and Turkey*